Management Research

Undertaking a research project for the first time can be a daunting prospect. Gaining the knowledge and skills needed to do research typically has to be done alongside carrying out the project itself. Students often have to conduct their research independently, perhaps with limited tutor contact. What is needed in such situations is a resource that supports the new researcher on every step of the research journey, from defining the project to communicating its findings.

Management Research: Applying the principles provides just such a resource. Structured around the key stages of a research project, it is designed to provide answers to the questions faced by new researchers but without neglecting the underlying principles of good research. Each chapter includes 'next steps' activities to help readers apply the content to their own live research project. The companion website provides extensive resources, including video tutorials, to support the development of practical research skills.

The text reflects the richness and variety of current business and management research both in its presentation of methods and techniques and in its choice of examples drawn from different subject disciplines, industries and organizations. *Management Research: Applying the principles* combines diversity of coverage with a singularity of purpose: to help students complete their research project to a rigorous standard.

Susan Rose is an Associate Professor in Marketing Management at Henley Business School, the University of Reading, UK.

Nigel Spinks is a Lecturer at Henley Business School, the University of Reading, UK.

Ana Isabel Canhoto is a Senior Lecturer in Marketing at Oxford Brookes University, UK.

Management Research
Applying the principles

Susan Rose, Nigel Spinks
and Ana Isabel Canhoto

Routledge
Taylor & Francis Group

LONDON AND NEW YORK

First published 2015
by Routledge
2 Park Square, Milton Park, Abingdon, Oxon OX14 4RN

and by Routledge
711 Third Avenue, New York, NY 10017

Routledge is an imprint of the Taylor & Francis Group, an informa business

British Library Cataloguing in Publication Data
A catalogue record for this book is available from the British Library

Library of Congress Cataloging in Publication Data
Rose, Susan.
  Management research: applying the principles/Susan Rose, Nigel Spinks
  and Ana Canhoto. – First Edition.
  pages cm
  Includes bibliographical references and index.
  1. Management – Research.   2. Quantitative research.   I. Title.
  HD30.4.R67 2014
  658.0072 – dc23
  2013047088

ISBN: 978-0-415-62811-2 (hbk)
ISBN: 978-0-415-62812-9 (pbk)
ISBN: 978-1-315-81919-8 (ebk)

Typeset in Sabon
by Florence Production Ltd, Stoodleigh, Devon, UK

Contents

List of figures   *ix*
List of tables   *xii*
List of Research in Practice boxes   *xiv*
List of Critical Commentary boxes   *xvi*
Preface   *xvii*
Acknowledgements   *xviii*
How to use this book   *xix*

PART I
Define   **1**

1 Researching in management and organizations   3

    1.1 Introduction 3
    1.2 Defining management research 4
    1.3 The relationship between research and practice 8
    1.4 The relationship between research and theory 11
    1.5 Research and philosophy 15
    1.6 Reflexivity and the researcher 20

2 Formulating your research problem   24

    2.1 Introduction 24
    2.2 A problem-solving view of research 24
    2.3 Choosing a research problem 29
    2.4 Developing your research questions 33

3 Reviewing the literature   44

    3.1 Introduction 44
    3.2 Undertaking a critical review 44
    3.3 Search 48
    3.4 Capture 56
    3.5 Synthesize 60
    3.6 Present 65

PART II
Design   **73**

4   Designing research   75

   4.1 Introduction 75
   4.2 Integrating theory into your research 76
   4.3 Time horizon 81
   4.4 Primary and secondary data 83
   4.5 Quantitative and qualitative research methods 84
   4.6 Quality in research 90

5   Linking research questions to research design   98

   5.1 Introduction 98
   5.2 Research designs for answering 'what' questions 98
   5.3 Research designs for answering 'why' questions 102
   5.4 Research designs for answering 'how' questions 110

6   Applying quantitative and qualitative research designs   117

   6.1 Introduction 117
   6.2 Quantitative research designs 117
   6.3 Qualitative research designs 126

7   Conducting research ethically   144

   7.1 Introduction 144
   7.2 Ethics in Research 144
   7.3 Avoidance of harm or loss of dignity 145
   7.4 Transparency and honesty 146
   7.5 Right to privacy 151
   7.6 Researcher integrity 153
   7.7 Ethics in online research 154
   7.8 Understanding the ethical dimensions of your own research project 155
   7.9 The role of codes of practice and ethics committees 158

8   Planning and managing your research project   163

   8.1 Introduction 163
   8.2 Selecting a research design 164
   8.3 Planning your research project 168
   8.4 Managing your research project 173
   8.5 Keeping a research diary 176
   8.6 Preparing a research proposal 178

PART III
Collect 185

9 Sampling 187

    9.1   *Introduction* 187
    9.2   *What is a sample?* 187
    9.3   *Sampling methods* 191
    9.4   *Sampling in quantitative and qualitative research* 195
    9.5   *Sample size* 197
    9.6   *Sampling and the Internet* 201
    9.7   *Gaining and maintaining access* 204

10 Collecting data using questionnaires 211

    10.1   *Introduction* 211
    10.2   *Why and when to use a questionnaire* 211
    10.3   *The questionnaire design process* 213
    10.4   *Identify relevant concepts/variables* 213
    10.5   *Formulate your questions and decide the level of measurement* 215
    10.6   *Structuring and laying out your questionnaire* 227
    10.7   *Pre-test and pilot the questionnaire* 231
    10.8   *Administrate and distribute the questionnaire* 232

11 Collecting data using in-depth interviews 236

    11.1   *Introduction* 236
    11.2   *Individual interviews* 236
    11.3   *Group interviews* 246
    11.4   *Capturing and storing your interview data* 251

12 Collecting data through observation, documents and artefacts 257

    12.1   *Introduction* 257
    12.2   *Collecting data by observation* 257
    12.3   *Collecting documents and other records* 266
    12.4   *Diaries and other researcher-instigated documents* 271
    12.5   *Artefacts* 273

PART IV
Analyse 277

13 Analysing quantitative data 279

    13.1   *Introduction* 279
    13.2   *Entering your data* 280
    13.3   *Preparing your data for analysis* 282
    13.4   *Exploring your data* 285

13.5 *Answering your research question 305*
13.6 *Presenting your findings 328*
13.7 *Summary of chart types used in this chapter 332*
13.8 *Summary of statistical tests used in this chapter 334*

14 Analysing qualitative data   335

14.1 *Introduction 335*
14.2 *The qualitative analysis of data 335*
14.3 *Organizing and preparing your data 336*
14.4 *Coding your data 338*
14.5 *Using computers in qualitative data analysis 346*
14.6 *Using visualization to make connections 348*
14.7 *Types of visual data display 349*
14.8 *Answering your research question 352*
14.9 *Drawing and verifying conclusions 360*
14.10 *Presenting qualitative data 363*

PART V
Communicate   367

15 Reporting your research   369

15.1 *Introduction 369*
15.2 *Writing for an academic qualification 370*
15.3 *Writing for a practitioner audience 378*
15.4 *The process of writing 380*
15.5 *Alternative forms of reporting 385*

Glossary   391
Author index   407
Subject index   410

Figures

1.1	The 5-stage model of research	6
1.2	Deductive and inductive approaches to research	14
2.1	Linking research problems, questions, design and findings	25
2.2	Looking for potential topics	30
3.1	Structure of an argument	47
3.2	The literature review process	47
3.3	Example literature map	63
3.4	Conceptual model of the expected relationship between advertising level and sales revenue	64
3.5	Types of conceptual model	64
4.1	Decisions in research design	76
4.2	Stages in the deductive research approach	77
4.3	Stages in the inductive research approach	79
4.4	Example mixed method designs	88
5.1	Independent and dependent variables	103
5.2	Mediating variable	104
5.3	Moderating variable	105
6.1	Quantitative research designs	118
6.2	Classic experimental design with treatment and control groups and pre- and post-test measurement	118
6.3	Qualitative research designs	126
6.4	Action research cycles	132
8.1	Factors influencing choice of research design	164
8.2	Example Gantt chart time schedule	171
9.1	Target population and sample	188
9.2	Generic sampling process	189
9.3	Probability and non-probability sampling methods	192
10.1	The questionnaire design process	214
10.2	Example checklist question	218
10.3	Example categorical scale questions	219
10.4	Example rank preference question	220
10.5	Example single-item Likert-type scale	220
10.6	Example semantic differential scale	221
10.7	Example single item response question	223
10.8	Example open question	223
10.9	Suggested questionnaire structure	227

10.10	Example of conditional routing	230
13.1	The quantitative data analysis process	280
13.2	Example data matrix created in Excel	281
13.3	Frequency table of respondent gender	287
13.4	Bar charts showing frequency of car driving	288
13.5	Histogram showing the age of medal winners in the 2012 Olympic Games	288
13.6	Example pie charts showing European Union EU27 electricity production by source, 2011	289
13.7	Calculating the median and interquartile range for a dataset	290
13.8	Normal distribution	292
13.9	Unimodal and bimodal data	293
13.10	Skewness	293
13.11	Kurtosis	293
13.12	Components of a typical box plot	295
13.13	Box plot showing the age of medal winners in the 2012 Olympic Games	295
13.14	Bar charts of mean satisfaction levels by customer age group	297
13.15	Multiple box plots of mean satisfaction levels by customer age group (data from Table 13.6)	297
13.16	Clustered bar charts of driving frequency by annual household income	300
13.17	Stacked bar chart of driving frequency by household income	301
13.18	100 per cent stacked bar chart of driving frequency by household income	301
13.19	Scatterplot of number of hits on seller website and number of copies sold online for 14 different book titles	302
13.20	Example scatterplots	302
13.21	UK Internet users, thousands	303
13.22	Time series plot showing per cent Internet users by gender, UK	304
13.23	Time series plot showing total retail sales (excluding motor vehicles) and electronic shopping and mail-order house sales as per cent of total retail sales, USA 2000–2012	304
13.24	Point and interval estimates	306
13.25	Chart of confidence intervals for mean satisfaction levels by customer age group	308
13.26	Hypothesis testing procedure	309
13.27	Type I and Type II errors	310
13.28	Scatterplots illustrating the strength of Pearson's correlation coefficient	321
13.29	Conceptual model of the relationship between website hits and book sales	323
13.30	Scatterplot, regression line and regression equation for website hits and online book sales	324
13.31	Regression analysis for book sales and website hits	325
13.32	Summary of statistical tests	333
14.1	Steps in the qualitative analysis of data	336
14.2	Using index cards for coding	341

14.3	Emerging themes	343
14.4	Level 1 and 2 codes	343
14.5	Creating sub-categories	343
14.6	Examples of a revised coding scheme	344
14.7	Coding hierarchy	345
14.8	Coding table created using a spreadsheet	347
14.9	Possible column and row headers for data matrixes	351
14.10	Example of a network display incorporating vertical and horizontal dimensions	352
14.11	Example of a simple social network display	354
14.12	Example of an events network	360
15.1	Example mind map	382

Tables

1.1	Definitions of research	4
1.2	Characteristics of pure and applied research	8
1.3	Philosophical orientations in research	16
2.1	Examples of the relationship between decision problems and research problems	27
2.2	Sources of ideas for your research problem	28
3.1	Potential literature sources	50
3.2	Where to search online	52
3.3	Reference data for common source types	57
3.4	Capturing reference and content information from a key literature source	58
3.5	Author-centric versus concept-centric structure	60
3.6	Concept matrix	61
3.7	Example bibliographic databases	71
4.1	The qualitative-quantitative distinction	85
4.2	Dimensions of validity	92
4.3	Dimensions of reliability	93
4.4	Trustworthiness criteria	93
4.5	Trustworthiness criteria, and proposed techniques for meeting them or confirming that they have been met	94
6.1	Example case studies	130
7.1	Key ethical principles in research	145
7.2	Key ethical questions to ask about your research	157
7.3	Research ethics: codes of practice and guidelines	158
8.1	Mapping research questions to research designs	166
8.2	Developing a plan for your research project	169
8.3	Typical activities in a student research project	169
8.4	Example risks in a student research project	172
8.5	Typical structure and components of a research proposal	180
9.1	Quantitative and qualitative sampling compared	195
9.2	Approaches to purposive sampling in qualitative research	197
9.3	Reported survey response rates by distribution method	200
10.1	How questionnaires may be used in different research designs	212
10.2	Levels of measurement	218
10.3	Common mistakes in questionnaire wording	224
10.4	Example data collection matrix	227

11.1	The role of interviews in different research designs	237
11.2	Potential benefits and problems of elite interviewing	238
11.3	Types of interview question	240
11.4	Example of a discussion outline for a focus group	249
12.1	The role of observation in different research designs	258
12.2	The role of documents and other records in different research designs	267
12.3	Example sources of online secondary data	269
13.1	Example codebook entry for a single question in a questionnaire	282
13.2	Example summated scale	284
13.3	Univariate descriptive statistics and graphical presentation techniques	286
13.4	Simplified frequency table showing frequency of car driving	287
13.5	Techniques for exploring more than one variable	296
13.6	Table of mean satisfaction levels by customer age group	297
13.7	Contingency table showing frequency of driving by driving licence holders aged 17 and household income, showing counts	299
13.8	Contingency table showing frequency of driving by driving licence holders aged 17 and household income, showing per cent of row totals	300
13.9	Customer satisfaction levels by age group showing confidence intervals for the mean	308
13.10	Example hypothesis statements	310
13.11	Example statistical test output (independent 2-sample *t*-test)	312
13.12	Significance tests (1): tests of difference	314
13.13	Measures and tests of association	318
13.14	Descriptors for correlation coefficient strength	321
14.1	Conversation analysis transcription symbols	339
14.2	Using tables to manage coding	342
14.3	Some functions typically performed by CAQDAS programs	347
14.4	Advantages and disadvantages of CAQDAS programs	348
14.5	Example of a data matrix	350
14.6	Example of an explanatory effects matrix	355
14.7	Tactics for getting meaning out of data	360
14.8	Testing and confirming your findings	362
14.9	Example showing respondent details	363
15.1	Typical structure and components of a report for an academic qualification	371
15.2	Structure and contents of a typical practitioner report	379
15.3	Advantages and disadvantages of web-conference research presentations	387

Research in Practice boxes

1.1	Using pure research to understand corporate reputation	9
1.2	The use of applied research to explore the practice of 'homeworking'	10
2.1	From managerial problem to research question	38
3.1	Literature review questions	54
3.2	Using tables to summarize and compare theories of corporate governance	62
4.1	Choosing a deductive approach	79
4.2	Choosing an inductive approach	80
4.3	A mixed method study of emotion and sales in convenience stores	89
5.1	A multidimensional classification scheme: structure in fives	100
5.2	Non-compliance in taking medication	106
5.3	A process model of how groups learn from other groups	112
6.1	The effects of shelf placement on consumer purchases of potato chips	120
6.2	Analytic survey: enterprise resource planning (ERP) systems and the manufacturing–marketing interface	121
6.3	A descriptive survey of executive coaching practices	123
6.4	A simulation study of co-ordination in supply chain management	124
6.5	A content analysis of the portrayal of women in James Bond films	125
6.6	An ethnography of subcultures of consumption	128
6.7	A grounded theory study of the influence of information about labour abuses on consumer choice	129
6.8	Multiple case study research on success factors for implementing customer relationship management systems	131
6.9	Action research study on the role of information systems in small business growth	133
6.10	Interview study of the characteristics of successful employer brands	134
6.11	Conversation analysis and streetwise sales	137
7.1	Deception in research	147
7.2	Example information sheet for face-to-face interviews	148
7.3	Example informed consent form for face-to-face interviews	149
7.4	Researching online shopping addiction	155
8.1	CEO as insider researcher	175
8.2	Example research diary format	177

8.3	Preparing a research proposal: Trickle Out	179
9.1	Theoretical sampling: researching supplier–client relationships in outsourcing	198
9.2	Sample access for participant observation within an online firm-hosted brand community	203
9.3	Accessing a sample in a sensitive research topic	207
10.1	Dimensions of service quality	214
10.2	Measuring affective commitment	222
10.3	Developing questions to measure variables in a conceptual model	225
10.4	Example filter questions	229
11.1	Interviewing using social media	245
11.2	Using Skype to conduct a text-based focus group	251
12.1	An observational study of customer-profiling practices at a UK-based financial institution	261
12.2	Examples of a structured observation coding schedule	264
12.3	Capturing social media comments	270
12.4	Using diaries for data collection	272
13.1	Outlier or not?	291
13.2	How satisfied are the customers?	307
13.3	Independent 2-sample *t*-test	315
13.4	Chi-squared test of association	318
13.5	Pearson's correlation coefficient	322
13.6	Factors influencing smartphone shopping adoption	326
14.1	Example of the coding process	340
14.2	Using a data matrix to display comparisons	350
14.3	Using a data matrix in an intestigation of success factors	356
14.4	Visualizing events and processes	358
15.1	Research titles	372
15.2	Writing your introduction	374

Critical Commentary boxes

1.1   Management research, management theory and management practice   11

2.1   The dictatorship of the research question   40

3.1   Systematic review   68

4.1   Mixing methods   90

5.1   A hierarchy of methods?   109

6.1   Critiques of quantitative and qualitative research   138

7.1   The growth of ethical regulation   159

8.1   How much planning is too much?   182

9.1   The use of research panels   203

10.1   Likert scale data: interval or ordinal?   217

11.1   The nature of interview data   253

12.1   Observer effects and unobtrusive measures   274

13.1   The cult of statistical significance   328

14.1   Limitations to data display techniques in qualitative research   353

15.1   Disseminating research   388

Preface

In writing this book we set ourselves a clear aim: to produce a textbook that would provide the practical and conceptual resources needed by students undertaking a research project in business and management. Our experience as tutors and supervisors on both Master's and doctoral programmes had shown us that such a book was needed. Our students struggled to find a single source that could help them to design and carry out research to answer the questions that interested them, whilst meeting the standards of a rigorous academic assessment. What we felt was required was a book that explained the principles underpinning research in business and management and that guided the reader through their application in practice.

This book is therefore aimed at students undertaking a research project as part of an academic or professional qualification in business and management, or related disciplines, at Master's level and above at a business school or similar institution. It is particularly suited to post-experience students who plan to carry out their research projects in their own organization or industry. We take an inter-disciplinary approach to support research in different subject areas, different industries and different sectors, including the not-for-profit sector. The book is designed to be read while preparing for and carrying out a research project and to act as a reference resource throughout. We have therefore included 'next steps' activities to guide the researcher on that journey. In addition, extensive online resources, including video, are available on the book's companion website to help at key points in the research process.

To achieve our stated aim in the book, we have structured it around the key stages of a research project. We place particular emphasis on how to design research that can help to answer the kinds of questions that, in our experience, students want to answer. Questions such as 'What is the impact of new contract arrangements upon employee relations?' 'Why do young people no longer use our brand?' or 'How are new services developed and implemented?' We therefore take a close look at how such questions can be researched and the types of research design that may be appropriate. In doing so we emphasize the different ways that such questions can be understood and the different ways that they can be investigated. Throughout the book we seek to show how research can be used to generate findings that are both useful and robust and to provide the reader with the knowledge and skills to carry it out. As such, it provides students of business and management with a comprehensive new resource.

Acknowledgements

The authors would like to acknowledge the important contribution made by a number of people to the completion of this book. The original idea for the book came from our experiences of writing course materials for MBA and MSc students, and from teaching and supervising them through their research projects. We would like to thank all of our students who have, over the years, provided thought-provoking insights as we worked alongside them in completing their research projects. Several of these projects appear in this book as practical examples of applied research and we would like to thank the following students for agreeing to our including their work: Arun Dhandayudham, Ann James, Volker Krön, Silvia Lang, Davin Mac Ananey, Beverley Pass, James Ramsey, Melanie Shapiro. Full reference information can be found in the chapter Notes sections.

Additionally we would like to acknowledge the contribution made by our academic colleagues, in particular Moira Clark and Anne Dibley of the Henley Centre for Customer Management; Kevin Money, Carola Hillenbrand and David Littlewood of the John Madejski Centre for Reputation and Sheilagh Resnick and Kim Cassidy at Nottingham Trent University for allowing us to use examples of their own research. Thanks also go to Phillip Samouel of Kingston Business School and Jeni Giambona for taking time to review and give feedback on early versions of our work and to Charlotte Boughen for her support during preparation of the manuscript.

We also acknowledge the role that both of our institutions – Henley Business School and Oxford Brookes University – have played in the completion of the book and thank them for providing the space and time to do this. Finally we would like to thank the editorial team at Taylor Francis, in particular Amy Laurens, Rosie Baron and Nicola Cupit, for their constant faith in our ability to deliver this book.

Any remaining errors are, of course, all our own.

Susan Rose, Nigel Spinks and
Ana Isabel Canhoto

How to use this book

Management Research: Applying the Principles includes a number of features to help you develop your research knowledge and skills. Here we give you a quick overview of these to help you to understand how to get the best out of the book.

Firstly, the book is structured around a simple five-stage model of the process of research (see figure). This model makes it easy to see where you are within the book, how the parts are related and where to look to find specific topics.

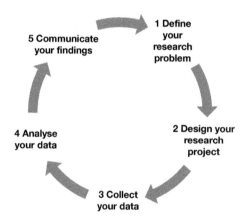

The 5-Stage model of research

Each stage is addressed in one the five parts of the book as shown below. Each part begins with a brief explanation of what is covered in the relevant chapters. The five parts of the book are:

1 *Define*: how to identify and define the topic of your research project.
2 *Design*: what to consider when drawing up your research design, ethical issues in research, and factors in planning and managing your project and how to capture your design in a proposal.
3 *Collect*: how to apply different methods for sampling and collecting data and how to decide upon the relevant ones for your project.
4 *Analyse*: how to analyse quantitative and qualitative data and draw robust conclusions.
5 *Communicate*: how to communicate your research to different audiences in either written or oral format.

Each chapter contains a consistent set of features:

- a brief list of key topics at the start of the chapter to help direct your reading
- 'Research in Practice' examples to provide short vignettes of research projects undertaken and illustrate key issues discussed in the text
- a 'Critical Commentary' introduces differing viewpoints and controversies on some topic addressed in the chapter to reflect the diversity of views on research
- 'Key learning points', which summarize the main points covered in the chapter
- 'Next steps', activities designed to help you apply the principles introduced in the chapter to your own research project
- a full reference list for those wanting to explore particular topics further.

A comprehensive glossary is included for reference.

In addition, the book is supported by a companion website that contains a range of student and instructor resources including: expanded content to certain chapters, teaching notes, PowerPoint slides, video content, further readings and guidance on the next steps you can take to apply your learning.

Part I

Define

Part I of the book contains three chapters, each of which relates to how you define your research problem. Chapter 1 is an introductory chapter that provides you with an orientation towards research and its purpose. We first define what we understand management research to be, its distinguishing features and why it is important to the management of organizations. We introduce the five-stage process model that forms the structure of the book and discuss the activities within each stage. We explore the relationship between management practice, theory and research, and discuss different philosophical stances that a researcher may adopt. Chapter 1 also encourages you to take a reflective stance towards your research and your role in it.

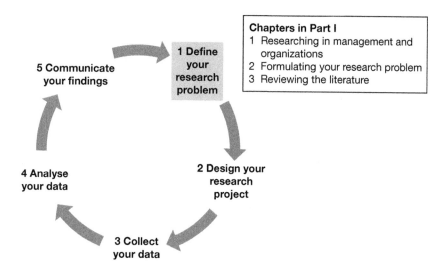

Our approach to research is to view it as providing solutions or insights to problems faced by theorists and practitioners. Chapter 2 introduces you to this problem-centred approach and guides you on identifying a research problem and developing suitable research questions. We examine different types of research questions, how they link to the overall aims of a research project and how to formulate them effectively. Before starting a research project, it is good practice to look at what we already know about the topic and how it has been investigated before. To do this we undertake a critical literature review and Chapter 3 explains the nature and purpose of a literature review in research and how to carry one out.

1 Researching in management and organizations

CHAPTER SUMMARY

The key topics covered in this chapter are:

- defining management research
- relating research to practice
- relating theory to research and practice
- comparing different philosophical orientations to research
- being reflexive about your research.

1.1 Introduction

Management research is an exciting way of learning more about the world of organizations and business. As a management researcher you will need energy, drive and a desire to see beyond the expected and the everyday. At this point, particularly if you are new to research, you will probably have more questions than answers about your project. What makes a good research topic? How should I design my research? Where and how will I get my data? How will I analyse my data and report my findings? What skills do I need? This book will help you answer these and many other questions about doing research. It introduces key principles that underpin rigour and relevance in research. It shows you how to apply these principles to your research in order to produce output that has impact and value, whilst making sure you complete your project within the time and resources available.

In this first chapter we begin by defining what we mean by research, identifying its characteristic features and why we do it. We then introduce a high-level model of the research process which both maps out the sequence of activities that go into a research project and forms the overall structure of the book itself. Next, we explore two important issues: the relationships between management research and practice and between theory and research. These topics prepare the ground for a discussion of different philosophical orientations that characterize present-day management research. Finally, we discuss the importance of reflection and learning from research practice and how this helps you to think through the impact you have had on the research process and to develop your knowledge, expertise and skills in research.

1.2 Defining management research

Management research is usually considered part of the social sciences, which is the field of enquiry concerned with human beings and how they behave and interact either as individuals or as a group. Like many other aspects of management studies, management research is a diverse field. It is used in many different contexts including commercial and not-for-profit organizations, different industries and different national and cultural settings. As well as its own, and growing, body of knowledge it draws on the theories and practices of other disciplines such as economics, sociology and psychology. But what do we mean by 'research'?

1.2.1 What do we mean by research?

Table 1.1 presents different definitions of research, drawn from a range of sources both academic and non-academic. We can see that they emphasize two different but related dimensions. First, that research is a systematic process of investigation and second, that it has the purpose of finding out information or knowledge about a specific problem or issue. Other authors have also emphasized the problem-solving nature of research (e.g. Van de Ven 2007). So we can define **research** as a purposeful, systematic process of investigation in order to find solutions to a problem.

1.2.2 Why do a research project?

Management research is used for many different purposes and in many different contexts. It can be done by academics and practitioners or by the two groups in

Table 1.1 Definitions of research

— 'The systematic investigation into and study of materials and sources in order to establish facts and reach new conclusions.'

(OED 2011: 1222)

— 'The systematic gathering and interpretation of information about individuals or organisations using the statistical and analytical methods and techniques of the applied sciences to gain insight or support decision making.'

(Definition of market research, including social and opinion research, ESOMAR 2013)

— 'a systematic process to solve real-world problems.'

(Gray 2009: 2)

— 'systematic investigation to find things out. It is the process by which we produce evidence or knowledge.'

(McGivern 2006: 4)

— 'Systematic study and investigation.'

(Robson 2011: 532)

— 'The systematic collection and interpretation of information with a clear purpose, to find things out.'

(Saunders et al. 2012: 600)

— 'An organised, systematic, critical, scientific inquiry or investigation into a specific problem, undertaken with the objective of finding answers or solutions thereto.'

(Sekaran and Bougie 2010: 398)

collaboration. As we will see, its aim may be to contribute to the body of management theory or to management practice. At this point, however, it is helpful to stop and consider the situation in which you are working as a researcher and why you are doing your research. This can help you understand the type of research you are likely to have to undertake, identify the stakeholders and their expectations and understand some of the challenges you may face during the project. We have found it is helpful to consider two key questions.

1   Are you doing the research for an academic qualification? If your research project forms part of an academic qualification programme of study you are taking the role of student researcher. You may be doing research as a final year project on an undergraduate or Master's programme, for a doctorate or perhaps as part of a work placement. For a student research project, the outcome will need to meet the assessment criteria of the academic institution in which you are studying as well as meet any commitments that you may have made to other stakeholders in the research. A major benefit of doing research as part of a qualification is the support available. You are likely to be working with an academic supervisor, who will give guidance and advice during your research project, as well as act as a mentor for your development as a researcher. In addition you will almost certainly have access to library and other study resources, and possibly to specialist software and technical advice. If you are not a student researcher you are likely to have to develop your contacts and networks to help support you during the process.

2   Are you doing the research in your own organization? If you are, you are taking on the role of insider researcher. This presents you with both opportunities and challenges. Opportunities arise because being part of an organization can make it easier to identify a suitable research topic and to gain support and help in getting access to research respondents, data sources and so on. Challenges arise because of the potential ambiguity of adopting a dual role as both researcher and organizational member. You may face difficulties, for example, because of the need to balance the commitments of a managerial position with the demands for your time as a researcher, or your choice of topic may be constrained by organizational expectations. Being an insider researcher may place particular demands on your ability to deal with a complex and ambiguous situation. Whilst you may avoid these sorts of problems if you are not an insider researcher, you may face greater challenges in gaining access to organizations, respondents or data. Here your network and personal and professional contacts will be invaluable during the project. If you are a student researcher your academic institution may be able to help with identifying potential projects or organizations looking for help with research.

Of course these roles are not mutually exclusive. You can be both an insider researcher and a student researcher, for example, a common position for those studying part time whilst working in an organization. Whatever your situation, it is important to recognize the implications for how you go about your project and the expectations that are placed on it. We return to these issues in Chapter 8 when we look at planning your research project.

Figure 1.1 The 5-stage model of research

1.2.3 *The research process*

Carrying out a research project involves undertaking a series of activities, linked together in a structured and logical process. Successful research is not haphazard and does not happen by chance. In Figure 1.1 we provide a high-level model of the research process, separated into five distinctive stages. The model identifies the principal activities involved in carrying out a research project. It provides a working template for planning and monitoring your own project. It also forms the structure for the book, as each of the five stages is covered in a different part of the book. We will now look at each stage in turn in terms of its objectives, key considerations and the relevant chapters within the book.

Stage 1: *Define*

In the first stage of your research you will need to identify and define the topic of your investigation. In Chapter 2 we introduce the idea of the research problem and how it provides the focus for you to determine the boundaries of your investigation and set the high-level questions your research will need to answer in order to address your chosen research problem. Having identified the focus of the research, it is important to spend time looking at what is currently known about your topic. Chapter 3 shows how to undertake a critical review of the academic, practitioner and policy literature that makes up the body of knowledge in your chosen field.

Stage 2: *Design*

In this part of the book we move on to look at the design of your research project. Chapter 4 introduces the elements of research design and the key decisions that determine the overall shape of your research and discusses how we can judge the quality of research. Chapter 5 looks at how qualitative, quantitative and mixed method research can be used to answer different types of research question and lays the groundwork for an introduction to specific quantitative and qualitative research designs in Chapter 6. Chapter 7 alerts you to ethical considerations that you will need to address when carrying out your research project, while Chapter 8 provides you with guidance on planning and managing your own research project, along with advice on how to prepare a research proposal at the outset of your project.

Stage 3: Collect

Data collection is one of the key practical tasks in any research project. Depending upon the type of research design you have chosen you will use a different data collection method(s) to collect data from different sources. We begin in Chapter 9 by discussing where and how much data you are going to collect, by introducing the idea of sampling. Chapter 10 looks at one of the most commonly used quantitative data collection methods, the questionnaire. Chapter 11 does the same for an important family of qualitative data collection techniques: in-depth individual and group interviews. In Chapter 12 we turn our attention to three important data sources: observation, documents and artefacts. In each chapter we discuss how to prepare for and carry out your chosen data collection method.

Stage 4: Analyse

Analysis is the heart of a research project and can often be the most exciting part of doing research. In this part of the book we look at how to prepare your data, carry out your analysis and draw appropriate, evidence-based conclusions. Chapter 13 is dedicated to quantitative analysis and in Chapter 14 we cover qualitative data analysis techniques.

Stage 5: Communicate

The audience for your research output may be your academic institution and/or other stakeholders for whom the research has been undertaken. Either way, you must ensure that you communicate your findings clearly, effectively and in a way that meets the needs of the audience. Communication is the subject of Chapter 15, which looks at how to prepare appropriate written or oral reports of your research findings.

1.2.4 Is research a sequential process?

For clarity the five-stage model has been shown as a sequential process with discrete stages. In practice, research is often much messier, especially early on in a project, where there may be iterations between the definition and design stages as the topic and practical aspects of the research design are clarified. In addition, some research designs are intentionally iterative. Nevertheless, we believe that it is useful to emphasize the high-level sequence of activities that make up the research process in order to make it easier to see the tasks that will need to be carried out to complete your project. Similarly, we have shown the process as a continuous one to stress the importance of being aware of and, where appropriate, building upon, the results of prior research, even though individual projects will use past research in different ways and to a different extent.

1.3 The relationship between research and practice

If research is about the application of a process to help solve problems, it is important to understand how management research relates to the practice of management and what this might mean for your own project. As we discuss in the Critical Commentary to this chapter, the relationship between research and practice is a controversial one in business and management. We can, however, distinguish two broad types of research that differ in terms of their primary focus, their intended audience and their relationship to management practice. Their key features are summarized in Table 1.2.

Table 1.2 Characteristics of pure and applied research

Pure research	*Applied research*
— Primary aim is to add to our theoretical knowledge of the topic area under investigation.	— Primary aim is to help to solve a problem or issue of concern to practitioners.
— Motivation for research is a particular problem or issue within the domain of theoretical knowledge.	— Motivation for research is a particular problem or issue within the domain of management practice.
— Research outputs contribute to the body of theoretical knowledge about the topic.	— Research outputs are used by managers and policy makers to inform decision making and action.
— Undertaken predominantly for an academic audience.	— Undertaken predominantly for a practitioner audience.
— Findings disseminated via academic conferences, journals and books.	— Findings disseminated via reports and practitioner publications but often restricted in terms of availability (e.g. for commercial reasons).
— Contribution to practice is usually indirect.	— Contribution to body of theoretical knowledge is usually secondary and indirect.

1.3.1 Pure research

Pure (or basic) research is often associated with an academic agenda and is aimed primarily at an academic audience. The motivation for the research is a problem, gap or anomaly identified in the body of theoretical knowledge about a topic. The main aim of the research is to address that problem and thereby extend our knowledge in the field. Findings of the research are likely to be disseminated via academic publishing routes such as conferences, academic journals and so on. Contribution to practice is likely to be indirect, through a 'trickle down' effect via routes such as higher education, researchers acting as consultants or specialist advisors or through non-academic publications. In Research in Practice 1.1 we give an example of pure research, along with attempts to relate findings to practice.

RESEARCH IN PRACTICE 1.1

Using pure research to understand corporate reputation

Researchers at the John Madejski Centre for Reputation at Henley Business School have been carrying out pure research into the topic of corporate reputation (CR) in order to understand what it is, how it can be measured and its role in the relationship with organizational stakeholders. A research paper by Money et al. (2012) illustrates the use of pure research to increase our understanding of an area of management theory. The purpose of the research was to understand how stakeholders affect organizations and are themselves affected by organizations. The research began with a literature review to identify existing knowledge in the field and from this a conceptual framework (called RELATE) was developed and a process for its application. The RELATE model was then tested using quantitative data collected via a postal questionnaire from 700 customers of a European service organization. The findings provided empirical support for the theory that there is mutual dependency between organizations and their stakeholders and that the way stakeholders relate to an organization is dependent on the way the organization relates to them.

Whilst these types of research outputs are the product of pure research following a highly theoretical development process, they have also been used to inform management practice. The researchers have worked closely with leading organizations to translate theory into practice by applying their frameworks and models to organizational situations. This results in three benefits. First, organizations are able to build evidence-based strategies to form relationships that benefit both stakeholders and the organization by encouraging positive behaviours found in the research such as loyalty and sustainable consumption; second, the transfer of knowledge from the academic domain to management practice; and third, the validation of the pure research findings by application and relevance in practice.

1.3.2 Applied research

Applied research, on the other hand, is likely to emerge as a direct response to a particular problem faced by practitioners and with the output being aimed directly at a practitioner audience. Note, however, that the research itself may be carried out by academics, practitioners or by commercial research specialists such as a consultancy or market research agency. In applied research the primary aim is to address the practical problem or issue and the output is usually intended to be used by practitioners, such as managers or policy makers, to inform decision making and action. Dissemination may be by publication (for example, for research commissioned by government or other public bodies) but the findings of applied research may also be very restricted in terms of its circulation, especially if it is commercially sensitive. Applied research varies also in the extent to which it engages with current theory and past research, but by its nature the contribution to the body of theoretical knowledge is likely to be a secondary goal for the research. Nevertheless, applied research can develop awareness of both research methods and theory within the wider management profession. Research in Practice 1.2 shows applied research in action.

RESEARCH IN PRACTICE 1.2

The use of applied research to explore the practice of 'homeworking'

The Henley Centre for Customer Management is an example of a research centre focused upon applied research. The centre consists of researchers and representatives of major companies who jointly explore contemporary topics relevant to customer relationships of importance to companies today. In 2011 the Centre turned its attention to the growing phenomenon 'homeworking', a practice by companies of using people who work from their own homes, particularly for call-centre work. It is important to companies, given the contact that such staff may have with customers. A research project (Harrington and Clark 2011) was set up with the aim of better understanding this practice and the benefits it presents for both the companies and the homeworkers. The project began with a review of the current status of homeworking in both the US and the UK by using a web-based search. To gain a deeper understanding of the practice the team then undertook a series of interviews with key managers in organizations that use homeworkers, as well as with homeworkers themselves who were part of the Homeworker Project Companies (HPC). The focus of the research was to understand the benefits of homeworking rather than to develop a theoretical explanation of it. The companies using homeworking stated the benefits as cost savings, increased flexibility, reduced absenteeism and improved customer satisfaction. Whilst homeworkers were generally happy with their way of working, a key challenge was the isolation that they experienced, given the lack of social contact with other colleagues that would happen in a traditional workplace. The findings of the research project provided companies in the HPC with insights as to how to leverage the benefits and develop potential solutions to the isolation problem for their homeworkers.

1.3.3 Implications for your research project

So what is the appropriate type of research for your project? The answer depends, of course, on your situation. If you are doing a doctorate you would typically be expected to demonstrate that your work makes a contribution to knowledge. Although this is rather difficult to define, it certainly means that you need to make sure that your research is grounded within the existing body of knowledge in your topic area, so your research is likely to fall within the category of pure research even if your project has a strong practice orientation. For Master's-level and undergraduate projects, requirements will vary according to the type of project you are doing, but most final projects will offer the opportunity of doing applied research. If you are not bound by the requirements of an academic qualification you are likely to be able to decide what is most appropriate in view of your reason for undertaking a research project. Whatever your circumstances, however, you should make sure your choice is compatible with the expectations of other stakeholders in your project.

CRITICAL COMMENTARY 1.1

Management research, management theory and management practice

In this chapter we present a generally positive view of the relationship between management research, management theory and management practice and, by implication, of the possibilities that the relationship offers for deepening our understanding of the business of management. Many commentators, however, are less confident. Van de Ven, for instance, suggests that the goal of advancing 'scientific and practical knowledge' through research 'remains an elusive ideal' (Van de Ven 2007: 2). In fact this topic has been the subject of a long-running debate in both the academic and the broader literature, but we will highlight two particular areas of concern in this short commentary.

The first concern regards the extent to which academic research is relevant and useful for practitioners. Bennis and O'Toole (2005: 98), for example, writing in the context of research at business schools, claim that 'some of what is published in A-list journals is excellent, imaginative, and valuable. But much is not. A renowned CEO doubtless speaks for many when he labels academic publishing a "vast wasteland" from the point of view of business practitioners.' Too much focus on the concerns of pure research runs the risk of a withdrawal into 'academic fundamentalism' (Tranfield and Starkey 1998: 350).

A second concern is the failure of practitioners to inform themselves of the latest findings in their area and adopt the results of recent research (Van de Ven 2007), or that they are too busy with the latest fad to focus on fundamentals (Weick 2001). Neither is it clear that reliance on applied research is the answer. As Tranfield and Starkey (1998: 350) warn, there is risk in letting the research agenda be driven by 'political priorities and processes, managerial fads and fashions' and the need for quick results.

A more positive view is taken by Hodgkinson and Rousseau (2009), who point to a number of initiatives and examples of collaborative working between academics and practitioners which, they argue, 'point cumulatively to a new zeitgeist of closer ties between research and practice' (Hodgkinson and Rousseau 2009: 543). We hope that your research project will be part of that zeitgeist!

1.4 The relationship between research and theory

In the previous discussion we noted that pure and applied research may differ in terms of how they relate to practice. We now move on to look at what we mean by 'theory' and how it relates to research and to practice.

1.4.1 *What is theory?*

Christensen and Raynor (2003: 68) define theory as 'a statement predicting what actions will lead to what results and why'. A more technical definition is offered by Gill and Johnson (2010: 43), who define theory as an 'abstract conceptual framework which allows us to explain why specific observed regularities happen'. A theory might explain, for example, why a particular leadership style is more effective than other leadership styles in particular situations or how customers choose between different products when shopping online.

Taking this further, Whetten (1989) argues that a theory should consist of four elements:

1   The concepts that make up the theory. A **concept** is a mental category that groups observations or ideas together on the basis of shared attributes. It can be relatively concrete such as 'age' or 'income', or more tangible, such as 'satisfaction' or 'leadership style'. Concepts form the 'building blocks' of theory (Strauss and Corbin 1998: 101).
2   A statement of how the concepts are related, for example, in terms of one causing another.
3   A logical explanation for the relationships between them; this provides the 'theoretical glue' (Whetten 1989: 491) that holds the theory together.
4   Identification of the contexts, such as the organizational situation, in which the theory applies.

Theory should therefore provide an explanation of a phenomenon in terms of the relevant concepts, how they are related, why they are related and in what contexts the theory would apply. As we discuss in Chapter 3, such theories are often depicted graphically as a conceptual model that shows the concepts and the relationships between them.

1.4.2 Theory and practice

Theory and practice sometimes seem to belong to separate worlds and the relevance of theory to everyday management practice is not always obvious. Christensen and Raynor make the point in a light-hearted way:

> Theory often gets a bum rap among managers because it's associated with the word 'theoretical', which connotes 'impractical'. But it shouldn't . . . Every action that managers take, and every plan they formulate, is based on some theory in the back of their minds that makes them expect the actions they contemplate will have the results they envision. But . . . most managers don't realise they are voracious users of theory.
>
> Christensen and Raynor (2003: 68)

Argyris and Schön (1974: 4) make a similar point in their study of theory and professional practice. They argue that any deliberate behaviour is the result of 'theories of action' that human beings hold and which guide those actions. Such theories of action, they suggest, take the form of: 'in situation S, if you want to achieve consequence C, do A' (Argyris and Schön 1974: 4). As humans we therefore find ourselves applying theories every day, whether or not we are aware of doing so.

The inevitability of using some form of theory in our everyday and professional lives means, as Henry Mintzberg puts it (2004: 250), that 'we use theory whether we realize it or not. So our choice is not between theory and practice as much as between different theories that can inform our practice'. In the view of some writers, theory is even more pervasive. It is a way of 'seeing and thinking about the world'

(Alvesson and Deetz 2000: 37) that shapes how we view reality. Even a simple description is not just a neutral account of what something 'is'. It implicitly involves the concepts, background knowledge and language available to us as observers. You cannot describe an executive board meeting, for example, without invoking the concepts and language of an executive board, of meetings, and so on (Thorpe and Holt 2008). Our observations therefore are influenced by the concepts and theories we hold. They are not theory neutral. However, if our theories influence our observations they do not determine them; instead, our observations can be thought of as 'theory laden' (Sayer 1992: 83). Being aware of our theories and how they may be influencing what we do and think is one of the reasons for taking a reflexive stance on research, as we discuss in more detail in Section 1.6.

1.4.3 The scope of theory

Theories can vary greatly in their scope. A commonly encountered categorization distinguishes three types of theory in terms of their scale.

Grand theories

Grand theories, sometimes known as meta-theories, are theoretical systems that apply to large-scale social phenomena. Marxist historical materialism and Freudian psychoanalysis are two familiar examples. Grand theory can provide a general orientation towards a problem area and suggest potential explanations for phenomena of interest. It may also be linked to a specific philosophical orientation and thereby incorporate a particular understanding of the nature of research and of the social world. Grand theory may, however, be difficult to test empirically or to use directly in a research project because of its high degree of abstraction, but it may provide an overall orientation for a study.

Middle-range theories

Middle-range theories have a more limited scope than grand theory and provide an explanation of a particular phenomenon, such as leadership or organizational change. As a result they can more readily be used to guide research efforts. Middle-range theories are likely to be important in guiding pure research efforts but they can also inform applied projects. An example of a middle-range theory is the Theory of Reasoned Action (Ajzen and Fishbein 1980), which explains the relationship between beliefs, attitudes, behaviour intention and actual behaviour. This theory has been used extensively in consumer research as the basis for explaining a range of purchase and consumption behaviours.

Substantive theories

Substantive theories apply to a specific phenomenon in a specific setting such as leadership in distributed teams or organizational change in entrepreneurial start-ups. Research in Practice 1.2 provides such an example. Their narrower scope means that they may not be applicable to other contexts, but their closeness to practical problems makes them especially relevant in applied research, where the focus may be a particular situation and the researcher has less interest in theorizing about other contexts.

For applied research, middle-range or substantive theories will probably be more directly relevant to the immediate needs of the research project. Even if you are carrying out pure research, with a strong theoretical focus, contributing to middle-range or substantive theory in the topic area is likely to be more feasible than aspiring to develop grand theory.

1.4.4 Theory and research

When commencing a research project you may already be familiar with existing theories in your topic area and you will encounter further theories as you start to read more about your subject. But how can theory contribute to your research? And how can your research contribute to theory? Figure 1.2 shows two different ways in which theory can be integrated into research.

With a **deductive** approach you start with theory, typically based on existing literature that proposes possible solutions to your research problem. This theory is then tested against data collected in the situation under investigation. The resulting findings provide both a test of the theory and potential solutions to your chosen problem. A deductive approach might be used, for example, to investigate the factors that influence customers' decisions to shop online. By drawing on existing theory to identify factors seen to influence online shopping behaviour and by collecting suitable data, you could test which factors were influential in the situation you were investigating.

When adopting an **inductive** approach, on the other hand, you begin the collection of data via observations of a specific phenomenon in response to your research problem and then build a theory about what is going on from those observations. For example, an inductive approach might be used to investigate the process by which innovative ideas are developed into a final product in a particular situation. Rather than test an existing theory, you could decide to gather data about what is going on by studying how particular products have been developed from the idea stage in one or more organizations. This would enable you to develop a more detailed understanding of how such product development is done, from which you could build a theory explaining the product innovation process. In an inductive approach theory is therefore

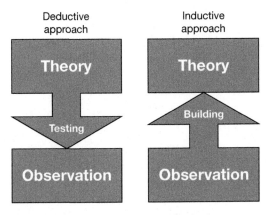

Figure 1.2 Deductive and inductive approaches to research

primarily an output; in a deductive approach it is a key input. The two approaches involve contrasting 'logics of enquiry' (Blaikie 2000: 8), using theory and literature in different ways and making use of different research designs, as we discuss in more detail in Chapter 4.

1.5 Research and philosophy

Behind any research lie our fundamental assumptions about the world we are researching. This is the domain of philosophy, and in particular the philosophy of social science. The debates in this area have divided research communities for decades (and even centuries). This is a fascinating area for those who are interested in it but can be mystifying to those who are not. We now introduce you to aspects of this topic that are particularly relevant to management research. Our aim is to assist you in making sense of philosophical issues that you will encounter during your research and to help you develop your own philosophical position in relation to your own project.

1.5.1 Epistemology and ontology

Discussion of research philosophy often proceeds by distinguishing between the **epistemology** and **ontology** of different philosophical positions. In social sciences, epistemology usually refers to questions of how we know what we claim to know. Since epistemology is concerned with the problem of how we know things its connection with research as an activity of findings things out is fairly obvious. To illustrate this, we will highlight two contrasting epistemological stances, **objectivism** and **subjectivism**. An objectivist epistemology assumes the possibility of gathering data through the theory-neutral (objective) and value-free observation of the social world by the application of appropriate methods. A subjectivist epistemology rejects this view and instead assumes that all observation is, at the very least, theory laden, thereby calling into question any claim to produce a value-free, objective account of something. Our epistemological assumptions have significant implications for how we go about evaluating the research that we and others produce.

Ontology is concerned with our beliefs about the nature of what is out there to know in the social world. At first sight the relevance of ontology to research may not be that clear. But if we think about it in terms of our assumptions about the nature of the world we are investigating we can see that it does matter. Again we can illustrate this by contrasting two ontological positions, realism and idealism. Ontological **realism** assumes the existence of a mind-independent reality. The tree outside the office window, for example, is there independently of our awareness of it. Ontological **idealism**, on the other hand, challenges that assumption. Idealism, as we use the term here, does not necessarily deny the existence of an object outside our window but it does suggest that its 'tree-ness' is not something intrinsic to the object but is instead a product, a construction, of cognitive and social processes that make it meaningful for us as humans. If we turn our attention from trees to social phenomena such as organization or culture, we can start to see the importance of ontological questions to research. Is an organization something 'out there' waiting for us to come along and describe and explain it, or is it something that can be understood by investigating the shared meanings of organizational members? How we answer such questions influences how we approach the problem of research in a social setting such as management.

1.5.2 Philosophical orientations

These epistemological and ontological assumptions combine in different ways to contribute to alternative philosophical orientations to business and management research. These alternative orientations have different emphases in terms of the primary goals of research, what constitutes an appropriate research approach and the preferred research methods. We summarize them in Table 1.3.

Table 1.3 Philosophical orientations in research

| | Philosophical orientation | | | |
	Positivism	Interpretivism	Social constructionism	Realism
Epistemology	Objectivist	Objectivist	Subjectivist	Subjectivist
Ontology	(Direct) Realist	Idealist	Idealist	(Depth) Realist
Emphasis of research	Explanation in terms of universal 'laws'	Understanding lived experience and shared culture	Understanding the process of social construction	Explanation in terms of causal mechanisms
Typical research approach	Deductive	Inductive	Inductive	Abductive/ inductive
Dominant research methods	Quantitative, with qualitative research in a subordinate role	Qualitative	Qualitative	Qualitative/ quantitative

Positivism

Positivism, at least as the term is used in the social science, usually refers to a philosophical orientation that looks to apply the methods of the natural sciences to the social sciences. Positivist research aims to establish causal explanations in the form of universal laws by means of controlled observation and measurement and deductive theory testing, in line with its objectivist epistemology. Rigorous and explicit procedures are advocated so as to avoid researcher bias and to ensure that the research is value-free. Positivism is closely associated with quantitative methods and research designs such as experiments. Positivism's ontological position is sometimes described as direct realism because it restricts claims about the world to those that can be observed. Claims about things that cannot be observed or about things about which suitable evidence cannot be gathered (such as some mental processes) are treated with scepticism. This emphasis on the central role of observation is sometimes referred to as **empiricism**, which term is sometimes used synonymously with positivism. Positivism is often depicted as the dominant research approach in business and management but it has come in for a great deal of criticism on both philosophical and practical grounds.

One response to the criticisms of positivism has been the emergence of **post-positivism** which has been described as a 'less arrogant form of positivism' (Crotty 1998: 29). Phillips and Burbules sum up the post-positivist position in the following terms:

> [Post-postivists] are united in believing that human knowledge is not based on unchallengeable, rock-solid foundations – it is conjectural. We have grounds, or warrants, for asserting the beliefs, or conjectures, that we hold as scientists, often very good grounds, but these grounds are not indubitable. Our warrants for accepting things can be withdrawn in the light of further investigation.
>
> Phillips and Burbules (2000: 26)

In addition to the quantitative methods typical of positivist research, post-positivist researchers also use qualitative research methods, particularly those that lend themselves to more structured analysis. Post-positivists may also employ mixed method research designs aimed at 'capturing as much of reality as possible' (Denzin and Lincoln 2000: 9). Nevertheless, post-positivism retains much of positivism's commitment to the goal of value-free, objective research.

Interpretivism

Intepretivism rejects the positivist assumption that the methods of the natural sciences apply to the social sciences, insisting instead that there are fundamental differences between the objects (such as chemicals and rocks) that natural scientists study and the reasoning human beings that social scientists study. People actively interpret the world around them and do so within a specific socio-cultural context. Understanding of the social world therefore requires understanding it from the point of view of the people directly involved in the social process (Burrell and Morgan 1979). We have therefore classified interpretivist ontology as a form of idealism, in order to stress the importance of meaning and understanding in this approach. Interpretivist researchers are also interested in the lived experience of individuals, in how they understand and make sense of their experiences. The resulting knowledge of particular groups and events in their specific context is often referred to as idiographic, in contrast to positivism's search for nomothetic knowledge in the form of universal laws. Given the very different way in which the nature of the social world is understood, it is not surprising that interpretivism questions the use of the methods of the natural sciences for social research, arguing instead that a different approach is needed. In place of the deductive, quantitative methods that characterize a positivist research, interpretivist research therefore typically adopts an inductive approach, combined with qualitative research methods, such as ethnography and in-depth interviews that allow the researcher to investigate phenomena in context and through the perspective of those involved.

In Table 1.3 we show interpretivism as adopting an objectivist epistemology. This is reflected in two commitments that are evident to varying degrees in interpretivist research (Hammersley 2013). The first is a commitment to the value of detailed and accurate observation via in-depth field research, including audio and even video recording where appropriate. The second is the need for researchers to put aside their presuppositions and own assumptions in favour of understanding the culture being researched on its own terms. This objectivist stance has led some writers to refer to this approach as neo-empiricism, on the basis that interpretivism shares to some degree positivism's empiricist orientation (Johnson et al. 2006), even though it is opposed to other aspects of positivist thought. This objectivist aspect of interpretivism has been challenged by the rise of social constructionism, to the point where today many interpretivist researchers are likely to adopt a more subjectivist epistemological position.

Social constructionism

Social constructionism is a more recent development than either positivism or interpretivism but has been very influential in both the philosophy and method of social science. As its name suggests, social constructionism emphasizes the 'constructed' nature of social reality. Phenomena like management, organization and personal identity are not determined by some internal essence that makes them what they are but are instead constructed through our social processes and, in particular, through interaction and language. Researcher interest therefore focuses on investigating the construction process, documenting, for example, how and in what ways things such as 'globalization' or 'competence' get constructed in some ways rather than others. Social constructionist research is generally qualitative and inductive and often with a particular interest in research that investigates language (spoken and written).

As we have seen, social constructionism shares interpretivism's ontological idealism, but it rejects its neo-empiricist leanings in favour of epistemological subjectivism. It thereby draws attention to the constructed nature of the researcher's own account of his or her own research. Social constructionist researchers have, for example, sought to show the processes through which scientific facts are constructed during the course of laboratory research (such as Latour and Woolgar 1986). This is a very radical move in many respects: if all accounts, including scientific ones, are socially constructed, what is the basis for preferring one over another? The extreme relativism implied by this question is not accepted by all social constructionists, let alone all researchers, but it draws attention to the problem of how we should decide whether a piece of research should be taken seriously. The problem of deciding on the quality of a piece of research is an important topic which we discuss further in Chapter 4.

Realism

Our final example of a philosophical orientation is realism. As we are using the term here, it refers to the relatively recent version of realism that goes under various headings such as critical realism, subtle realism and scientific realism. As its name suggests, it is characterized by a form of ontological realism. It replaces the direct realism of positivism, however, with a **depth realism** that draws a distinction between the events we can observe (the empirical) and the potentially unobservable mechanisms and processes that give rise to them (the real). Explanation, in this view, involves identifying the causal mechanisms that generate the regularities that we observe in the natural and social world. For example, we may observe that gunpowder ignites when it comes into contact with a flame. From a realist point of view, an explanation of this phenomenon would require that we identify the mechanisms, such as gunpowder's chemical composition, that bring this about, and the contexts, such as the presence of oxygen, in which it occurs. Identification of such causal mechanisms, along with the contexts in which they are triggered, is a key component of realist research. The research methods for doing this can be qualitative or quantitative, although realists are often critical of the ways in which quantitative methods are used in positivist research. Realism also questions both the deductive and inductive approaches to research in favour of what is sometimes called abduction, a topic we discuss in more detail in Chapter 4.

Realism also departs from positivism in adopting a subjectivist epistemology. In doing so it accepts that we can only know the world through our descriptions of it. Unlike social constructionism, which also espouses a subjectivist epistemological position, realism insists that there is a reality independent of our knowledge of it and this reality constrains the ways in which we can construct our world and offers the possibility of being able to decide which accounts of reality are more adequate than others. Observation in the realist view is always theory laden but it is not theory determined.

1.5.3 Axiological assumptions

Axiology deals with questions of value (Saunders et al. 2012). In terms of philosophical positions in research, positivism is traditionally associated with the idea that research should be value free. The researcher's neutrality is achieved through the application of appropriate research methods and techniques. Other philosophical orientations acknowledge the inevitability of researcher involvement in the research process and thus are more sceptical of the extent to which research can be free of the explicit or implicit values of the researcher. One response to this loss of certainty has been to emphasize the need for researchers to be aware of their own role in and impact upon the research process. This awareness is often referred to as reflexivity, a topic we discuss in more detail later in the chapter.

Values are also at the heart of another debate in business research; namely, on whose behalf and in whose interests is the research being done? We have so far taken it for granted that research that generates knowledge that improves management and organizational practice is a 'good thing'. This is not a view shared by everyone. There is a long tradition in both academic and popular writing that is critical of capitalism in its various manifestations. In business and management research what are sometimes known as critical management studies have been inspired by various influences, particularly Marxism and feminism, and question what they see as research that operates in the interests of management or other dominant groups. Researchers taking this approach aim to surface issues such as gender imbalance, discrimination and worker exploitation. We explore this further in Chapter 7 when we discuss the ethical aspects of management research and the emergence of participatory research.

1.5.4 Taking it forward

Although we may not be explicitly aware of it, our philosophical orientation shapes the way we frame a research problem and the possible solutions to it. It influences how we go about investigating it in terms of the overall approach and the specific research methods and techniques that we adopt. This is one reason why academic research, especially for dissertations and theses, often includes a discussion of philosophical issues as part of the research report. But where do we start? Our experience is that most new researchers do not begin with strong awareness of, let alone commitment to, a particular philosophical orientation. Instead, this develops over time as they learn more about research methods and as they look at research carried out from different philosophical positions. At this early stage, therefore, do not worry if you do not have a sense of where you stand in relation to the philosophical aspects of research. As you read, talk about and, above all, reflect on your research project you will develop your own thinking on this complex but fascinating aspect of research.

We conclude this section on a note of caution. It is very easy to get lost in philosophical debate about and lose sight of the research itself. If you find yourself getting into this situation, the advice of Tashakkori and Teddlie is worth noting:

> For most researchers committed to the thorough study of a research problem . . . the underlying world view hardly enters the picture, except in the most abstract sense . . . [Philosophical] considerations are not as important in the final analysis as the research question that you are attempting to answer.
>
> Tashakkori and Teddlie (1998: 21)

1.6 Reflexivity and the researcher

A growing awareness of the impact of the researcher on the research process has led to calls for researchers to pay greater attention to this aspect of their work. This is often talked about in terms of reflexivity and involves 'a focus on how does who I am, who I have been, who I think I am, and how I feel affect data collection and analysis' (Pillow 2003: 176). In this sense reflexivity goes beyond simply reflecting upon the technical details of our research, to think more deeply about how our underlying assumptions influence what we do and how we do it and how those assumptions are affected in turn by our experiences.

1.6.1 Types of reflexivity

Reflexivity is not constrained by any single aspect of our research but operates on multiple levels simultaneously, as shown by the following examples (Lynch 2000, Johnson and Duberley 2003, Haynes 2012):

- Theoretical reflexivity. How do our existing theories shape our framing of the research problem and our approach to it? How are these theories themselves shaped as the project unfolds?
- Methodological reflexivity. How are our assumptions and preferences about research methods influencing and influenced by the research?
- Philosophical reflexivity. How do our philosophical commitments (epistemological, ontological and axiological) shape how we go about our research? How are these, in turn, influenced by the research project?
- Standpoint reflexivity. How does our own political, cultural, social and emotional standpoint influence our approach to the research?

We suggest that reflexivity about our own standpoint in relation to the research is particularly relevant when we are doing research about which we have strong personal feelings or close personal involvement. Such situations can easily arise for the insider researcher doing research in their own organization; reflexivity is therefore important not just with respect to the technical details of the research but also in terms of engagement with stakeholders who may influence or be affected by the research or its findings.

1.6.2 *Being reflexive*

What can we do to be more reflexive about our research? Making time and space to think and reflect is the first step, but to develop our skills in reflexivity takes more than that. As part of your research project we encourage you to keep a research journal or diary (see Chapter 8). This is the ideal place to start writing reflexively. Alongside recording 'factual' information such as the date that an interview took place or the details of a decision that was made, record also your emerging thoughts and feelings about what was happening, why you took a particular decision, how you carried out a particular task and so on. Use the diary to reflect on the implications of what you are doing, both for the research and yourself. Not only will this help you develop your reflexive skills, it will also provide a valuable record of your actions and thoughts during the research when it comes to writing up your project, especially if you are required or decide to include a reflective component in your final report.

KEY LEARNING POINTS

- Research is a purposeful systematic process of investigation in order to find solutions to problems or issues.
- Pure (or basic) research is focused on adding to the existing body of theoretical knowledge that exists in relation to a particular topic or domain. Its output is primarily aimed at an academic audience. Applied research addresses particular questions or problems faced by practitioners, with the output being aimed at a practitioner audience.
- Theory is an explanation of a phenomenon in terms of relationships between two or more concepts. The role of theory in a research project can vary. With a deductive approach we begin with theory and test it against data. With an inductive approach we begin by collecting data and then build theory from our observations.
- The philosophy of research helps us to understand the fundamental assumptions about the world that lie behind our approach as a researcher. Four important philosophical orientations are positivism, interpretivism, social constructionism and realism.
- Reflexivity is important to researchers. It involves the researcher in not only reflecting upon the technical details of a project but also thinking more deeply about how underlying assumptions have influenced what we do and how we do it. Researchers should also reflect upon how these assumptions are themselves affected by the experiences of research.

NEXT STEPS

1.1   Familiarizing yourself with the terms of reference for your project. We recommend that you start your research project by looking at the specification (often called 'terms of reference') of your project. This may be set by your academic institution and/or the organization instigating the project.

1.2   Identifying challenges and issues in your project. Identify any questions or challenges that you have with regard to your intended project. Note these down so that you can review them as you read later chapters.

1.3   Reflecting on your research. Review the types of reflexivity listed in Section 1.6.1. Note down your thoughts with respect to each one to help you develop your awareness of your position with respect to research and your research project.

Further reading

For further reading, please see the companion website.

References

Ajzen, I. and Fishbein, M. (1980). *Understanding attitudes and predicting social behaviour.* Englewood Cliffs, NJ: Prentice Hall.

Alvesson, M. and Deetz, S. (2000). *Doing critical management research.* London: Sage.

Argyris, C. and Schön, D. A. (1974). *Theory in practice. Increasing professional effectiveness.* San Francisco, CA: Jossey-Bass.

Bennis, W. G. and O'Toole, J. (2005). 'How business schools lost their way', *Harvard Business Review*, 83(5), 96–104.

Blaikie, N. (2000). *Designing social research.* Cambridge: Polity.

Burrell, G. and Morgan, G. (1979). *Sociological paradigms and organisational analysis.* Aldershot: Ashgate Publishing Ltd.

Christensen, C. M. and Raynor, M. E. (2003). 'Why hard-nosed executives should care about management theory', *Harvard Business Review*, 81(9), 67–74.

Crotty, M. (1998). *The foundations of social research.* London: Sage.

Denzin, N. K. and Lincoln, Y. S. (2000). Introduction: The discipline and practice of qualitative research. *In:* Denzin, N. K. and Lincoln, Y. S. (eds) *Handbook of qualitative research.* 2nd edn. Thousand Oaks, CA: Sage.

ESOMAR (2013). *Market research explained* [online]. ESOMAR. Available from: www.esomar.org/knowledge-and-standards/market-research-explained.php [Accessed 31 October 2013].

Gill, J. and Johnson, P. (2010). *Research methods for managers.* 4th edn. London: Sage.

Gray, D. (2009). *Doing research in the real world.* Los Angeles, CA: Sage.

Hammersley, M. (2013). *What is qualitative research?* London: Bloomsbury.

Harrington, T. and Clark, M. (2011). *Homeworking.* Reading: The Henley Centre for Customer Management, Henley Business School.

Haynes, K. (2012). Reflexivity in qualitative research. *In:* Symon, G. and Cassell, C. (eds) *Qualitative organisational research.* London: Sage.

PART I

Hodgkinson, G. P. and Rousseau, D. M. (2009). 'Bridging the rigour–relevance gap in management research: It's already happening!', *Journal of Management Studies*, 46(3), 534–46.

Johnson, P. and Duberley, J. (2003). 'Reflexivity in management research', *Journal of Management Studies*, 40(5), 1279–303.

Johnson, P., Buehring, A., Cassell, C. and Symon, G. (2006). 'Evaluating qualitative management research: Towards a contingent criteriology', *International Journal of Management Reviews*, 8(3), 131–56.

Latour, B. and Woolgar, S. (1986). *Laboratory life: The construction of scientific facts*. Princeton, NJ: Princeton University Press.

Lynch, M. (2000). 'Against reflexivity as an academic virtue and source of privileged knowledge', *Theory, Culture & Society*, 17(3), 26–54.

McGivern, Y. (2006). *The practice of market and social research: An introduction*. Harlow: Prentice Hall.

Mintzberg, H. (2004). *Managers not MBAs*. Harlow: Pearson Education.

Money, K., Hillenbrand, C., Hunter, I. and Money, A. G. (2012). 'Modelling bi-directional research: A fresh approach to stakeholder theory', *Journal of Strategy and Management*, 5(1), 5–24.

OED (2011). Research. *In:* Stevenson, A. and Waite, M. (eds) *Concise Oxford English Dictionary*. Oxford: Oxford University Press.

Phillips, D. and Burbules, N. C. (2000). *Postpositivism and educational research*. Lanham, MD: Rowman and Littlefield.

Pillow, W. (2003). 'Confession, catharsis, or cure? Rethinking the uses of reflexivity as methodological power in qualitative research', *International Journal of Qualitative Studies in Education*, 16(2), 175–96.

Robson, C. (2011). *Real world research*. 3rd edn. Chichester: Wiley.

Saunders, M., Lewis, P. and Thornhill, A. (2012). *Research methods for business students*. 6th edn. Harlow: Prentice Hall.

Sayer, A. (1992). *Method in social science*. 2nd edn. London: Routledge.

Sekaran, U. and Bougie, R. (2010). *Research methods for business*. 5th edn. Chichester: John Wiley and Sons.

Strauss, A. and Corbin, J. (1998). *Basics of qualitative research*. 2nd edn. Thousand Oaks, CA: Sage Publications.

Tashakkori, A. and Teddlie, C. (1998). *Mixed methodology*. Thousand Oaks, CA: Sage.

Thorpe, R. and Holt, R. (eds) (2008). *The Sage dictionary of qualitative management research*. London: Sage.

Tranfield, D. and Starkey, K. (1998). 'The nature, social organization and promotion of management research: Towards policy', *British Journal of Management*, 9(4), 341–353.

Van de Ven, A. H. (2007). *Engaged scholarship*. Oxford: Oxford University Press.

Weick, K. E. (2001). 'Gapping the relevance bridge: Fashions meet fundamentals in management research', *British Journal of Management*, 12 (Special Issue), S71–S75.

Whetten, D. A. (1989). 'What constitutes a theoretical contribution?', *Academy of Management Review*, 14(4), 490–5.

2 Formulating your research problem

CHAPTER SUMMARY

The key topics covered in this chapter are:

- seeing research as a problem-solving activity
- identifying and refining a research problem for your project
- selecting and formulating your research questions
- evaluating your research questions.

2.1 Introduction

Your **research problem** is the specific issue or opportunity that forms the subject of your research. It should give a clear and compelling reason for doing the research and provide the basis for developing the research questions that you need to answer in order to solve the problem. Research questions in turn provide the basis for developing your overall research design. Identifying a suitable problem is therefore a critical stage of your project. It is one of the most challenging aspects of undertaking research, especially for novice researchers, so this chapter takes a step-by-step approach to doing so. We begin by looking at how to take a problem-centred approach to research and how to identify a suitable research problem for your own project. Next we examine different types of research questions and how they relate to the overall aims of your research. We conclude by looking at what makes a good research question.

2.2 A problem-solving view of research

One way of thinking about research is to see it as a problem-solving activity. Research, according to this view, 'aims to increase our understanding of complex problems or phenomena that exist under conditions of uncertainty found in the world' (Van de Ven 2007: 72). It applies to both applied and pure research because a research problem may arise from a practical issue or opportunity experienced by practitioners (including the researcher) or it may be the result of anomalies or gaps identified in the theoretical literature. Note that we are using the word 'problem' in a broad sense so it should not be understood only in negative terms as something harmful or unwelcome; it can equally be an opportunity that merits further investigation, such as the potential offered by a new technology or new form of organization. A research problem may also have an exploratory aspect in response to a situation about which little is known.

2.2.1 The role of the research problem

Your research problem forms the crucial link between the practical or theoretical problem that has motivated your project and the design and conduct of the research itself. It provides the basis for framing clear research questions that will drive how you design your research in order to deliver useful research findings. Those findings ultimately help you to resolve your original practical or theoretical problem. Solving the research problem provides the rationale for undertaking your research and helps you to demonstrate the significance of your results (Creswell 2009). We depict these relationships in Figure 2.1.

Formulating a clear, well-focused research problem is not a simple or quick task. There are likely to be false starts, multiple iterations and revisions as you read around your potential topic, discuss it with colleagues, supervisors or others involved in the situation. Given that the process may require input from multiple stakeholders, negotiating access to potential research sites and even carrying out a preliminary review of the literature in your topic area, it is not surprising that this can take weeks or even months. Be prepared to invest the necessary time and energy into this crucial stage of your research project.

Taking a problem-centred approach draws attention to a more subtle and complex issue in choosing a research subject: problems are a matter of perception and

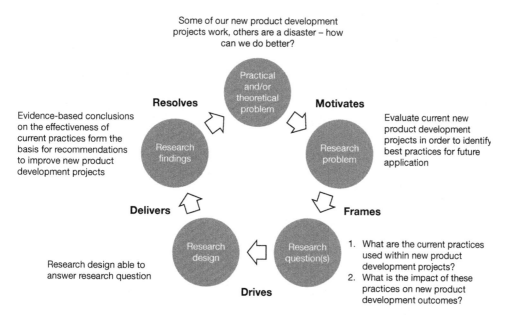

Figure 2.1 Linking research problems, questions, design and findings

interpretation and formulating them involves a process known as framing. Van de Ven explains this in the following way:

> All problems, anomalies, or issues motivating a study begin with a perception that something requires attention. Problems are not given by nature, but by how, whom, and why they are perceived ... That being the case, any formulation of a problem is a partial representation reflecting the perspectives and interests of the observer.
>
> Van de Ven (2007: 74)

How you frame a problem has a big influence on how you try to solve it. It also affects whether other people share the view that it is a problem. Framing it in a particular way may also blind you to other possible ways of looking at the problem. If you frame a problem in terms of human resources, for example, you will draw attention to some features of the situation and away from others. If someone else sees the same issue in terms of operations management, their perspective may be very different. As well as being aware of how different stakeholders perceive a particular situation, you also need to reflect on your own position and role in the research process. This involves developing a reflexive awareness of yourself as a researcher, as we highlighted in the previous chapter.

2.2.2 Research problems in pure research projects

In pure research, which aims at making an explicit contribution to theory, problem formulation typically involves the identification of some theoretical puzzle that the research is intended to address. In this kind of project, a review of literature (see Chapter 3) plays a central role in refining both your research problem and subsequent research questions. Alvesson and Sandberg (2011: 247) identify 'gap spotting' and 'problematization' as two possible strategies for generating research topics from the literature. Gap spotting, as its name suggests, involves identifying gaps in the literature or opportunities to extend current theories in some way or other. Problematization involves a more fundamental investigation of the assumptions that underlie existing theories. Problematization, according to Alvesson and Sandberg (2011), can lead to more interesting and influential theories. If successful, it may also lead to more radical theoretical innovation in the topic area. However, radical innovation in research is potentially risky and subject to high failure rates (Voss 2003). If you are new to research, you are probably best advised to take a more incremental and cautious approach, focusing on gaps or anomalies in existing theories that a well-scoped research project could address rather than trying to develop a radically new theory-of-everything.

2.2.3 Research problems in applied research projects

In applied research, your research problem is likely to originate directly from a practical issue or opportunity facing management or other stakeholders. If you are commissioned by a third party to carry out a project, whether on a commercial basis or as part of an academic course of study, the research problem is, to some extent, presented to you. One difficulty, however, is that the problem may not actually be formulated in research terms or even in a way that is researchable. Churchill (1999:

Table 2.1 Examples of the relationship between decision problems and research problems

Management decision problem	Research problem
Selection of offshore distribution channels	Evaluate channel structures and channel members in each of the countries being considered in order to determine their potential
Addressing variable level of performance in new product development	Evaluate new product development practices in order to identify practices for future application
Reducing employee turnover	Identify factors influencing employee turnover in order to identify options for policy changes
Building consumer trust in the online brand	Understand consumer perceptions of the online brand in order to identify improvement opportunities

78) discusses this challenge in terms of the need to move from the 'decision problem' to a 'research problem'. The decision problem relates to the situation faced by the organization and the decisions that management need to take in order to address it. The research problem is 'essentially a restatement of the decision problem in research terms' (Churchill 1999: 77). Table 2.1 illustrates this distinction. Churchill argues that this restatement is enabled by the researcher working closely with those involved to understand the 'total decision situation'.

Problem or symptom?

Understanding the total decision situation can help you to distinguish between surface symptoms and underlying problems. Suppose, for example, that a company's customer service team is making frequent mistakes when processing customer orders. As a result of the mistakes many customers have complained and stopped using the company's services. In response the company is offering compensation in an effort to retain them. You will no doubt recognize this as a classic case of treating the symptom rather than the problem. Whilst immediate action to retain customers may be necessary, only by focusing on the root causes of the mistakes in order processing will the problem really be solved.

Similar situations can arise when defining your research problem, particularly in applied research projects. Do not just take the initial statement of the problem for granted. Instead be prepared to do some preliminary investigation to ensure that you understand the situation in sufficient depth to be able to formulate your research problem adequately. Van de Ven (2007: 78) calls this 'grounding the problem'. Careful discussion with stakeholders is a useful starting point for getting a better understanding of what is going on and deeper insights into the problem space. Dialogue with those involved is also essential to ensure a common understanding of the problem and the expected outputs of the research. At this stage, even in applied projects, a preliminary review of literature on the topic area, including existing theories and models, can help you to understand the problem and identify relevant dimensions for subsequent investigation. Remember, however, that you are not expected to solve the problem at this point.

Is your research problem suitable?

Even once your problem is specified in research terms, you will still have to decide whether it is appropriate for you to take on. If you are doing commercial research the decision will primarily be a business one. If your project is part of an academic course such as a Master's degree, you will need to ensure that it meets the terms of reference set by your institution for your qualification. You should therefore make sure that you fully understand those terms of reference before accepting the task. You will also need to consider whether the proposed research is compatible with your personal goals and can be achieved within the time, word count and any other resource constraints you are working under. Lastly, regardless of the type of project, you must think through the ethical dimensions of the proposed research, a topic discussed in more detail in Chapter 7.

2.3 Choosing a research problem

You may already have a good idea of what research problem you would like to investigate, but equally you may be struggling to come up with a suitable subject. Even where you have a general idea or have even been asked to carry out a particular research project, the problem will still need to be refined and developed. In this section we present some suggestions for choosing your research problem and guidance on how to refine it.

2.3.1 Sources of ideas for your research problem

Many writers have offered suggestions for identifying research topics. What follows is drawn from their suggestions and our own experience and is summarized in Table 2.2.

- A good starting point is to reflect on your own personal experiences and interests. Work or career-related situations can offer a huge source of possible topics but other areas of personal life such as hobbies, voluntary work or community activities also provide plenty of scope for projects. A useful approach, in keeping with the problem-solving view of research, is to look for anomalies, puzzles, opportunities or the unexpected in your experiences with organizational and professional life.
- Discussion with practitioners, academics and other researchers can often generate potential topics. Talking to work colleagues and your broader social and

Table 2.2 Sources of ideas for your research problem

- Personal experiences and interests
- Discussions with practitioners, academics and colleagues
- Academic and practitioner literature, including popular media
- Past projects
- Projects of opportunity
- Seeking a sponsor/client

professional network can also throw up interesting ideas. Such discussions can lead to a direct request for help with a problem, a concrete suggestion of a topic or just more ideas to add to the emerging list of options.

- Read practitioner and academic journals and papers to see what is attracting attention. This is likely to be most fruitful when you have some idea of a general topic area, but practitioner publications can be particularly useful in identifying what is happening in your industry or profession. The general business media can also be a good source of potential topics. There is a risk of picking up on a transient management fad rather than a sound research topic, but this can be checked by further reading and discussion to see whether the topic has real substance.

- Look at past research projects. Past projects can be a useful source of inspiration for ideas, not least because researchers often identify where further research is needed. Looking at previous projects is particularly important if your project has to take a particular form such as a Master's dissertation or doctoral thesis because it will help you to get a better understanding of the scope, depth and complexity of what is expected.

- Look out for projects of opportunity. These are projects that just appear out of the blue from time to time. These can arise at work when a particular problem needs investigating, or you may hear about possible projects through your personal contacts. Many academic institutions have close relations with businesses and other organizations and may receive requests for help with issues that they are facing.

- Actively seek a potential client or sponsor organization for which you could conduct a research project. This can also provide you with an opportunity to get in touch with a potential future employer or simply to offer your services to an organization, such as a charity, that you would like to help. Your negotiation skills will be at a premium, as you may well be trying to reach agreement on the research problem, access to data and respondents, and the format of any deliverables, such as a research report, all at the same time.

Techniques such as mind mapping or brainstorming can also be helpful, especially if you are trying to move from a general idea to a specific, researchable problem. Whatever sources and techniques you use – and if you are starting from scratch you will probably need to use more than one – keep a record of your thoughts and emerging ideas. You will find it useful to start a research diary at this point, noting down ideas as they come to you so that they are not forgotten (we discuss keeping a research diary in Chapter 8).

A suitable research problem often emerges as a result of bringing together different perspectives. Figure 2.2 shows a simple Venn diagram that can help you to come up with a potential research problem. It brings together four areas of interest.

1   Professional interests. What issues or opportunities have you come across in your professional experiences that are of particular interest to you? Are there any particular skill sets or areas of knowledge that you want to acquire or develop?
2   Career interests. What areas of business and management are interesting for your future career development? Is there a particular topic area in which you want to raise your profile?

3   Employer interests. What issues or opportunities are important for your employing organization (or possible employer)?
4   Theoretical interests. What areas of management or organizational theory do you find particularly interesting?

Record your thoughts on each of these areas and look for any overlaps or interesting juxtapositions. Areas of overlap may suggest topic areas where there is synergy between different aspects of your life. These may be particularly fruitful in terms of the personal benefits they offer. They may also be easier to carry out from a practical point of view if they build on your existing knowledge, skills and professional and personal network.

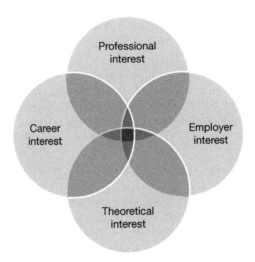

Figure 2.2 Looking for potential topics

2.3.2 *Refining your problem*

In our experience, if you use the techniques we have discussed it is not too hard to find a general topic area. The challenge comes in trying to refine a general idea into a clear, focused research problem. One way forward is to ask yourself how your research will contribute to resolving your chosen theoretical or practical problem. In particular, ask yourself what it is that you want to know at the end of the project that you do not now know. If you cannot give a clear answer to this question it probably means that you have not defined your problem clearly enough in research terms. At this point reading around the topic area and talking to practitioners, academics (including your supervisor, if you have one) and colleagues can help you to refine your thinking and identify researchable problems within a general topic area.

Once you have an initial idea for your research problem you need to ensure that it is clear and well defined. Van de Ven (2007) discusses this in terms of the problem's focus, level of analysis and scope. The focus of the project determines who or what is in the foreground and who or what is in the background of the research. A research study into stress at work, for example, might foreground those individuals experiencing stress, whilst treating the organization or management as the background or context. Alternatively, it might foreground managers involved in managing stressed individuals. It is likely that the audience for whom the research is intended (e.g. the client, the funding body or the academic institution) will influence the focus of the problem.

Your level of analysis (individual, group, organizational or industry) will also shape where the emphasis of the project lies and help you to identify the **unit of analysis** for your project. The unit of analysis refers to the level of aggregation of the data used during analysis and for reporting your results. Your unit of analysis can be at any level from individual (e.g. a consumer in marketing research), through group (e.g. a project team) or organization (e.g. a firm) to industry or geographical or political region. Being clear on your unit of analysis is important because it will affect how and where you collect your data, how you will carry out your analysis and how you will report your findings.

Once your level and unit of analysis are chosen, higher levels of aggregation will tend to be treated as context, whilst lower levels become components of the problem domain itself. Suppose, for example, that you were investigating the performance of project teams. The project teams would form your unit of analysis. The organizational and industry levels would be the context in which those project teams operate, whilst the individual project members would be of interest primarily in their role as part of the project team and as potential sources of data on aspects of their team's performance.

You will also need to decide the scope of your project by setting boundaries to determine what is 'in' and what is 'out'. This is rather like putting up a tent. You have to be very clear about what is inside the tent and what is going to be outside and accept that your tent cannot hold everything. As well as setting boundaries at the outset, you will also need to be very careful about scope creep as the project unfolds. This is a very common problem in dissertations and theses, especially once the literature review is underway. As you learn more about your problem area you will spot connections with other interesting subjects and it is very tempting to incorporate these, pushing out the boundaries of your project. Before long, if you are not careful, you will have lost focus and ended up with something unmanageable. Try to keep within your project scope and shift the boundaries only after careful consideration of the implications.

Scope creep can also be a problem when conducting research for a third party, especially if the research context is very dynamic, as it may be in applied projects in an organizational context. Client demands can change and grow as the project proceeds, particularly if the problem was not clearly defined at the outset. In such situations Markham's (2004) advice on handling scope creep in consultancy projects is worth following.

- Assess the implications of the proposed change for the project.
- Discuss these with the client (and your supervisor/tutor if applicable).
- Document the change, noting any changes to deliverables, timings and resource requirements (and fees for commercial projects).

2.3.3 What makes a good research problem?

A good research problem should be clear, tightly focused and well scoped. Sekaran and Bougie (2010) suggest that it should also be relevant, feasible and interesting. Relevance is achieved if the problem relates to a definite need in the domain of either practice (applied research) or theory (pure research) that is recognized by appropriate stakeholders, such as practitioners in a particular work situation or the academic community to which the findings of the research will be addressed. Feasibility addresses two related aspects. Firstly, it must be possible to address the problem through research, and secondly, it must be possible for you to carry out that research within the constraints of ethical conduct, access, time and other resources. Feasibility is therefore closely connected to the scope of the research. Lastly, the research problem must be interesting to you and to other relevant stakeholders. Sustaining enthusiasm throughout a research project can be a real challenge; make sure that you at least start off interested and enthused by your chosen problem.

When finalizing you research problem, do take time to consider your own motivations and objectives in undertaking it. If you are doing an assessed project as part of an academic course of study, then you may be motivated by the qualification towards which you are working. Beyond the immediate goals of the research project and any qualification, you may have other reasons for undertaking a particular piece of research work. You might want, for example, to learn about a new technology, investigate a new trend in organizational development or explore an industry sector other than your own. Alternatively, you may want to acquire or develop your skills in a particular type of research. Other benefits can also accrue from careful choice of research problem. You may want to raise your profile in a particular subject area or to use the research to help you make a career change. Whatever the case, a research project can offer great opportunities for personal development, so do not overlook these when choosing your research problem.

2.3.4 Writing down your research problem

As you think about your research problem, capture your thoughts by writing them down. Doing so will help you to develop and clarify your thinking around your topic. Ideas that are written down will also be easier to share and discuss with other people, such as colleagues or your supervisor. They will also be input for a written research proposal (Chapter 8) and even for your final report. In the early stages we have found the following simple structure useful to capture the essence of your research problem.

1 *Background* (a statement of the theoretical or practical problem, issue or opportunity motivating the research).
2 *This research will* (the overall aim of the research) *in order to* (how the research will address the problem).

For example:

1 The Company has been successful in attracting online customers but is unable to retain them.
2 This research will identify the factors influencing online customer retention in order to make recommendations to the Company for improvement.

The structure of the statement is designed to encourage you to think not just about the overall problem but also how your research will contribute to solving it. You will build upon this as you develop your research questions.

2.4 Developing your research questions

Research questions are the specific questions that your research needs to answer in order to resolve your research problem. As Maxwell (2013: 73) puts, it they show 'what you specifically want to understand by doing your study'. They form the bridge between your research problem and your research design (Figure 2.1). Clearly formulated, they provide direction for your investigation and selection of a suitable research design. Research questions also help to confirm the boundaries of your study and keep it manageable. They are also important because without clear questions it is very difficult to have clear answers and therefore to know whether your research has achieved its aims by answering them. Lastly, research questions also help to communicate to the reader what your research is intended to find out.

2.4.1 Research questions and investigative questions

One difficulty that novice researchers often encounter is distinguishing between research questions and **investigative questions** (Saunders et al. 2012). The latter are those questions that are used in interviews or questionnaires in order to collect the data needed to answer the research question. The difference is easily illustrated by distinguishing between a research question such as 'what is the average IQ (intelligence quotient) of a group of students?' and the investigative questions included in a test designed to measure the IQ of each individual. In many cases, as in the IQ example, the research question is not actually answerable in a single investigative question because IQ measurement requires more than one investigative question. Research questions and investigative questions are rarely the same. They are likely to be worded differently and to be at very different levels of generality. When formulating research questions you should be aware of this distinction.

2.4.2 Categorizing research questions

Different writers have proposed different ways of categorizing research questions. Our approach is to distinguish three generic types of question that not only generate different insights into the problem under investigation but require different research designs: 'what', 'why' and 'how' questions.

'What' questions

'What' questions seek to generate a detailed description of the characteristics and attributes of some phenomenon of interest. Examples might include:

- What is the level of satisfaction amongst our customers?
- What is the attitude of employees to the new information system?
- What are the experiences of people participating in a coaching programme?
- What are the characteristics of online shoppers?

- What are consumers saying about our products on social media websites?
- What leadership styles are displayed by project managers in our organization?

'What' questions can also encompass such questions as 'who', 'when', 'how much' and 'how many' (Yin 2009: 9), but all have the same purpose: to describe the phenomenon under investigation. Description can take many different forms. It may involve the quantitative measurement of the attributes of a large population or it may require the in-depth investigation of the experiences of a small number of people involved in a particular situation. Descriptive research often includes an element of comparison; for example, it might involve comparing the difference in customer satisfaction levels across different retail sites or the range of ways in which employees make sense of a change programme. Alternatively, it may seek to compare over time, for instance, to identify trends in social media use or changing attitudes to environmental issues. Descriptive research would not, however, seek to answer 'why' or 'how' such differences had come about. That would require a different type of research question and a different research design.

Description is 'fundamental to the research enterprise' (de Vaus 2001: 1), as it forms the basis on which further research can be built. Description may also be required to inform practical action. You might, for example, use research to develop a detailed description of the behavioural or demographic characteristics of your firm's customers in order to focus future marketing efforts. In evaluation, descriptive research methods can be used to gain an understanding of the situation being evaluated, to find out what policy measures are currently in place or to measure programme outcomes. Descriptive studies can also provide a 'call for action' (Yin 2011: 214) to draw attention to the need for a policy change, although care needs to be taken to avoid the accusation that the research is biased by the policy-making agenda. Descriptive research can also be undertaken as an end in itself. In some cases a topic may be sufficiently novel or interesting for no further justification to be needed. In many cases, however, description is not the end point of the research but provides an impetus and basis for further research into why and how a phenomenon exists. The relationship is not one way. Not only does good description provoke 'why' and 'how' questions; the answers to those questions can in turn help to add to the significance of the descriptive component of your research project.

'Why' questions

'Why' questions are concerned with explaining phenomena. de Vaus (2002) suggests three basic forms that such questions can take.

1   Why is something happening? For example, you observe that employee turnover rate is higher than the industry average; your research question may then be aimed at identifying the reasons why.
2   What are the consequences of something? What, for instance are the consequences of high employee turnover; your search is therefore for the effects of some phenomenon.
3   What is the effect of something on something else? Here the focus shifts to investigating a relationship between two phenomena. You might, for example, investigate whether employee satisfaction is impacting on employee turnover and, if so, by how much.

Example 'why' questions include:

* Why do some mergers and acquisitions fail?
* What are the effects of long-term unemployment?
* Why do people get involved in voluntary work?
* What is the effect of performance-related pay on employee motivation?
* What is the impact of online advertising on sales?

The wording is not always as straightforward as in the examples above. Common variations include expressions such as 'what factors influence/affect/impact . . .?' or 'what are the determinants of . . .?' In other situations the explanatory component is implied rather than explicit. For example, evaluating whether or not a particular management initiative works in the way intended means establishing and explaining the linkages between the initiative and the expected outcomes (Patton 2008). Similarly, investigating 'success factors' for something implies an explanatory component in order to determine the nature of the relationship between the supposed success factors and the outcome of interest.

Why is explanation of interest to researchers? Aneshensel (2002) suggests that it is prompted by the findings of descriptive research arousing curiosity about why things are as they are. 'The search for scientific understanding, therefore, tends', she argues, 'to evolve in the direction of explanation' (Aneshensel 2002: 4). Pure research often involves building or testing theories about why something is happening. Similarly, many applied research problems are related to issues of explanation. Behind this often lies the assumption that explanation may help in practical situations: if we can explain something we may be able to predict it and possibly control (or at least influence) it. In practice, the extent to which such prediction and control are feasible, or even desirable, within complex social systems like an organization is debatable, but, given the practical possibilities of knowing why something happens, it is not surprising that the answers to 'why' questions are of interest to practitioners as well as academics.

'How' questions

Answers to 'how' questions offer a different form of explanation by taking a process view. The focus of research may be on investigating the sequence of events or activities by which entities such as people or organizations change over time. Alternatively, it may take a more micro-level perspective, focusing on how 'things' such as organizing, leading and strategizing actually get done and how social reality is constituted, reproduced and maintained through social processes. A process perspective can also contribute to an understanding of causality by identifying the steps through which a cause produces an effect, and so complement 'why' type questions. Example 'how' questions could include:

* How do high technology start-ups develop over time?
* How do customers select an online insurance provider?
* How is strategy formulated in companies?

Historically, 'how' questions have undoubtedly been neglected in the management literature in favour of other forms of explanation. Nevertheless they have been used in a wide range of applications and have generated a substantial body of research and thinking. They also have significant practical relevance. As Langley and Tsoukas (2010) point out, even well-established answers to 'why' questions may be difficult to put into practice. Knowing, for example, that one particular organizational structure outperforms another in a specific situation does not tell you how you might change your own organization to that new structure. Neither is that knowledge likely to capture the complex sequence of actions and interactions and potential unintended consequences that could arise during such a change. We therefore need process studies not just out of academic curiosity about the world but in order 'to better understand how to act within it' (Langley and Tsoukas 2010: 10). Process knowledge thereby complements the knowledge gained in response to 'why' questions. Effective management practice, we suggest, requires an understanding of 'how' as well as 'why'.

Mixing research questions

A research project is not, of course, limited to one type of research question. In practice, you will often need answers to 'what' questions before you can go on to address 'why' or 'how' questions. To identify factors influencing employee turnover (a 'why' question), for instance, you might first need to get detailed knowledge of turnover levels by employee group, attitudes to various aspects of conditions in the workplace and so forth (answers to 'what' questions). Successful use of the resulting 'why' knowledge may depend in turn on understanding 'how' the factors arose in the first place and opportunities for addressing them. The research question types should therefore be seen as complementary rather than mutually exclusive.

'Should' questions

As we noted earlier, practical problems in applied research may not be formulated in research terms. One aspect of this is that solutions to practical problems frequently require explicit or implicit value judgements, often expressed in terms of whether or not we 'should' or 'ought to' take a particular action. Such questions are sometimes referred to as normative questions; they are concerned with what ought to be rather than what is. Whilst they are important questions, they cannot be addressed empirically because there is no correct answer and, as a result, should be avoided as research questions (White 2009). In this connection, Maxwell (2013: 28) makes the useful distinction between what he calls the 'intellectual' and 'practical' goals of a project. Intellectual goals are concerned with understanding what is going on in a situation in terms of what, why or how. Practical goals typically involve accomplishing something, such as making a change or achieving some performance objective. Whereas either may be legitimate aims of your project, practical goals cannot typically be translated directly into questions which research can answer. Instead Maxwell recommends that you ask yourself 'what data could I collect, and what conclusions might I draw from these, that would help me accomplish this goal?' (Maxwell 2013: 76–7). Therefore he suggests framing your research questions so that they provide the information and understanding that will help you to achieve your practical goals or to develop recommendations that will allow you to do so.

To illustrate this approach, suppose that you were asked to investigate whether or not your organization should develop a particular type of product. The practical goal of such a project is to answer the question whether or not the product should be developed. How could research contribute to achieving that goal? Possibilities include researching the size of the potential market, customer attitudes to the proposed product, the likely impact of the proposed product on existing product sales and so on. Discussion with relevant stakeholders could be used to identify what research output would be most helpful to the decision-making process and thereby refine both your problem and your research questions.

2.4.3 Formulating your research questions

Like your research problem, your research questions need to be carefully formulated and this can be a time-consuming and challenging task. You will almost certainly have to go through several iterations in order to get them right. Start by reading around your topic, especially the academic or more theoretically oriented practitioner publications, because this will help you to refine the conceptual dimensions of your problem as well as develop your awareness of the questions that have already been answered or are seen as particularly important by other researchers. You will also come across examples of how research questions are formulated in your topic area. At this stage take every opportunity to discuss and share your emerging ideas with colleagues and, if you have one, your supervisor. Robson (2011: 65) writes about 'going public' by producing a review paper, talking in a seminar or presenting to colleagues 'whose comments you respect (or fear)'. As well as providing feedback on your research questions, such events can also be an opportunity to generate fresh insights into your problem area, especially from those with different areas of expertise and interest. As always, ensure that you capture these ideas so that you can refer to them later. In Research in Practice 2.1 we show the process of formulating research questions from an initial idea.

How many research questions?

Most research problems, even if tightly scoped, can generate multiple questions that may warrant investigating. This is generally a good thing at the start because it helps you to explore the problem area to the full, but at some point you will need to decide what questions you can feasibly answer within your project. Andrews (2003) suggests writing down all the possible questions that you have identified and then examining how they are related. Is there overlap or duplication between them? Is one question more central than the others? Does one question logically have to be answered before another? Examining your research questions in this way can help you to identify the main question that your research must answer, along with possible subsidiary questions that will need to be answered in order to answer the main question. You should also look out for redundant or overlapping questions that can be eliminated or combined with others. As a result you may have:

- a single research question that will address the research problem
- a principal research question with some subsidiary questions (probably not more than 3–7 unless the project is very large) that, taken together, will allow you to answer the main research question and thereby address the research problem
- more than one independent main research question, each of which must be answered to address the research problem.

RESEARCH IN PRACTICE 2.1

From managerial problem to research question

The research project started with a question asked in a forum on customer management: 'What should we do when people talk about our company on social media sites like Facebook and Twitter?' Further discussion in the forum showed that the motivation for the question was a general lack of knowledge about what to do. Should companies respond? If so, in what way? What was good practice? What did customers expect?

A review of practitioner literature and conversations with marketing professionals revealed an emphasis on how to deal with crises. The managers in the forum, on the other hand, were more interested in how to handle things on a day-to-day basis and avoid reaching crisis point, rather than in waiting until things got out of control. The academic literature on social media was also limited on how to handle feedback in social media. Much of what was available looked at complaint handling. There was some information on who was using social media and the sorts of things they were saying on social media sites. This would be helpful background and context but it was not the solution to the problems the forum had raised.

Clearly there was a gap here between the theory and practice of handling social media. Two researchers took up the challenge and kicked off a research project with the goal of helping companies make decisions about how they should handle online customer feedback. Initially they thought that the research questions should focus on identifying best practice within the companies actively engaging with customers in social media. It soon became clear that there was too little knowledge and experience within the companies to make this a viable research approach. Instead, after further discussion, they decided to begin by exploring the problem from a customer perspective. Their unit of analysis would be individual customers who were active social media users. The final research question reflected their focus: 'What are social media users' perceptions of best practice in handling customer feedback online?'

The first two cases can typically be managed by a single researcher. Problems can arise, however, where there are multiple, independent questions to be answered. Lack of time and resources to complete the project is the most obvious difficulty but multiple questions may indicate that the research problem itself is inadequately focused or that it is simply too large for you to address in a single project. In such situations consider reformulating your research problem or prioritizing particular aspects of the problem. By doing this the process of developing your research questions can help you to focus your research efforts even more precisely.

Wording your research questions

As you formulate your research questions, you will need to think carefully about how to word them. As well as helping you to clarify what your research is about, clear and unambiguous wording makes it easier to communicate with other stakeholders and to manage their expectations in terms of the research output. Try to keep your questions simple and straightforward. Use a single sentence: if you have to use more, it may indicate that you are actually asking two questions in one. Avoid unnecessary technical language or jargon: when you make use of technical concepts make sure that you can define them clearly. As a guide, in most research projects the research questions should make sense to an informed reader without elaborate explanation.

One key decision when preparing your questions is how open they should be. This is important because it is an indicator of what research method may be appropriate. Research questions associated with quantitative research designs are often quite specific and narrow, being structured around specific concepts and how they are related (Creswell 2009), for example, 'What is the impact of customer satisfaction on customer loyalty?' Questions of this type are often linked to the testing of existing theory about those relationships. Questions associated with qualitative research, on the other hand, may be worded in more general terms so as to permit a greater degree of exploration of the central issue (Creswell 2009) whilst still putting some boundaries around the study (Marshall and Rossman 2006). An example might be 'How do customers relate to our brand?' Such open questions may indicate a more exploratory approach, be linked to building new theory or reflect research that seeks understanding a situation from the perspective of those involved. We will discuss the relationships between research question and research design in more detail in Chapter 5.

When to formulate your research questions

Formulating the research questions can be a lengthy process, but when should it take place? Our stress on the importance of the research question and its role in the research design suggests that they should be developed first, with everything else flowing logically and in a straight line from there. In practice it is rarely quite so straightforward. There are also differences between different research approaches. On the one hand, in research designs using a deductive approach, the need to measure concepts quite precisely means that the research questions have to be clear prior to data collection getting underway, although final wording may not be confirmed until after the review of literature. In research designs using an inductive approach, on the other hand, researchers may prefer to start with more open research questions that are refined and developed as the research itself proceeds. Nevertheless, even in inductive research, formulating your research questions should be seen as 'a first and central step' (Flick 2009: 98), even if your initial questions are subject to what Strauss and Corbin (1998: 41) call 'progressive narrowing'. Regardless of the research method, our advice is to develop research questions early on, whilst accepting that they may need refining as your project progresses.

2.4.4 Research objectives

Some writers advocate developing specific research objectives from research questions. Whilst this can improve precision and focus, it is not necessary (or even appropriate) in all situations and, in our experience, can cause considerable confusion in distinguishing between the overall aim of the project and the specific, detailed objectives derived from the research questions. Research objectives are likely to be

CRITICAL COMMENTARY 2.1

The dictatorship of the research question

In this chapter we emphasize the key role played by the research question in providing direction for developing a suitable research design. According to this view, choice of research method is subordinate to choice of research question, a position memorably summed up in the phrase 'the dictatorship of the research question' (Tashakkori and Teddlie 1998: 20). We believe that this is a useful approach, especially for the novice researcher, because it can help to encourage careful attention to the alignment between research design and the problem being studied. It does, however, simplify what is in reality a more complex process. It downplays, for example, the role of other influences on the choice of method. One of these is the philosophical orientation held either consciously or unconsciously by the researcher, which can influence both the framing of the research problem/questions and the choice of research method. Individual researchers may also have preferences for particular types of research method, and consequently choose research questions that are appropriate for their preferred method. Those who are more comfortable working with quantitative methods, for example, may formulate research questions in a way that supports the use of a quantitative research design. Other potentially important influences on the choice of research method include the expectations of funding bodies, the preferences of policy makers and the traditions of the subject discipline regarding what is 'acceptable knowledge' (Bryman 2007: 17). Of course none of these things renders research questions irrelevant but they do highlight the complexity of research in practice.

most useful when the research questions themselves can be formulated in very specific terms, for example, in a theory-testing study. In the early stages of a research project, our advice is to stick to research questions, but check what is expected by your own institution if doing an academic project.

2.4.5 *Features of a good research question*

Although research questions differ according to the needs of the project, it is possible to offer some guidelines as to what makes a good research question (Andrews 2003, Van de Ven 2007, White 2009, Robson 2011). Your research questions should:

- Address the research problem that you have identified. If you have more than one research question they should be linked in a coherent way.
- Be clear and unambiguous so that they are understood by the reader. Get feedback from others and use it to help you refine the wording of your research questions.
- Be researchable. As with the overall research problem, your research questions must be answerable by research and that research must be feasible in the light of practical and ethical considerations. The latter means that the questions must be appropriately scoped, so that they are neither too broad nor too narrow.
- Be non-trivial so that they justify the time that will be spent on them. This is linked to the selection and significance of the research problem. If your research

questions look insignificant and uninteresting, you may need to revisit your research problem.

- Be questions and not statements. Statements do not give direction to the study, nor translate into research designs. Make sure your research questions really are in question format.

Some writers also emphasize that good research questions should also be connected with existing theory. This is obviously the case in pure research, where the relationship between your research problem and existing theory needs to be very clear. In applied research, where the motivation for the research comes from a practical problem, the relationship with theory is likely to be less direct, but knowledge of existing theory is essential to help you develop clear and useful research questions and to locate your research within the existing body of knowledge in your topic area.

Once you have drafted your research questions review them against the criteria we have identified. It is hard to overestimate the importance of getting this part of your project right, so we will conclude this chapter with a quote from Flick (2009) to underline the point:

> The less clearly you formulate your research question, the greater is the danger that you will find yourself in the end confronted by a mountain of data helplessly trying to analyse them.
>
> Flick (2009: 98)

KEY LEARNING POINTS

- Research can be understood as a problem-solving activity. The research problem provides the context for framing the research questions, which in turn determines the research design able to deliver research findings to resolve the original theoretical or practical problem that motivated the project.
- In pure research the research problem is derived from and grounded in existing theory; in applied research the research problem emerges in response to a practical problem.
- Potential sources of ideas for your research problem include personal experiences and interests; discussions with academics, practitioners and colleagues; academic, practitioner and even popular media; past projects of opportunity or through seeking a potential sponsor or client.
- Personal motivations for a particular project can come from professional, theoretical, career and current or future employer interests.
- Research questions link your research problem to your research design and provide the yardstick against which the success of the project can be judged.
- There are three generic types of research question. 'What' questions focus on description. 'Why' questions focus on explanation for why things are happening. 'How' questions focus on explaining how things change and develop over time. Different types of research questions can be combined in a single project.
- Good research questions address the chosen research problem, are clear and unambiguous, researchable, non-trivial and formulated as questions.

NEXT STEPS

2.1   Identifying a problem. Use one or more of the techniques below to generate a list of potential research problems. Review the potential research problems in terms of their relevance, feasibility and interest. Select one that looks most promising.

2.2   Research problem statement. Formulate a statement of your research problem in three sentences:

  a) *Background* (a statement of the theoretical or practical problem, issue or opportunity motivating the research).
  b) *This research will* (the overall aim of the research) *in order to* (how the research will address the problem).

2.3   Personal goals. What are your personal goals (career, professional, skills, knowledge, etc.) in undertaking this project? How will the chosen research problem help you to achieve those goals?

2.4   Research questions. Now start formulating your research questions:

  a) What do you need to know in order to resolve your research problem? Is the knowledge in the form of answers to 'what', 'why' or 'how' questions?
  b) Make a list of possible research questions that, if answered, would provide that knowledge.
  c) Use the evaluation criteria in Section 2.4.5 to refine your research questions.

Further reading

For further reading, please see the companion website.

References

Alvesson, M. and Sandberg, J. (2011). 'Generating research questions through problematization', *Academy of Management Review*, 36(2), 247–71.

Andrews, R. (2003). *Research questions*. London: Continuum.

Aneshensel, C. S. (2002). *Theory-based data analysis for the social sciences*. Thousand Oaks, CA: Pine Forge.

Bryman, A. (2007). 'The research question in social research: What is its role?', *Social Research*, 10(1), 5–20.

Churchill, G. A., Jr. (1999). *Marketing research: Methodological foundations*. 7th edn. Fort Worth, TX: Harcourt.

Creswell, J. W. (2009). *Research design*. 3rd edn. Los Angeles, CA: Sage.

de Vaus, D. (2001). *Research design in social research*. London: Sage.

de Vaus, D. (2002). *Surveys in social research*. 5th edn. Abingdon: Routledge.

Flick, U. (2009). *An introduction to qualitative research*. 4th edn. Los Angeles, CA: Sage.

Langley, A. and Tsoukas, H. (2010). Introducing 'perspectives on process organization studies'. *In*: Hernes, T. and Maitlis, S. (eds) *Process, sensemaking and organizing*. Oxford: Oxford University Press.

Markham, C. (2004). *The top consultant.* 4th edn. London: Kogan Page.

Marshall, C. and Rossman, G. B. (2006). *Designing qualitative research.* 4th edn. Thousand Oaks, CA: Sage Publications.

Maxwell, J. A. (2013). *Qualitative research design: An interactive approach.* 3rd edn. Los Angeles, CA: Sage.

Patton, M. Q. (2008). *Utilisation-focused evaluation.* 4th edn. Los Angeles, CA: Sage.

Robson, C. (2011). *Real world research.* 3rd edn. Chichester: Wiley.

Saunders, M., Lewis, P. and Thornhill, A. (2012). *Research methods for business students.* 6th edn. Harlow: Prentice Hall.

Sekaran, U. and Bougie, R. (2010). *Research methods for business.* 5th edn. Chichester: John Wiley and Sons.

Strauss, A. and Corbin, J. (1998). *Basics of qualitative research.* 2nd edn. Thousand Oaks, CA: Sage Publications.

Tashakkori, A. and Teddlie, C. (1998). *Mixed methodology.* Thousand Oaks, CA: Sage.

Van de Ven, A. H. (2007). *Engaged scholarship.* Oxford: Oxford University Press.

Voss, G. B. (2003). 'Formulating interesting research questions', *Journal of the Academy of Marketing Science*, 31(3), 356–9.

White, P. (2009). *Developing research questions: A guide for social scientists.* Basingstoke: Palgrave Macmillan.

Yin, R. K. (2009). *Doing case study research.* 4th edn. Thousand Oaks, CA: Sage.

Yin, R. K. (2011). *Qualitative research from start to finish.* New York, NY: Guilford Press.

3 Reviewing the literature

3.1 Introduction

Before starting your research you need to find out what is already known about your problem. Perhaps there are relevant theories or research methods you could use. Perhaps your research questions have already been answered and the research is no longer needed. These are some of the reasons why a critical review of the literature is a key component of many research projects. In the review, you present a critical analysis of literature in your problem area. It is where you examine theories relevant to your research problem and review prior research or other studies that can help you to get a deeper understanding of your problem. This chapter addresses how to conduct a critical review. We begin by discussing the nature and purpose of a literature review, before looking at the steps involved in carrying one out.

3.2 Undertaking a critical review

The seventeenth-century natural philosopher Isaac Newton once wrote that 'if I have seen a little further it is by standing on the shoulders of giants'. The idea that knowledge can be cumulative, that we can add to and build on the contributions of those who have gone before, has long been an influential one in science. It is one of the reasons why academic researchers are expected to review literature in their topic area before actually carrying out their research. According to Boote and Beile:

> 'Good' research is good because it advances our collective understanding. To advance our collective understanding, a researcher or scholar needs to understand

what has been done before . . . A researcher cannot perform significant research without first understanding the literature in the field.

Boote and Beile (2005: 3)

3.2.1 Aims of the literature review

An important objective of your literature review is to ground your own project in previously undertaken research and writing in your topic area. However this is not the sole purpose, or value, in reviewing literature, as we now explore.

Literature and your research problem

Literature can help you when formulating your research problem and research questions. This is particularly important in academic research where the contribution to theoretical knowledge is emphasized. Early on in your project you can use literature to identify gaps in previous research which you might fill with your own work. The review can also help you to avoid duplicating earlier research. In applied research projects, literature can help you to clarify your thinking, define key concepts that you are using and open up different perspectives on your topic that you may have overlooked. Literature can also help your project by providing background information on the broader context of your research topic. Government statistics, industry surveys, practitioner journals, consultant reports and even newspapers can provide useful input for the introduction to your report and for setting the scene for your fieldwork.

Literature and theory

Literature is the key source of theories and models that will be useful in investigating your research problem. If you are adopting a deductive theory-testing approach, your literature review will be where you elaborate the theory that your research will test. If you are taking a more inductive approach, the literature review can provide an important source of ideas for developing your study. Literature can also be used to help you interpret your findings upon completion of the project. In academic research, linking findings back to existing theory is necessary in order to show the contribution your research has made. In applied research, it is the opportunity to provide evidence-based findings to inform current thinking on practice and policy.

Literature and practice

The emphasis on academic theory in many guides to doing a literature review can overshadow the significance of practice and policy literature in your topic area. Such literature is likely to be a major part of any applied project which aims to make recommendations for practice. Identifying what is currently perceived as good practice by practitioners and policy makers and reviewing the evidence of its effectiveness can be an important role for the literature review in applied research projects. A review of practice literature also provides an opportunity to explore links between academic theory and practice. In addition, it can familiarize you with the terminology and language used by practitioners when discussing your chosen topic area, which will be very helpful when carrying out your own research and when writing up.

Literature and research methods

There are two main ways in which literature can help you to design your own research. Firstly, other researchers in your subject area may have used research methods that would be useful for your own project. In some cases this may extend to replicating a previous study in a different context. More likely, you might make use of specific research techniques and tools (such as questions in a questionnaire) that have proved effective in previous studies. Remember that there is no need to reinvent the wheel when it comes to research design, although you must always acknowledge the contribution of others through correct referencing and ensure that, where required, you have permission to use their material. Secondly, you will probably need to draw on literature about research methods in order to develop your own research skills. This might include specialized literature that deals with particular research techniques in greater detail as well as general research methods textbooks such as this one.

Literature and academic qualifications

If you are carrying out a research project as part of a course of academic study, the literature review is the place where you 'demonstrate a familiarity with the approaches, theories, methods and sources used in your topic area' (Grix 2004: 38). Your mastery of this aspect of your topic can form a significant part of the final grade awarded, so ensure that you understand the assessment requirements for your particular project to see whether a literature review is expected and, if so, in what format.

3.2.2 Adopting a critical stance in your literature review

Any literature review, whether intended for academic purposes or not, should adopt a critical stance. By 'critical' we do not mean simply drawing attention to flaws or pointing out that a certain writer is 'wrong'. Instead, a critical review involves the exercise of careful judgement and the judicious evaluation of your sources, the theories and ideas they use, the arguments they deploy and the conclusions they reach. To do so you may have to develop your own skills in analysing an argument. In Figure 3.1 we show the basic structure of an argument based on the work of Toulmin (1958). It consists of three components: the claim being made, the data or other evidence presented in support of the claim (or on the basis of which the claim has been made), and the warrant. The warrant provides the justification for linking the evidence and the claim.

Separating out the components of an argument in this way allows us to look more critically at what is being claimed and the justification for the claim. In evaluating an argument, consider the following.

- The claim. Establish what is being claimed. Is the claim clearly stated and coherent?
- The evidence. Is appropriate evidence provided? What type of evidence is presented? Is that evidence credible? What was its source?
- The warrant. Is the claim justified on the basis of the evidence? Is the link between the evidence and the claim robust?

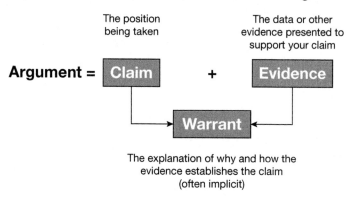

Figure 3.1 Structure of an argument (after Toulmin 1958)

Developing your skills in argumentation analysis will stand you in good stead not only in your literature review but also when you come to write up: you should use the same approach to evaluate the strength of your own arguments.

3.2.3 The literature review process

The process of doing a literature review can be broken down into four stages (Figure 3.2):

1 Search for appropriate literature sources.
2 Capture information from individual texts, including evaluating their quality and relevance.
3 Synthesize the body of literature into a coherent, critical review.
4 Present your review to show how it informs your research project.

The remainder of this chapter is devoted to a discussion of these four stages.

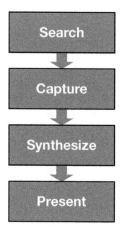

Figure 3.2 The literature review process

3.3 Search

Searching involves finding relevant literature. The challenge you face in doing so has been described as finding the 'right stuff' whilst avoiding getting too much of the 'wrong stuff' (Petticrew and Roberts 2006: 83).

3.3.1 What is literature?

We will define **literature** as the body of written material on a particular topic. Written material includes digital and print formats and both academic and non-academic writing. Wallace and Wray (2011: 95) offer a useful categorization of literature types in terms of the kind of knowledge they embody:

1   Theoretical literature, which addresses theories and models relevant to the topic area.
2   Research literature, which presents the results of research into the topic area.
3   Practice literature, which is written by practitioners about their own or about other practitioners' practice.
4   Policy literature, which evaluates and proposes changes to current practice.

Depending on your research topic, you may draw on any of the categories in your review. If you are conducting pure research, theoretical and research literature is likely to feature prominently. A critical understanding of such literature will also be important in applied research but you will probably need to provide a thorough review of applicable practice and policy literature as well.

3.3.2 Literature sources

It is not possible to present a comprehensive review of subject-specific literature sources here, as this would have to run to many thousands of items. In any case, identifying relevant material is your role as the reviewer/researcher. Instead, we will look more broadly at what literature sources are available and how and where to find them.

Peer review

Before doing so we need to clarify how quality is controlled in academic writing. Whilst all kinds of literature can have a place within your project, if your research is part of an academic qualification you will be expected to draw heavily on academic journal articles that have been peer reviewed prior to publication. **Peer review** (or refereeing) is a quality control process in many academic journals. Articles submitted for publication are sent out for review by other specialists in the field. Often this is double blind so that neither the author nor the reviewer know each other's identity. This process attempts to maintain some objectivity in judging which articles should be published. Submissions may be rejected; others have to be reworked, sometimes extensively, before being accepted for publication. That does not, of course, place a piece of writing above criticism in your review. It may have been overtaken by later work or had its conclusions challenged by authors with alternative views, but in selecting an article from a peer-reviewed journal for your literature review you can at least be confident that the content has been subject to a level of critical scrutiny.

Not all academic journals are peer reviewed. If you are unsure you can check by visiting the journal's home page on the Internet, where publishers usually indicate whether or not a journal is peer reviewed. Alternatively, a review of the journal's submission procedures will normally reveal the review process. Many online bibliographic databases also include the option of restricting a search to peer-reviewed articles.

Potential sources

Many different literature sources can contribute to your research project. Table 3.1 reviews some of the main sources, with supporting commentary on how and where you might use them. Most of the sources types listed will not have been through any kind of peer-review procedure so you will have to undertake much of the analysis of their credibility yourself. You should also be aware that a great deal of 'recycling' goes on. A short article in a newspaper or practitioner journal may just be a summary of something the author (or someone else) has published in more detail elsewhere. Where possible, always go back to the original sources, which will allow you to investigate the arguments in more depth.

3.3.3 Where to search

The Internet is the obvious place to start searching, but do not restrict yourself to your favourite web browser. To help you, Table 3.2 gives some guidance, in rough order of priority, on places to look online for different sources of literature.

The Internet seems such a natural place to search that it is easy to overlook other very useful ways of finding relevant literature. These include:

- Reference lists in books and articles. These provide invaluable guides to earlier work on your topic. Many online bibliographic databases allow these to be searched electronically for publications in the database.
- Your personal network. An important aspect of doing research is joining the community of academics and practitioners working in your field through conferences, professional organizations and informal contacts. As you progress your research project, you will build up a network of contacts of people sharing your interests. Your network can become an important way of sharing ideas and accessing sources, especially literature that may not be widely available.
- Library staff. Librarians, particularly in academic or other specialist libraries, can usually suggest places to look for relevant literature. Their expertise is particularly valuable when it comes to developing your literature search skills or when you are trying to locate a hard-to-find book or article.
- Course material and academic staff. If your project is part of a course of study, course material and reading lists will often provide a helpful starting point for searching. Your supervisor, if you have one, can also be a useful source of suggestions about where to search or even of recommendations for specific sources.

Table 3.1 Potential literature sources

Source	Comments
Peer-reviewed academic journals	The 'gold standard' for an academic literature review, covering both theory and research. Most articles will include extensive reference lists which help with further searching. Perhaps the biggest drawback is that because of long publishing lead times new or emerging topics may be less well covered.
Non-peer-reviewed academic journals	Articles in these journals may have many of the characteristics of peer-reviewed articles but are likely to vary in quality, so you will have to rely more on your own judgement as to their rigour.
Academic books	Books (or sections of edited books) by academic authors in your topic area can be an important source of ideas, but note that there is generally less quality control than under the journal peer review system. Academic textbooks can be very helpful in introducing you to a topic area but you will often still need to consult the original literature on which they were based. Handbooks and edited collections of journal articles can be useful in getting an overview of a topic area. Specialist encyclopaedias and dictionaries can provide useful summaries of particular themes as well as suggestions for further reading. General encyclopaedias (including Wikipedia) can also be helpful, as you get to know your topic, but you should not rely on them as principle sources for your literature review.
	Obtaining academic books can sometimes be difficult, particularly for highly specialized texts, unless you have access to an academic library or can use a library loan system. Prices also vary, although online search can often reveal low-cost options, including second-hand copies or even digital copies that can be read online.
Working papers from reputable academic institutions	Many academic institutions publish working papers. These are often work in progress, reporting research work that is currently underway, some of which subsequently finds its way into journals. As a result, they can be useful sources of current research and thinking. Accessibility varies and in some cases authors may place restrictions on whether they can be quoted without permission.
Conference papers from leading academic conferences	Conference papers, like working papers, can have the advantage of dealing with on-going and current research topics. There may be some form of review prior to acceptance but you will still need to make your own judgement regarding quality. Accessibility can be a problem unless the proceedings are published online or you attend the conference yourself.
Theses and dissertations	By their nature, theses tend to be highly specific but can be useful sources, especially for academic research. Getting full-text access can be difficult, although some are now available online. Note that there may be restrictions on using material, including quotations, from a dissertation or thesis without permission.

Table 3.1 continued

Source	Comments
Research reports	There is a huge variation in quality, quantity and accessibility of research reports. These can include studies commissioned or carried out by governments, non-governmental organizations (NGOs), consultancies, lobby groups etc. Some are of a high standard and carried out by leading authorities in the area, whilst others are much less robust, especially in terms of the quality or reporting of empirical research. Copies of research reports for government departments are often available free of charge (as is some NGO literature), whilst commercial consultancy reports can be very expensive. A particular issue with commissioned research can be the problem of bias in either the conduct or reporting of the research. A further problem is that not all reports give details of how the research was carried out (although these are sometimes published separately). You will have to use your own judgement in assessing such sources.
Practitioner/consultancy literature	Business and management generates an enormous literature from practitioners and consultants. These sources tend to be more practical, less theoretical and often without a strong empirical content (perhaps based on the authors' experiences of management or consulting). They are also often written in an accessible style. Examples of such sources include: • professional/trade journals • white papers by consultancies/companies • non-academic books aimed at the practising manager/ general reader • autobiographies of business leaders. Some of this material can be very useful in helping you to identify a topical research question and for identifying current practice and practitioner views in your research area. It may also be the only source for new topics for which little or no academic writing is available. Quality, however, can be very mixed, as can accessibility.
Newspapers	Newspapers and news magazines can be good ways of identifying topical issues but their content is, of course, driven by editorial and other concerns rather than by academic criteria. Usually they report things as they happen and may therefore be unable to offer in-depth, critical or retrospective analysis. As a result, they are probably best avoided as principal sources for your literature review but they can help you to pick out potential topic areas. In addition, they can be valuable sources of information for background or commentary on public debates.
Everything else	Finally, there is everything-else-out-there, and thanks to the Internet there is an awful lot of it, including blogs, tweets and other opinion pieces. At this point it will fall almost entirely on your shoulders to judge the quality of material you find. Very often your time would be better spent looking for more academic articles than trawling hopefully through the Internet.

Table 3.2 Where to search online

Location	Comments
Bibliographic databases	Bibliographic databases are one of the most important sources available, especially for academic journal articles. They provide a searchable index of journal articles and other material, giving abstracts and citations. Access may also be given to the full text or links to where the full text can be obtained. Most databases are accessible online, although commercial ones usually require a subscription for full-text access. Universities and business schools typically include a range of such bibliographic databases as part of their library services. Other organizations, such as professional institutions, may also offer access to specific collections. Public databases are usually accessible to anyone but may have limited or no full-text sources.
	A list of commercial and public databases that are particularly relevant for organization and management research can be found in the further reading on this book's companion website.
Library databases	Library databases (such as the British Library, www.bl.uk) can be used to search for available books and other material on your topic area. University libraries may also hold other publications such as working papers. Worldcat (www.worldcat.org/) provides a searchable database covering thousands of libraries around the world and can help you to find the library nearest to you that holds a book for which you are searching.
Google Scholar	Google Scholar (http://scholar.google.co.uk/) provides the facility to search for academic and other scholarly articles. It offers some of the capability of bibliographic databases, although coverage is not as systematic. In some cases links are included to where a full-text version can be found.
Citation indexes	Citation indexes are a particular form of bibliographic database. They provide an index of the citations between publications, such as journal articles, to allow you to see who has cited a particular article. In literature searching they are very useful to see how an article has been used by other writers and to follow the development of a line of thinking over time. Bibliographic databases often include citation links for articles that they reference, as does Google Scholar. You may also be able to access the ISI Web of Science, a subscription citation index, through a university or other library.
Index to theses	Index to Theses (www.theses.com) provides an index of theses accepted for higher degrees by universities in the United Kingdom and Ireland since 1716. Access is via subscription and includes abstracts and full text where available.
Google Books	Google Books (http://books.google.com) offers the ability to search across a large number of books. Some books can be previewed and some are available for download.

Table 3.2 continued

Location	Comments
Industry, business and market research databases	Industry, business and market research databases offer access to market reports and to industry and company data. Your university or other organization may have subscriptions to relevant databases. They can be particularly useful for background and context literature.

Other places to search online

Academic institutions' websites	These can be used to locate working papers and specialist research centres (which often have their own working paper/research paper series).
Individual academics' home pages	Academics often have their own websites. In some cases you can access copies of their earlier work and work in progress or find references to other work they have authored. When you identify a key author in your area, it is well worth checking to see whether they have their own website.
Government/professional associations/trade bodies/ NGO websites	These sites can be very helpful for locating research reports, policy papers, official statistics etc., although bear in mind the comments made earlier about possible bias. Some professional associations offer extensive access to library resources for their members.
Publishers' websites	Some journal publishers' websites have access to journal contents pages, which can supplement other search strategies for journal articles. This is also normally where individual copies of articles can be purchased if they cannot be accessed in any other way.
Consultancy/company websites	Consultancies and other commercial organizations publish research reports or white papers that can be of interest and which sometimes can be downloaded or read online for free.

3.3.4 How to search

We have addressed what sources you might want to use and where you might look for them, but how do you organize and carry out your search?

Literature review questions

It is hard to search effectively or efficiently without knowing what you are looking for. Wallace and Wray (2011) suggest formulating questions that your literature review should answer. These can help you focus your reading. For example:

- How are the key concepts in your research project defined in the literature?
- What theories/models are being used in relation to your topic?
- How are those theories related to one another (e.g. supporting/contradicting, etc.)?
- What empirical studies have been made of this topic? What were their findings?
- What research methods are used in this topic area? (Answers to this question can also inform your investigation design.)

- What management practices or policies are relevant to the topic area? What evidence is there for their use or effectiveness? (These questions can be particularly important in applied research projects.)

Research in Practice 3.1 provides an example of literature review questions for a specific topic.

RESEARCH IN PRACTICE 3.1

Literature review questions

To illustrate the application of literature review questions, suppose your research question was 'How does job satisfaction influence employee commitment?' Possible questions to answer in your literature review could include the following.

- How is job satisfaction defined in the literature? What are the key dimensions of job satisfaction?
- How is employee commitment defined in the literature? What are the key dimensions of employee commitment?
- What theories are there about the relationship between job satisfaction and employee commitment?
- What does prior research show about the relationship?

  - What concepts (variables) were used and how were they measured?
  - In what context (e.g. industry, type of organization)?
  - What were the findings?
  - What research methods were used (and can I use them for my study)?

Choosing your search terms

For searching electronic databases and for general online searching, you will need to identify appropriate search terms or keywords. Initially these can be taken from the concepts included in your research problem, your research questions and literature review questions. For example, if your research question asks how job satisfaction influences employee commitment, your initial search terms might be 'job satisfaction' and 'employee commitment'. You may find, however, that these terms are too restrictive and that you need either to expand them or to include synonyms in your search. 'Job satisfaction', for instance, may need to be supplemented with 'employee satisfaction'. Alternatively, some of your terms may be too broad, so additional words need to be included in the search to refine the scope. Simply searching on 'satisfaction' without a qualifier, for instance, is likely to produce a lot of irrelevant hits. Adding 'job' or 'employee' should reduce that number. In addition to using additional concept descriptors, particular theories and even the names of key authors in the field can be useful search terms.

As you search, pay attention to the terminology used in your topic area. Look at keywords used by the authors of the articles you are reading. You may find that the terms you are using are not universally recognized. The term 'queue', for example, is common in British English but 'waiting line' is often preferred in US English. Differences can also exist between academic and practitioner literature. In marketing, for example, academics may refer to customer segmentation, whereas practitioners might describe the same phenomenon as profiling or modelling.

If you find that your search generates a huge number of hits, many of which are totally irrelevant, you have a number of options. Many search engines use Boolean operators such as AND, OR and NOT. Adding more terms using the AND operator will reduce the number of hits. Using the NOT operator with a search term will exclude references containing that term. If you are still getting a lot of irrelevant hits, you may be able to confine the search to article titles and abstracts; this is usually possible in bibliographic databases. Another option is to use search limiters such as date range, industry, geographic sector, language or publication type (e.g. peer reviewed).

If, on the other hand, your search gets very few hits you will need to adopt a different strategy. Reducing the number of terms included in your search, making terms more general (e.g. changing from 'employee commitment' to 'commitment') or replacing the AND operator with OR will generally produce more hits. Removing any search limiters should have a similar effect. You should also review the search terms you are using. Are they appropriate, or are there other terms that are in more common use? Has terminology changed over time? Try searching more than one database and even general web searching. This can be a frustrating point in the search process, but perseverance combined with some creative thinking will usually win through. In our experience, once you have found one or two sources you can use their reference lists or check using a citation index to see where they have been cited to identify other references.

A particular problem arises when you are searching a cutting-edge topic where there may be very little published material and you are struggling to identify relevant academic theory. In this situation you need to think about what other situations might offer useful insights. In the early days of research on e-commerce, for example, many researchers used literature on direct mail as the reference literature and complemented it with sources looking at the context of the phenomenon, in this case the Internet, in terms of what the web was being used for, how it was being used and by whom. A bit of imagination and lateral thinking is sometimes needed at this point.

Starting and stopping your search

There is some debate over whether it is better to start your search by searching for peer-reviewed journals in bibliographic databases or by looking at more general reference literature, such as encyclopaedias or textbooks. In practice it probably depends on your level of background knowledge. If you are reasonably familiar with your topic you may be able to start searching academic literature straight away. If, on the other hand, you are new to the topic area you will probably want to begin with more general, introductory literature to help you formulate appropriate literature review questions, generate relevant search terms and identify authors, journals and other literature sources on which you can base a more in-depth search.

Getting started is not always easy, but neither is deciding when to stop. In some projects it can seem that there is no limit to the sources that might be relevant to your study, but clearly you have to conclude your search at some point. Deciding when to do so is a balance between your project timetable and your search progress to date. Whilst it is difficult to suggest universal stopping criteria, we suggest an appropriate stopping point may be approaching when:

- you have answered the literature review questions you have set yourself
- searches of additional bibliographic and library databases fail to find new literature
- examination of literature and reference lists already located does not reveal gaps in your search coverage
- you have identified a range of perspectives on your topic of interest
- theories and models described in non-academic literature are grounded, where possible, in appropriate academic sources.

Your personal network of subject experts, other researchers and your supervisor may also be able to help you decide whether you have reached an appropriate stopping point.

3.4 Capture

As you search, you need to capture appropriate information from the sources relevant to your study. This stage involves three key tasks: evaluating your sources, capturing relevant information and managing the material.

3.4.1 Evaluating your sources

Your searches can generate a very large amount of material, not all of which will be applicable to your topic. When you first locate a source you should therefore make a preliminary assessment of its relevance to your project. This can be done quickly by scan-reading it and we find the following sequence useful.

1 Read the abstract or executive summary if there is one.
2 Read the introduction and conclusion.
3 Review the table of contents, main headings, figures and tables.
4 Review the reference list, if there is one, to check the coverage of other literature.

As you scan, review the source against your literature review questions to help you assess its likely relevance. If it is clearly not applicable it can be put aside. If you are not sure about its relevance, we suggest that you review it again later when you are more familiar with the topic. Relevant sources should be flagged for further evaluation.

You will need to evaluate sources in terms of two dimensions. The first is the quality of the source itself. If it is an empirical study you will need to evaluate the quality of the research; if the work is peer reviewed you may be more confident about its rigour but you will still need to look at the study's limitations. If it is a work that has been widely cited elsewhere this may be a positive indication of its quality or suggest that it holds some important place within the body of literature in a topic area. The second dimension is how the source can contribute to your own project.

Use your literature review questions to help you make that evaluation. A relevant source is likely to contribute in one or more of four general areas:

1   problem formulation and context
2   theories and models
3   practice and policy
4   research methods.

3.4.2 *Capturing relevant information*

Two different types of information need to be captured when you find a relevant source: the reference data and content information.

Reference data

Reference data are needed to allow you to reference a literature source accurately within your report. Table 3.3 shows the data required in order to reference some common source types. As you are likely to be reviewing a large amount of material, you should note down the referencing details of each literature source as you go, even if you subsequently decide not to use it. This will help you to keep track of the literature and avoid problems when you come to write up. Online databases usually provide citations in different formats that can be copied and pasted into your records. This process can be made easier by using reference management software. Further details on referencing and reference management software are given later in this chapter.

Table 3.3 Reference data for common source types

Journal article	Book	Chapter of edited book	Report/working paper	Website
Author(s)	Author(s)	Author(s)	Author(s)	Author(s) or originator (e.g. company name)
Year	Year	Year	Year	Year
Title	Title	Title	Title	Title
Journal	Place published	Editor(s)	Series	Publisher
Volume	Publisher	Book title	Publishing institution	Uniform Resource Locator (URL) or Digital Object Identifier (DOI)
Issue		Place published	Place published	Date accessed
Pages		Publisher	Uniform Resource Locator (URL) or Digital Object Identifier (DOI) (if online version)	
		Pages	Date accessed (if online version)	

Table 3.4 Capturing reference and content information from a key literature source

Information required	Your notes
Full reference details	Note here the full reference details in the correct format.
Keywords	Record the keywords used for your search and any useful keywords used by the author.
Brief summary of the study	Make a brief summary of the study. Use the abstract/ executive summary if there is one.
Type of literature (theoretical, research, practitioner or policy)	Note the type of literature. This can be useful when comparing how your topic is discussed by different sources.
Purpose of the study (e.g. the aims of the study/ research questions)	What is the author trying to achieve in the study?
Theories/concepts/models described or reviewed	What are the key theories, concepts and models discussed in the source? How are they treated (e.g. supported, critiqued)?
Practices/policies described or reviewed	What are the key practices and policies discussed in the source? How are they treated (e.g. supported, critiqued)?
If it is a research study, research methods used	What research methods are used in the study (e.g. quantitative/qualitative; sampling; data collection instrument; data analysis techniques etc.)?
Study findings	What are the major findings or conclusions of the study? What are its limitations?
Your evaluation	Note your evaluation of the source in terms of its quality and its likely contribution to your project in terms of theories/models, practice/policies, research methods and background/context). Use your literature review questions to help you decide on the potential relevance of the study.
Any other comments	Record here any other comments or thoughts.

Content information

Content information includes key points from the source itself and the results of your evaluation of the source. Capture this information systematically as you read. Avoid the temptation just to keep on reading. Unless you record what you are discovering as you work, you will find it very difficult to synthesize and present your review later on. Table 3.4 shows a suggested format for capturing content information in a structured way. Not all sources will need to be recorded to this level of detail, but make sure that you capture the contribution of your main sources. If you come across any pieces of text or data that you think you may wish to quote verbatim in your write-up, note these down, including the number of the page from which they were taken. Remember that the aim at this stage is not just to summarize the source but to evaluate it critically, particularly with respect to its quality and likely relevance for your project.

3.4.3 Managing the review material

Data management is a big part of any research project, and the literature review stage is no exception. You will need to decide how to manage the material that your review generates.

Managing your sources

You can easily get overwhelmed by the results of your search efforts. Your first task is managing the sources themselves. Printed material needs to be stored securely and archived in a way that allows easy and quick access. The same applies to digital sources. If you are downloading material, allocate each document a logical filename. A simple approach is to use citation reference details (i.e. author, date). Ensure that you back-up digital data. Online storage can be useful for this, especially if you need access the material from more than one computer or other device. If you are not downloading a source, make sure you bookmark it and note details of the **Uniform Resource Locator** (URL) or **Digital Object Identifier** (DOI). You will also need to keep track of your material in a structured way. You can build up a simple database in a spreadsheet to record all reference details and where the source is located. Alternatively, you could consider using specialist reference management software.

Reference management software

A large number of reference management software packages are available. These typically act as a database in which you record details of individual references, and provide an interface with word-processing software (such as Microsoft Word) to allow easy insertion of in-text citations and the automatic creation of a reference list directly from the database. Many also allow you to import reference details directly from online bibliographic databases, Google Scholar and so on. Some also offer additional functionality, such as annotation of Adobe Acrobat (pdf) documents, or have interfaces with mobile devices. Details vary, depending on the particular software. EndNote (www.endnote.com) and Biblioscape (www.biblioscape.com) are examples of commercial products; versions of Zotero (www.zotero.org) and Mendeley (www.mendeley.com) can be downloaded for free. Microsoft Word also has a referencing facility built in, although this does not offer the database capabilities of full reference management programs. If you are a student, your institution may offer referencing software, and training on how to use it. Reference management software is definitely worth considering if you are going to do a lot of reference work. For smaller projects a spreadsheet or a table in a word-processing package is usually adequate to manage your references.

Managing your notes

You will also need to manage the notes that you generate during your review. We strongly recommend that you do not just scribble notes on a paper or electronic copy of the document. Instead, record your analysis in a structured format, preferably digital, because this will make it easier to write up. The headings in Table 3.4 can be used to organize your notes. Tabular summaries can also be useful, as we discuss in the next section.

3.5 Synthesize

As you read your sources you should start to notice connections between them. Some sources may support the views of others; some sources may give alternative perspectives. You may see that there are common ways of researching your topic. You may find that different policies or practices referred to in your literature group together into clear families or categories. When you begin to see such patterns, you are starting to synthesize the literature. You are moving from understanding sources in isolation to understanding the body of literature in your topic area.

3.5.1 From author-centric to concept-centric

A review of literature is not an uncritical listing of previous research in the manner of

> A laundry list of previous studies, with sentences or paragraphs beginning with the words, 'Smith found . . .', 'Jones concluded . . .', 'Anderson stated . . .', and so on.
>
> Rudestam and Newton quoted in Silverman (2010: 324)

The 'laundry-list' approach is what Webster and Watson (2002: xvi) call author-centric. They contrast this with a concept-centric approach in which the concepts provide the organizing logic for the review, as shown in Table 3.5. Moving from an author-centric to a concept-centric understanding of your reading is a key step in the process of synthesising your literature.

Table 3.5 Author-centric versus concept-centric structure (adapted from Webster and Watson 2002: xvii)

Author-centric structure	*Concept-centric structure*
Author A argues . . . concept/theory x	Concept/theory x. . . [Author A, Author C]
According to Author B . . . concept/theory y	Concept/theory y. . . [Author B, Author E]
Author C suggests . . . concept/theory x	
Author D identifies . . . concept/theory z	Concept/theory z. . . [Author D]
Author E critiques . . . concept/theory y	

As you capture content information from your literature try to group different sources and authors according to the way in which they approach your topic in terms of concepts and theories that they use. Also note whether authors explicitly support or critique a particular approach to your topic. By comparing and contrasting the support for different theories from a range of authors, you can create a more powerful and coherent critical argument than is possible by sequentially reiterating the findings of individual authors. Ordering the literature conceptually also gives you a ready-made framework when it comes to writing up. Each of the main theories or concepts can form a sub-section of your review and you can discuss the arguments for and against each approach as reflected in the literature you have studied.

Using matrices to synthesize your findings

Tables and matrices provide a useful practical way of developing such a framework, as shown in Table 3.6. The visual layout of the table allows you to see the different contributions to the theories within the literature you have reviewed. You can build tables such as these in a word-processing or spreadsheet package. The cells in the table can contain short summaries, direct quotations or symbols, as here. Additional dimensions can be added as required.

Table 3.6 Concept matrix (content based on Mintzberg et al. 1998, after Webster and Watson 2002: xvii)

Source	Strategy as planning	Strategy as positioning	Etc.
Ansoff (1965)	X		
Henderson (1979)		X	
Porter (1980)		X	
Steiner (1969)	X		
Stewart (1963)	X		
Etc.			X

Matrices are generally useful ways of organizing, analysing and displaying textual data and we look at their use in more detail in the context of qualitative data analysis in Chapter 14. Appropriately organized and edited tables and matrices also provide a useful summary device when presenting your literature review, as we show in Research in Practice 3.2. In this example, the matrix cross-tabulates major theories with relevant dimensions of the topic.

Graphical techniques

You may also find graphical techniques useful for exploring the interrelationships in your literature. Literature maps (Creswell 2009) are one way of investigating and displaying the relationships between different concepts and different authors. Figure 3.3 shows an example related to strategic management which uses a tree structure.

Concept maps can also be used to help you synthesize the literature you have studied and to develop a theoretical framework for your research (Maxwell 2013). Concept maps show relationships between concepts. They provide a way of helping you to visualize how the concepts you have identified in your literature fit together. Another option is to use mind maps to help you organize your thinking and to synthesize a body of literature. Note that suitable tables and graphics can also be used in your final write-up to help the reader grasp the essence of your review. Remember, however, that matrices and figures do not themselves constitute a synthesis of the literature (Petticrew and Roberts 2006): you will still need to present a narrative summary of your critical review.

RESEARCH IN PRACTICE 3.2

Using tables to summarize and compare theories of corporate governance

In a critical review of corporate governance, Letza et al. (2004) employ a matrix to summarize and compare four theories (labelled as 'models') of corporate governance in terms of nine dimensions. Their review includes a commentary on the matrix that expands key points of interest. The following table, adapted from Letza et al. (2004: 246), presents a simplified version of the original, showing only five of the nine dimensions to illustrate the principle of using matrices in this way in a literature review.

	The principal-agent model	The myopic-market model	The abuse of executive power model	The stakeholder model
Major contributor	Jensen and Meckling (1976); Manne (1965)	Charkham (1994); Sykes (1994)	Hutton (1995); Kay and Silberston (1995)	Freeman (1984); Blair (1995)
Purpose of corporation	Maximization of shareholder wealth	Maximization of shareholder wealth	Maximization of corporate wealth as a whole	Maximization of stakeholder wealth
Problem of governance	Agency problem	Excessive concern with short-term market value	Abuse of executive power for their own interests	Absence of stakeholders' involvement
Cause	Shareholders do not have enough control	Ineffective market forces	Institutional arrangements leave excessive power to management	Governance failure to represent stakeholders' interests
Proposition	Market efficiency	Importance of long-term relationship	Manager as trustee	Social efficiency of economy

3.5.2 Developing a conceptual model

A more formal way of synthesizing and presenting literature is through the use of a conceptual model. Such models play a very important part in management and organizational research. They can act as a bridge between theory and the real-world phenomenon you are investigating, making it easier to relate the one to the other.

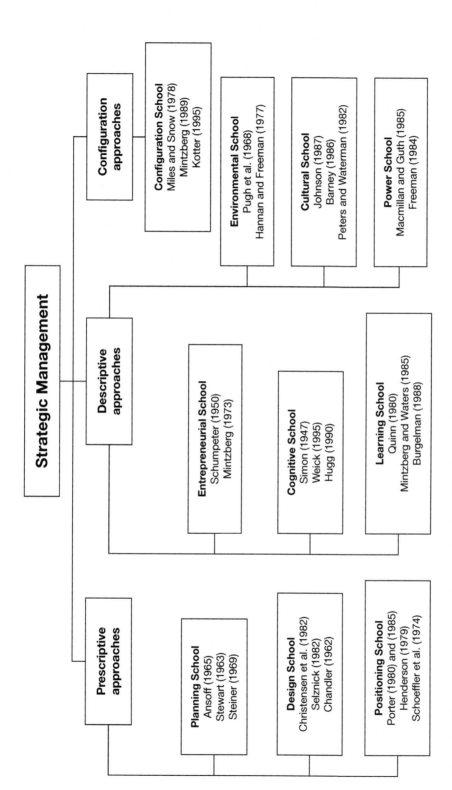

Figure 3.3 Example literature map (content based on Mintzberg et al. 1998)

What is a model?

The term **model** is a common one and is used in many different ways. It can be employed simply as another word for theory. It can refer to a mathematical representation of a theory or of some real-world phenomenon. Queuing models are a good example of this type of model; they can be used to represent or to simulate the behaviour of real waiting lines. Most importantly for current purposes, however, the term is used to refer to a diagrammatic representation of a theory or some real-world phenomenon. This type of model represents visually the features of a theory or of a phenomenon that are relevant to the purpose for which the model has been created. In the case of research, of course, the purpose will be determined by the research questions. Such diagrammatic models are often referred to as **conceptual models**, a term we will use here. Modelling conventions vary but, typically, conceptual models show the key elements/concepts in the theory and how they are related. We give a very simple example in Figure 3.4, which shows the possible relationship between advertising level and sales revenue. The + sign indicates that the relationship is positive: as the advertising level increases, so does sales revenue. The model thereby provides a clear, visual depiction of a possible theory about the impact of advertising on sales.

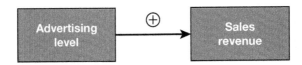

Figure 3.4 Conceptual model of the expected relationship between advertising level and sales revenue

Types of conceptual model

Conceptual models vary enormously in their form, depending on the theory or phenomenon they are intended to model. Nevertheless it is possible to identify some generic types of model that you may come across during your reading or use in your own research. We consider three of them here (Figure 3.5).

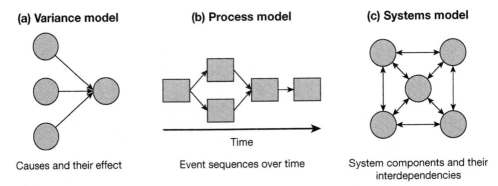

Figure 3.5 Types of conceptual model

- **Variance models.** One of the most common types of conceptual model in research depicts cause-and-effect relationships between concepts, for example, the impact of advertising on sales as we discussed above. In its basic form the causes are shown on the left and connected to the effect by a single-headed arrow. Models like this are sometimes referred to as variance models because they focus on explaining the variability or change in some outcome on the basis of changes in other factors (Mohr 1982). They are very widely used in explanatory research when answering 'why' type questions, and we discuss them in more detail in Chapter 5.
- **Process models.** Process models show the sequence of events or activities by which things such as people or organizations change over time, for example, in change programmes, mergers and acquisitions or innovations. Each step in the model represents an event or activity. A well-known example of a simple process model is Lewin's (1952) three-stage Unfreeze-Move-Refreeze model of planned change. We discuss process theories in relation to answering 'how' type questions in Chapter 5.
- **Systems models.** Systems models make up another important, and very diverse, family of conceptual models. They reflect an equally diverse heritage in systems thinking and systems theory. Not intended to represent any particular system model, our simple diagram illustrates the interdependence of system components (via the double-headed arrows) and the emphasis on taking a holistic view that is a feature of much system thinking. Well-known examples of systems thinking in management include Senge's (1990) systems approach to the learning organization and Checkland's soft systems methodology (Checkland and Scholes 1999).

Using conceptual models in your research

Conceptual models can play different roles in your research, depending on your research problem and the research approach you adopt. In deductive research it is common practice to develop a conceptual model from the theory that is to be tested. The model depicts the concepts and the relationships between them in a very clear way that supports the design of the research and the formulation of suitable hypotheses for testing, as we discuss in Chapter 4. If you are using an inductive approach, it is more likely that a conceptual model will be an output as part of theory building during your analysis, although you might use a preliminary conceptual framework based on the literature to help guide your data collection and analysis. Note that in inductive research such models are not subjected to formal testing as in the deductive approach, but serve as tentative starting points for your field research.

3.6 Present

The final stage of the literature review process is to present your findings. General aspects of presenting your research are discussed in Chapter 15, but here we draw attention to some points particularly relevant to presenting your review of the literature.

3.6.1 *What the review should cover*

Coverage of your review will depend on its purpose, the audience for which it is intended and the amount of space allowed. A review that forms part of a dissertation or thesis, for example, might be expected to:

- demonstrate your critical understanding of the issues which writers and researchers consider important in your topic area
- provide a critical overview and evaluation of relevant previous work; depending on the topic, this may include:
    - o   key concepts and their definitions
    - o   relevant theories and models
    - o   relevant policies and practices
    - o   a review of research findings from relevant empirical studies
- give a clear demonstration of the link between work you have reviewed and your own research.

3.6.2 *Integrating your review*

One of the decisions you will need to take is how to integrate your review into the overall research report. In academic reports such as journal articles, dissertations or theses, a literature review usually forms a separate chapter or section within the main body of the report, generally just prior to the research design section. Its role and where it is sited in the report are, however, influenced by the research approach that you have taken.

In deductive research approaches the review is typically positioned immediately before the chapter or section describing the research design. It is where you present your development of the theory to be tested in your research. You should clearly identify the concepts (variables) to be used in the study, the relationships between them and any hypotheses to be tested. The theory can be summarized in the form of a conceptual model, which may be located at the end of the review or in a separate chapter or section.

In inductive research there is more variability in the role of the literature review, depending on how prior theory is being used in your research. One option is to use the literature review to 'frame' the research problem (Gray 2009: 124). This can involve reviewing the theoretical background to the topic or identifying broad themes that might be relevant, perhaps including a tentative conceptual framework. In such cases, your review can be positioned before the research design section. A second option is to position the literature review later in the report when discussing the findings. The role here is to compare the theory developed during your research with existing theory in the topic area.

In applied research reports intended for a non-academic audience, the position of your literature review can vary even more. In some cases, you may choose to follow traditional academic practice and include it in the main body of the report, before the research design chapter. An alternative, useful if the audience is less interested in the theoretical aspects of your topic, is to include the review as an appendix rather than as part of the main body. In other cases, especially for very large projects, your review may be published or issued separately. Chapter 15 discusses different report formats in more detail.

If you are doing a research project for an academic qualification, check your institution's guidelines on where to position your literature review in the final report. If there are none, the default option is to include your review prior to the research design chapter or section.

3.6.3 Structuring your review

In writing up your review, give careful thought to the structure of your argument. Ordering literature by concept will help, but you will still need to develop a clear overall structure and line of argument. Saunders et al. (2012) suggest thinking of your review as a funnel which progressively focuses in on your key themes. Begin by setting the broader scene, introducing the core theories and concepts in your topic area, before narrowing down the discussion to the specific aspects in which you are interested. Here you should discuss in detail the key theories or ideas that relate to your research problem. Finally, you should lead the reader into later sections of your research report.

3.6.4 Writing style

The writing style you adopt will depend on the purpose of your review and the intended audience. It should also conform to the writing style used for your report as a whole. This is discussed in Chapter 15 but the following points are particularly relevant to a literature review.

- *Tense*. When writing a literature review it is standard practice to use the present rather than the past tense so 'Jones (2013) argues . . .', 'Patel (2008) reports that . . .' rather than 'Jones (2013) argued . . .' or 'Patel (2008) said . . .'.
- *Direct quotations*. Taking direct quotes from key authors is a useful way to emphasize an important point or take advantage of a particularly clear definition or powerful turn of phrase. They should be used sparingly and very long extracts are generally best avoided. Embed shorter quotes in the body of the text and use separate text blocks only for longer extracts. You should always cite both the source and the number of the page where the quotation appears, so remember to record the page number of any quotations when making notes.
- *Tone*. Although you are doing a critical review, you should avoid setting a tone that is too negative and dismissive of other people's works. It is important to recognize limitations in what has been done, but this can be achieved while still treating others' work with respect.
- *Concept focus*. We have stressed the importance of structuring your review around concepts. An indication that your review is insufficiently concept-centric is when you have a large number of paragraphs that begin with phrases such as 'As so and so says . . .' or 'According to so and so . . .'.

3.6.5 Referencing

As noted earlier in the chapter, knowledge builds on the contributions of earlier scholars, and we acknowledge that debt by referencing their work. Referencing is also important to ground the credibility of your own claims and to allow the reader to refer directly to important or interesting material. You are expected to reference any of the following:

- direct quotations from another source
- paraphrased text based on someone else's work
- data/information/statistics from other sources
- theories/ideas/interpretations from someone else's work
- facts for which the reference provides the evidence.

You do this by means of a referencing system that provides rules for how to cite the work of others in the text of report and rules for how to format a **reference list** that shows all sources cited in your text. Reference systems vary and academic institutions, publishers and other organizations have their own preferences. To illustrate the basic principles, we give an introduction to referencing using two different systems in the companion website: the Harvard system and the Vancouver system. The Harvard system is an author-date system similar to the one used in this book. The Vancouver system is a numbered system which is widely used in medical and other sciences. Ensure that you understand the referencing system you are required to use so that you can collect all of the bibliographic information needed for your final reference list. You should also check whether you are expected to provide a reference list or a **bibliography**. A reference list contains only those works cited in your text. A bibliography lists all works you have consulted in preparing your report. Unless you have been explicitly asked to provide a bibliography, a reference list is more appropriate for most reports.

Plagiarism

Appropriate referencing is also essential to avoid the accusation of **plagiarism**. You commit plagiarism when you represent someone else's work as your own. 'Work' does not just mean published text but includes ideas, images or models and so on. It applies to work you have paraphrased as well as direct quotations. The 'someone else' could be a well-known public figure, an anonymous author of a website or another student. As well as being in breach of ethical standards, plagiarism is a very serious offence in academia and can lead to your dismissal from your programme of study. If you are a student, you should make sure you understand the rules on plagiarism for your institution. You should also take care to ensure that your work does not breach the copyright of another author.

CRITICAL COMMENTARY 3.1

Systematic review

The type of literature review that we have described here requires you to take a structured approach to developing a critical review of the relevant writing in the chosen topic area to support your research project. Reviews produced using this traditional approach, sometimes referred to as narrative reviews, have been criticized as failing to show how and why sources were selected and what assessment criteria were used to evaluate them and draw conclusions. As a result, according to critics, such reviews 'can be biased by the researcher and often lack rigour' (Tranfield et al. 2003: 207). A further criticism of traditional reviews is that they are not oriented to the needs of policy makers and practitioners in terms of guidance for policy decision making and implementation.

In the light of these criticisms, **systematic review** has been advocated as an alternative to the traditional approach. Originating from the field of medical science and closely associated with the evidence-based management movement, systematic review seeks to provide a systematic, transparent and reproducible method for locating, appraising and synthesizing all of the relevant studies in the chosen topic area. To achieve this, systematic review emphasizes the need to prepare a detailed protocol that sets out the research question that the review will answer and the procedures to followed, including the search strategy to be used, the inclusion/ exclusion criteria for studies and the methods for assessing the quality of studies and synthesizing the findings (CRD 2009). A feature of some systematic reviews is an approach known as **meta-analysis**, which is the use of statistical techniques to synthesize the findings from multiple studies to provide a single quantitative estimate.

Systematic review is not appropriate in every situation. Petticrew and Roberts (2006) suggest that it is particularly useful as a tool for reviewing existing evidence on whether or not a particular policy or intervention is effective, or where there is a need to get a more accurate picture of previous research to inform future research. Carrying out a systematic review, however, can be a major undertaking: a study of 37 systematic reviews that included meta-analysis found that they took on average 1,139 hours to complete (reported in Petticrew and Roberts 2006). Critics have also drawn attention to systematic reviews' perceived positivist leanings in the way that they evaluate studies and the extent to which they are seen to privilege policy-oriented studies over other forms of research (Hammersley 2001).

KEY LEARNING POINTS

- A critical review of literature is a component of academic and many other research projects. It provides the opportunity to build on the contribution of others and can help you to formulate your research problem, identify relevant theory, practices and policy and develop a suitable research design.
- Literature reviewing involves a systematic process of search, capture, synthesis and presentation of relevant theoretical, research, practice and policy literature.
- The literature review requires a critical evaluation of the arguments put forward in your sources and a structured synthesis of the findings from your own review.
- Conceptual models play an important role in research as graphical representations either of theory or of some real-world phenomenon of interest. Variance, process and systems models are three common types of conceptual model used in research.
- Clear and accurate referencing is essential to acknowledge the contributions of others, to ground your own claims and to avoid committing plagiarism.

NEXT STEPS

3.1   Formulating your literature review questions. Based on your research problem and research questions, formulate questions that your literature review should answer that will help you to (1) develop your understanding of theory and practice in your topic area, (2) design a suitable research approach.

3.2   Places to look. Review Table 3.2 and identify databases and other online areas that you can search for sources. Check which of these you can access via your academic institution, professional body or other organization.

3.3   Preparing to search.
  a) Confirm the reference format you are required to use. If there is no specific requirement, you will have to make your own choice.
  b) Use Tables 3.3 and 3.4 to develop your own template for capturing information from the sources you find.
  c) Familiarize yourself with any reference management software you intend to use or decide how you will record reference information.

3.4   Start searching. Make a list of search terms/keywords and the databases and other search locations to use to start searching. Capture your findings using your template created in the previous activity.

3.5   Developing a concept-centric review. As you evaluate and capture individual sources, start looking for patterns and themes in your reading. Use a table and/or graphical technique such as a literature map to develop a concept-centric view of your literature.

3.6   Developing a conceptual model. If you are adopting a deductive research approach, develop a conceptual model and formulate appropriate hypotheses for testing (this activity should be done after deciding on your research design and studying Chapters 4–6).

3.7   Make a presentation on your review findings. Find a suitable forum where you can make a presentation on your literature review findings to peers and colleagues. Use the opportunity to refine your overall argument and to get feedback on its structure and coherence.

Further reading

For further reading, please see the companion website.

Bibliographic databases

The table below shows a selection of bibliographic databases. In addition, most journal publishers have their own databases.

Table 3.7 Example bibliographic databases

Name	URL	Type
ABI/INFORM Complete (ProQuest)	www.proquest.co.uk	Bibliographic database
Business Source Complete (EBSCO)	www.ebscohost.com/academic/business-source-complete	Bibliographic database
Directory of Open Access Journals	www.doaj.org	Database of open-access journals
Emerald Insight	www.emeraldinsight.com	Bibliographic database
ERIC (Education Resources Information Center)	www.eric.ed.gov	Public database of education-related research and information; limited full-text availability
Ingenta Connect	www.ingentaconnect.com	Bibliographic database
JSTOR	www.jstor.org	Bibliographic database with full-text journals going back to date of first issue; recent issues less likely to be available
Science Direct	www.sciencedirect.com	Bibliographic database
Social Science Research Network	www.ssrn.com	Collaborative database of open-access and other publications

References

Boote, D. N. and Beile, P. (2005). 'Scholars before researchers: On the centrality of the dissertation literature review in research preparation', *Educational Researcher*, 34(6), 3–15.

Checkland, P. and Scholes, J. (1999). *Soft systems methodology in action: A 30-year retrospective*. Chichester: Wiley.

CRD (2009). *Systematic reviews*. University of York: Centre for Reviews and Dissemination.

Creswell, J. W. (2009). *Research design*. 3rd edn. Los Angeles, CA: Sage.

Gray, D. (2009). *Doing research in the real world*. 2nd edn. London: Sage.

Grix, J. (2004). *The foundations of research*. Basingstoke: Palgrave.

Hammersley, M. (2001). 'On "systematic" reviews of research literatures: A "narrative" response to Evans and Benefield', *British Educational Research Journal*, 27(5), 543–54.

Letza, S., Sun, X. and Kirkbride, J. (2004). 'Shareholding versus stakeholding: A critical review of corporate governance', *Corporate Governance: An International Review*, 12, 242–62.

Lewin, K. (1952). *Field theory in social science*. London: Tavistock Publications.

Maxwell, J. A. (2013). *Qualitative research design: An interactive approach*. 3rd edn. Los Angeles, CA: Sage.

Mintzberg, H., Ahlstrand, B. and Lampel, J. (1998). *Strategy safari*. London: Prentice Hall.

Mohr, L. B. (1982). *Explaining organisational behaviour*. San Francisco, CA: Jossey-Bass.

Petticrew, M. and Roberts, H. (2006). *Systematic reviews in the social sciences*. Oxford: Blackwell.

Saunders, M., Lewis, P. and Thornhill, A. (2012). *Research methods for business students*. 6th edn. Harlow: Prentice Hall.

Senge, P. M. (1990). *The fifth discipline: The art and practice of the learning organization*. London: Random House.

Silverman, D. (2010). *Doing qualitative research. A practical handbook*. 3rd edn. London: Sage Publications.

Toulmin, S. (1958). *The uses of argument*. Cambridge: Cambridge University Press.

Tranfield, D., Denyer, D. and Smart, P. (2003). 'Towards a methodology for developing evidence-informed management knowledge by means of systematic review', *British Journal of Management*, 14(3), 207–22.

Wallace, M. and Wray, A. (2011). *Critical reading and writing for postgraduates*. 2nd edn. London: Sage.

Webster, J. and Watson, R. T. (2002). 'Analysing the past to prepare for the future: Writing a literature review', *MIS Quarterly*, 26(2), xiii–xxiii.

Part II

Design

Part II contains five chapters, each of which focuses on helping you at the design stage of your project. In Chapter 4 we begin by laying out key considerations in research design, including how you can integrate theory into your project, the choice of time frame, data type, overall research methods and quality criteria. In Chapter 5 we explore how the nature of your research questions will influence the type of research design that may be appropriate and in Chapter 6 we introduce you to a range of quantitative and qualitative designs that you can apply to your own project.

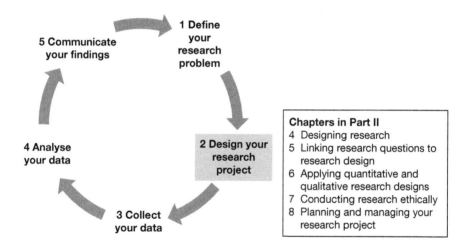

A key consideration for all researchers today is the ethical implications of their work and we review ethical issues in research in Chapter 7. Chapter 8 moves on to look at how you select an appropriate research design, plan your project and ultimately manage it. This chapter also introduces you to a crucial part of the planning process – the research proposal. We look at how to write one and provide you with a template for its structure and content.

4   Designing research

CHAPTER SUMMARY

The key topics covered in this chapter are:

- relating research design to theory
- selecting the time horizon for your research
- recognizing the characteristics of primary and secondary data
- choosing between quantitative, qualitative and mixed methods
- understanding quality in research.

4.1 Introduction

Your research design is the plan that you will adopt for your research in order to answer your research questions. It lays down both the overall structure for your research and the specific methods and techniques that you will use to collect and analyse your data. Research methods refer to the general form of your data collection and analysis procedures, in particular whether they are quantitative or qualitative. Research techniques are the specific tools and techniques, such as a particular type of statistical analysis or interview procedure.

Designing your research therefore requires decisions at increasing levels of detail to cover each stage of your project. This involves answering a series of questions as shown in Figure 4.1, where each is linked to chapters in this book where the topics are covered in more depth. At each level your decisions must be aligned so that the overall plan is consistent and coherent. The sort of data you collect, for example, has major implications for the data analysis techniques you can use. Conversely, the analysis techniques you plan to use will influence your choice of data collection procedure. Mistakes made at one stage can be difficult or even impossible to fix later on. Design is therefore a crucial stage in the overall research process.

Before you can begin a detailed design, you will need to think about your overall research approach. This involves addressing four broad issues that are the topic of this chapter. The first is the relationship between research design and theory, building on the distinction between deductive and inductive approaches that we introduced in Chapter 1.The second is the time horizon embedded in the research: do you intend

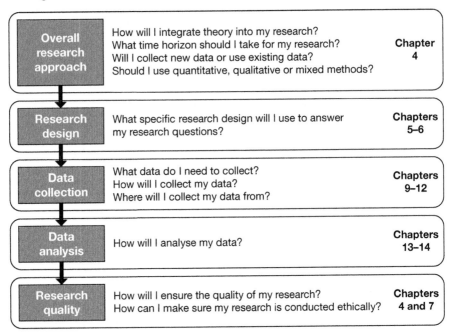

Figure 4.1 Decisions in research design

to track events through time or to take a snapshot of what is happening right now? The third relates to the origin of the data: will you collect new data or make use of data that exists already? The fourth concerns whether you will adopt quantitative, qualitative or mixed research methods for your project. In addition to addressing these issues, and regardless of what research design you adopt, you will want to have confidence in your findings and for them to be taken seriously by others. We therefore conclude this chapter with an introduction to a very contentious subject: criteria for judging quality in research.

4.2 Integrating theory into your research

In this section we expand on the relationship between research and existing theory and what it means for research design. We start by revisiting the distinction between deductive and inductive approaches introduced in Chapter 1, as these are the approaches most commonly encountered in business and management research. Later we will also consider a third approach known as abduction.

4.2.1 Deductive research approaches

A deductive (or **hypothetico-deductive**) research approach involves testing theory against observational data, thereby moving from the general (the theory to be tested) to the specific (actual data). In Figure 4.2 we show this proceeding through a series of closely connected sequential steps.

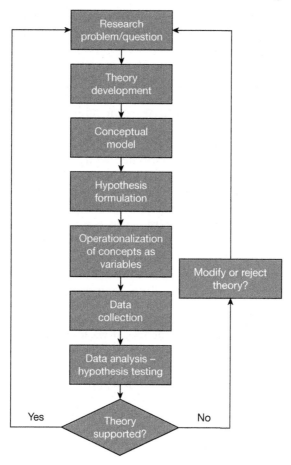

Figure 4.2 Stages in the deductive research approach

1   The process begins with development of a theory that potentially explains the problem under investigation. The theory must be articulated in a way which allows you to specify the concepts of interest, how they are related and why. This is often done by developing a conceptual model as described in Chapter 3.

2   Next, specific hypotheses are formulated, derived from the theory. In this context a **hypothesis** can be defined as a testable proposition about the expected association between two or more concepts in the theory. Based on theory, you might, for example, develop the hypothesis that customer satisfaction and customer loyalty are positively related.

3   The concepts identified in the hypotheses are then translated into measurable variables, a process known as **operationalization**. The term **variable** is an important one, particularly in quantitative research, and refers to any characteristic or attribute of something that can take on different values. Such values can be numerical (such as the level of customer satisfaction or customer loyalty) or categorical (such as a respondent's gender or nationality).

4   Suitable data are then collected to measure each variable, for example, by measuring satisfaction and loyalty amongst a randomly chosen sample of customers.

5   The hypotheses are then tested using an appropriate statistical procedure to see whether or not the hypotheses are supported by the data.

6   The results of the hypothesis testing may lead to the rejection of the theory, its modification or its retention. Either way, the findings are then used to address your original research question.

The deductive approach is closely associated with positivism and the idea of the scientific method and is frequently applied to answer 'why' type research questions. This involves using quantitative research designs such as experiments and survey studies to test theories about the associations between variables in order to determine whether or not a causal relationship exists. This is a very important application of the deductive approach, so we discuss it in more detail in Chapter 5, while the technical details of statistical hypothesis testing are covered in Chapter 13.

Although the deductive approach may appear at first sight to offer a high degree of precision and objectivity, a very important point needs to be made in connection with the truth status of the findings in this type of research. To explain this we draw on the work of the philosopher of science Karl Popper. Concerned by the ease by which our theories can be 'proved' to be true if we look for evidence that confirms or verifies them, Popper (2002: 48) proposed that the only 'genuine test' of a theory was an attempt to falsify or refute it. The aim of theory testing is therefore the falsification of theories, not their verification. Applying this perspective, we do not prove theories to be true, we fail to reject them. Thus, whilst a theory that has been refuted should be modified or abandoned, those theories that have survived testing should be seen as provisional rather than 'true' in any simplistic sense. As Blaikie (2000: 105) puts it, 'all knowledge is tentative and subject to ongoing critical evaluation'.

We illustrate the choice to take a deductive approach in Research in Practice 4.1.

4.2.2 *Inductive research approaches*

In contrast to the theory testing of a deductive approach, an inductive research approach seeks to build theory on the basis of observations. Theory is therefore the outcome of the research. The process begins with data collection in response to a problem or question (Figure 4.3). Inductive research designs favour open-ended and flexible data collection methods, such as in-depth interviews, rather than the pre-specified measurement techniques typical of deductive approaches. Similarly, instead of applying predetermined categories to the data, analysis in inductive research typically proceeds by searching for themes and patterns which form the building blocks of the emerging theory. The resulting theory can then be used to address the original research problem. At this point it is common to compare the findings with existing literature and theory, as we discussed in Chapter 3 and as shown diagrammatically in Figure 4.3.

When you adopt a deductive approach, prior theory determines what data you need to collect. How should you proceed when working inductively? One view is that you should approach the task of data collection without any presuppositions as

RESEARCH IN PRACTICE 4.1

Choosing a deductive approach

For his final year project, MBA student Davin Mac Ananey decided he wanted to learn more about the factors that motivate consumers to use mobile devices such as smartphones to shop online.[1] His began his project by conducting a literature search that generated a significant number of articles around the subject of consumer behaviour in relation to online shopping, the use of mobile telephony to shop online and, specifically, theories of technology adoption. Given the quality of existing theory that was relevant for his topic, Davin chose to adopt a deductive approach to his research. He used existing theory and prior research to create his own conceptual model of the factors that may influence consumers' adoption of smartphones to shop online. The model was tested using statistical analysis of quantitative data derived from a sample of online shoppers in the UK collected via an online survey. The findings showed that four of the six factors identified in the conceptual model had a significant influence on using smartphones for online shopping. Adopting a deductive approach for his research allowed Davin to build on existing theories to develop his own conceptual model of the factors influencing the use of smartphones for online shopping and to test his model against data, thereby contributing to our understanding of an important aspect of mobile commerce.

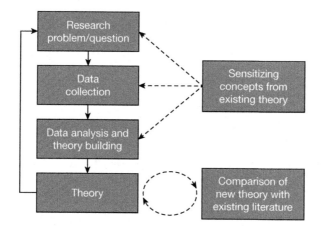

Figure 4.3 Stages in the inductive research approach

to what might be important, thereby avoiding imposing your own biases on the data you gather. If, however, we accept that observation is always to some extent theory laden we have to recognize that 'presuppositionless' observation is not really possible (Blaikie 2000: 103). In addition, from a practical point of view, we have to make sure that our data collection efforts generate useful results in whatever time we have available. As a result, many researchers make use of what Blumer (1954: 7) calls **sensitizing concepts**. Sensitizing concepts, which can be developed from the literature review, are not fixed and formally defined in advance as in deductive research. Instead they are seen as tentative, subject to change and added to or discarded as the research proceeds. They can guide data collection by suggesting initial lines of enquiry and can help to structure your data analysis, as we discuss further in Chapter 14.

An inductive approach suits pure research projects where the topic area is not well understood and there is little or no prior theory to act as a guide. Flick (2009) suggests that this is increasingly necessary, as rapid social change means that researchers are confronted with new contexts. Inductive approaches are also relevant to applied research projects where the problem under investigation may initially be poorly structured or is completely novel. Moreover, because theory is developed from the data, an inductive approach is attractive to researchers seeking to develop an in-depth understanding of a situation from the perspective of those involved in a situation. This focus on understanding, coupled with the nature of both data collection and analysis, means that qualitative methods are the most common to use when taking an inductive approach, and we introduce a range of suitable research designs in Chapter 6. Research in Practice 4.2 provides an example of a researcher choosing an inductive approach.

Inductive research involves an attempt to move from specific observations to more general theory, but, as Blaikie (2000: 104) warns us, 'all attempts to generalise must be tentative . . . Consistent findings can support generalization but never prove it to be true.' Just as with deductive approaches, therefore, we should regard our inductive findings as fallible and therefore provisional and subject to revision.

RESEARCH IN PRACTICE 4.2

Choosing an inductive approach

An important area of consumer research for management researchers is the link between an individual's values and their behaviour. As part of her PhD research, Anne Dibley (reported in Dibley and Baker 2001) was interested to investigate how certain types of brands, such as snack foods, can appeal to the personal values of consumers in the so-called 'tween' group (around 11 to 12 years old), an important consumer group for many brands. The aim of the research was to understand how brands relate to the value system of the young 'tween' group. The product category of snack foods was chosen as this is popular with young people.

Given the personal nature of our values and the sensitivities of discussing them, the researchers chose an inductive approach that enabled them to investigate the research participants' own understanding of the topic and allow them to discuss their feelings and attitudes openly. In-depth, qualitative interviews were chosen as the research method. The choice of an inductive approach in this research was motivated by the desire to generate deep insights into the topic from the respondents' perspective; a more structured, deductive approach using predetermined measures the research would not have been able to achieve this level of insight.

4.2.3 Abductive research approaches

Abduction (also known as **retroduction**) offers a third way that involves the interplay of observation and theory during the research process. The term is associated with the philosopher Charles Peirce, who used it to describe a form of reasoning that he called 'inference to the best explanation' (Honderich 1995: 1). We can illustrate this process with a simple example. Suppose that one morning your car does not start. Faced with this anomaly, you start to theorize why not. If the engine does not turn over you might decide that a flat battery is a plausible explanation. You could test your new theory by looking for other symptoms of a flat battery, such as the car lights not working. If you found such symptoms you would have more confidence in your theory. If you did not, you might decide that your original theory was wrong and look for an alternative explanation. Your flat battery theory might also prompt you to think more deeply about why the battery was dead in the first place. The process of abduction would thereby lead you on to more theory development as a result of encountering the original anomaly.

Several writers have drawn attention to the possibilities of using abductive reasoning in research but its application in research practice is not as well documented as either deduction or induction. When considering an abductive approach there are two requirements to think about beforehand. Firstly, you will need to collect data that is detailed and rich enough to allow you to develop your tentative theory. Secondly, the research process needs to be sufficiently flexible to support the iteration between theory and data. These requirements suggest the use of qualitative or mixed method research designs. Grounded theory is one research design that can employ abduction in its method of constant comparison between data and emerging theory (Reichertz 2007). Abductive reasoning can also have a role in the cyclical process of action research and in multiple case study designs (see Chapter 6).

4.2.4 Implications for your research

What does your approach to theory mean for your research? Each approach embodies a different overall logic to the way in which theory, data collection and data analysis are combined to answer a research question. They provide a way of thinking about how to align these elements in order to produce a coherent overall plan for your research.

4.3 Time horizon

The second important decision to take early in your project is the time horizon for your proposed study. Do you want to track events through time or take a single cross-sectional 'snapshot' of the current situation? This decision is driven by your research question and has major implications for your research design. There are three main options, as we explain here.

4.3.1 Cross-sectional studies

Cross-sectional studies (also known as one-shot studies) involve gathering data on your topic at a single, specific point in time. Whilst the term is often linked to quantitative survey research, qualitative studies, such as in-depth interviews, also use cross-sectional designs. Cross-sectional studies can be used to address a range of research questions where the focus is on the current state of the phenomenon of interest, for example, current levels of customer satisfaction or attitudes to a new product. Although in practice you might have to carry out data collection over several days or weeks, due to practical constraint, the nature of cross-sectional studies means that data collection is time-bounded, which brings practical benefits for the researcher. Nevertheless cross-sectional designs face a major problem when it comes to investigating situations where you need to assign some chronological sequence to events. This can arise, for example, in explanatory research where you want to be sure that a potential cause precedes an effect and not the other way around. Similar problems identifying chronological sequence occur when researching how things change over time. An alternative solution is to carry out a **longitudinal study** to gather data on subjects or events over time.

4.3.2 Prospective studies

A longitudinal research design that follows events as they happen is known as a **prospective study**. Prospective studies do not necessarily involve continuous data gathering. Instead data may be collected by making repeated observations at specific points in time using cross-sectional techniques, for instance before and after a change management initiative. **Panel studies**, which follow a group of subjects over a time, are classic examples of this type of prospective study. The British Household Panel Survey (ISER 2013a), for instance, has collected data by questionnaire annually from a representative sample of over 5,000 households in the United Kingdom since 1991. Ethnography (Section 6.3), on the other hand, is an example of a longitudinal qualitative research design where data collection is done during the more continuous presence of a researcher in the research setting.

   Longitudinal research provides a way of investigating the effects of time, as well as in some cases allowing you the opportunity to immerse yourself in the research setting. By definition, however, data collection for prospective longitudinal studies will take longer than for cross-sectional ones. There are also other issues that can jeopardize the findings, such as loss of access to the research site or the withdrawal of participants during the study. In addition, some events of importance are not known about in advance, so that a prospective longitudinal study is not feasible. Natural or other disasters fall into this category. In such situations, you may have no option but to study events retrospectively.

4.3.3 Retrospective studies

A **retrospective study** is a form of longitudinal research design that takes place after the events of interest have happened. This raises the challenge of gathering data on past events. Where reliance is placed on the memory of respondents, serious concerns can arise regarding the accuracy of their recall. According to Miller et al. (1997: 189), problems can arise from 'inappropriate rationalisation, oversimplification, faulty post hoc attribution and simple lapses of memory', to which they add the problem of respondents giving answers to present themselves or their organizations in a 'socially desirable' way. In some situations you may be able to use multiple respondents or other sources of data such as company records or other contemporary documents in order to corroborate your findings. Although this can reduce the problems of relying on human recall there may still be gaps or inconsistencies in retrospective data, so careful attention needs to be paid to data collection.

4.3.4 Implications for your research

During your research design you will need to decide the time horizon for your project. The key driver should be your research question. Can it be answered using a cross-sectional design or is a longitudinal study needed? If the latter, is a prospective or a retrospective design appropriate? Practical considerations will also play a part in the decision. Particularly if you are doing your research for an academic award or for an external client, the time allowed for your project is likely to be fixed, so you will need to make sure that you can complete data collection in the time available. In addition, you should be aware of any problems that may arise during the course of data collection, such as loss of access to the research site.

4.4 Primary and secondary data

The next decision area involves whether to collect new data for your project or to use existing data that have been collected for a different purpose. This is the distinction between primary and secondary data.

4.4.1 Primary data

The term **primary data** refers to any data that are collected specifically for the purposes of the research project being undertaken. The data have therefore been collected to answer your own specific research questions and you are the first user of that data. Primary data can be quantitative or qualitative. In most cases (particularly in a student research project) you are likely to be playing an active role in the actual data collection process. In other situations data collection may be outsourced, for example, to a market research agency. Nevertheless, the term 'primary data' is still applicable.

4.4.2 Secondary data

Secondary data refers to data that were collected, usually by someone else, for purposes other than your own investigation. Examples of secondary data include government statistics, such as census data, or research generated by other research projects such as the British Household Panel Survey that we mentioned earlier. Another important category of secondary data is the data generated by organizational activities, such as customer and employee data and company financial or operating records. Data of this kind are sometimes referred to as administrative or bureaucratic data and are a valuable source for business and management researchers. **Secondary data analysis** (also known as **secondary analysis**) is the re-analysis of such data to answer a research question that is distinct from that for which the data were originally collected. The Institute for Social and Economic Research website (ISER 2013b), for example, lists over one thousand journal articles that have made use of British Household Panel Survey data. Although much of this sort of data is quantitative, available qualitative datasets, for example, from earlier qualitative research projects, can also be subject to secondary analysis (Seale 2011).

4.4.3 Choosing your data type

In choosing what type of data to use, you need to consider the relative advantages and disadvantages that each offers. The main benefit of using primary data is the ability to target data collection precisely to the needs of your research project, thereby ensuring that you have relevant data in the format you want. Additionally, you will be familiar with the data and the quality of the collection process. Against this you have to weigh issues of access, cost and time that may limit your ability to collect yourself the data that you need. Using secondary data potentially offsets some of these disadvantages. In particular it may offer access to much larger and better-quality datasets than you would otherwise be able to obtain. Secondary data that have been collected over a period of time can also be used for retrospective analysis. Problems with secondary data can include the size and complexity of the dataset, lack of familiarity with the data and the collection methods used. Moreover, because the data were not specifically gathered for your current project, not all relevant variables may be included or those that are may be defined differently. Administrative secondary data that have been collected by organizations in the course of their normal activities are also more likely to reflect the collector's interests than yours and may tell you more about the way the organization works than what the data are supposed to represent (Gomm 2008). Issues of privacy and data protection must also be addressed when using organizational data such as customer records. You are not, however, limited to choosing only one type of data in your project: mixing data types is not unusual and offers further opportunity for **triangulation**, although it can complicate aspects of data collection and analysis. We look at secondary data collection in more detail in Chapter 12.

4.5 Quantitative and qualitative research methods

The fourth decision area concerns the broad choice of research method. So far in the book we have referred in passing to quantitative and qualitative methods. As we will see, the distinction between these two types of research is complex and controversial but is very widely used both in general textbooks and in more specialized treatments of research methods. It does also provide a helpful framework for classifying research designs discussing important aspects of both designing and carrying out management research. We will start by reviewing some of the perceived differences between the two families of method.

4.5.1 The quantitative–qualitative distinction

Table 4.1 summarizes some of the ways in which quantitative and qualitative research may be seen as different. Our starting point is to distinguish between the type of data used, with quantitative researchers collecting and analysing numerical data and qualitative researchers using non-numeric data, primarily words but also images and video. The types of data preferred involve quantitative researchers using statistical analysis procedures, whilst qualitative researchers use techniques such as thematic

Table 4.1 The qualitative–quantitative distinction

Quantitative research	Qualitative research
Collects and analyses numeric data	Collects and analyses non-numeric data
Tests theory deductively	Builds theory inductively or abductively
Uses structured, pre-specified, fixed procedures	Uses emergent, flexible procedures
Is variable oriented	Is case oriented
Is concerned with aggregate properties and statistical inference	Is concerned with depth, diversity and context
Uses researcher's categories (etic approach)	Uses local actors' categories (emic approach)
Works in artificial and/or controlled settings	Works in natural settings
Researcher is at a distance	Researcher is closely involved

analysis to interpret their data. The distinction is not so precise in practice. Text (such as advertisements, reports etc.) can be analysed quantitatively, whilst qualitative researchers may make explicit or implicit use of some quantification in their analysis. Nevertheless this difference is widely acknowledged and has significant practical implications for how you design and carry out your research, as well as the skills you will need to develop to do so.

Quantitative and qualitative research are often distinguished in terms of their relationship to theory. As we mentioned earlier in the chapter, quantitative research designs are widely used for deductive theory testing, and indeed the hypothetico-deductive approach is so strongly associated with the quantitative methods that the two can appear to be synonymous. Qualitative methods, on the hand, are more closely associated with inductive or abductive theory building. Use of qualitative methods does not, however, rule out a deductive approach and quantitative researchers can and do make use of inductive reasoning in their research. Nevertheless the deduction–induction split is widely encountered both in books about research methods and in the actual practice of researchers. It is also connected to other perceived differences between quantitative and qualitative methods.

One of these differences is the extent to which the procedures to be followed in the research are specified in advance or are developed as the research unfolds. Quantitative research is commonly characterized as having structured, predetermined and fixed research designs. A fixed design is consistent with the need to operationalize concepts as measurable variables and to pre-specify appropriate data collection and analysis procedures when taking a deductive approach. Qualitative research does not work under the same strictures, so that research designs can be more flexible, evolving as the research itself unfolds. Cooper et al. (2012: 243) refer to this as a 'developmental' mode of investigation and emphasize its iterative character in support of inductive or abductive theory building. Much quantitative research, on the other hand, operates in what they call 'simultaneous' mode, where all the data are brought together and then analysed simultaneously.

Quantitative research is often characterized as having a 'variable orientation'. By operationalizing concepts of interest as measurable variables and specifying the expected association between them, quantitative researchers can apply statistical techniques for analysis, including theory testing. This approach is combined with an interest in the aggregate properties of whatever is being investigated, which often involves a process of statistical inference by which statistical techniques are used to draw conclusions about a larger population on the basis of data drawn from a sample of that population. Qualitative research, on the other hand, tends to adopt a 'case-oriented' or 'case-focused' approach in which the focus is on the 'heterogeneity and particularity of individual cases' (Ragin 1987: xii). Instead of the aggregate properties of large groups, qualitative researchers usually investigate a small number of cases in depth and in their local context to understand the diversity and complexity of a phenomenon.

Important differences can also be seen in the origin of the conceptual categories used in research. Quantitative research typically adopts an 'outsider' or **etic** perspective in which concepts are specified by the researcher, based for example, on the theory being tested. Qualitative research, on the other hand, often seeks to take the perspective of those involved in the situation being investigated by adopting what is sometimes called an 'insider' or **emic** view. This can involve either staying close to the language and interpretations used by participants in a given situation or actively attempting to understand the lived experience of those involved in a situation. Qualitative research thereby offers a way of 'exploring and understanding the meaning individuals or groups ascribe to a social or human problem' (Creswell 2009: 4). This interest is shared with the philosophy of interpretivism, which has traditionally been associated with qualitative research and contrasts with the positivist orientation that characterizes much quantitative research. As always, however, we need to exercise caution. Some quantitative researchers, for example, in psychology, are interested in 'how people make sense of their experience' (Gomm 2008: 7) and not all researchers who use qualitative methods seek an interpretivist understanding of phenomena.

The final distinctions we will draw relate to the research environment and the role of the researcher. Qualitative research is often seen as preferring to conduct research in natural settings, such as the participants' homes or workplace, whilst quantitative research uses artificial ones, such as a laboratory, in which the researcher can control aspects of the environment. In practice this distinction does not always hold but it does indicate a difference in emphasis in some research designs. Another difference is how to deal with the influence of the researcher on the research findings. In most quantitative designs the aim is to minimize researcher impact by keeping 'physical and emotional distance from the study' (Robson 2011: 84). This is sought by careful attention to pre-specified procedures and protocols and the use of standardized data collection techniques. In qualitative research, however, methods of data collection such as face-to-face interviews or participant observation mean that 'the researcher is essentially the main "measurement device" in the study' (Miles and Huberman 1994: 7). Qualitative researchers therefore typically accept that they will have an impact on the research process and stress the need to reflect on the nature of that impact. This is an aspect of reflexivity, a topic we introduced in Chapter 1. Note, however, that both quantitative and qualitative methods share a general awareness of researcher effects even if the way in which such effects are understood and addressed varies considerably.

We must be careful not to exaggerate these differences. Particular qualitative and quantitative designs will display these tendencies to different degrees and in different combinations. There is also as much variation between different qualitative or different quantitative designs as there is between quantitative and qualitative research as a whole. Nevertheless, the distinction does provide a framework for discussing important aspects of research design and practice as they relate to choice of method. In addition, the distinctive features of quantitative and qualitative methods suggest different ways in which each may be used to answer particular research questions. We develop these ideas in Chapter 5, before presenting specific research designs in Chapter 6.

4.5.2 Is it possible to mix methods?

Up to now we have made the implicit assumption that choosing a research design will involve choosing either a quantitative or a qualitative method. Research that uses only one family of methods (e.g. only quantitative or only qualitative) is described as **mono method**. Given their different characteristics, however, it might seem sensible to seek to combine the two methods in some way to take advantage of the features of both. The combination of quantitative and qualitative methods in a single study is commonly referred to as a **mixed method** study.

4.5.3 Reasons for mixing methods

Advocates of mixed methods have identified a number of possible benefits in combining methods. Greene et al. (1989), for example, identify five reasons for doing so.

1 *Triangulation.* The idea of triangulation in mixed methods research is to corroborate the findings of one method with those of the other to give more confidence in the results.
2 *Complementarity.* The findings of one type of research can be used to clarify, elaborate upon or illustrate the findings of the other method.
3 *Development.* The output of one method is used to support the development of the other method, for example, qualitative interviews used to inform the preparation of a quantitative questionnaire.
4 *Initiation.* The questions or results of different methods are used to offer different perspectives or to uncover contradictions and paradoxes. The desire to gain new perspectives can also lead to the combination of methods, even when the assumption is that they are incompatible philosophically (see Critical Commentary 4.1).
5 *Expansion.* The scope and range of the study can be increased by adopting different methods as appropriate for different research questions within the study.

Behind these potential benefits is the assumption that, as Creswell (2009: 4) puts it, mixed method research 'is more than simply collecting and analysing both kinds of data'. Instead, both methods should be combined in such a way that the resulting study is stronger than it would have been, had a mono method approach been employed.

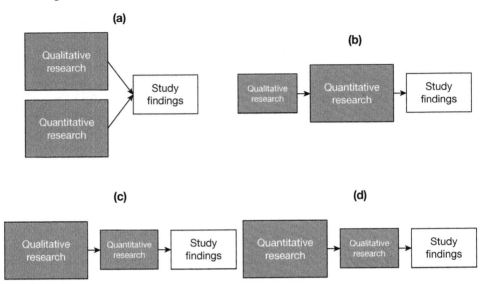

Figure 4.4 Example mixed method designs (adapted from Tashakkori and Teddlie 1998: 44)

4.5.4 Mixed method design options

Mixed method researchers have suggested a range of options for combining quantitative and qualitative methods. A helpful starting point has been proposed by Morgan (1989), who identifies two dimensions of mixed methods designs: priority and sequence. Priority refers to the weighting attached to the different methods. Are they equal or is one predominant over the other? Sequence refers to the ordering of the research methods. Will one follow the other or will they be done in parallel? This generates a range of options, four of which are illustrated in Figure 4.4.

In the first example in Figure 4.4(a) the researcher is using quantitative and qualitative methods in parallel and with equal weight. The objective may be to achieve methodological triangulation in order to corroborate the findings; alternatively, the approach may be one of 'initiation' (in the terminology used by Greene et al. 1989: 260), whereby the researcher uses different methods to reveal different aspects of a phenomenon. The second example, in Figure 4.4(b), illustrates how one method may be used to support the development of another, for example, the use of qualitative focus groups to help refine a questionnaire as part of a larger quantitative survey study. This is a sequential design with the qualitative research coming first but with the quantitative research taking the dominant position with respect to the ultimate findings. An alternative sequential design is given in the third example, Figure 4.4(c), where quantitative research is being used to elaborate the findings from a qualitative study. Such research might, for example, involve investigating one dimension of a qualitative study's findings in more breadth by carrying out a survey study, perhaps to establish the prevalence of a particular phenomenon identified by the qualitative research. The fourth example, Figure 4.4(d), uses a qualitative study to elaborate upon or help explain the findings of a quantitative study. We give an example of a mixed method study using this design in Research in Practice 4.3.

RESEARCH IN PRACTICE 4.3

A mixed method study of emotion and sales in convenience stores

(Sutton and Rafaeli 1988)

In a classic mixed methods study, Sutton and Rafaeli (1988) analysed quantitative data gathered by structured observation from a sample of 576 convenience stores to test the hypothesis that there was a positive relationship between employees' display of positive emotions to customers and store sales. Behind the research lay the assumption by the company's executive team that enhancing employee courtesy could give competitive advantage over rivals by improving customer service. Surprisingly, the data analysis showed a negative relationship: displays of positive emotion were negatively related to store sales.

To find out why, Sutton and Rafaeli carried out a second, qualitative inductive study. This involved case studies of stores, working as a store clerk, interviews and informal conversations with staff at different levels and store visits. Analysis of the qualitative data led the researchers to conclude:

> Sales is an indicator of a store's pace, or the amount of time pressure on clerks and customers, and that pace leads to displayed emotions, with norms in busy settings supporting neutral displays [of emotion] and norms in slow settings supporting positive displays.
>
> Sutton and Rafaeli (1988: 461)

Sutton and Rafaeli re-analysed the quantitative data and found that it confirmed their findings from the qualitative study. Their study shows the potential power of combining the insights from both quantitative and qualitative research designs in a single research project.

4.5.5 Opting for mixed methods research

Despite growing interest in mixed method research and its apparent attractions, it does not follow that mixed method research represents some ideal. Certainly not all research projects would benefit from, let alone require, a mixed method study. Neither is it clear that all the philosophical or technical issues around mixing methods are resolved (see Critical Commentary 4.1). Practical factors intrude as well. The researcher, especially a student researcher, always has finite time and other resources. Spreading those resources too thinly may result in a lower-quality piece of work than if effort had been focused on a single research method. A similar problem comes when reporting research, because of word count or other limits. You will also need to develop the skills to carry out mixed method research, which may be a particular challenge if you are new to research.

If you are considering adopting a mixed method approach, you should think carefully about the logic of doing so. Map out how the different methods are related

PART II

in terms of sequence and priority. Ask yourself how they combine to answer your research questions. Consider what your mixed method design offers that a mono-method approach would not. Review the practical implications of your research design. Do you have the time, skills and word count to carry it out successfully? Finally bear in mind that using more than one method is not a substitute for sound research design and execution.

CRITICAL COMMENTARY 4.1

Mixing methods

Although mixed methods have attracted increased attention over the last few years, there is still some controversy over their role in research. Cooper et al. (2012: 8–9) identify four main perspectives on using mixed methods. The first holds that quantitative and qualitative research represent incompatible paradigms based on fundamentally different philosophical assumptions (such as positivism versus inter-pretivism), with supporters of one approach dismissing the other as valueless (or at best subordinate) in terms of producing useful knowledge. This is an example of methodological monism, where one particular approach is seen as the exemplar for all branches of social science. In this view there can be no meaningful mixing of methods. The second position also sees a paradigmatic difference between quantitative and qualitative approaches but accepts each as 'legitimate in its terms, to be selected as a matter of fundamental, and therefore necessarily non-rational, commitment by researchers' (Cooper et al. 2012: 8). We might think of this as a 'separate spheres' view of the possibility of mixing methods. Cooper et al.'s third position on the quantitative and qualitative divide represents a softer version of the separate spheres view in which the characteristics of the methods make them suitable for answering different types of research question but within any given study a single method would be used. The fourth position goes much further in terms of its methodological pluralism, rejecting any paradigmatic or other incompatibility between quantitative and qualitative methods and, instead, combining them in a single study in order to incorporate the strengths of both approaches. Positions three and four therefore see the issue of mixing methods more in technical than in philosophical terms, placing emphasis on the characteristics of the methods and their relationship to the research question. The view we take in this book is closer to position four, whilst acknowledging the philosophical and technical questions that have been raised about mixing methods.

4.6 Quality in research

What does it mean to do good research? One way of answering this question might be to lay down fixed criteria for what constitutes 'good' research. For some writers this means taking the natural sciences as a model, adopting what is sometimes characterized as the 'scientific method', often equated with the hypothetico-deductive approach. As you may imagine, this view is not shared by all researchers. The assumption that the methods of the natural sciences are applicable to the social sciences is contested by many (Guba and Lincoln 1989), whilst others question whether the standard image of the scientific method is applicable even to the natural sciences, let alone the social sciences (Bhaskar 1989). Other writers have called into question the possibility of 'objective' science that many accounts of the scientific method emphasize (Johnson and Duberley 2000) and its association with deduction and, by implication, quantitative research. Behind much of this debate lie competing philosophical worldviews, as we discuss in Chapter 1. However, as Silverman (2010: 274) points out, 'short of reliable methods and valid data conclusions, research descends into a bedlam where the only battles that are won are by those who shout the loudest'.

In the face of such disagreements, Robson (2011: 14) proposes that researchers should take what he calls a 'scientific attitude'. As discussed in Chapter 1, this involves doing research systematically (thinking carefully about what you are doing, how and why), sceptically (subjecting your findings to scrutiny and possible disconfirmation) and ethically (conducting your research so as to ensure the interests of participants are respected). These three criteria would seem a sound guide for research, regardless of your chosen research method or philosophical position. Seale (1999: x) takes a similar stance in advocating 'methodological awareness', emphasizing that you should be 'always open to the possibility that conclusions many need to be revised in the light of new evidence'. Thus the reaction against the assumption of a unified scientific method does not inevitably mean the abandonment of rigour in research or that anything goes.

4.6.1 Quality criteria

Disagreements over status of the 'scientific method' show how difficult it is to establish commonly agreed quality criteria against which we can judge our own research and that of others. Therefore, although we begin by introducing the traditional quality criteria of validity, reliability and generalizability, you should be aware that these are closely associated with quantitative research and are by no means universally accepted. To complement them we therefore conclude this section by looking at an alternative framework that has been proposed, particularly in the context of qualitative research projects.

Validity

At its most basic, **validity** is about whether your research findings are really about what they claim to be about. Quantitative researchers in particular have developed a complex conceptualization of validity, supported by a range of techniques to assess validity. Some of these focus on the validity of any measures used in the research, such as questions in a questionnaire. Here a key question is whether or not the measures actually measure what they are supposed to measure. For example, does a set of questions in a questionnaire really measure customer satisfaction? Other validity criteria focus more on the validity of the overall research design, in particular the extent to which any causal claims are valid. Table 4.2 summarizes some of the main aspects of validity, particularly as used within quantitative research.

Table 4.2 Dimensions of validity

Dimension	Definition
Content construct validity	The extent to which a measure actually measures the underlying concept it is intended to measure
Construct content validity	The extent to which a measure captures all of the dimensions of the concept it is intended to measure
Convergent validity	The extent to which a measure for one concept is correlated with another measure that measures the same underlying concept. Contrast with discriminant validity
Criterion validity	The extent to which a measure of a chosen variable predicts the value of another variable known to be related, for example, how well a score on a course entry test predicts performance on that course
Discriminant validity	The extent to which a measure for one concept is not correlated with another measure that measures a different underlying concept. Contrast with convergent validity
Ecological validity	The extent to which findings from research in an artificial environment, such as a laboratory, hold in natural settings, such as the home or workplace
External validity	The extent to which research findings are applicable to people, time or settings other than those in which the research was conducted. Also known as generalizability
Face validity	A subjective judgement of the extent to which a measure appears 'on the face of things' to measure what it is supposed to measure
Internal validity	The extent to which causal inferences about the relationship between two or more variables can be supported by the research design

PART II

Reliability

Reliability in quantitative research is concerned with the stability and consistency of the measures that researchers use. In the case of a set of questions in a questionnaire, for example, you would want to be confident that they gave the same results if the measure were repeated. As with validity, a number of different dimensions of reliability can be identified, as summarized in Table 4.3.

Generalizability

Generalizability (also known as **external validity**) concerns the extent to which your research findings are applicable to people, time or settings other than those in which the research was conducted. In quantitative research this is often done using a process of statistical inference to make generalizations about the population from which the research sample was drawn. Technically, this is the limit of generalization that is possible statistically (Bryman and Bell 2007). An alternative approach that does not rely on statistical inference is known as analytic or theoretical generalization. Yin (2011) sees this as a two-stage process in which the researcher proceeds via the

Table 4.3 Dimensions of reliability

Dimension	Definition
Internal consistency reliability	The extent to which items in a multi-item scale are related. Often measured using Cronbach's alpha
Inter-rater (or inter-observer/ coder) reliability	The degree of consistency between two or more coders when coding the same set of data. Also known as inter-coder reliability
Test-retest reliability	The extent to which a measure will give the same result if it is repeated

development of theory on the basis of research findings to draw out the implications for other settings in which such theory might be relevant. Yin cites the example of a well-known case study of the 1962 Cuban missile crisis to show how a single study can inform understanding of superpower confrontation in other situations.

4.6.2 *Alternative quality criteria*

Imposing a one-size-fits-all universal framework raises both theoretical and practical problems. The theoretical problems relate to the appropriateness of using a single set of criteria to judge very different forms of research, sometimes motivated by different philosophical worldviews. The practical problems relate to the difficulty of applying criteria created, for example, for a quantitative survey study to a qualitative ethnography. Not surprisingly, alternative criteria have been proposed, particularly with respect to evaluating qualitative research. Some of these are based on philosophical assumptions that are very different to those claimed to underpin the 'traditional' quality criteria. Here we will illustrate one well-known framework proposed by Lincoln and Guba (1985) in their book *Naturalistic Inquiry*. Lincoln and Guba (1985: 290) argue that researchers need to establish the 'trustworthiness' of any research findings in order to demonstrate that research findings are worth paying attention to. This, they argue, involves addressing four criteria (Table 4.4).

Table 4.4 Trustworthiness criteria (Lincoln and Guba 1985)

Criteria	Dimensions
Credibility	Giving confidence in the 'truth' of the findings, in terms of the alignment between the researcher's findings and the lives and experiences of respondents
Dependability	Demonstrating that the findings are consistent and could be repeated
Confirmability	Showing that the findings of the study are shaped by the respondents and not by researcher bias, motivation or interest
Transferability	Providing sufficient information to allow the reader to assess the findings' relevance to other contexts; analogous to generalizability (external validity) in traditional criteria

PART II

Helpfully, Lincoln and Guba also put forward a range of techniques that can be used to help researchers meet the criteria or confirm that they have been met. These are summarized in Table 4.5.

Table 4.5 Trustworthiness criteria, and proposed techniques for meeting them or confirming that they have been met (Lincoln and Guba 1985)

Trustworthiness criteria	Proposed techniques
Credibility	1 Prolonged engagement with the field and respondents
	2 Persistent observation, especially of features that appear to be particularly relevant
	3 Triangulation of sources, methods and investigators to cross-check data
	4 Peer debriefing, exposing ideas to a non-involved peer who can help to keep the researcher honest and act as 'devil's advocate'
	5 Negative case analysis, looking for negative cases to test emerging theory
	6 Member checking (also known as respondent validation), feeding emerging and final findings back to participants for commentary and review
Dependability	Keeping an audit trail and having external audit of the processes used in the research
Confirmability	Keeping an audit trail and having external audit of the data and analysis
Transferability	Sufficient detail, including contextual information, to allow the reader to assess the relevance of the research findings for other situations

Lincoln and Guba's framework has been critiqued, not least by the originators, but it provides a helpful alternative perspective to complement validity, reliability and generalizability as the dominant language and yardstick for quality in research. Further details on the practical aspects these techniques are given in Chapter 14 when we discuss qualitative data analysis.

4.6.3 *Implications for your research*

Both as part of your research design and as part of your final write-up, you will need to demonstrate the quality of your research. In the first place, regardless of your preferred research design, you will need to show rigour in its conceptualization and execution. Second, you will need to address appropriate dimensions of research quality as they relate to your own research findings. Further guidance is given in the chapters on data analysis (Chapters 13 and 14).

KEY LEARNING POINTS

- Your research design is your plan for your research in order to answer your research questions; it provides the overall framework for the research and specifies the research methods and techniques to be used to collect and analyse the data.
- Deductive, inductive and abductive approaches are three ways in which theory can be integrated into research. Deductive research emphasizes theory testing; inductive research is concerned with theory building; abductive research involves the iterative interplay of theory and data. Whatever approach is used, however, findings should always be open to further revision in the light of new evidence.
- The time horizon of a research study can be cross-sectional or longitudinal. If the latter, it can involve studying events prospectively, as they unfold, or retrospectively after, they have happened.
- Quantitative research designs emphasize quantification and measurement in the collection and analysis of data; qualitative research designs emphasize the collection and analysis of data non-numerically. Other distinctive characteristics can also be identified but the degree to which they are present for a given design varies and the quantitative–qualitative distinction is a controversial topic.
- Mixed method research designs in which qualitative and quantitative methods are combined in a single study can be characterized in terms of the sequencing and priority given to the different methods.
- Quality is a contentious subject in research. Traditional criteria of validity, reliability and generalizability are widely used but have been challenged, particularly for qualitative research, where alternative criteria for establishing trustworthiness have been proposed. Nevertheless, you will still need to think about how you will establish the credibility of your research.

NEXT STEPS

4.1 **Theory and research design**. Select one or more research articles from the literature you have reviewed so far in your topic area. Identify the approach used by the authors to integrate theory into the research design (deductive, inductive or abductive). Why is this approach adopted? How does it help the authors answer their research questions? Would the approach be suitable for your research project?

4.2 **Time horizon**. Review the research articles that you have identified so far in your topic area. What time horizon is adopted in each study? Why was this time horizon chosen? How does it help the authors answer their research questions? What time horizon would be most suitable for your research project?

4.3 **Choice of data type**. Review the research questions for your project and identify the data you will need in order to answer them. What potential data sources (primary/secondary) are available? What are the strengths and weaknesses of each for your particular project?

> **4.4   Research methods**. Review the research articles that you have identified so far in your topic area. What research method (quantitative, qualitative, mixed methods) are adopted in each study? Why was that method chosen? How does it help the authors to answer their research questions? What research method would be most suitable for your research project?
>
> **4.5   Research quality**. Select one or more research articles from the literature you have reviewed so far in your topic area. How do the authors address the quality of their research? What quality criteria do they refer to in their article? How does this help to establish the credibility of their research for the reader?

Further reading

For further reading, please see the companion website.

References

Bhaskar, R. (1989). *The possibility of naturalism*. 2nd edn. Hassocks, NY: Harvester.

Blaikie, N. (2000). *Designing social research*. Cambridge: Polity.

Blumer, H. (1954). 'What is wrong with social theory?', *American Sociological Review*, 19(1), 3–10.

Bryman, A. and Bell, E. (2007). *Business research methods*. 2nd edn. Oxford: Oxford University Press.

Cooper, B., Glaesser, J., Gomm, R. and Hammersley, M. (2012). *Challenging the quantitative–qualitative divide*. London: Continuum.

Creswell, J. W. (2009). *Research design*. 3rd edn. Los Angeles, CA: Sage.

Dibley, A. and Baker, S. (2001). 'Uncovering the links between brand choice and personal values amongst young British and Spanish girls', *Journal of Consumer Behaviour*, 1(1), 77–93.

Flick, U. (2009). *An introduction to qualitative research*. 4th edn. Los Angeles, CA: Sage.

Gomm, R. (2008). *Social research methodology: A critical introduction*. 2nd edn. Basingstoke: Palgrave Macmillan.

Greene, J. C., Caracelli, V. J. and Graham, W. F. (1989). 'Toward a conceptual framework for mixed-method evaluation designs', *Educational Evaluation and Policy Analysis*, 11(3), 255–74.

Guba, E. G. and Lincoln, Y. S. (1989). *Fourth generation evaluation*. London: Sage.

Honderich, T. (ed.) (1995). *The Oxford companion to philosophy*. Oxford: Oxford University Press.

ISER (2013a). *British Household Panel Survey* [online]. University of Essex. Available from: www.iser.essex.ac.uk/bhps [Accessed 17 September 2013].

ISER (2013b). *BHPS publications* [online]. University of Essex. Available from: www.iser.essex.ac.uk/bhps/publications [Accessed 17 September 2013].

Johnson, P. and Duberley, J. (2000). *Understanding management research*. London: Sage.

Lincoln, Y. S. and Guba, E. G. (1985). *Naturalistic inquiry*. Beverly Hills, CA: Sage Publications.

Miles, M. B. and Huberman, M. A. (1994). *Qualitative data analysis*. 2nd edn. Thousand Oaks, CA: Sage.

Miller, C. C., Cardinal, L. B. and Glick, W. H. (1997). 'Retrospective reports in organisational research: A reexamination of recent evidence', *Academy of Management Journal*, 40(1), 189–204.

Morgan, D. L. (1989). 'Practical strategies for combining qualitative and quantitative methods: Applications to health research', *Qualitative Health Research*, 8(3), 362–76.

Popper, K. (2002). *Conjectures and refutations.* London: Routledge.

Ragin, C. C. (1987). *The comparative method.* Berkeley and Los Angeles, CA: University of California Press.

Reichertz, J. (2007). Abduction: The logic of discovery of grounded theory. *In:* Bryant, A. and Charmaz, K. (eds) *The Sage handbook of grounded theory.* London: Sage.

Robson, C. (2011). *Real world research.* 3rd edn. Chichester: Wiley.

Seale, C. (1999). *The quality of qualitative research.* London: Sage.

Seale, C. (2011). Secondary analysis of qualitative data. *In:* Silverman, D. (ed.) *Qualitative research.* 3rd edn. London: Sage.

Silverman, D. (2010). *Doing qualitative research: A practical handbook.* 3rd edn. London: Sage Publications.

Sutton, R. I. and Rafaeli, A. (1988). 'Untangling the relationship between displayed emotions and sales: The case of convenience stores', *Academy of Management Journal*, 31(3), 461–87.

Tashakkori, A. and Teddlie, C. (1998). *Mixed methodology.* Thousand Oaks, CA: Sage.

Yin, R. K. (2011). *Qualitative research from start to finish.* New York: Guilford Press.

Note

1   Mac Ananey, D. (2013). *An investigation into the factors that drive online shopping adoption through smartphones in the United Kingdom.* MBA dissertation submission. Henley Business School, University of Reading.

5   Linking research questions to research design

CHAPTER SUMMARY

The key topics covered in this chapter are:

- designing research to answer 'what' questions
- designing research to answer 'why' questions
- designing research to answer 'how' questions.

5.1 Introduction

In Chapter 2 we introduced three generic categories of research question: 'what', 'why' and 'how' questions. In Chapter 4 we looked at key dimensions of research design. We now bring these two perspectives together to consider how different research questions can be investigated using different research designs that employ quantitative, qualitative or mixed methods. We address each type of research question in turn, examining the implications for how we go about answering them. This chapter provides the background to the presentation of specific research designs in Chapter 6 and the foundation for your choice of design for your own project.

5.2 Research designs for answering 'what' questions

Answers to 'what' questions are essentially descriptive. To describe means to give a detailed account of something. In research, description involves identifying and describing the characteristics of, and patterns in, a phenomenon of interest. Descriptions can be relatively concrete, such as the age or gender mix of your customer base, or relatively abstract, such as their attitudes or values. They can be qualitative or quantitative, cross-sectional or longitudinal. They can be relatively simple, such as a description of customer satisfaction, or more complex, such as a description of customer satisfaction by customer age and the type of product purchased. Answers to descriptive questions do not attempt to provide explanations of phenomena in terms of 'why' or 'how' they happen, but good description is not just reportage or 'mindless fact gathering' (de Vaus 2001: 1). Instead it involves drawing conclusions about the phenomenon of interest on the basis of a set of observations in order to reduce a mass of data into something more manageable and useful.

5.2.1 Description and comparison

Description of something in isolation can raise the question 'so what?' because without some frame of reference it can be difficult to make sense of your findings. Knowing, for instance, that the average spend per customer visit to your website is €38.99 may not be very useful on its own. Is 38.99 a big number? Should you be pleased? Concerned? One way of making sense of such data is by making comparisons. For example:

- between groups or sub-groups within your own data, for instance, by comparing differences in spend between one customer group and another
- between the same group at different points in time, for example, by comparing how the level of customer spending has changed over time
- against a predetermined reference, such as comparison of the average customer spend against organizational sales targets or other relevant (internal or external) benchmarks.

Comparison is not just done in quantitative terms. It can also be qualitative, comparing, for example, different experiences of organizational change or different ways in which customers relate to a company's brand. Comparison has obvious practical application in organizational research, for instance when evaluating current practices relative to an external benchmark or when seeking a deeper understanding of how groups differ in their perceptions, values and beliefs. Unexpected or unwelcome findings may prompt further research to find out why or how the situation has arisen and how to close any gap.

5.2.2 Description and classification

Another approach to description is to use a classification scheme to divide things into groups or categories according to their similarities and differences. As Bailey (1994: 1) describes the process, 'we arrange a set of entities into groups so that each group is as different as possible from all other groups, but each group is internally as homogenous as possible'. The 'entities' to be categorized might be individuals, organizations, events or some other phenomenon of interest. The resulting classification scheme should be mutually exclusive and exhaustive so that each entity is in one and only one group. At their best, classification schemes can provide a powerful way of reducing the complexity of your data whilst helping you to identify key distinctions with practical and theoretical relevance.

Classification schemes can be developed using both quantitative and qualitative analysis techniques. Classification can be done along a single dimension such as age or marital status, but more interesting classificatory schemes are likely to be multidimensional. Research in Practice 5.1 illustrates a multidimensional classification scheme for organizations proposed by Mintzberg (1983). Classifications schemes can be built inductively from the data, in which case they are often referred to as **taxonomies,** or they can be developed in advance from existing theory and then applied to the data as a categorizing device, when the expression **typology** is sometimes preferred. You can use a classification scheme to reduce descriptive complexity but it can be used to help in answering 'why' and 'how' questions, for example, by classifying different patterns of causal factors or types of process.

RESEARCH IN PRACTICE 5.1

A multidimensional classification scheme: structure in fives

Mintzberg's (1983) well-known typology of organizational designs classifies organization types on the basis of three dimensions:

1 the prime mechanism used to coordinate work in the organization
2 the key part of the organization
3 the type of decentralization used in the organization.

Each of these has, in turn, five dimensions so that there are, for example, five basic parts of an organization (strategic apex, middle line, operating core, support staff and technostructure). Theoretically this gives a rather large number of possible combinations. According to Mintzberg, however, the different dimensions cluster together into five different design configurations in each of which 'a different one of the coordinating mechanisms is dominant, a different part of the organization plays the most important role, and a different type of decentralization is used' (Mintzberg 1983: 152). The five structural configurations are:

1 simple structure
2 machine bureaucracy
3 professional bureaucracy
4 divisionalized form
5 adhocracy.

Mintzberg discusses the implications of his classification scheme in terms of four different applications to theory and practice.

5.2.3 Is description enough?

Despite the importance of description, a word of warning is necessary, particularly to those undertaking research for academic assessment: just describing something may not be seen as making sufficient contribution, especially at Master's or doctoral level. So, while description will almost certainly be a component of any research project, it will not necessarily be the endpoint. In many cases, you will want to go further and build on description as you go on to develop answers to 'why' and 'how' questions. For student research projects, we recommend that you clarify what is expected with your supervisor.

5.2.4 Quantitative approaches to description

Some descriptive research questions naturally imply quantification as a component of the answer. Questions such as 'what is the level of . . .?' 'what is the frequency of . . .?' 'how many . . .?' or 'what proportion of . . .' all suggest quantitative description. At its simplest, such description seeks to identify and describe something in terms of the distribution (e.g. frequencies or average) of one or more variables of interest for a particular **population**. Suppose, for example, that you wanted to know the average number of store visits per week made by customers in different age groups. Since it may not be possible or practical to get data from every single customer, you might find this out by administering a questionnaire to a randomly selected sample of store customers and then use appropriate statistical techniques to draw conclusions about your overall customer base in terms of frequency of visit by age group.

From this simple example we can identify four general features that typify a quantitative approach to description:

1   The pre-specification of the concepts of interest (such as age, income, attitude, etc.) so that they can be operationalized as measurable variables for data collection.
2   The use of a standardized data collection instrument, such as a questionnaire, to gather quantitative or quantifiable data on the chosen variables.
3   The selection of a representative sample in a way that will support statistical inferences about the population from which the sample was drawn.
4   The use of statistical techniques to generate a description of the aggregate properties of the population, including any relevant sub-groups or classes, based on analysis of the sample data.

Although descriptive research may not involve any formal theory testing, you will notice that these features align closely to the deductive research approach and the general characteristics of quantitative research that we described in Chapter 4.

In Chapter 6 we describe two quantitative research designs that are particularly well suited to answering 'what' questions. The first is a survey study which can be used for a wide range of descriptive purposes. The second is content analysis, a design that can be used to describe the message content of different forms of text, such as online documents, advertising and even video material. Secondary data, such as organizational operating data, are also a useful data source for answering 'what' questions, especially for developing retrospective descriptions.

5.2.5 Qualitative approaches to description

Qualitative approaches to description shift the focus of the research away from the aggregate characteristics of a population in terms of key variables to the in-depth study of a small number of cases in terms of their range and diversity (Jansen 2010). This allows you to develop a richer and more detailed description of something than is typically possible with a quantitative study. This is helped by the flexible and open-ended nature of most qualitative data collection methods, which leaves more scope to discover the unexpected. Such flexibility is also very useful in exploratory research either to develop a preliminary description of a topic that is novel or poorly understood or as part of a mixed methods research design to help identify relevant dimensions for inclusion in a follow-up quantitative study.

Another distinctive characteristic of qualitative description is its preference for taking an emic viewpoint emphasizing the experiences and perspectives of those involved in a situation. In this approach, 'the aim [of description] is to grasp in some way what it is like to be the people under investigation and to go through the experiences as they go through them' (Thorpe and Holt 2008: 7). A further development of description in qualitative research is the idea of 'thick' description, a term popularized by the ethnographer Clifford Geertz (1975). **Thick description** is more than just a very detailed description. It provides the basis for understanding the meaning of actions in a particular context. It enables us to know, for example, whether someone closing one eye is suffering from a nervous tic or is signalling a friend by winking Geertz (1975). Developing a thick description involves moving beyond reporting simply what is observed to interpreting the meaning, motivation and understanding involved in what is seen and how these are related to the context (Hammersley and Atkinson 2007).

The flexible nature of qualitative research means that many of the research designs we introduce in Chapter 6 can be used for descriptive purposes. Case study is particularly suited for in-depth description of individual cases and ethnography for studies taking an emic perspective with an emphasis on thick description. Interview studies can be used in a wide range of descriptive research projects but their flexibility and open-endedness makes them particularly useful in exploratory research projects and for investigating the experiences and perspectives of respondents in their own words. Qualitative content analysis can be used for the descriptive analysis of messages, such as advertising, Internet postings and printed text.

5.3 Research designs for answering 'why' questions

Answers to 'why' questions are concerned with explanations for something. What form such an explanation might take, how to produce one and even whether explanation is feasible are extremely controversial topics in social science. Nevertheless, as we argued in Chapter 2, explanation is an important part of much business and management research so in this section we take a closer look at different ways of answering 'why' type research questions. We will begin by looking at approaches that seek explanation in terms of cause and effect relationships to identify, for example, what factors are causing some observed phenomenon (the effect).

5.3.1 Criteria for inferring causality

Four criteria are commonly suggested for inferring causality:

1   Cause and effect should co-vary. If an independent variable is causally related to a dependent variable they should co-vary so that as one variable changes, the other systematically changes with it.
2   The cause should precede the effect in time. Establishing the time sequence of cause and effect can help to address the **directionality problem**, which is the problem of deciding, if two variables co-vary, which one is the cause and which is the effect.
3   Alternative potential causes have been ruled out. The researcher must control for the effects of factors other than the presumed cause that might influence the observed outcome.
4   There should be a plausible explanation for the relationship. There should be a theoretical account of why the cause produces the observed effect.

Identifying co-variance, establishing the time sequence of cause and effect and controlling for the effects of **extraneous variables** can give you more confidence that a causal relationship exists, but they do not really explain why it is happening. This is the difference between **causal description** and **causal explanation** (Shadish et al. 2002). The former involves identifying *that* a causal relationship exists; the latter involves explaining *why* it exists. Shadish et al. (2002) illustrate this by contrasting the difference between *knowing* that throwing a light switch causes a light to go on (causal description) and *understanding* how and why throwing the light switch causes the light to go on (causal explanation). If the light does not work, explanatory knowledge could help us to work out why not and potentially to fix the problem. Both kinds of knowledge are potentially useful. A robust causal description may have practical relevance, even if we cannot provide a full causal explanation; similarly, a potential causal explanation may stimulate further research to establish whether or not there is a causal effect in practice.

5.3.2 The language of explanation

Before going further, it will be useful to introduce some widely used terminology which will help subsequent discussion.

Figure 5.1(a) depicts a simple causal relationship where one variable (X) is shown as causally related to another variable (Y). The arrow in the diagram shows the direction of the causal relationship, which runs from X (the cause) to Y (the effect). The term **dependent** or **outcome variable** refers to the effect in a causal diagram; it is *dependent* on changes in other variables. Conventionally it is labelled as the Y variable. The **independent** or **predictor variable** is the variable that is identified as the cause of changes in the dependent variable. In experiments it is often called the **treatment variable** because it is the variable that is manipulated by the researcher. It is labelled as the X variable. In some situations there will be more than one independent variable, in which case they are usually labelled $X_1, X_2 \ldots X_n$, as shown in Figure 5.1(b). You will recognize this as a conceptual model of the variance type that we introduced in Chapter 3. Such models are closely associated with positivist and quantitative approaches to causal explanation.

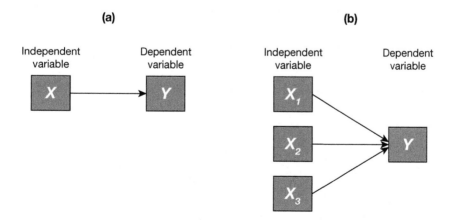

Figure 5.1 Independent and dependent variables

Mediating variables and causal paths

We can extend the basic model in Figure 5.1(a) by identifying the process through which the proposed cause operates to bring about the effect. This can allow a more complete explanation of how the independent variable affects the dependent variable. Suppose, for example, you were investigating the relationship between customer satisfaction and sales revenue and you observed that there was a strong positive association between the two: as customer satisfaction increases, so does sales revenue. A possible explanation for this relationship is that satisfied customers are more likely to make repeat purchases, which in turn drives increases in revenue. We depict this sequence in, Figure 5.2 where repeat purchase behaviour is shown as a **mediating** or **intervening variable** (labelled Z) between the independent and dependent variables, thereby forming a causal path.

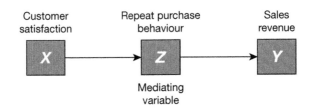

Figure 5.2 Mediating variable

Moderating variables and context

When investigating causal relationships it is important to understand in what contexts they pertain. You can think of this as addressing the question of 'where' something works as well as why. Does a causal relationship identified in one situation hold for other contexts in terms of people, settings or time? One way of incorporating context into explanatory research is to treat it as a moderating variable. A **moderating variable** influences the nature of the relationship between the independent variable and the dependent variable, as we show in Figure 5.3. Suppose, for example, that consumers' income levels (X) influence whether or not they use a smartphone (Y). This relationship, however, could be affected by the consumer's age (Z), as, regardless of income level, older consumers might be less likely than younger ones to buy such a phone. Age therefore acts as a moderating variable since it influences the relationship between income and smartphone purchase. Note the difference between how a moderating variable is depicted in a causal diagram, as shown in Figure 5.3, as compared to the way a mediating variable is shown, in Figure 5.2.

5.3.3 Alternative approaches to causal explanation

The causal criteria we have identified are closely associated with positivism but their origins can be traced back to the work of the eighteenth-century philosopher David Hume. Hume argued that causation itself was unobservable and that we could only infer a causal relationship on the basis of observing the 'constant conjunction' of events between a presumed cause and its effect (Maxwell 2012: 34). This approach,

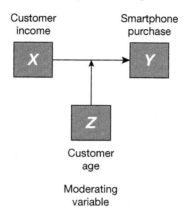

Figure 5.3 Moderating variable

sometimes referred to as the regularity or successionist view of causation, is arguably still the dominant view of causality in business and management research but is not the only way in which causal explanation can be understood.

A generative view of causality

An alternative approach to causal explanation, associated with the philosophical orientation known as realism, rejects the regularity view of causation in favour of what is sometimes referred to as a generative view of causality. In this approach, explanation depends on 'identifying causal mechanisms and how they work, and discovering if they have been activated and under what conditions' (Sayer 2000: 14). Causal mechanisms are the underlying causal 'powers' in things, people or social structures that can bring about – generate – some outcome. Whether or not a particular mechanism is triggered, thereby realizing its causal potential and leading to a particular outcome, depends on the context, including the action of other mechanisms. For example, we might identify that raising skills by workforce training (a mechanism) has the potential to raise productivity (an outcome), but that this occurs only if the organization of the working environment (the context) permits use of the new-found skills. According to the realist view, in an open system such as an organization where there are many causal mechanisms operating simultaneously, we cannot necessarily expect to see the constant conjunction of cause and effect required by the regularity view of causation. Moreover, the same mechanism might produce different outcomes, depending on its interaction with other mechanisms. The generative view of causality therefore frames the problem of explanation in terms of configurations of causal mechanisms, the contexts in which they are triggered and the outcomes that they generate. The emphasis is therefore on causal explanation rather than causal description.

Reason explanation

In everyday situations we are quite used to citing people's reasons or beliefs to explain their actions: 'he went to the shop because he wanted to buy some milk', or 'they purchased an electric car because of their beliefs about global warming', and so on. One way of incorporating people's beliefs, values and reasons in explanatory research is to treat them as variables in causal models of the type shown in Figure 5.1 in the same way as other (non-reason) variables. When doing so it can be helpful to think of reasons as dispositions, a 'tendency to respond in a certain way under designated circumstances' (Rosenberg 1968: 14). A disposition such as a particular set of beliefs about the environment, for instance, might be included as an independent variable in order to explain behaviour, such as the adoption of energy-saving technology, which is then treated as the dependent variable. We can therefore see this option as an extension of the regularity view of causation. For some critics, however, the cause–effect model appears to leave little room for human agency: 'people are by implication reduced to robots . . . with little capacity for creative deliberation' (Gergen 1999: 92). An alternative approach, without abandoning explanatory ambitions altogether, is to adopt a more emic stance in an attempt to understand social actors' own reasoning into research on why things are happening and the consequences as experienced by individuals in particular settings. The potential value of this approach is illustrated in Research in Practice 5.2, which shows a qualitative interview study being used to help understand non-compliance in drug treatment from the perspective of the patients.

RESEARCH IN PRACTICE 5.2

Non-compliance in taking medication

Patient non-compliance with medication regimes has been seen as a major problem around the world, with implications for both patient health and healthcare resources (Pound et al. 2005). Quantitative studies have identified over 200 variables but none that consistently predicts non-compliance (Vermeire et al. 2001). An alternative research approach is to use qualitative methods to understand patients' own ideas about adherence to medication, an example of which is Britten's (1994) interview study carried out amongst 30 patients drawn from two different areas in London. The research identified three main themes with respect to patients' attitudes to medicines and adherence to medication. The study showed strong negative images of medicine that the author suggests may differ from the assumptions of many doctors. It also identified a number of reasons for non-adherence, including a preference for avoiding taking medicines if at all possible, a desire to avoid side-effects and the role of patients' own judgement as to the risks and benefits. The study drew out three implications for practice when assessing whether or not a proposed treatment regime is appropriate. Firstly, that doctors should not assume that medication is an acceptable treatment for all patients; secondly, that they should seek to understand any fears the patient might have about taking medicine; and, thirdly, that they should be aware of the patient's social context in case that might affect adherence.

Causal complexity

Some critics have argued that the regularity view of causality struggles to deal with causal complexity (Hammersley 2012). According to this view of causality, it is a combination of causal conditions that generates a particular outcome. Several different combinations may produce the same outcome and, depending on the context, a given outcome may result from a condition when it is present and also when it is absent. To study these combinations using conventional statistical techniques is challenging in terms of both data collection and analysis. Some researchers have concluded that in the face of such complexity the whole idea of causal explanation should be abandoned (Lincoln and Guba 1985). Others have turned to qualitative research methods, which they see as better able to handle complexity (Miles and Huberman 1994), while other researchers have opted to study causality through computer simulation, a topic that we address later in this chapter.

5.3.4 Using quantitative methods to answer 'why' questions

Quantitative research methods are closely associated with the regularity view of causation and use of the hypothetico-deductive approach to test an explanatory theory expressed as a conceptual model of the type shown in Figure 5.1. The **experiment** in which the researcher manipulates an independent (treatment) variable to observe the effect it has on a dependent (outcome) variable is the classic example of a research of this kind. According to Shadish et al. (2002: 6), 'no other scientific method regularly matches the characteristics of causal relationships so well'. In practice, however, there are many situations in which an experiment cannot be used, for instance, when it is either not practical or not ethical to manipulate the independent variable (such as making someone redundant to observe what happens). In such cases, researchers may turn to a range of quantitative non-experimental explanatory research designs. As their name suggests, **non-experimental designs** do not involve manipulation of an independent variable by the researcher but rely on observation of situations which have occurred more or less naturally. A researcher interested in the impact of a new management technique on performance, for example, might compare organizations in which the technique had been introduced with those where it had not, to see whether the technique had made a difference. Statistical rather than experimental techniques are used to control for the influence of extraneous variables. In Chapter 6 we discuss experimental and quantitative non-experimental explanatory research designs in more detail, along with their potential applications.

5.3.5 Using qualitative methods to answer 'why' questions

The relationship between qualitative research and explanation is not straightforward. Researchers influenced by the regularity view of causation and quantitative methods have tended to see the role of qualitative research as primarily one of exploration and discovery, with any causal claims being treated as 'speculative' (Maxwell 2012: 35). At the same time, qualitative researchers adopting an interpretivist approach often reject the positivist search for causal explanation in favour of an idiographic understanding of people and events in their local contexts. This is signalled by a move away from the language of 'cause' and 'explanation' in favour of that of 'under-standing' and 'meaning'.

Despite this, many qualitative studies do take an interest in why things are happening and what the consequences are (Hammersley 2013) and other researchers have stressed the potential for using qualitative methods to answer 'why' questions. Miles and Huberman make the point very strongly:

> We consider qualitative analysis to be a very powerful method for assessing causality . . . Qualitative analysis, with its close-up look, can identify *mechanisms* going beyond sheer assumptions. It is undeterringly *local*, and deals with the *complex* network of events and processes in a situation. It can sort out the *temporal* dimension, showing clearly what preceded what, either through direct observation or *retrospection*.
>
> Miles and Huberman (1994: 147, italics in original)

The language being used here is that of causal explanation rather than causal description, and sees qualitative methods providing ways of developing causal explanation. Writing from a realist perspective, Maxwell (2012: 38) identifies three specific areas where qualitative methods can help with explanation:

1   identifying causality in single cases through, for example, investigating the mechanisms and processes involved
2   understanding the role of context in causal explanation
3   incorporating the meanings, beliefs and values of social actors in causal explanation.

A range of qualitative research designs are candidates for answering 'why' questions. Both grounded theory and case study designs have been used for explanatory research. Ethnography has potential to offer explanatory insights, even if that is not necessarily a primary concern for ethnographers. Interview studies can be used to deepen our understanding of actors' motivations and reasoning, as we saw in Research in Practice 5.2. Action research provides a way of investigating why things are happening through direct intervention. Each of these research designs is discussed in more detail in Chapter 6.

5.3.6 Using mixed methods to answer 'why' questions

Mixed methods designs can also be used to answer 'why' type research questions. One option, as Teddlie (2005) suggests, is to use quantitative research for what we have called causal description and qualitative research for causal explanation. Other options include qualitative research in parallel with a quantitative study to gain a fuller understanding of what is happening and why, using qualitative research to help design and shape an experiment or other quantitative study, or employing a qualitative study to elaborate on the findings of a quantitative study. An example of the latter, in which qualitative research was used to explain the findings of a quantitative study, was given in Sutton and Rafaeli's (1988) study of convenience stores discussed in Research in Practice 4.3.

5.3.7 The limits of explanatory research

Regardless of the research designs we employ, we should use the outputs of our explanatory research with due awareness of their potential limitations and be cautious about any causal claims we make. In practice, our ability to make causal inference with absolute certainty will always be limited because in social science we are dealing with complex situations with many interacting and interdependent factors influencing what is happening. These challenges have contributed to a move away from understanding causality in a deterministic way in which X always leads to Y

CRITICAL COMMENTARY 5.1

A hierarchy of methods?

As we have seen, causality is a complex and controversial topic in business and management research and there is a lot of debate over the best way to investigate causal questions. Experimental designs, particularly the **randomized controlled trial**, are sometimes portrayed as the 'gold standard' for causal research because of their perceived ability to address the requirements for inferring causality that we identified in this chapter. For some writers, non-experimental research designs are simply not able to demonstrate causality because of the difficulty of achieving high levels of control over extraneous influences. Gravetter and Forzano (2012: 167), for example, advance this view very forcefully, claiming that 'only the experimental strategy can establish the existence of cause-and-effect relationships; other strategies cannot'.

There are, however, many situations in management research when an experiment is not possible or not ethically desirable. Moreover, as Gorard (2002: 63) suggests, 'there remain many useful strategies of a non-experimental nature that enable us to increase our confidence in perceived causal relationships'. Non-experimental designs, whether quantitative or qualitative, can therefore play a valuable role in helping us to answer 'why' questions. They are neither irrelevant nor the final answer to explanatory research. Instead, they should be seen as a tool to use, alongside experimental designs and rigorous theorizing, to help in the search for useful explanations of why things are happening. Gorard illustrates this point in connection with the relationship between smoking and lung cancer:

> The statistical conjunction [of smoking and lung cancer] and the observations from laboratory trials were elucidated by the isolation of carcinogens in the smoke, the pathological evidence from diseased lungs and so on. From this complex interplay of studies and datasets emerges an explanatory theory . . .
> Gorard (2002: 61)

In the complex world of organizations and management no single research technique, whether quantitative or qualitative, is likely to be able to address all the 'why' questions that we may wish to answer. We have therefore chosen to emphasize the strengths and weaknesses of different approaches in order to support an informed decision on research design when investigating why things are happening.

and replacing it with a probabilistic notion of causality in which, instead of certainty, 'we work at the level that a given factor increases (or decreases) the probability of a particular outcome' (de Vaus 2001: 5). Having a Bachelor's degree, for example, increases the probability of a higher salary on leaving university, but it does not make it certain. Even with a probabilistic understanding of causality, however, researchers are often very cautious in the language they use, preferring to use terms such as prediction, correlation, co-variation and impact, without mentioning the word cause. Although absolute certainty is never possible we can, with carefully designed and executed research, deepen our understanding of some fundamental questions for business and management: what works, for whom, under what circumstances and why?

5.4 Research designs for answering 'how' questions

In the previous section we introduced 'why' explanations. This section focuses on a different form of explanation, one that seeks to understand *how* things come about in terms of process. In business and management we often use the term 'process' quite narrowly to refer to the ways in which organizations go about producing goods and services. Here we will be using the term more broadly to refer to the sequences of events, actions and activities through which phenomena, such as organizations or innovations, change and develop over time and in context. Viewing a topic through the lens of process involves 'considering phenomena dynamically – in terms of movement, activity, events, change and temporal evolution' (Langley 2007: 271).

We have already seen one application of process thinking when looking at the sequence of variables linked together to form a causal path. In this section we will explore three other applications where you may find a process approach helpful in answering 'how' questions.

1   The first application is in studying how entities (people, organizations, etc.) change and develop over time, for example, in the context of organizational change, innovation or mergers and acquisitions.
2   The second application focuses on how 'things' such as organizing, leading and strategizing actually get done and how social reality is constituted, reproduced and maintained through social processes including everyday social interaction.
3   The third application is the use of simulation to deepen our understanding of how phenomena behave dynamically over time. As we saw in the previous section, simulation is also of interest when answering 'why' questions in the face of causal complexity.

Although features of process, such as frequency of communication or stakeholder participation, can be included as independent variables in causal models, researchers adopting a process orientation usually investigate process more directly. This typically involves gathering data on how the process unfolds over time by adopting either a prospective or a retrospective longitudinal design. Choice of a specific design, however, depends on the focus of your research, so we will look at options in relation to each of the three applications of process thinking.

5.4.1 Researching change and development processes

You will probably already be familiar with examples of process thinking in the context of managing change and development. Models of product and organizational life cycles or stage models of innovation and change are all examples of this approach. Research in this area involves identifying an entity, such as an individual, an organization or innovative idea that goes through a series of 'events' over time. Unlike cause-and-effect theories that explain outcomes in terms of independent and dependent variables, process theories explain them in terms of sequences of events: do A, then B to get to C (Langley 1999). Events rather than independent and dependent variables are therefore the building blocks of this kind of process theory. They can include activities such as meetings, administrative reviews, communications, people-related events such as changeover of personnel or roles, changes in the external environment, or outcomes of the process.

The research design can be deductive to test an existing process theory, or inductive or abductive to build process theory. It may use qualitative, quantitative or mixed methods for collecting and analysing the data. Despite these differences, we can nevertheless identify common features of this approach.

- Collecting data that will offer insights into process, context and development over time. Data collection can involve a range of techniques, including interviews, observation, questionnaires, archival or other documentary data and participant diaries using the logic of triangulation (Pettigrew 1990).
- Analysing the data to identify events that are relevant to the process. Event identification can be done deductively, based on event types drawn from prior theory or carried out inductively from the data (Van de Ven 2007).
- Developing a time-ordered sequence of events.
- Explaining what is causing the event sequences that are observed. This is the domain of process theorizing and can involve looking for common patterns across different cases and explaining how and why process and context interact to produce differences in outcomes across different cases (Pettigrew 1992).

A range of research designs are available for investigating process. Qualitative methods are particularly useful when building process theories. Case study designs lend themselves to this kind of research as they facilitate in-depth analysis of individual cases, the use of multiple data sources, retrospective analysis and both qualitative and quantitative data. Another useful research design is grounded theory, particularly for building process theories. Quantitative methods can also be used when investigating process, for example, by testing causal pathways. In Chapter 13 we offer an introduction to time series data and in the further reading section for this chapter on the companion website we suggest sources dealing with some of the more advanced quantitative techniques that fall outside the scope of this book. Research in Practice 5.3 gives an example of a qualitative research study that takes a process perspective on group learning.

PART II

RESEARCH IN PRACTICE 5.3

A process model of how groups learn from other groups

Although prior research has indicated that group performance can be enhanced as a result of learning from other groups – so called vicarious group learning – less attention has been paid to the process by which this happens. Bresman's (2013) study of research and development (R&D) teams sets out to address that gap by investigating how groups change their way of working by using vicarious learning.

The research is a multiple case study examining eight R&D teams across two different sites in a pharmaceutical company recently formed from the merger of two smaller firms. In the absence of sufficient prior theory, the researcher adopted an inductive approach, starting 'with specific observations from which general patterns are identified and theory developed' (Bresman 2013: 39). Data were collected using a combination of semi-structured and informal interviews, observation, attendance at meetings and other events, along with secondary data such as project reports and process manuals. Analysis was carried out by developing individual case histories, with attention being paid to the sequence of events in each case, before moving on to cross-case analysis. The research identified a four-stage process model of vicarious learning consisting of:

1   identification of another group with relevant experience
2   translation of the knowledge of the other group to assess its value
3   adoption of the knowledge by the learning group in the form of a change in its routines
4   continuation in which the learning group decides whether to continue to use the new routine.

The study concludes that the process of vicarious learning by groups is more varied than previously believed and is 'rarely a matter of simply finding and copying best practice routines exactly and in full, but instead is better seen as a set of distinct interlinked activities unfolding over time, each with its own unique demands' (Bresman 2013: 58).

5.4.2 Investigating social processes and practices

An alternative to looking at process in terms of the stages through which things develop and change over time is to focus on social practices and processes at a more detailed level. This can include analysing patterns of behaviour and meaning-making in a given situation in order to arrive at an understanding of the social processes at work (Locke 2001, Corbin and Strauss 2008). Putting such social processes under the microscope allows us to see how 'things', such as leadership or strategizing, actually get done by people in day-to-day interactions and settings. Interest in this approach has been stimulated by the so-called 'practice turn' (Llewellyn and Hindmarsh 2010: 10) in social science. An example of this is the field of strategy-as-practice. Strategy, in this view, is not 'something an organization *has* but something its members *do*' (Jarzabkowski et al. 2007: 6). Researchers adopting this approach focus on how strategy is done by studying who is involved and how they go about doing it. The practice turn raises further interesting areas for investigation, such as how practices are actually used in day-to-day situations and the role of practitioners themselves in a given phenomenon. It also invites us to take a closer look at language, how it is used in social interactions and, from a social constructionist perspective, its role in the construction of meaning.

A range of research designs, primarily qualitative, are applicable to the study of social processes and practices. Ethnography and grounded theory both provide ways of investigating social interaction, while conversation analysis focuses specifically on talk-in-interaction. Different forms of discourse analysis offer a way of investigating language from a social constructionist perspective and in Chapter 6 we discuss one variant, critical discourse analysis, to illustrate the approach.

5.4.3 Simulation and process

A third approach to investigating processes is to use **computer simulation**. Simulation can be used to deepen understanding of processes involved in a particular phenomenon or to predict how that phenomenon may develop dynamically (Gilbert and Troitzsch 2005). It can be particularly useful for investigating phenomena that behave in non-linear ways (Davis et al. 2007). Many quantitative analysis methods used in research assume that the relationship between variables is linear, in other words that outputs are proportionate to inputs. In non-linear systems this proportionality may not hold. Instead small changes can lead to disproportionately large effects; conversely, large changes may have little effect. Harrison et al. (2007) suggest that non-linear behaviour is a feature of organizational situations where there are multiple interdependent processes in operation.

Simulation can be used to investigate the behaviour of complex systems using techniques such as multi-agent modelling, in which the behaviours of interacting, adaptive actors (agents) are simulated over time. Other simulation methods are used to model the behaviour of phenomena such as queuing systems, supply chains and service systems. We provide an introduction to simulation studies in Section 6.2.

KEY LEARNING POINTS

- Answers to 'what' questions seek to describe the key characteristics and patterns in phenomena of interest. Descriptive research often involves comparison and the development and application of classification schemes.
- Descriptive research may be used to explore something novel, generate insights or deeper understanding of a situation, to provide a stimulus for action or as the basis for answering 'why' or 'how' questions.
- Quantitative descriptive research emphasizes measurement, pre-specification of variables of interest, use of standardized instruments and statistical inference to draw conclusions about a population on the basis of sample data. Qualitative descriptive research emphasizes in-depth study of small samples, exploration of diversity and heterogeneity, taking an emic perspective and the generation of thick description.

- Answers to 'why' questions are about explaining phenomena in why something is happening. Interest may focus on the causes or consequences of a phenomenon or on investigating specific relationships between variables. Research differs in whether it emphasizes causal description, establishing that a causal relation exists, or causal explanation, explaining why it exists.
- The regularity view of causation, associated with both positivism and quantitative methods, identifies four criteria for establishing causality: co-variation between cause and effect, time sequence, elimination of extraneous variables and the existence of a plausible explanation for the relationship.
- Alternative perspectives on answering 'why' questions include investigating the causal mechanisms that generate an outcome in particular contexts, understanding the reasons and beliefs of social actors involved in a particular situation and investigating the complex interactions of causal factors that give rise to a phenomenon of interest.
- Quantitative, qualitative and mixed method research designs may be used to answer 'why' questions, but there is debate over the ability of non-experimental designs to establish causal claims.
- Answers to 'how' questions are concerned with explanation in terms of the processes through which things come about. Process can be understood in terms of causal pathways, as sequences of events or stages through which entities such as organizations develop and change over time, or in terms of the processes and interactions through which social reality is created, maintained and changed.

NEXT STEPS

5.1   Research designs used by prior research in your topic area. Review the research articles that you have identified so far in your topic area.

a) What type of research questions ('what', 'why' and 'how) have been addressed?

b) What research designs have been used?

c) What are the strengths and weaknesses of those designs in terms of answering the research questions posed in the articles?

d) Are any of the research designs potentially useful for your own project?

5.2   Developing a research design for your own questions. Revisit your own research questions. For each question:

a) What type of question ('what', 'why' and 'how') is it?

b) What research designs (quantitative, qualitative, mixed method) could be suitable?

c) Why might they be suitable? What are their potential strengths and weaknesses?

Further reading

Chapter 6 provides more detail of particular research designs discussed in this chapter. For further reading, please see the companion website.

References

Bailey, K. D. (1994). *Typologies and taxonomies. An introduction to classification techniques.* Thousand Oaks, CA: Sage.

Bresman, H. (2013). 'Changing routines: A process model of vicarious group learning in pharmaceutical R&D', *Academy of Management Journal*, 56(1), 35–61.

Britten, N. (1994). 'Patients' ideas about medicines: A qualitative study in a general practice population', *The British Journal of General Practice*, 44(387), 465–468.

Corbin, J. and Strauss, A. (2008). *Basics of qualitative research.* 3rd edn. Thousand Oaks, CA: Sage.

Davis, J. P., Eisenhardt, K. M. and Bingham, C. B. (2007). 'Developing theory through simulation methods', *Academy of Management Review*, 32(2), 480–99.

de Vaus, D. (2001). *Research design in social research.* London: Sage.

Geertz, C. (1975). *The interpretation of cultures.* London: Hutchinson.

Gergen, K. (1999). *An invitation to social construction.* London: Sage.

Gilbert, N. and Troitzsch, K. G. (2005). *Simulation for the social scientist.* 2nd edn. Maidenhead: Open University Press.

Gorard, S. (2002). 'The role of causal models in evidence-informed policy making and practice', *Evaluation & Research in Education*, 16(1), 51–65.

Gravetter, F. J. and Forzano, L.-A. B. (2012). *Research methods for the behavioural sciences. International edition.* 4th edn. London: Wadsworth.

Hammersley, M. (2012). What's wrong with quantitative research? *In:* Cooper, B., Glaesser, J., Gomm, R. and Hammersley, M. (eds) *Challenging the quantitative–qualitative divide.* London: Continuum.

Hammersley, M. (2013). *What is qualitative research?* London: Bloomsbury.

Hammersley, M. and Atkinson, P. (2007). *Ethnography, principles in practice.* 3rd edn. London: Routledge.

Harrison, J. R., Zhiang, L. I. N., Carroll, G. R. and Carley, K. M. (2007). 'Simulation modeling in organizational and management research', *Academy of Management Review*, 32(4), 1229–45.

Honderich, T. (ed.) (1995). *The Oxford companion to philosophy.* Oxford: Oxford University Press.

Jansen, H. (2010). 'The logic of qualitative survey research and its position in the field of social research methods', *Forum Qualitative Sozialforschung/Forum: Qualitative Social Research* [online], 11(2). Available from: www.qualitative-research.net/index.php/fqs/article/view/1450/2946 [accessed 29 April 2014].

Jarzabkowski, P., Balogun, J. and Seidl, D. (2007). 'Strategizing: The challenges of a practice perspective', *Human Relations*, 60(1), 5–27.

Langley, A. (1999). 'Strategies for theorizing from process data', *Academy of Management Review*, 24(4), 691–710.

Langley, A. (2007). 'Process thinking in strategic organization', *Strategic Organization*, 5(3), 271–82.

Lincoln, Y. S. and Guba, E. G. (1985). *Naturalistic inquiry.* Beverly Hills, CA: Sage Publications.

Llewellyn, N. and Hindmarsh, J. (2010). Work and organisation in real time: An introduction. *In:* Llewellyn, N. and Hindmarsh, J. (eds) *Organisation, interaction and practice: Studies in ethnomethodology and conversation analysis.* Cambridge: Cambridge University Press.

Locke, K. D. (2001). *Grounded theory in management research.* London: Sage.

PART II

Maxwell, J. A. (2012). *A realist approach for qualitative research*. Thousand Oaks, CA: Sage.

Miles, M. B. and Huberman, M. A. (1994). *Qualitative data analysis*. 2nd edn. Thousand Oaks, CA: Sage.

Mintzberg, H. (1983). *Structure in fives: Designing effective organizations*. Upper Saddle River, NJ: Prentice Hall.

Pettigrew, A. M. (1990). 'Longitudinal field research on change: Theory and practice', *Organization Science*, 1(3), 267–92.

Pettigrew, A. M. (1992). 'The character and significance of strategy process research', *Strategic Management Journal*, 13(S2), 5–16.

Pound, P., Britten, N., Morgan, M., Yardley, L., Pope, C., Daker-White, G. and Campbell, R. (2005). 'Resisting medicines: A synthesis of qualitative studies of medicine taking', *Social Science & Medicine*, 61(1), 133–55.

Rosenberg, M. (1968). *The logic of survey analysis*. New York: Basic Books.

Sayer, A. (2000). *Realism and social science*. London: Sage.

Shadish, W. R., Cook, T. D. and Campbell, D. T. (2002). *Experimental and quasi-experimental designs for generalized causal inference*. Belmont, CA: Wadsworth Cengage Learning.

Sutton, R. I. and Rafaeli, A. (1988). 'Untangling the relationship between displayed emotions and sales: The case of convenience stores', *Academy of Management Journal*, 31(3), 461–87.

Teddlie, C. (2005). 'Methodological issues related to causal studies of leadership: A mixed methods perspective from the USA', *Educational Management Administration & Leadership*, 33(2), 211–27.

Thorpe, R. and Holt, R. (eds) (2008). *The Sage dictionary of qualitative management research*. London: Sage.

Van de Ven, A. H. (2007). *Engaged scholarship*. Oxford: Oxford University Press.

Vermeire, E., Hearnshaw, H., Van Royen, P. and Denekens, J. (2001). 'Patient adherence to treatment: Three decades of research. A comprehensive review', *Journal of Clinical Pharmacy and Therapeutics*, 26(5), 331–42.

6 Applying quantitative and qualitative research designs

CHAPTER SUMMARY

The key topics covered in this chapter are:

- introducing quantitative research designs
- introducing qualitative research designs.

6.1 Introduction

In this chapter we introduce a range of quantitative and qualitative research designs that are used in business and management research. Each design is discussed in terms of its main characteristics and potential applications. Our aim in the chapter is to provide information to help you decide whether it may be suitable for your own research project. More details on how to carry out each design are presented in the companion website, along with suggestions for further reading, and data collection and analysis techniques are covered later in the book in Parts III and IV.

6.2 Quantitative research designs

In this section we describe a number of research designs that use quantitative methods. To varying degrees they share the general characteristics of quantitative research that we introduced in Chapter 4. We begin with experimental designs, before looking at a range of non-experimental approaches (Figure 6.1).

6.2.1 Experimental and quasi-experimental designs

The key feature of an experimental research design is that you deliberately vary something in order to find out what happens to something else in order to 'discover the effects of presumed causes' (Shadish et al. 2002: 6). Using the terminology we introduced in Chapter 5, you manipulate one or more independent variables to discover the effect on a dependent variable. Other characteristic features of experimental designs include a deductive approach, the use of experimental controls to

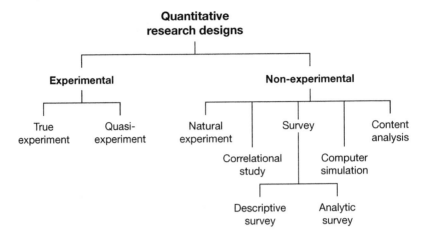

Figure 6.1 Quantitative research designs

eliminate extraneous influences, measurement of the effects of the manipulation and the comparison of the resulting measures.

Figure 6.2 shows these features applied to a 'classic' experimental design that has a single **treatment group**, a **control group** and pre- and post-treatment measures. The levels of the dependent variable are measured for each group both pre- and post-treatment but only the treatment group receives the treatment. Analysis focuses on the difference in pre- and post-treatment scores for the treatment group, as compared to the difference in pre- and post-treatment scores for the control group. If the change is greater in the treatment group, you would infer that this was due to the treatment, i.e. the manipulation of the independent variable.

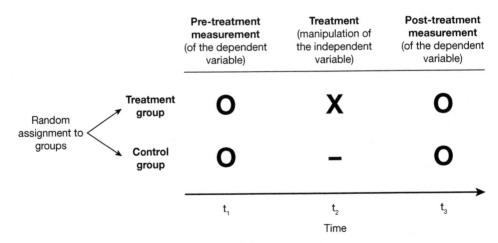

Figure 6.2 Classic experimental design with treatment and control groups and pre- and post-test measurement

The extent to which you can be confident in making this causal claim is a function of the internal validity of the design. Even with the simple example in Figure 6.2, there are several potential threats to internal validity. There may be inaccuracies or inconsistencies in the measurement or the way the treatment is administered. If some participants leave during the course of the research or reject treatment, their dropping out may influence the results. Alternatively, particularly if the research is running over a long period, time alone may be introducing changes in participants, giving rise to what are known as **maturation effects**. The researcher may deliberately or unwittingly bias the results through their actions by, for example, behaving differently towards the treatment group, as compared to the control group, thereby leading to what are called **experimenter-expectancy effects**. Additionally, research participants may themselves react to the experience of being in an experiment. Some participants, for example, may be enthusiastic about taking part and this could influence the outcome, regardless of the actual treatment, creating what are referred to as **subject-expectancy effects**. Experienced experimenters are, of course, well aware of these (and other) issues and seek to address them through careful design and conduct of the experiment.

To achieve high levels of internal validity you could conduct your experiment in a laboratory or highly controlled environment. However, such experimental conditions may well be different to the normal lives of participants and the naturally occurring conditions of the phenomenon of interest. The term ecological validity is used to describe the degree to which the experiment is representative of the real world. One solution is to conduct your experiment in a natural setting. Such **field experiments** can have higher ecological validity than equivalent **laboratory experiments** but it may be harder to achieve equally high levels of internal validity because of reduced control over the sort of threats discussed above.

There are many variations in experimental research designs but we can usefully distinguish between **true experiments**, which feature random assignment of participants to groups, and so-called **quasi-experiments**, which do not. The logic behind random assignment is that, with a sufficiently large sample size, random selection will ensure that the groups are comparable before treatments are applied, thereby reducing a potential threat to internal validity (Cook and Campbell 1979). A quasi-experimental design may be the only option if random assignment is not possible, in which case careful attention has to be given to sampling procedures.

Applications of experimental designs

Experimental designs are primarily used for answering questions about cause and effect. Whilst some organizations, such as pharmaceutical or research and development companies, use experiments as part of their normal business activity, experimental research designs are relatively rare in organization and management research (Gill and Johnson 2010). Despite this, an understanding of the logic of experimental designs is essential to a critical understanding of other ways of doing causal research. Research in Practice 6.1 provides an example of a field experiment.

PART II

RESEARCH IN PRACTICE 6.1

The effects of shelf placement on consumer purchases of potato chips

Sigurdsson et al. (2009) used a field experiment to evaluate the effects of shelf placement on consumers' purchases of potato chips. The experiment involved an alternating treatment design in which the target brand of potato chip was placed on the high, middle or low shelf in two budget stores. The dependent variable was the proportion of all unit sales of potato chips accounted for by the target brand. The treatment variable was the shelf placement; this was randomized over the course of the experiment to reduce threats to internal validity. Prices of the target brand were kept constant, as were other factors in the marketing mix. Researchers visited each store at least once a day to check on shelf placement and to note possible extraneous variables. In addition, the researchers also collected data on sales prior to the experiment to act as a baseline. The research found that the highest percentage of purchases was recorded when the potato chips were placed on the middle shelf, as compared to the high or low shelf. In their conclusions, the authors suggest that this might be due to lower response effort required by consumers. This research supports the findings from proprietary commercial research into the effects of shelf placement.

6.2.2 *Natural experiments and correlational studies*

Natural experiments, despite their name, are not really experiments in the true sense because the independent variable is not manipulated. For this reason they are classified as non-experimental. Instead, the researcher looks for naturally occurring comparison between a treatment and a control condition that is as close as possible to those that would have been created in an experiment. An example would be a study that compares one factory in which a new quality programme has been introduced (the treatment group) against one in which it has not (the comparison group), in terms of their respective quality levels (the outcome). In **correlational studies** the researcher measures two or more variables as they exist naturally for a set of individual cases (e.g. people) and then tests the relationship between them, for example to investigate the relationship between individual customers' satisfaction levels and their likelihood of making further purchases. Analytic survey studies (see below) are typical examples of this type of research. (Note that, despite their name, the analysis procedures used in correlational studies are not limited to correlation but can include regression and other statistical techniques as presented in Chapter 13.)

Depending on the chosen design, non-experimental studies can be cross-sectional or longitudinal. Longitudinal designs may be prospective, following developments over time, or retrospective, researching what has already happened, sometimes in order to set a baseline against which the current situation can be compared. Like experiments, they take a deductive approach, pre-specifying the hypotheses to be tested and emphasizing measurement and comparison. However, since experimental control is not possible, non-experimental explanatory designs rely on statistical control to deal with extraneous influences. For this reason, as noted in Chapter 5, caution is needed when making causal inferences.

Applications of natural experiments and correlational studies

Non-experimental designs of this kind are widely used in both pure and applied research. Two applications stand out.

1   *Theory testing:* the theory is often depicted as a conceptual model of the variance type and the hypotheses are expressed in terms of relationships between independent and dependent variables, as discussed in Chapter 5.
2   *Prediction* of the value of a dependent variable from knowledge of the value of one or more independent variables in order, for example, to measure the impact of one variable on another to determine the size of the effect and, in many cases, to compare it relative to other possible factors. In such cases, determining whether any observed relationship is really causal may not be of interest.

From a practical point of view, a non-experimental design of this sort may be appropriate in situations where an experiment is not an option. Such situations are commonly encountered in practice, so it is not surprising that non-experimental designs are so widely used. Research in Practice 6.2 presents an example of a correlational design using an analytic survey.

RESEARCH IN PRACTICE 6.2

Analytic survey: enterprise resource planning (ERP) systems and the manufacturing–marketing interface

Interdependence between marketing and manufacturing is seen as an important issue in operations management, especially under conditions of market or product uncertainty, but the role of information technology in facilitating this interface has not received much attention. Enterprise resource planning (ERP) information systems are intended, amongst other things, to integrate management information across the enterprise, thereby improving coordination and, ultimately, performance. Gattiker (2007) set out to investigate the relationship between marketing–manufacturing interdependence, improved coordination thanks to ERP and the overall business impact of ERP on the manufacturing plant. A conceptual model and hypotheses were developed which were tested in the research.

The research design was a non-experimental explanatory correlational study using a questionnaire-based analytic survey. A range of methods are reported by which potential respondents were identified, including a professional association and ERP user groups; responses were screened to remove those not meeting appropriate criteria regarding, for example, ERP use, resulting in a total of 124 usable responses. Multivariate statistical analysis was used to establish the reliability of the scales and test the research hypotheses. The author concludes that the findings 'support the general proposition that interdependence is one factor that influences the degree to which organisations reap benefits from their ERP investments' (Gattiker 2007: 2895).

6.2.3 Survey studies

The word survey is used in many different ways in research. It is frequently used as a synonym for a **questionnaire** or to refer to a research design that uses a questionnaire. Although questionnaires are widely employed in survey studies, their use is not the determining characteristic of the design. Instead, we can identify three features that typify a **survey study**.

1   It produces quantitative (or quantifiable) data on the variables of interest for the population being studied; the population may be individuals, groups, organizations or some other entity, such as a project or product.
2   Data are collected using predefined, structured collection procedures. Data are often gathered by questionnaire but structured observation or secondary data can also be used; some survey studies use more than one source of data.
3   Data are usually collected from only a sample of the population of interest; statistical analysis techniques are then used to generalize the findings to the wider population.

More generally, survey studies fall into the category of non-experimental quantitative research designs.

Applications of survey study design

The survey study is a very versatile research design and is widely used in both pure and applied research for a range of tasks. There are two primary uses of survey study designs.

1   **Descriptive surveys**, which provide a description of a phenomenon in terms of the distribution of relevant variables within a particular population either at a single point in time (cross-sectional) or comparatively over time (longitudinal) by using repeat surveys. An example of a cross-sectional descriptive survey is given in Research in Practice 6.3.
2   **Analytic surveys** (also known as theory-testing or explanatory surveys), which aim to test theories about a phenomenon by examining and testing the associations between variables. Analytic surveys are a common form of correlational, non-experimental explanatory research design, as shown in Research in Practice 6.2.

Survey studies can also have an exploratory role (Forza 2002, Easterby-Smith et al. 2008), in which exploratory statistical techniques such as **cluster analysis** are used to identify underlying patterns in the data. The development and availability of exploratory quantitative analysis techniques have increased the potential for more open-ended exploration of quantitative data, especially with large datasets.

6.2.4 Simulation-based research

In Chapter 5 we introduced simulation as an option for studying how complex processes behave dynamically. In this context, a simulation can be defined as 'a method for using computer software to model the operation of "real-world" processes,

RESEARCH IN PRACTICE 6.3

A descriptive survey of executive coaching practices

Bono et al.'s (2009: 386) study sets out 'to describe the current state of executive coaching practices with a special emphasis on comparing the practices of psychologist and non-psychologist coaches'. The research design adopted was a questionnaire-based descriptive survey study. The questionnaire was divided into four sections, looking at coaching practices, coaching outcomes, coaches' backgrounds and coaching competencies. Section 1, for example, asked questions on such practices as assessment tools, approaches to coaching and methods of communication. Respondents rated each on a 5-point scale indicating frequency of use. Selection of the sample of respondents was done in two stages. In the first stage, screening emails were sent to members of organizations to which coaches are often affiliated to identify executive coaches. In stage two, those identified as executive coaches were invited by email to take part in a web-based survey. This procedure generated 428 usable responses from the 1,260 coaches who were emailed in stage two. Analysis involved summary statistics of responses by sub-group (psychologists and non-psychologists) and inferential statistical tests of inter-group differences. The findings show that differences between psychologists and non-psychologists are generally quite small and there are as many differences between different types of psychologist as between psychologists and non-psychologists.

systems, or events' (Davis et al. 2007: 481). In simulation studies of this kind, the researcher develops a model of the phenomenon under investigation and then chooses an appropriate simulation method. The model specifies the concepts of interest and the 'theoretical logic' (Davis et al. 2007: 481) that links them together so that they can be coded into computer software. The model can then be run many times under various conditions to observe the outcomes. In this sense, simulations are sometimes seen as akin to virtual experiments, although in a simulation the researcher is experimenting with the model rather than the actual phenomenon.

Application of simulation research

Computer simulations are used in training, teaching or entertainment. In research, Gilbert and Troitzsch (2005) claim that simulation can be used to help us get a better understanding of a phenomenon of interest and for the purposes of prediction, for example, when modelling demographic change or the behaviour of a planned production system. They also argue that simulation is valuable for social science as a tool for formalizing theory. According to Gilbert and Troitzsch (2005: 5), the process of specifying and building the computer simulation, which 'involves being precise about what the theory means and making sure it is complete and coherent, is a very valuable discipline in its own right'. Simulation, they suggest, has advantages over traditional mathematical modelling when the interest is in processes and mechanisms rather than associations between variables. Simulation may be particularly suitable

RESEARCH IN PRACTICE 6.4

A simulation study of co-ordination in supply chain management

Modern supply chains are complex networks of suppliers and partners on which firms rely to deliver goods to their customers in increasingly uncertain and cost-sensitive markets. Datta and Christopher (2011) use a simulation study to investigate different information-sharing and coordination mechanisms for improving performance under such conditions of uncertainty. Their chosen method is a simulation of a paper-tissue manufacturing supply chain using a technique known as agent-based modelling (ABM). In ABM, a system such as a supply chain is modelled as a collection of autonomous decision-making entities, called agents. Agents can represent distribution centres, planners or factories within the system. Each agent makes its decisions autonomously, based on a set of rules. In addition, over time, agents can learn and evolve. In Datta and Christopher's study, a simulation is run for five different configurations of the supply chain, a baseline model which represents the actual set-up and four additional models with different configurations of coordination and information-sharing mechanisms. The baseline model is validated against historical data and by testing with experienced managers. The results from the simulations of each configuration are then compared to understand the effectiveness of different information-sharing and coordination mechanisms.

when dealing with complex, non-linear phenomena and has been used in research in process analysis and evaluation in operations research, investigating diverse topics such as patient appointments in healthcare, supply chain dynamics and production control systems. Research in Practice 6.4 presents an example of a simulation study.

6.2.5 Content analysis

Content analysis refers to a family of procedures for the systematic, replicable quantitative analysis of text. In essence it involves the classification of parts of a text through the application of a structured coding scheme from which conclusions can be drawn about the message content. By clearly specifying the coding and other procedures, content analysis is replicable in the sense that other researchers could reproduce the study. Content analysis can be applied to all kinds of written text such as speeches, letters or articles, whether online or in print. It can also be used to analyse text in the form of pictures, video, film or other visual media. Content analysis can be carried out quantitatively but also qualitatively. We will focus on quantitative content analysis here and discuss qualitative approaches to message analysis in the next section.

Applications of content analysis

Content analysis provides a structured way of analysing data that are typically open ended and relatively unstructured. Applications include:

- Description. Here the focus is on describing features of the message content. Jain et al. (2010), for example, study how the ways in which celebrities were presented in Indian television commercials varied according to the category of products they were promoting. Descriptive content analysis can be cross-sectional or longitudinal.
- Prediction. Here the main aim is to predict the outcome or effect of the messages being analysed. A study by Naccarato and Neuendorf (1998), for example, investigated how different features of print media advertising affected recall, readership and evaluation in a business-to-business context.

Content analysis has been applied to a wide range of social science topics, including gender and race, media reporting and political communication; it has obvious applications in the analysis of business communication, particularly marketing. The rise of the Internet also creates opportunities for using content analysis techniques to analyse online communication, such as Gebauer et al.'s (2008) analysis of online user reviews to identify requirements for mobile technology. If using content analysis, however, you should be careful, when drawing conclusions, not to go beyond what your data will support. Do job advertisements, for instance, tell us something about real changes in job skill or do they tell us only about the way in which skill is portrayed in advertising? Researchers interested in, for instance, the impact of advertisements on consumers can choose to combine content analysis with other research approaches such as surveys or experiments.

Research in Practice 6.5 gives an example of a quantitative content analysis study.

RESEARCH IN PRACTICE 6.5

A content analysis of the portrayal of women in James Bond films

How women are portrayed in the media has long been a subject of interest to researchers. Neuendorf et al.'s (2010) study uses quantitative content analysis to investigate how women are depicted in the long-running and very popular series of James Bond films. Data analysis focused on female characters who met certain criteria (e.g. they speak or are spoken to) and the coding scheme defined a range of variables to be measured for each character, such as race, hair colour, body size, physical attractiveness, along with aspects of sexual activity and violence by and against the character. Eight coders were used to code 20 films, with tests being carried out to measure the reliability of coding between the different coders. Research findings showed clear links between sex and violence in the way women are portrayed in Bond films. According to the authors, 'the collective body of Bond films ... stands to serve as an important source of social cognitive outcomes regarding appropriate role behaviour for women – still stereotyped, with persistent allusions to violence and sex (and their linkage), and with unrealistic standards of female beauty' (Neuendorf et al. 2010: 758–9).

6.3 Qualitative research designs

We now turn our attention to research designs that use primarily qualitative methods, as shown in Figure 6.3.

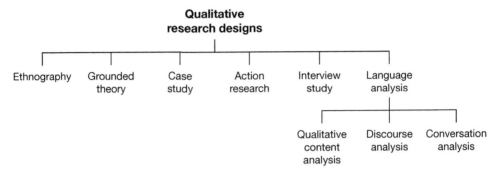

Figure 6.3 Qualitative research designs

6.3.1 Ethnography

Ethnography involves an in-depth field investigation through which the researcher seeks to describe and interpret 'the shared and learned patterns of values, behaviours, beliefs and language of a culture-sharing group' (Creswell 2009: 68). Typically this is done by the researcher acting as a participant-observer in the situation under study, sometimes for a prolonged period of time. The origins of ethnography lie within anthropological studies and can be traced back over a century. Ethnography has since developed and diversified and, as a result, the term defies easy definition. We can, however, identify a number of characteristics of an ethnographic study in terms of what ethnographers do (Hammersley and Atkinson 2007).

- People's actions and interactions are studied in the field, in their natural settings as they go about their daily activities rather than in an artificial environment.
- Emphasis is placed on **participant-observation** and/or informal conversations at first hand, by the researcher, although other data collection methods may be used as well.
- Field methods are relatively unstructured and have a flexible character, developing as the research proceeds.
- Research is usually focused on a small number of cases, sometimes a single group or setting, to facilitate in-depth study.
- Analysis is inductive in the sense that conceptual frameworks are generated from the data analysis, rather than being imposed on the data by the researcher.

The output of an ethnographic study traditionally involves what the anthropologist Clifford Geertz (1975: 6) labelled 'thick' description. As we pointed out in Chapter 5, this is more than just a very detailed description and involves moving beyond reporting simply what is observed to providing an understanding of the meaning of a phenomenon from the perspective of those involved.

Applications of ethnography

A relevant application of ethnographic research in business and management is in the area of organizational ethnography. Within this very broad body of work, it is possible to identify three different categories (Brewer 2004). First, research has focused on occupational careers and identities. Studies have included such diverse subjects as police officers, factory workers and nightclub hostesses. One example among many is Delbridge's (1998) study of worker experience of the 'Japanese model' of production management. The second category explores control in organizations. A classic work in this tradition is Roy's (1952) research on the range of informal mechanisms used by machine-shop workers to control output. Control is also the subject of researchers engaging in critical ethnography where the focus is on understanding power in organizations or other social situations (Creswell 2009). The third category of organizational ethnography addresses 'the practical reasoning skills of people coping at the bottom of bureaucracies' (Brewer 2004: 314). Studies in this area have highlighted both the routine nature of much professional work and the skilled coping strategies employed by workers in routine jobs.

Ethnography is also used in market research, where its advocates claim that ethnography can be used to understand customers and markets more fully in order to learn about product or service use in its natural context (Arnould and Price 2006). A more recent development is the use of ethnographic methods to gain an in-depth understanding of online communities. This is known variously as **netnography**, virtual ethnography, online ethnography or even webethnography (Prior and Miller 2012). The diversity of online communities means that there is considerable scope for such research to explore topics from online gaming to healthcare.

Research in Practice 6.6 gives an example of an ethnographic study.

6.3.2 Grounded theory

Grounded theory was originally expounded by Barney Glaser and Anselm Strauss in their 1967 book, *The Discovery of Grounded Theory* (Glaser and Strauss 1967). Reacting against what they saw as the dominance of hypothetico-deductive, theory-testing approaches, they proposed grounded theory as a way of building theory systematically, using data obtained from social research. Since its first appearance, grounded theory has gone on to become 'currently the most widely used and popular qualitative research method across a wide range of disciplines and subject areas' (Bryant and Charmaz 2007: 1).

A characteristic of grounded theory is that data collection and analysis are interrelated and iterative, with the analysis beginning as soon as the first data are collected and shaping further data collection. Usually the overall approach is described as inductive, but some writers (e.g. Reichertz 2007) argue that grounded theory also employs abductive logic in its iteration between data and emerging theory. Key features of grounded theory include:

* Rather than being fixed in advance, as in most quantitative studies, data collection is adjusted in response to emerging theory; additional data might be collected, for example, to allow a particular concept to be investigated in more detail.

- Grounded theory can involve multiple data collection methods, including in-depth interviews and observation, as well as document analysis, offering the possibility of triangulation of sources and aiming to gather 'rich data [that] get beneath the surface of social and subjective life' (Charmaz 2006: 13).
- Grounded theory adopts a **coding** approach to data analysis. This is a process in which the researcher derives and develops concepts from the data which are then given a conceptual label, called a code. The coded concepts form the building blocks of the emerging grounded theory. Variants of coding play a central role in much qualitative analysis and we review them in more detail in Chapter 14.
- Throughout the coding process, the researcher iterates between data and emerging theory. This is known as **constant comparison** and involves constantly comparing coded data with other pieces of similarly coded data.
- The cycles of data collection and analysis continue until no new insights or new dimensions to categories are being identified. This is the point of **theoretical saturation**.

RESEARCH IN PRACTICE 6.6

An ethnography of subcultures of consumption

In their ethnographic study of Harley-Davidson motorcycle owners, Schouten and McAlexander (1995) sought to understand the phenomenon of subcultures of consumption from the perspective of consumer behaviour. Over the three years of the research, the authors report moving from being outsiders to becoming insiders, 'deeply immersed in the lifestyle of the HDSC [Harley-Davidson-oriented subculture of consumption]' while 'making a conscious effort to maintain scholarly distance' (Schouten and McAlexander 1995: 44). Sampling involved multiple research sites, including motorcycle rallies, club meetings and bikers' homes, and multiple sources of data, including formal and informal interviews, participant and non-participant observation, photographs and documents such as magazines and newsletters. Sampling developed in response to the researchers' deepening understanding of the field. Analysis took a coding/thematic approach (see Chapter 14) to develop a conceptual framework that identified four key topics with respect to a subculture of consumption: its social structure, its ethos, the process self-transformation in becoming a member and the opportunities for 'symbiotic relationships' (Schouten and McAlexander 1995: 59) with marketers. In their article, the authors discuss the question of transferability of their findings, arguing that the 'concept of the subculture of consumption is robust enough to encompass virtually any group of people united by common consumption values and behaviours' (Schouten and McAlexander 1995: 59).

Applications of grounded theory

Versions of grounded theory are widely encountered in organization and management research, including information systems, organizational change and leadership, where the aim is theory building. In terms of our earlier categorization of research questions, grounded theory is particularly suited to investigating 'how' questions. This can include a focus on micro-level actions and interactions in response to a situation or problem as well as stage models of change and development. 'Why' research questions can also be addressed using grounded theory. For example, Dey (2007: 178) argues that causal explanation is 'central' to the method. Grounded theory may be particularly helpful when looking at causality through the lens of human agency, for example managers' decision making (Partington 2000).

Research in Practice 6.7 gives an example of a grounded theory study.

RESEARCH IN PRACTICE 6.7

A grounded theory study of the influence of information about labour abuses on consumer choice

Valor's (2007) grounded theory study investigates how information about labour abuses in the clothing industry influences consumer choice. Concerned that previous studies had tended to oversimplify the purchasing process, the author chose grounded theory because it could 'explain a complex, multi-faceted problem, without reducing *a priori* the number and type of variables involved' (Valor 2007: 677). The chosen data collection method was in-depth interviews with participants being selected on the basis of their lifestyles. Interview questions focused on past buying decisions and not asking directly about labour abuses, so as to avoid introducing social desirability bias. Each interview was transcribed and analysed prior to conducting the next interview; sampling was continued until theoretical saturation was reached, which was after a total of 11 interviews. Data analysis was carried out using a coding approach and emerging analytic categories were recorded in memos. The findings are presented in the form of a graphical model supported by quotations from the interviews and discussion of the findings in relation to existing literature. The author discusses the implications for practice from the perspective of both (commercial) companies and non-governmental organizations campaigning for change in the industry.

6.3.3 *Case study research design*

The word 'case' means 'an instance of' and the central feature of **case study** research design is an investigation of one or more specific 'instances of' something that will be the cases in the study. A case in a case study can be something relatively concrete such as an organization, a group or an individual, or something more abstract such as an event, a management decision or a change programme. Other common features of case study include (Gomm et al. 2000, Yin 2009):

Table 6.1 Example case studies (based on Eisenhardt 1989: 535)

Study	Number and description of cases	Research topic	Data sources
Leonard-Barton (1992)	Twenty new product and process development projects across five companies	Core capabilities and core rigidities in new product development	Interviews Archives
Wilson et al. (2002)	Five projects in five different companies	Success factors in implementing customer relationship management systems	Interviews
Olsson et al. (2008)	Two companies engaged in offshoring	Client–vendor relation-ships in two-stage offshoring	Interviews Workshops with practitioners from case companies
Ozcan and Eisenhardt (2009)	Six entrepreneurial firms in the same industry	The origins of alliance portfolios	Archives Interviews Industry conferences Some observation

- in-depth study of a small number of cases, often longitudinally (prospectively or retrospectively)
- collection and analysis of data about a large number of features of each case
- studying cases in their real-life context; understanding how the case influences and is influenced by its context is often of central interest to case researchers
- naturally occurring cases, in the sense that they are not manipulated as in an experiment
- employing multiple sources of data, including interviews, observation, archival documents and even physical artefacts to allow triangulation of findings.

Case studies are most commonly associated with qualitative research and qualitative data but this need not be so and quantitative data can readily be incorporated into a case study where appropriate.

A brief comment is needed on the topic of case studies in teaching, since they are so widely used in business and management education. It is important to realize that academic case study research serves a different purpose. Teaching cases are written to highlight particular issues for teaching and to stimulate debate in class. Research case studies also differ from the short, descriptive 'vignettes' popular in textbooks and many policy reports. The case study method in research demands a high degree of depth, breadth and rigour, with careful attention to showing the way in which evidence supports the conclusions reached.

Applications of case study design

Case studies have been used in many different areas of management research, including strategy, information systems, innovation and organizational change, reflecting the versatility of the design. Their ability to investigate cases in depth and to employ multiple sources of evidence makes them a useful tool for descriptive studies where the focus is on a specific situation or context where generalizability is less important. Case study designs can also be employed in applied research, for example, in evaluating the effects of a programme or policy. It is in answers to 'how' and 'why' questions, however, that case study research comes into its own (Yin 1998), for both theory building and theory testing. In explanatory research, for instance, case studies offer the possibility of investigating causal mechanisms and the specific contexts in which they are activated (George and Bennet 2005). Case study research can also facilitate a holistic perspective on causality because it treats the case as a specific whole. It thereby offers the possibility of investigating causal complexity where there are many relevant factors but few observations. Case study can also be used to research questions about process because the use of multiple data sources supports the retrospective investigation of events. A flavour of the diversity of case study topics is given by the different examples shown in Table 6.1.

Research in Practice 6.8 gives an example of multiple case study research.

RESEARCH IN PRACTICE 6.8

Multiple case study research on success factors for implementing customer relationship management systems

Wilson et al. (2002) used a multiple case study to investigate how to ensure the successful implementation of an IT-enabled CRM (customer relationship management) system. Drawing on existing literature, the authors identified a range of (potential) success factors which were to be tested in the research. 'But', they noted, 'we did not wish to exclude the possibility that the factors might need modification, or that additional factors might emerge, given the evolving nature of this application area and the relatively sparse previous research' (Wilson et al. 2002: 202). They therefore wanted a research design that could combine elements of theory testing and theory generation. Five examples of CRM implementations were selected to provide variation in the industry sector, the nature of the CRM application and the perceived project success. Primary data collection was by qualitative interview with a total of 23 managers being interviewed. The success-factor framework was compared against each case in turn and developed progressively during the analysis using a process known as analytic induction. Each factor was weighted according to its presence and influence and the whole then summarized in a summary table. The authors then drew conclusions on success factors and their relative impact.

6.3.4 Action research

'Research that produces nothing but books will not suffice' (Lewin 1946: 35). These were the words of the social psychologist Kurt Lewin in a paper in which he advocated a 'type of action-research [*sic*]' that would lead to social action. Lewin proposed a cyclical, iterative approach to research involving planning what was to be done, taking action and fact finding about the results. Lewin's ideas have since become one of the key influences in what is now known as **action research**. Over time, action research has taken different directions but we can nevertheless identify key features of the approach as we are using it here.

- The close relationship between knowledge acquisition and action; action research is 'research *in action* rather than research *about action*' (Coghlan and Brannick 2010: 4). Action is taken to improve practice and the research generates new knowledge about how and why the improvements came about.
- Action research is conducted as a collaborative partnership between the researcher and a group in an organization or community who participate in the process of the action research. Research proceeds as a cycle of joint planning, action, observation and reflection, where the reflection phase paves the way for further cycles of planning, acting, observing and reflecting in a spiral of learning (Figure 6.4).
- The results are shared amongst participants and for action research in an academic context the output typically also includes a report such as a dissertation or thesis.
- The output is 'actionable knowledge' that is useful to both the practitioner and academic communities (Coghlan 2007: 293).

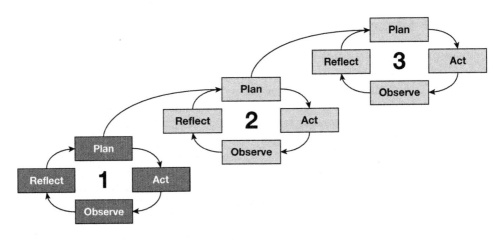

Figure 6.4 Action research cycles

Applications of action research

Applications of action research reflect the different directions in which the method has been taken, although its action orientation makes it appropriate for investigating 'why' and 'how' questions where the focus is on producing solutions to problems encountered in practice. Within organizations and management, some of the early action research projects investigated issues around autonomous work groups in organizations, and action research has continued to be applied in organizational development and change. Action research has also been used as a research method by management students who are studying while working and who undertake the research in their own organization, an approach Coghlan (2007: 294) calls 'insider action research'. Another approach, sometimes known as participatory action research, has been to emphasize the collaborative and democratic possibilities of action research to exploit its emancipatory potential.

Research in Practice 6.9 gives an example of an action research study.

RESEARCH IN PRACTICE 6.9

Action research study on the role of information systems in small business growth

Street and Meister (2004) used action research to investigate how and why a management team in a small business developed an information system (IS) to support its growth needs. The project was carried out in collaboration with five managers at a Canadian electronics manufacturing company (referred to as ELCO) that was seeking to grow its business. The practical goal of the project was to recommend potential changes to the organization's IS in support of those growth plans.

The research team adopted a five-step action research cycle consisting of action planning, action taking, evaluating, specifying learning and diagnosing. Three iterations of the cycle were used, involving baseline analysis, strategy planning and the development of a requirements specification for a new IS solution. One of the findings from the project was the importance of internal transparency of information within the organization. In addition, the researchers developed a process model drawing on the theory of punctuated equilibrium to help understand the experiences at ELCO and the relationship between internal transparency, IS and business growth.

6.3.5 Interview studies

The word 'interview' is used in different ways in research, including the face-to-face or telephone administration of a quantitative questionnaire as part of a survey study. Here we will use it to refer to the in-depth interviews used in qualitative research. Such interviews play an important role as a data collection technique in many different qualitative research designs, including case study and ethnography, but often alongside other data collection methods such as observation. There are, however, many qualitative research projects in which interviews are the sole data source. As a result it is legitimate to talk about an **interview study** as a research design in its own right. (Kvale and Brinkmann 2009). Interview studies can use a variety of interview formats, including individual and group interviews, and can be carried out face to face or remotely, for example, by telephone.

Applications of interview study designs

An interview study design is appropriate in situations where a qualitative interview is suitable as the sole data collection method. Qualitative interviews, and by extension interview studies, offer the possibility of investigating respondents' points of view and the meaning and understanding they attach to their experiences (Kvale and Brinkmann 2009). An interview study may therefore be an appropriate design where your research focus is on the individual, subjective lived experience of your participants (Marshall and Rossman 2006). Interviews, particularly focus groups, are widely used in market research; for example, to understand how consumers react to and relate to products and brands. As well as facilitating an emic perspective in the research, interview studies are valuable for investigating novel, ill-defined topics where more structured data collection techniques are not feasible or where the ability to follow up emergent issues is likely to be important. Given the widespread use of interviews, we explore their use as a data collection method more fully in Chapter 11.

Research in Practice 6.10 gives an example of an interview study.

RESEARCH IN PRACTICE 6.10

Interview study of the characteristics of successful employer brands

Moroko and Uncles undertook an interview study in order to 'examine the perceptions of industry experts of the characteristics of employer branding success as a starting point to bridge the gap in our understanding and to add to the body of theory in this area' (Moroko and Uncles 2008: 162). The study consisted of 17 in-depth, semi-structured interviews with 13 senior industry experts from the fields of internal marketing, human resources, communications, branding and recruitment. According to the authors, 'expert informants were seen as appropriate participants for the study as they offered an efficient way to gather perspectives on employer branding success based on experience across a number of companies, industry sectors and countries' (Moroko and Uncles 2008: 162). Interviewees were identified using theoretical, purposive sampling.

Interviews were transcribed and coded using thematic analysis to identify principal themes and develop the final conceptual framework. The findings were validated with four of the original respondents. The analysis identifies two key dimensions of success for an employer brand: attractiveness and accuracy allowing a four-factor typology to be proposed in the form of a 2 x 2 matrix. The authors discuss the practical and theoretical implications of the findings.

6.3.6 *Qualitative approaches to language analysis*

Language is central to qualitative research because of the focus upon words rather than numbers. In many cases such words are analysed for what they can tell us about what is happening in a given situation. You might study a corporate annual report, for example, for information about what the company has been doing, or collect interview data in order to learn about participants' experiences in a particular situation. In this way, language is treated as a resource through which we can learn about the world. An alternative approach is to see language itself as a topic for analysis. Instead of analysing the corporate report for what it tells us about the company, we might instead analyse it for what it tells us about how the company communicates with its shareholders, how it presents itself and uses words and images to achieve certain effects. In this section we will look at three different qualitative research designs that investigate language and language use primarily as a topic rather than a resource. Each takes a different perspective on language and other symbols, whether verbal or written, and uses a different basic research design to achieve its aim.

Qualitative content analysis

Qualitative content analysis (QCA) is a variant of the (quantitative) content analysis approach we introduced in the last section. The expression 'content analysis' is used in a variety of ways in the context of qualitative research but we will use the term QCA to refer to one particular approach. This involves analysing text in a way that retains the quantitative content analysis preference for systematic analysis. It involves classifying textual material by following a methodical, sequential procedure in which a coding system and the rules for applying it are developed separately from their application to the bulk of the material to be analysed (Schreier 2012). Where QCA differs from quantitative content analysis is in its greater emphasis on developing the coding system from the data rather than primarily from prior theory, along with a recognition that frequency may not always be the best indicator of importance when analysing the content of text (Mayring 2000). The systematic analysis approach does, however, mean that QCA can be extended to include quantitative analysis of the data if appropriate. Like quantitative content analysis, QCA can be used to analyse both verbal and visual text material in either paper or digital format, including online material.

Discourse analysis

Discourse analysis represents a very different approach to analysing language, compared to QCA. The term discourse is used in a wide variety of ways in research and this is reflected in different forms of discourse analysis. In this section we will focus on a version of discourse analysis that has been influenced by the work of the French philosopher and historian Michel Foucault, who drew attention to the constitutive power of discourse (Fairclough 2010). Rather than passively reflecting reality, discourse actively constructs meanings for it:

> Discourses do not just reflect or represent social entities and relations, they construct or 'constitute' them; different discourse constitute key entities (be they 'mental illness', 'citizenship' or 'literacy') in different ways, and position people in different ways as social subjects (e.g. as doctors or patients) and it is these social effects of discourse that are focused upon in discourse analysis.
>
> Fairclough (1992: 3–4)

One approach to analysing discourse that seeks to investigate its social effects is **critical discourse analysis** (CDA). CDA provides a method for tracing the relationships between text and talk and wider social relations, practices and structures (Fairclough 2010). It is 'critical' both in the sense of looking to expose the ways in which language is implicated within relations of power and dominance and in the sense of advocating social change. In order to achieve this, CDA brings together both the social and the linguistic aspects of discourse. Fairclough (2005) argues that CDA can productively be used to understand the discursive component of organizational change, such as how new discourses emerge, how a particular discourse becomes dominant or how a dominant discourse is enacted in the organization. Doolin (2003), for example, explores how different discourses were employed during a change management programme in a hospital in an attempt to reconstitute clinical care as 'patient flow management' and doctors as 'clinicians-as-managers'. The latter conflicted with a view of the doctor as 'medical professional' and the management role was resisted by clinicians.

Conversation analysis

Although it is sometimes classified as a type of discourse analysis, our third approach to analysing language is a very distinctive one that focuses on talk in interaction. Known as conversation analysis (CA), it studies how talk is organized sequentially during the course of social interaction. Characteristics of CA include (Titscher et al. 2000, ten Have 2007):

- a focus on oral communication involving more than one person
- fine-grained analysis of detailed transcripts of language being used in naturally occurring situations
- local understanding of context in which the analyst seeks to understand an utterance in relation to the sequence of interactions that preceded it
- recording of macro-social phenomena are only when they are demonstrably relevant to the speakers' understanding during the course of the conversation.

Although conversation analysts can and do draw on a body of knowledge about talk in interaction, there is a preference for inductive, data-driven, rather than theory-driven, analysis.

The term conversation analysis and the emphasis on naturally occurring talk may suggest that the primary concern of CA is informal conversation, but CA has in practice been applied to a wide range of other settings, including what is referred to as institutional talk or institutional interaction. Applications have included strategizing (Samra-Fredericks 2003), political speaking (Atkinson 1984) and using standardized forms in service encounters (Moore et al. 2010). We present an example in Research in Practice 6.11 which shows CA being applied to street vending.

RESEARCH IN PRACTICE 6.11

Conversation analysis and streetwise sales

The Big Issue is a weekly magazine that is sold on the streets of the UK by people who are homeless and who apply to become vendors and can keep the profit on the sales. Llewellyn and Burrow (2008) used conversation analysis (CA) techniques in a study of the interactions between a *Big Issue* vendor and passers-by, thereby contributing to an understanding of 'streetwise sales'. Data were captured using video-audio recording and the authors present both CA-style transcripts and photographic imagery in the write-up. The following detailed transcript (see the end of this box for an explanation of the transcription symbols) is one example of an interaction with a passer-by who has bought a copy of the magazine (cover price £1.50 at that time) with a £10 note leaving £8.50 change due. The vendor is counting out the change:

1	Vendor:	four, five, six, seven
2		(1.2)
3		↑ eight
4		(1.0) ((vendor hands over eight pounds))
5	Passer-by:	that's fine
6	Vendor:	arh's the'fine? Arh bl[ess you
7	Passer-by:	[yeah]
8		(3.2)
9	Vendor:	thank you very much, thank you

In their analysis of this interaction, Llewellyn and Burrow (2008: 575–6) draw attention to a number of points. They highlight, for example, how the vendor counts back the change, presenting the passer-by with a choice about what to do; the word 'eight' is said with a rising pitch and the vendor hands over the eight pounds. At this point the passer-by says 'that's fine', which is taken as an indication that no more change need be given. Thus the vendor sells this copy for £2.00 rather than £1.50. As Llewellyn and Burrow explain, the phased return of the money did not force the passer-by to decline the change due but it did 'generate distinctive sequential possibilities (a slot where such action could be performed) and, potentially, new normative considerations. The passer-by is placed in a situation where they are awaiting not £8.50, but (a homeless person to present them with) fifty pence' (Llewellyn and Burrow 2008: 576).

Symbols used in the transcript:

(0.0) = time gaps, in seconds
↑   = higher pitch after the arrow
[ ]   = overlapping talk

CRITICAL COMMENTARY 6.1

Critiques of quantitative and qualitative research

In Chapter 4 we discussed how the quality criteria for quantitative and qualitative research may differ, reflecting both technical features of the research and different philosophical orientations. In this brief commentary we will highlight some of the general criticisms of quantitative and qualitative research.

Criticism of quantitative research is often linked to its perceived association with positivism. For researchers working from an interpretivist perspective, for example, quantitative research can be seen as failing to pay sufficient attention to meaning and to understanding of social actors in their particular contexts. A more radical version of this critique is that the data generated by questionnaires is 'constructed' in the process of respondents making sense of the questions, rather than reflecting some real underlying state, thereby casting doubt on the objective character of the data. Some critics also question the dominant role given to variables in quantitative research. This 'variable orientation' is often linked to the positivist/regularity view of causation and subject to criticism from those who adopt different views on the nature of causality in social systems. Concerns are also raised about the emphasis placed on tests for statistical significance in quantitative research. Despite its widespread use, aspects of such testing are controversial, for example, because it downplays practical significance. We explore this point more fully in Chapter 13.

Qualitative research is also subject to criticism. Mays and Pope sum up three common charges:

> Firstly, that qualitative research is merely an assembly of anecdote and personal impressions, strongly subject to researcher bias; secondly, it is argued that qualitative research lacks reproducibility – the research is so personal to the researcher that there is no guarantee that a different researcher would not come to radically different conclusions; and, finally, qualitative research is criticised for lacking generalisability.
>
> Mays and Pope (1995: 109)

To a great extent these three criticisms are based on a particular understanding of what constitutes 'good' research that is in line with the tenets of positivism and, by association, with quantitative research, rather than the philosophical orientations, such as interpretivism, underpinning much qualitative research.

Awareness of general criticisms of this kind is important because it draws attention to some of the challenges that researchers can face when their work is assessed according to quality criteria (see Chapter 4) more suited to other research methods or by researchers with a very different philosophical orientation.

KEY LEARNING POINTS

- Experiments involve the manipulation of a treatment variable to observe its effect. True experiments involve random assignment of subjects to groups, quasi-experiments do not. Experimental designs can have very high internal validity for inferring causality but are subject to practical and ethical constraints.
- Natural experiments and correlational studies are examples of non-experimental explanatory research designs that can be used for testing explanatory theory and for predicting the value of a dependent variable based on the value of one or more independent variables. The extent to which causality can reliably be inferred from non-experimental designs is controversial.
- Survey studies use pre-specified, structured data collection procedures (such as a questionnaire) to collect quantitative data on variables of interest to the researcher, often from a sample drawn from a larger population. Descriptive surveys generate descriptions of a phenomenon in terms of the distribution of relevant variables. Analytic surveys are used to test theories for explanatory or predictive purposes by investigating relationship between variables.
- Simulations can be used to investigate how phenomena behave dynamically and to predict the pattern of that behaviour, especially for complex systems or when empirical data are lacking.
- Quantitative content analysis provides a way of systematically and quantitatively analysing text through the application of a structured coding scheme for purposes of description or prediction. Content analysis on its own has limited ability to draw conclusions about the world beyond the text.
- An ethnographic study involves in-depth investigation of a culture-sharing group in which participant-observation and/or informal interviews play a significant role with the aim of generating 'thick description' of the phenomenon under investigation.
- Grounded theory is a research design in which the aim is to build theory systematically from data through an iterative process of constant comparison between emerging theory and data which proceeds until theoretical saturation is reached. Grounded theory offers the opportunity to investigate topics in depth and context and to shed light on new or existing topics.
- Case study research design involves the study of a relatively small number of naturally occurring cases, in depth and in context, often using multiple sources of evidence, particularly when the aim is to answer 'why' or 'how' questions.
- Action research involves a collaborative partnership between the researcher and a group of practitioners in a cyclical process of joint planning, action, observation and reflection that contributes to actionable knowledge for both the practitioner and academic communities.
- An interview study is one in which qualitative, in-depth interviews are the means of data collection. Variations include the use of individual or group interviews and face-to-face or remote interviewing. Interview studies are a flexible and potentially efficient design but careful thought needs to be given to the suitability of the design for the chosen project.

PART II

- A range of qualitative approaches can be used to analyse language and text in detail. Qualitative content analysis is a variant of traditional quantitative content analysis distinguished by a greater emphasis on a data-driven coding system, more stress on the importance of context and interpretation of meaning, and recognition that frequency may not always be the best indicator of importance in text analysis. Critical discourse analysis is a form of discourse analysis that recognizes the constitutive properties of discourse and investigates the relationships between discourse and wider social relations, practices and structures. Conversation analysis focuses on the detailed analysis of talk-in-interaction to understand how talk is organized sequentially during the course of social interaction.

NEXT STEPS

6.1   Research designs used in your topic area. Review the research articles that you have identified in your literature review.

   a) What specific research designs are used in your topic area?
   b) What types of research question are they used to answer?
   c) What are the strengths and weaknesses of these designs in relation to your topic area?
   d) Evaluate the contribution made by different research designs in your topic area.

6.2   What research design may be suitable for your own project? Review your research questions and your answers to Next steps activity 5.2 in Chapter 5.

   a) What specific research designs could be used to answer your research question?
   b) What would be the strengths and weaknesses of those designs for your project?
   c) Evaluate the suitability of the research designs you have identified for answering your research questions.

Further reading

More details how to carry out the designs introduced in this chapter can be found on the companion website, along with suggestions for further reading.

References

Arnould, E. J. and Price, L. L. (2006). 'Market-oriented ethnography revisited', *Journal of Advertising Research*, 46(3), 251–62.

Atkinson, M. J. (1984). *Our masters' voices*. London: Routledge.

Bono, J. E., Purvanova, R. K., Towler, A. J. and Peterson, D. B. (2009). 'A survey of executive coaching practices', *Personnel Psychology*, 62(2), 361–404.

Brewer, J. D. (2004). Ethnography. *In:* Cassell, C. and Symon, G. (eds) *Essential guide to qualitative methods in organizational research.* London: Sage.

Bryant, A. and Charmaz, K. (2007). Introduction to grounded theory research: Methods and perspectives. *In:* Bryant, A. and Charmaz, K. (eds) *The Sage handbook of grounded theory.* London: Sage.

Charmaz, K. (2006). *Constructing grounded theory.* London: Sage.

Coghlan, D. (2007). 'Insider action research doctorates: Generating actionable knowledge', *Higher Education*, 54(2), 293–306.

Coghlan, D. and Brannick, T. (2010). *Doing action research in your own organization.* 3rd edn. London: Sage.

Cook, T. D. and Campbell, D. T. (1979). *Quasi-experimentation: Design and analysis for field settings.* Chicago, IL: Rand McNally.

Creswell, J. W. (2009). *Research design.* 3rd edn. Los Angeles, CA: Sage.

Datta, P. P. and Christopher, M. G. (2011). 'Information sharing and coordination mechanisms for managing uncertainty in supply chains: A simulation study', *International Journal of Production Research*, 49(3), 765–803.

Davis, J. P., Eisenhardt, K. M. and Bingham, C. B. (2007). 'Developing theory through simulation methods', *Academy of Management Review*, 32(2), 480–99.

Delbridge, R. (1998). *Life on the line in contemporary manufacturing.* Oxford: Oxford University Press.

Dey, I. (2007). Grounding categories. *In:* Bryant, A. and Charmaz, K. (eds) *The Sage handbook of grounded theory.* London: Sage.

Doolin, B. (2003). 'Narratives of change: Discourse, technology and organization', *Organization*, 10(4), 751–70.

Easterby-Smith, M., Thorpe, R. and Jackson, P. R. (2008). *Management research.* 3rd edn. London: Sage Publications.

Eisenhardt, K. M. (1989). 'Building theories from case study research', *Academy of Management Review*, 14(4), 532–50.

Fairclough, N. (1992). *Discourse and social change.* Cambridge: Polity Press.

Fairclough, N. (2005). 'Peripheral vision: Discourse analysis in organization studies: The case for critical realism', *Organization Studies*, 26(6), 915–39.

Fairclough, N. (2010). *Critical discourse analysis.* 2nd edn. Harlow: Longman.

Forza, C. (2002). 'Survey research in operations management: A process-based perspective', *International Journal of Operations & Production Management*, 22(2), 152–94.

Gattiker, T. F. (2007). 'Enterprise resource planning (erp) systems and the manufacturing-marketing interface: An information-processing theory view', *International Journal of Production Research*, 45(13), 2895-2917.

Gebauer, J., Tang, Y. and Baimai, C. (2008). 'User requirements of mobile technology: Results from a content analysis of user reviews', *Information Systems & e-Business Management*, 6(4), 361–84.

Geertz, C. (1975). *The interpretation of cultures.* London: Hutchinson.

George, A. L. and Bennet, A. (2005). *Case studies and theory development in the social sciences.* Cambridge, MA: The MIT Press.

Gilbert, N. and Troitzsch, K. G. (2005). *Simulation for the social scientist.* 2nd edn. Maidenhead: Open University Press.

Gill, J. and Johnson, P. (2010). *Research methods for managers.* 4th edn. London: Sage.

Glaser, B. G. and Strauss, A. (1967). *The discovery of grounded theory: Strategies for qualitative research.* Chicago, IL: Aldine.

Gomm, R., Hammersley, M. and Foster, P. (eds) (2000). *Case study method.* London: Sage.

Hammersley, M. and Atkinson, P. (2007). *Ethnography, principles in practice.* 3rd edn. London: Routledge.

Jain, V., Roy, S., Daswani, A. and Sudha, M. (2010). 'How celebrities are used in Indian television commercials', *Vikalpa: The Journal for Decision Makers*, 35(4), 45–52.

Kvale, S. and Brinkmann, S. (2009). *Interviews*. Thousand Oaks, CA: Sage.

Leonard-Barton, D. (1992). 'Core capabilities and core rigidities: A paradox in managing new product development', *Strategic Management Journal*, 13(Special Issue, Summer), 111–25.

Lewin, K. (1946). 'Action research and minority problems', *Journal of Social Issues*, 2(4), 34–46.

Llewellyn, N. and Burrow, R. (2008). 'Streetwise sales and the social order of city streets', *The British Journal of Sociology*, 59(3), 561–83.

Marshall, C. and Rossman, G. B. (2006). *Designing qualitative research*. 4th edn. Thousand Oaks, CA: Sage Publications.

Mayring, P. (2000). 'Qualitative content analysis'. *Forum Qualitative Sozialforschung / Forum: Qualitative Social Research* [online], 1(2). Available from: www.qualitative-research.net/index.php/fqs/article/view/1089.

Mays, N. and Pope, C. (1995). 'Qualitative research: Rigour and qualitative research', *BMJ*, 311(6997), 109–12.

Moore, R. J., Whalen, J. and Gathman, E. C. H. (2010). The work of the work order: Document practice in face-to-face service encounters. *In:* Llewellyn, N. and Hindmarsh, J. (eds) *Organisation, interaction and practice: Studies in ethnomethodology and conversation analysis*. Cambridge: Cambridge University Press.

Moroko, L. and Uncles, M. D. (2008). 'Characteristics of successful employer brands', *Journal of Brand Management*, 16(3), 160–75.

Naccarato, J. L. and Neuendorf, K. A. (1998). 'Content analysis as a predictive methodology: Recall, readership, and evaluations of business-to-business print advertising', *Journal of Advertising Research*, 38(3), 19–33.

Neuendorf, K. A., Gore, T. D., Dalessandro, A., Janstova, P. and Snyder-Suhy, S. (2010). 'Shaken and stirred: A content analysis of women's portrayals in James Bond films', *Sex Roles*, 62(11–12), 747–61.

Olsson, H. H., Ó Conchúir, E., Ågerfalk, P. J. and Fitzgerald, B. (2008). 'Two-stage offshoring: An investigation of the Irish bridge', *MIS Quarterly*, 32(2), 257–79.

Ozcan, P. and Eisenhardt, K. M. (2009). 'Origin of alliance portfolios: Entrepreneurs, network strategies and firm performance', *Academy of Management Journal*, 52(2), 246–79.

Partington, D. (2000). 'Building grounded theories of management action', *British Journal of Management*, 11(2), 91–102.

Prior, D. D. and Miller, L. M. (2012). 'Webethnography', *International Journal of Market Research*, 54(4), 503–20.

Reichertz, J. (2007). Abduction: The logic of discovery of grounded theory. *In:* Bryant, A. and Charmaz, K. (eds) *The Sage handbook of grounded theory*. London: Sage.

Roy, D. (1952). 'Quota restriction and goldbricking in a machine shop', *The American Journal of Sociology*, 67(2), 427–42.

Samra-Fredericks, D. (2003). 'Strategizing as lived experience and strategists' everyday efforts to shape strategic direction', *Journal of Management Studies*, 40(1), 141–74.

Schouten, J. W. and McAlexander, J. H. (1995). 'Subcultures of consumption: An ethnography of the new bikers', *Journal of Consumer Research*, 22(1), 43–61.

Schreier, M. (2012). *Qualitative content analysis in practice*. London: Sage.

Shadish, W. R., Cook, T. D. and Campbell, D. T. (2002). *Experimental and quasi-experimental designs for generalized causal inference*. Belmont, CA: Wadsworth Cengage Learning.

Sigurdsson, V., Saevarsson, H. and Foxall, G. (2009). 'Brand placement and consumer choice: An in-store experiment', *Journal of Applied Behavior Analysis*, 42(3), 741–5.

Street, C. T. and Meister, D. B. (2004). 'Small business growth and internal transparency: The role of information systems', *MIS Quarterly*, 28(3), 473–506.

ten Have, P. (2007). *Doing conversation analysis*. 2nd edn. London: Sage.

Titscher, S., Meyer, M., Wodak, R. and Vetter, E. (2000). *Methods of text and discourse analysis*. London: Sage.

Valor, C. (2007). 'The influence of information about labour abuses on consumer choice of clothes: A grounded theory approach', *Journal of Marketing Management*, 23(7/8), 675–95.

Wilson, H., Daniel, E. and McDonald, M. (2002). 'Factors for success in customer relationship management (CRM) systems', *Journal of Marketing Management*, 18(1–2), 193–219.

Yin, R. K. (1998). The abridged version of case study research: Design and method. *In:* Bickman, L. and Rog, D. J. (eds) *Handbook of applied social research methods*. Thousand Oaks, CA: Sage.

Yin, R. K. (2009). *Doing case study research*. 4th edn. Thousand Oaks, CA: Sage.

PART II

7 Conducting research ethically

CHAPTER SUMMARY

The key topics covered in this chapter are:

- understanding the importance of ethical conduct in research
- applying the principles of ethical research
- identifying ethical concerns in your own research
- securing ethical approval.

7.1 Introduction

Ethical dilemmas in management have become widely discussed in the academic and practitioner literature, as well as in the wider media (Melé 2012). Organizations and industries such as food technology, pharmaceutical and medical devices have developed rigorous ethical guidelines to ensure that research projects conducted in relation to their products or services reach expected ethical and regulatory standards. Similarly, as a researcher today you also need to be aware of ethical dimensions of your own research.

Ethics concerns what is right or wrong about a particular course of action (Singer, in Remenyi et al. 1998). When carrying out a research project you must ensure that you fully understand the ethical implications of your decisions and how your actions may impact both on those directly involved in the research and on the wider community. In this chapter we introduce the topic of research ethics and highlight the importance of ethical behaviour in management research. We then discuss a set of ethical principles in relation to the research process to help you apply those principles to your own research. Special consideration is given to ethical aspects of Internet-based research. Finally, we discuss the role of codes of practice and regulatory standards, and the importance of gaining ethical approval prior to commencing your research.

7.2 Ethics in research

Research ethics is concerned with the appropriate conduct of research in relation to participants and to others affected by it. Over recent years, the research community has developed an increasingly formalized approach to ethical conduct in both social and business research. Organizations such as ESOMAR, the US Academy of Management, the UK's Market Research Society, for example, provide guidelines regarding ethical conduct both towards those participating in a research project and towards fellow researchers in their community or organization.

As a starting point for understanding your ethical responsibilities as researchers it is useful to adopt a multi-stakeholder perspective. We can begin by identifying the key stakeholder groups who are impacted upon by the research process. These include the participants in the research study, the organization or institution on whose behalf the study is being undertaken, the wider society that may be affected by the research and also the researcher. This categorization helps you to understand the range of perspectives that need to be taken into account when conducting our research.

A number of ethical principles can be identified that underpin guidelines for ethical behaviour in research that address these different stakeholder perspectives. In Table 7.1 we summarize them as four key principles and indicate the main issues that the researcher needs to consider. These principles provide a useful structure to help you identify the ethical issues you should consider when designing your research project, as well as specific actions that you may need to take while carrying it out. They should be borne in mind throughout your study: before, during and after your research project.

Table 7.1 Key ethical principles in research

Key principle	*Issues to consider*
Avoidance of harm or loss of dignity	• Protection from physical or psychological harm • Protection of personal dignity
Transparency and honesty	• Openness regarding the nature of the project • Informed consent • Absence of deception • Full disclosure of researcher affiliations
Right to privacy	• Anonymity • Confidentiality • Data protection
Researcher integrity	• Personal conduct of the researcher • Misrepresentation of findings • Reciprocity

7.3 Avoidance of harm or loss of dignity

You have a duty of care as a researcher to ensure that anyone involved in your research remains free from physical and/or psychological harm. This is not limited to the actual respondents taking part but extends to those commissioning the research, recipients of the output of the research as well as you or others who carry out the research.

Physical harm may result, for example, from some form of direct testing of a service or product, such as skin creams or hair dyes, upon participants. Alternatively it may arise from insufficient safeguards for the safety of the respondents or the researcher in terms of the research site itself, such as meeting in an unsafe or isolated location. Psychological harm may occur where your research results in anxiety, stress, embarrassment or loss of self-esteem to others. Such conditions might arise, for example, as a result of insensitive or inappropriate questions during an interview or from a lack of respect for the dignity of others involved in the research. As researchers we therefore need to be aware of cultural differences in the perception of dignity and respect. For example, in some cultures it may be inappropriate for researchers to interview participants of a different gender or to do so without an escort. It is your responsibility as the researcher to consider the nature of your topic and how you intend to investigate it and whether, in so doing you are likely to cause psychological harm to others.

Potentially harmful outcomes may be difficult for the researcher to recognize, given that they may be highly personal to the individual participant. As the researcher you need to try to step into the participants' shoes and look at the nature of the research, the wording of questions and any activities in which they will be involved, and identify potential harm. Prior discussions and pre-testing of the research with those familiar with the research context can help you to identify potential sources of harm, as well as ways of avoiding them. When planning your research you should document the safeguards you are putting in place to ensure the care and safety of those involved in your study, including yourself.

7.4 Transparency and honesty

Transparency and openness are important in a research study. Tricking respondents into taking part in your research or misleading them about the nature of the study is unethical. Openness and transparency require that participants are made fully aware of the topic of the research, its overall purpose, what they will be required to do and how long it will take. It is also unethical to deceive people into believing they are taking part in research when in fact the objective of the activity is sales promotion or fundraising – which have become known as sugging and frugging, respectively (McGivern 2006). Any form of deception not only alienates your respondents but also, in the longer term, can have a negative impact upon the reputation of management research by seriously undermining the acceptance and participation of the public in management and marketing research.

7.4.1 Informed consent

One way of achieving transparency and honesty is to ensure that participants are able to make an informed decision as to whether or not they wish to participate in your research. Informed consent is achieved when participants are given enough information about the research to make an informed decision about their involvement and then give their consent on that basis. The principle of informed consent is therefore intended to prevent the use of deception as a means of recruiting people to take part in research. Additionally, it is intended to prevent coercion and to ensure that participants are involved of their own free will. They must therefore be given the right to withdraw from the study if they wish to do so, without facing any repercussions (even though this may be disruptive to your data collection).

Informed consent may be particularly important in business and management research where an employee may feel obliged to take part, or be told that they have to do so by their line manager. The situation of the military servicemen shown in

RESEARCH IN PRACTICE 7.1

Deception in research

In January 2008, the United Kingdom government announced that it would pay a total of £3 million in compensation to a group of 369 military veterans who had launched a legal action against the British government. The veterans had been required to take part in tests carried out by researchers at the Porton Down defence research establishment during the Cold War. The research into chemical warfare had left the veterans suffering from a range of health problems, ranging from respiratory and skin diseases to cancer and psychological problems. Legal representatives of the veterans claimed that they had been tricked into taking part in the tests, which many thought were being undertaken with the aim of finding a cure for the common cold. The UK Defence Minister offered a full apology saying: 'The Government sincerely apologises to those who may have been affected' (Smith et al. 2008).

Research in Practice 7.1 is an example of participation due to organizational obligation combined with deception, and illustrates the ethical and legal hazards of failing to follow the principle of informed consent.

The process for establishing informed consent typically involves two steps. Firstly, you will need to generate an information sheet providing information about the nature of the research. This should provide sufficient information to the participant in order to decide whether or not they wish to take part. We provide a template based on one in use in one of the authors' own institutions as an example in Research in Practice 7.2.

Secondly, you should confirm participants' willingness to take part. Such consent should be obtained before you start data collection and is typically required for all research studies involving human participants. The method of evidencing consent depends on the method of data collection, for example:

- For data collection by self-completed questionnaire (for example, online or by post), a disclaimer statement can be included in the introduction to the questionnaire. This should make it clear that by completing and submitting the questionnaire participants will be understood to be giving their consent to take part (see also Chapter 10).
- If the research involves face-to-face contact (such as an interview), evidence of consent is provided by signing a consent form.

In Research in Practice 7.3 we provide you with an example of a consent statement for face-to-face interviews.

If interviews are being conducted remotely, for example, over the telephone, evidence of consent can be provided in advance by email or by return of a paper copy of the signed consent statement. If you are administering a closed-ended questionnaire by telephone and no personal data or other identifying information are being collected, a verbal agreement by the participant in response to a suitably worded

RESEARCH IN PRACTICE 7.2

Example information sheet for face-to-face interviews

_____ (*Title of research project*)

This research project investigates _____ (*brief topic statement*) in order to _____ (*broad aims of the research*). The research forms part of my _____ qualification at _____ (*name of institution*). As part of the research I am interviewing people who _____ (*are involved with particular situation/topic, have knowledge/experience of, etc.*) and for this reason, I would like to invite you to take part. If you agree, you will be asked to participate in an interview of about ____ (*number*) minutes. During the interview I will ask you questions on _____ (*brief non-technical outline of subjects to be covered*). You can choose not to answer any particular questions and you are free to withdraw from the study at any time. With your permission, I would like to _____ (*record/video the interview/take notes*) for later analysis. The data will be kept securely and destroyed on completion of the project. Your name and identifying information will not be included in the final report. The identity of your organization will not be included in the final report. [*Delete if not applicable*] A copy of the completed _____ (*project/ summary of the project/summary of findings*) will be available on request. [*Delete if not applicable*]

If you have any further questions about the project, please feel free to contact me at the email address below.

Name of researcher: _____

Email address: _____

Date: _____

disclaimer statement by the researcher may be seen as adequate evidence of informed consent (on the grounds that the respondent can break off the phone call at any time). We recommend, however, that you confirm the requirements of your own organization or academic institution.

If you are conducting your research as part of an academic qualification it is likely that your institution has its own guidelines and templates for use when evidencing informed consent. You should ensure that you understand and comply with the requirements of your institution with respect to informed consent.

Providing evidence of informed consent is a requirement for many organizations and institutions. At first sight, it may seem onerous or likely to impede your ability to get an appropriate number of respondents. In practice, however, the process of gaining informed consent signals to potential participants that you are aware of ethical

RESEARCH IN PRACTICE 7.3

Example informed consent form for face-to-face interviews

_____ (*Title of research project*)

1 I have read and had explained to me by _____ (*name of researcher*) the information sheet relating to the project and any questions have been answered to my satisfaction.

2 I agree to the arrangements described in the information sheet insofar as they relate to my participation.

3 I understand that my participation is entirely voluntary and that I may withdraw from the project at any time.

4 I agree to the interview being video/audio recorded. [*delete if not applicable*]

5 I have received a copy of this consent form and of the accompanying information sheet.

6 I am aged 18 or older.

Name of participant: _____

Signed: _____

Date: _____

issues. This can play an important role where a research topic is particularly sensitive and where it is likely that participants may have concerns about the confidentiality of the data being collected. Similarly, informed consent is a mechanism to protect those such as children or the elderly who may be viewed as particularly vulnerable. When interviewing children (under 18 years of age) or those unable to give informed consent, perhaps due to incapacity, you should observe any local protocol or procedure and ensure that you have obtained permission via the informed consent of a parent, guardian or carer. If your data collection is outsourced to a third party agency you should ensure that informed consent is obtained by it.

7.4.2 Collecting data covertly

There may be occasions when a researcher wishes to collect data without the awareness of respondents that this is happening. This can occur, for example, in an ethnographic study where the researcher does not wish to be identified to a community or group, or in designs that include covert observation such as mystery shopping, which is used in the service sector where an organization such as a retailer wishes to undertake observational work of customer/staff interactions in a store, uncontaminated by the known presence of a researcher. Covert observation is sometimes recommended on the grounds that awareness of the researcher can influence the normal behaviour of those being observed, so undermining the validity of your research.

The problem, of course, is that this goes against the principle of informed consent and the right to privacy. Differing views exist amongst researchers of the ethical position of such techniques and their effect upon those being observed. In the case of mystery shopping, for example, Wilson (2001) points out that it can be viewed as involving deception (e.g. service employees being led to believe that the customer is a real customer when they are not) and invasion of the right to privacy (e.g. staff being observed without their knowledge or without consent being given). Guidelines for mystery shopping studies (see ESOMAR 2005) recommend that service employees are always notified in advance that such research will be taking place over a designated period, and in some countries there is a legal requirement to do so. Wilson (2001) argues for the importance of openness with employees in cases where mystery shopping is used and that best practice is to gain their acceptance prior to studies commencing and to share findings with the staff in an open and transparent way. With respect to covert observation in general, the UK's Economic and Social Research Council (ESRC) gives the following guidance:

> The broad principle should be that covert research must not be undertaken lightly or routinely. It is only justified if important issues are being addressed and if matters of social significance which cannot be uncovered in other ways are likely to be discovered.
>
> ESRC (2012: 30)

You should be very cautious and seek further guidance if you are contemplating covert observation as part of your research project.

7.4.3 Researcher affiliation

Often research will be conducted on behalf of a particular organization, industry body or association. Such organizations may provide funding or other forms of support. Consideration should be given to the degree to which such affiliations or connections are made explicit to participants, and also to those reading the findings, given the effect that such support may have upon the research outcome. Bell and Bryman (2007) point out that whilst research affiliation, particularly if it involves funding, has the potential to affect the research agenda and how findings are presented, identification of affiliation is not common in management research reporting (academic or practitioner). This is in contrast, for example, to researchers in the medical field, who must declare any affiliations or financial relationships with organizations involved in a research study, such as with a pharmaceutical or healthcare company. In the design and implementation of your study you should be aware of the effect of affiliation, for example when collecting data from competitors, who may feel they should be informed about all organizations connected to the project at the informed consent stage. You should also be aware of the subjective impact of your own personal affiliations upon your work as a researcher and of any conflicts of interest. In such situations, you will need to take special care with respect to the principle of openness and transparency.

Affiliations and conflicts of interest should be clearly stated when presenting findings either in report form or by oral presentation (for example, at an academic conference).

7.4.4 Incentivization

Incentives are sometimes used to encourage participation. They may be in the form of financial incentive, a small gift (such as a pen) or entry into a draw for a prize. Whilst such incentives may encourage participation they can also create a form of bias. Incentives may encourage participation by those not falling within the chosen target population but who agree to take part for the reward only. Alternatively, they may distort the way in which participants respond, for example, by encouraging particular answers for fear of losing the reward. As a researcher you should give careful consideration to the use of incentives and the effect they will have upon your sample's participation and the quality of the data. You should also be aware of the ethical issues that incentives raise. The UK's ESRC offers the following guidance in its ethics framework:

> In some instances, it may be justified to use techniques such as a free prize draw or book vouchers, to encourage survey responses . . . Incentives may be permissible, but anything which implies coercion is not.
>
> ESRC (2012: 51)

If you are thinking of offering incentives to potential participants you should ensure that they are consistent with ethical codes of practice governing your research, and any incentivization methods must be described in your final report.

7.5 Right to privacy

Privacy was originally defined in 1890 by Warren and Brandeis, writing in the *Harvard Law Review*, as 'the right to be let alone' (Nairn 2009). Today we may view privacy in broader terms in relation to our personal space, but also in terms of our personal information. As a researcher you should respect the privacy of participants at all times. This means being aware of issues relating to anonymity and confidentiality.

7.5.1 Anonymity

Anonymity protects the personal identity of those taking part in research. This means ensuring that personal information about them as individuals and the data they have provided as part of your study cannot be identified by others. Anonymity may be easily achieved in large-scale survey study where personal contact details (e.g. name, address, email address) are not collected, so it is not possible to link a response to a particular individual and all results are reported in the aggregate. Maintaining anonymity can be more problematic in qualitative research. At the data collection stage, with relatively small samples the identity of the participant will be known to the researcher, so anonymous data collection is not really possible. Particular care must be given when reporting findings to ensure that it is not possible to work out the identity of a particular participant by the responses given. Various techniques

PART II

can be used to protect anonymity, such as using pseudonyms (e.g. by referring to organizations as Company A, TELCO, PHARMACO and so on) and by replacing specific job titles with generic job descriptions (e.g. senior manager rather than Finance Director) when completing the final report.

7.5.2 Confidentiality

Confidentiality relates to the protection of the data provided by participants, who will expect that their views, opinions or information they provide remain confidential and are not communicated to other individuals or organizations. As a researcher you will become privy to a lot of information and be responsible for its confidentiality. A particular issue in a business research context is that the information revealed may be commercially sensitive and therefore raise concerns regarding disclosure to competitors. Alternatively there may be instances where release of respondent inform-ation could result in someone being denied a service, such as a welfare benefit, a loan or a product upgrade. More serious ethical dilemmas can arise where the researcher becomes aware of information that should be reported to external authorities regarding illegal activity such as child abuse. In such situations you will need to balance ethical issues regarding confidentiality with your legal and moral position.

You will need therefore to think about the security of your data, whether it is online, held on your computer or other storage device, or in print or hand-written format. In addition to your ethical and legal obligations, this is also good practice to avoid loss or corruption of data disrupting your project. You will also need to decide what will be done with the data upon completion of the study. Depending on agreements made when the data were collected, a number of options are available, including:

- destroying the data in a secure environment on completion of the project (for an academic qualification this should normally be done only once the award has been confirmed)
- secure storage for later re-analysis (subject to agreement at the time of collection)
- return to the owner of the data and secure destruction of any copies.

Ensure that you understand the rules of your parent institution regarding data handling and destruction of data.

7.5.3 Data protection

In addition to an ethical obligation to respect confidentiality, legal and regulatory controls exist in most countries regarding data protection. For example, in the UK the Data Protection Act (1998) covers confidentiality in both the collection and use of personal data. It protects the personal details of an individual that are held on a database from being passed on to a third party or viewed without the consent of the individual. Regulations also apply to data held by organizations and should be taken into account if your research involves accessing company databases on customers or employees. You will need to work with those responsible in the company for managing the data to identify what is allowed in terms of access to and use of such data. Remember that as a researcher it is your responsibility to be familiar with data protection regulations and to adhere to them. If you are researching in different countries, you should also ensure that you are familiar with any local legislation regarding data protection for the site at which you are conducting your study.

7.6 Researcher integrity

Our final key ethical principle relates to the personal behaviour of ourselves as researchers. As researchers we must always act with integrity regarding the way in which we design, implement and report research. You should always conduct research in a way that upholds the previous principles we have discussed, that is to say, act in an honest and respectful way, with an awareness of your responsibility for the care and protection of all stakeholders and/or their data involved in your research.

7.6.1 Misrepresentation of findings

Researchers should take care to ensure that they do not, intentionally or unintentionally, misrepresent the findings. We are responsible for ensuring that the integrity and quality of a research project are not jeopardized by our own actions. The US Academy of Management (AoM 2006), for example, requires that its members 'do not fabricate data or falsify results in their publications or presentations' [but] 'report their findings fully and do not omit data that are relevant within the context of the research question(s)'. As researchers we should take every care to ensure that our research is rigorous and professional and that we do not mislead the audience regarding the status of our research findings. We should also be mindful of our own influence on the research process. We can develop this awareness through reflexive practice, as discussed further in Chapter 1.

7.6.2 Reciprocity

Research involves one person, or group of people, investigating and exploring the world of another group of people. Often when this occurs, particularly within an organization, a significant difference in the power relationship will exit. Respondents may be less well informed and more vulnerable than the researcher, who may benefit from both their status as an 'expert' researcher and, in some cases, the perceived or actual backing of more powerful stakeholders. This may be a particular concern if the researcher is also a manager in the organization and is conducting the research amongst more junior staff, who may feel obligated to take part or to respond in certain ways. Principles such as informed consent, honesty and transparency are essential to protect the respondent in such cases (we present an example of managing this in Research in Practice 9.3).

Another response to this situation is to emphasize the need for reciprocity in the relationship between the researcher and respondent, in which the research that is done is beneficial to both parties. One version of this is sometimes referred to as **participatory research**. This is not a particular method but instead represents a commitment by the researcher and participants to collaborate with respect to the goals, process and outcomes of the research project. The degree of collaboration can vary from 'shallow' forms of participation in which the researcher still takes the lead, to 'deeper' modes of participation in which researcher and participants jointly own the agenda and process for the research (Cornwall and Jewkes 1995). An example of a research design that is well suited to this type of approach is action research, which we introduced in Chapter 6.

7.7 Ethics in online research

The Internet has become an increasingly important medium for researchers as an object of research (such as in online ethnography), as a source of data (such as blogs or online databases) or as a channel for collecting data (such as online surveys). Whilst the general ethical principles still apply, online research raises some particular issues. Writing about online communities, for example, Hair and Clark (2007: 793) argue that 'researchers should not assume that members of communities accept the voyeuristic nature of their discussions'. In other words, whilst an individual may recognize that they are posting in a public space they may not expect or want their comments to be used for other purposes, such as a research project. We therefore need to consider our ethical principles in the online context, which we will do by looking at them from the perspective of data collection and data reporting.

7.7.1 Collecting online data

When collecting data via the Internet it is the researcher's responsibility to ensure that the ethical principles discussed so far are followed. Administration of an online questionnaire, for example, would still require informed consent procedures to be followed and for the researcher to observe commitments to confidentiality and data protection. Similarly, the informed consent procedures when using a Internet telephone service such as Skype for telephone interviews would be little different to those used when conducting remote interviews over a standard telephone line.

Other types of data collection, however, may be more problematic from an ethical point of view. An example would be for a researcher to join an online community and then to use the discussions and conversations as sources of data without making the other members of the community aware that their comments were being used as research data. Such practices do not meet the principle of transparency and honesty and can undermine the relationship of trust between the research community and other stakeholders. If you are intending to participate in an online community as a researcher (for example, in online ethnography), Harwood and Ward (2013) recommend that you always make your role as a researcher clear. This can be by direct contact with each participant (via email or an online posting) or via a more widely disseminated announcement on a bulletin board.

Ethical issues also arise for the researcher wishing to make use of the data sources that are now available online in the form of user-generated videos, photographs, blogs and discussion board postings. In this context the notion of privacy is an interesting one. On the one hand, individuals have chosen to place their data in a public domain, open for all to see. On the other hand, as Hong and Thong (2013) point out, in doing so they have made their personal information more vulnerable. Moreover, despite the public nature of such postings, participants may nevertheless regard them as 'private' (Lomborg 2013: 23). Thus, although it is possible to argue that such comments are made on a public platform, and hence available for use, an alternative viewpoint is that the comments made by an individual were not made for research purposes and it cannot be inferred that there is an automatic right to view them as data in our research. This debate is still ongoing, but, as online researchers, it is our responsibility is to be aware of such ethical issues and always to ensure that in the collection, storage and reporting of data analysis we do not infringe on the anonymity, privacy and confidentiality of our respondents.

7.7.2 Reporting of online data

When reporting online data, as in the offline environment, you are similarly responsible for adhering to the ethical principle of transparency in the final reporting of data. In particular you should consider carefully whether to report your findings with or without verbatim comments, as this may conflict with the anonymity of an individual and thus with the principle of protecting the personal identity of respondents and avoiding distress or harm. Remember that a section of text in a research report can be copied into an Internet search engine and the originator identified as a result. Hair and Clark (2007) recommend that online researchers report the approach they have adopted with regard to ethical aspects of their work in order that the research practices and protocols used can be appropriately understood and assessed.

7.8 Understanding the ethical dimensions of your own research project

In order to help you to identify key ethical dimensions of your own research project we provide in Table 7.2 a series of questions that you can ask yourself before, during and after your study. We cannot be prescriptive in terms of providing answers to these questions because ultimately these are your decisions to take as the researcher, but these questions should help you by prompting you to think about ethical aspects of your work. As you look through them you may see that there are conflicts in terms of your ethical responsibility towards different stakeholders. For example, maintaining the confidentiality of a respondent regarding the information discussed in an in-depth business-to-business interview may conflict with the expected level of final reporting agreed by you with an organization. These issues should be identified and addressed during the planning stage. As a researcher you have to ensure that you consider all ethical principles and make appropriate decisions, irrespective of how they may affect or constrain your original research intentions. An illustration of the experience of dealing with ethical issues in a sensitive research topic area is given in Research in Practice 7.4.

RESEARCH IN PRACTICE 7.4

Researching online shopping addiction

With the rapid rise of the Internet, a growing area of interest to researchers today is the changes in consumer behaviour in relation to online shopping. This form of shopping has many new features to it that change the nature of the experience for the individual, in particular making it easier, more convenient and in some respects more enjoyable. As researchers looking at such human behaviour, we are sometimes interested to look at it along a normal–abnormal continuum. A study conducted by Dhandayudham and Rose (2013) sought to understand the phenomenon of problematic online shopping, which is where a shopper may be exhibiting compulsive or, more seriously, addictive online shopping behaviour.[1]

In order to undertake this investigation, the researchers needed to make contact with a large sample of online shoppers whose behaviour fell along the continuum of normal–abnormal behaviour. Given the sensitive nature of this research topic, the researchers considered a number of ethical issues when designing and implementing their study. They did this by considering the four ethical principles considered in this chapter. The research was the subject of ethical approval by the two separate institutions within which the two researchers worked.

The avoidance of harm, particularly from a psychological perspective, was a key consideration. A survey research design which used a paper-based questionnaire to collect data was applied. It was important to consider the avoidance of psychological harm which might have been caused by creating anxiety, distress or worry to the respondents when answering the questions. Linked to this was the need to be transparent and honest with participants regarding the research subject matter. The participants all responded to a notice calling for volunteer respondents to a study of online shopping. No coercion was involved and the participants could withdraw from the project at any point, even after taking part in the survey. A detailed explanation of the nature of the research was provided and the questionnaire was distributed face to face so that verbal explanations could also be given. Informed consent was obtained from each participant. In addition to these preventative actions, the researchers also took action to protect participants after they had completed the questionnaire. A 'helpline' telephone number was provided which allowed a participant to speak to an experienced counsellor should they feel that they had been negatively affected by any of the content or questions in the questionnaire or if the questionnaire had raised concerns in their mind about their own online shopping behaviour. At the beginning of the study, the participants' right to privacy was considered. Participants were reassured regarding the security of their personal details and responses. No personal information was collected and therefore a participant could not be identified individually in relation to their responses regarding their online shopping behaviour. The data was stored securely and destroyed after completion of the study.

Finally, the researchers needed to consider the overall integrity of the study and their responsibility within it. First, the justification for conducting such research was considered. The researchers justified the research on the grounds that such behaviour is important to understand from both a clinical and commercial (retail) perspective. The outcomes would help to improve clinical responses to such abnormal behaviour and also inform retail practice. Second, it is interesting to consider whether the researchers had a moral responsibility to act should the data indicate severely addictive behaviour by an individual participant. Given the deliberate lack of a link between personal details and data, it was not possible to identify any specific individual's behaviour. The researchers felt that their responsibility was towards the security of the data and that a duty of care towards the participants was met by the provision of the counselling support.

Table 7.2 Key ethical questions to ask about your research

What should I consider before the study?	What should I consider during the study?	What should I consider after the study?
• Will any physical or psychological harm be caused by my research?	• Do any of the respondents appear to be upset or distressed?	• Have I retained the informed consent forms for safe keeping, should there be any subsequent query?
• Have I put in place appropriate measures for the safety of participants and anyone else involved in the research?	• Am I aware of everyone's safety, including my own?	• Have I declared any affiliations when reporting my research?
• Have I pre-tested to check that I understand the impact of my research on respondents?	• Am I treating everyone with respect and dignity?	• Have I maintained the anonymity and confidentiality of the respondents in my final report?
• How will I ensure that coercion is not involved?	• Am I ensuring that participants are fully informed of the nature of the research?	• Have I met my obligations regarding data destruction, continued storage or return?
• Have I prepared information sheets and informed consent forms?	• Have I collected all the informed consent forms?	• If relevant, have I ensured the dissemination of my findings to the wider community?
• Have I ensured that the research is free of deception?	• Am I disclosing any researcher affiliations to participants?	• Have I met all my obligations to all stakeholders regarding the project?
• Have I put measures in place to ensure the anonymity and confidentiality of all participants?	• Am I complying with requirements for anonymity and confidentiality?	• Is the final research report free of misleading statements or misrepresentation of the data?
• Have I put in place arrangements for secure data storage?	• Am I storing data securely?	• Have I complied with all relevant ethical guidelines?
• Am I familiar with relevant Data Protection legislation?	• Am I compliant with Data Protection legislation?	
• Do I have permission to collect data from a particular source?	• Are my research activities adversely affecting anyone in the wider community?	
• Will there be any impact on the wider community or society by the implementation of my research project?	• Am I complying with relevant ethical guidelines?	
• Have I obtained relevant ethical approval?		

7.9 The role of codes of practice and ethics committees

Ethical guidelines and codes of practice are provided by many research and industry associations or governing bodies. They have emerged alongside a general increased awareness of ethical responsibilities and, specifically within the research community, concerns about the impact of unethical research. Ethics codes of practice provide guidance and procedures with respect to the conduct of research. DeLorme et al. (2001) suggest that they can serve a number of purposes. Firstly, they aim to protect participants from harm or distress, but they also set expectations for participants as to how they will be treated by researchers. Secondly, from a researcher's perspective they are intended to encourage appropriate ethical behaviour by providing guidelines for them, but also guarding them from moral and/or legal problems. Finally, they create awareness of best practice within the research community and thereby encourage those in society to support what researchers do. In Table 7.3 we provide links to different organizations' codes of practice or ethical guidelines. In addition, your own organization or professional body may have its own code of practice and, if you are studying at a university, your academic institution almost certainly will do so. Make sure that you are familiar with any applicable guidelines before starting your research.

Table 7.3 Research ethics: codes of practice and guidelines

Organization	Link to website
Academy of Management (US)	http://aom.org/About-AOM/Ethics.aspx
American Marketing Association (US)	www.marketingpower.com/AboutAMA/Pages/Statement%20of%20Ethics.aspx
The Association of Internet Researchers (AoIR)	http://aoir.org/reports/ethics2.pdf
British Psychological Society (UK)	www.bps.org.uk/what-we-do/ethics-standards/ethics-standards
Economic and Social Research Council (ESRC)	www.esrc.ac.uk/about-esrc/information/research-ethics.aspx
ESOMAR (World guidelines)	www.esomar.org/publications-store/codes-guidelines.php
The Market Research Society (UK)	www.mrs.org.uk/standards/code_of_conduct/

7.9.1 Research ethics committees

Many organizations, including most universities in the UK, have **research ethics committees** (RECs) or an equivalent body which is responsible for ensuring that appropriate ethical standards of research conduct are maintained. In a university, for example, this may involve the formulating and maintaining of ethical guidelines and codes of practice, reviewing research applications from an ethical point of view and providing advice on matters relating to research ethics. There is considerable variation in the roles and responsibilities of RECs within universities, for example, in terms of what types of research are subject to formal review and to what degree of detail, but if you are a student researcher you should familiarize yourself early on in your project with any requirements that will be placed on your research.

7.9.2 Gaining ethical approval

Alongside the development of codes of ethics, many organizations, particularly academic institutions, have developed formal requirements for the ethical approval of proposed research projects. Approval typically involves the researcher in submitting a written request for ethical approval. Depending on the nature of the research and the policies in place, this may be very detailed, describing all aspects of the proposed research in full. Alternatively, it may be a brief summary of the proposed research which is then reviewed to see whether further ethical clearance is necessary. The latter might happen, for example, if the proposed project involved working with vulnerable groups and it was felt that closer scrutiny was required.

It is your responsibility as the researcher to be aware of your institution's procedure for approval and what is required of you. Make sure that you take ethical considerations into account at the planning stage so that you can design a research project that meets the requirements of ethical research. If your research is in an ethically sensitive topic (such as experiments on humans or research with vulnerable groups) you will need to be particularly clear regarding your plans and be prepared for further scrutiny before being allowed to proceed. If you are unsure about any ethical matters relating to your proposed project, you should seek advice from your supervisor or a representative from your institution's REC. Do not begin your research proper until you have secured approval to do so. Note that in some cases you may also have to get approval from more than one body (for example, research in healthcare environments may also require approval of the relevant healthcare authority).

7.9.3 Following rules or behaving ethically?

Codes of practice, ethics committees, approval processes and so on have been developed with the purpose of alerting individuals to the ways in which their decision making or behaviour may contradict ethical criteria or impact on the rights of others. It is relevant to question whether or not this serves to develop ethical behaviour or just blind rule following. Bell and Bryman (2007: 63) point out that the imposition of codes of practice upon individuals 'may encourage instrumental compliance with minimal ethical obligations'. We have to recognize the distinction between merely following ethical procedures (such as completing approval forms or obtaining informed consent forms) and actively recognizing and accepting our responsibility for the rightness of our actions within a particular situation and adjusting our behaviour accordingly. We debate this issue further in Critical Commentary 7.1.

CRITICAL COMMENTARY 7.1

The growth of ethical regulation

The ethical regulation of social and managerial research is not without its critics. Martyn Hammersley, for example, questions the rise of 'ethical enthusiasm' and the movement in social research that 'treats ethicality as the pre-eminent requirement' (Hammersley 2009: 213). Ethical regulation first emerged in the field of healthcare and medical research, where the potential for harm is far greater, given the physical nature of many of the areas of investigation, such as drug trials. Hammersley argues that social researchers have adopted the same medical model, even though the potential for harm within the social sciences is considerably less. Instead he suggests that journalism is perhaps a more appropriate model for comparison, as both pursue social enquiry and yet the ethical demands of social research are far more stringent. Whilst we must recognize that we have a duty of care and the need to adhere to ethical standards such as in relation to privacy, confidentiality and honesty, Hammersley questions whether there is a need for the level of authority and control that is currently enforced via university ethical approval committees or funding bodies such as the Economic and Social Research Council (ESRC), which, in the UK, insists on compliance by organizations wanting to receive research funding. Furthermore, Hammersley asks, what is the basis for assuming that their expertise in ethical decision making is superior to the capability of an individual researcher? As researchers are we not capable of making autonomous decisions based on our own judgement and expertise?

These are interesting questions for us to consider and Hammersley (2009) suggests that there are three consequences of the current level of ethical regulation and requirement for approval. First, it has created an increased level of administrative burden, particularly when conducting funded research. Second, it may discourage researchers from undertaking certain forms of research and in some instances research may not now be feasible for many researchers (e.g. involving children). Third, we can question whether heavy regulation encourages researchers to feel that their own ethical responsibility has been transferred to an ethics committee and encourages a tick box mentality towards adherence.

Whilst we raise these alternative views, we emphasize that it is a requirement to meet ethical standards, to follow ethical regulations and obtain ethical approval for your researcher project. However, we must be aware of the distinction between merely following ethical instructions and taking responsibility ourselves for behaving ethically as researchers.

KEY LEARNING POINTS

- Ethics in research is concerned with the rights and wrongs of how we conduct a research project. Ethical considerations should be made in relation to all stake-holders who are involved in, or affected by, a particular project.
- There are four key ethical principles to consider when planning a research project: avoidance of harm or loss of dignity; transparency and honesty; right to privacy; and researcher integrity. Each should be considered in terms of four key stakeholder groups: the researcher; the participants in the research study; the organization or institution on whose behalf the study is being undertaken; and the wider society or community.
- The rise of the Internet as a medium for research means that researchers should be alert to how the four ethical principles apply in that context. We must still respect

the privacy, anonymity and confidentiality of respondents and maintain transparency and honesty in the handling and reporting of data.
- Ethical considerations should be identified at the planning stage of a research
  project and documented during the planning stage.
- Ethical codes of practice and guidelines have been produced by the leading
  research bodies. Academic institutions and funding bodies will have their own
  ethical regulation and approval procedures. It is imperative that a research project
  is compliant with such regulation and that appropriate ethical approval is obtained
  prior to commencing a research project.

NEXT STEPS

7.1   **Preparing the ground**. Familiarize yourself with any ethical guidelines or codes
of practice that are relevant for your project, for example, those of the academic
institution at which you are studying or of the organization or professional body
of which you are a member.

7.2   **Identifying ethical issues**. Before undertaking this activity, look again at Table
7.2, where we provide you with a series of questions to ask yourself about the
ethical context before, during and after your research project. Then consider
which of the following four aspects of your research design may raise an ethical
issue for you: avoidance of harm or loss of dignity; transparency and honesty;
right to privacy; and researcher integrity. Think about how you are going to
address them.

7.3   **Preparing to apply for ethical approval**. Confirm the ethical approval process
that applies to your project and start preparing the necessary documentation,
including information sheets and consent forms.

Further reading

For further reading, please see the companion website.

References

AoM (2006). *Code of ethics* [online]. Briarcliff Manor, NY: Academy of Management. Available
from: http://aom.org/uploadedFiles/About_AOM/Governance/AOM_Code_of_Ethics.pdf
[Accessed 13 November 2013].

Bell, E. and Bryman, A. (2007). 'The ethics of management research: An exploratory content
analysis', *British Journal of Management*, 18(1), 63–77.

Cornwall, A. and Jewkes, R. (1995). 'What is participatory research?', *Social Science &
Medicine*, 41(12), 1667–76.

DeLorme, D. E., Zinkhan, G. M. and French, W. (2001). 'Ethics and the internet: Issues
associated with qualitative research', *Journal of Business Ethics*, 33(4), 271–86.

Dhandayudham, A. and Rose, S. (2013). An exploratory study of the indicators of online shopping addiction. *First International Conference on Behavioral Addictions.* Budapest.

ESOMAR (2005). *ESOMAR world research codes and guidelines. Mystery shopping studies* [online]. ESOMAR. Available from: www.esomar.org/uploads/public/knowledge-and-standards/codes-and-guidelines/ESOMAR_Codes-and-Guidelines_MysteryShopping.pdf [Accessed 7 August 2013].

ESRC (2012). *ESRC framework for research ethics (FRE) 2010. Updated September 2012* [online]. Swindon: Economic and Social Resarch Council. Available from: www.esrc.ac.uk/_images/Framework-for-Research-Ethics_tcm8–4586.pdf [Accessed 13 November 2013].

Hair, N. and Clark, M. (2007). 'The ethical dilemmas and challenges of ethnographic research in electronic communities', *International Journal of Market Research*, 49(6), 781–800.

Hammersley, M. (2009). 'Against the ethicists: On the evils of ethical regulation', *International Journal of Social Research Methodology*, 12(3), 211–25.

Harwood, T. G. and Ward, J. (2013). 'Market research within 3D virtual worlds: An examination of pertinent issues', *International Journal of Market Research*, 55(2), 247–65.

Hong, W. and Thong, J. Y. L. (2013). 'Internet privacy concerns: An integrated conceptualization and four empirical studies', *MIS Quarterly*, 37(1), 275–98.

Lomborg, S. (2013). 'Personal internet archives and ethics', *Research Ethics*, 9(1), 20–31.

McGivern, Y. (2006). *The practice of market and social research: An introduction.* Harlow: Prentice Hall.

Melé, D. (2012). *Management ethics: Placing ethics at the core of good management.* Basingstoke: Palgrave Macmillan.

Nairn, A. (2009). 'Research ethics in the vitual world', *International Journal of Market Reseach*, 15(2), 276–8.

Remenyi, D., Williams, B., Money, A. and Swartz, E. (1998). *Doing research in business and management: An introduction to process and method.* London: Sage Publications.

Smith, L., Bowcott, O. and Evans, R. (2008). Porton Down veterans awarded £3m compensation [online]. *Guardian.* Available from: www.theguardian.com/politics/2008/jan/31/politicalnews.uk1 [Accessed 17 October 2013].

Wilson, A. M. (2001). 'Mystery shopping: Using deception to measure service peformance', *Psychology and Marketing*, 18(7), 721–34.

Note

1   Dhandayudham, A. (2012). *Problem online shopping behavior: Definition, investigation and codes of conduct.* MBA dissertation submission. Henley Business School, University of Reading.

8 Planning and managing your research project

CHAPTER SUMMARY

The key topics covered in this chapter are:

- selecting your research design
- planning your research project
- managing your research project
- keeping a research diary
- writing a research proposal.

8.1 Introduction

Carrying out a research project is not just an intellectual activity. It requires the application of practical management skills, effective engagement with multiple stakeholders and the commitment of time and other resources. A successful research project involves a series of decisions at both the planning and implementation stages. In this chapter we look at how you reach these decisions. We start with guidance on how to select the most appropriate research design for your project and the factors that you should consider when making your decision. Having selected your research design, you will then need to plan your project in terms of the activities you need to carry out and the time and other resources you will need, so we discuss what to consider at the planning stage. You will also need to think about how to manage your project once it is underway, so we move on to look at the various activities that are involved in doing so effectively. As you work you will need to keep track of your thoughts and reflections on your project and your role in it. To help you do this we introduce the idea of a research diary or journal. Finally, we look at how to prepare a research proposal. This is a document written at the start of your project, for review by a supervisor, client or funding body, that sets out your proposed research and how you will carry it out. We provide you with guidance as to the structure and content of an effective research proposal.

8.2 Selecting a research design

Before you can begin detailed planning, you will need to decide what type of research design is appropriate for your research project. Your decision will be influenced by a number of factors as we show in Figure 8.1. Some of these relate to the nature of the research problem itself, others to practical aspects of the project or to you as the researcher. As you consider each in turn, write down your thoughts, as these will help you when it comes to describing and justifying your research design in your final report. These notes will also be useful to you as the basis of your research proposal.

8.2.1 Research question(s)

The starting point for choosing a design should be your research questions. This is because the design must be capable of providing you with appropriate data from which to answer your research questions and so resolve your research problem. To help you to link your choice of research design to your research questions, Table 8.1 maps different research designs onto the three generic research question types identified

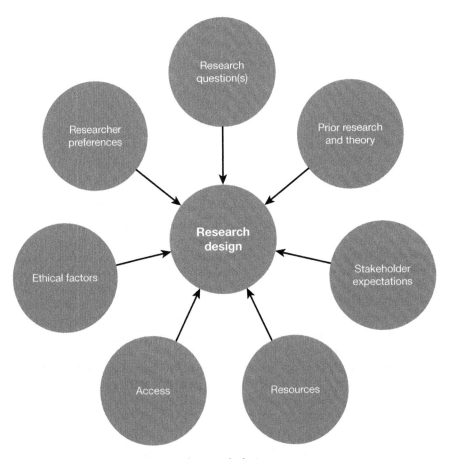

Figure 8.1 Factors influencing choice of research design

in Chapter 2 and discussed in Chapter 5. In Table 8.1 we have split out quantitative and qualitative research methods to emphasize that they each offer different insights into the research question(s) under investigation. Mixed method designs may also be appropriate where a single method will not be adequate to address all aspects of your research questions. For further details on each design, you should refer back to the relevant sections in Chapter 6.

Guidelines such as in Table 8.1 provide a useful starting point for thinking about how to align your research design with your research questions. However, they should not be treated as a prescriptive framework in which the required design is simply 'read off' from the table. Developing a research design requires careful thought and reflection about your research problem, along with a sound understanding of the options available. Your decision process must also take into account the many other factors that can influence the final choice of research design and which we explore next.

8.2.2 Prior research and theory

Your critical review of literature will give you a thorough understanding of the research problem, including how it has been researched in the past. Prior research can be a useful source of inspiration and methods for your own project. For example, you may decide to replicate a study found in the literature in a different context (with, of course, appropriate acknowledgement to the original research). Alternatively, you may make use of specific elements of an earlier study, such as measurement scales in a questionnaire, that have been shown to be useful and reliable. At the same time, prior research can also help you to identify whether certain approaches to research are commonly used or widely accepted in a particular field. Your chosen research field may have developed specific research designs that are particularly appropriate to the nature of the problem under investigation, thereby providing you with a useful starting point when selecting your own research design.

8.2.3 Stakeholder expectations

As a researcher, decisions about your research design are rarely taken in isolation. For many research projects, key stakeholders will have to give explicit approval before the project can proceed. Gaining such approval may be necessary in a variety of situations. As a student researcher you will probably have to submit a research proposal and gain agreement from your supervisor before starting your research project. In such cases you will have to ensure that your proposed research design meets the requirements for your programme of study. Alternatively, approval may be required if you are applying for research funding or if you are conducting research for and on behalf of another body such as your own organization as an insider researcher. In such situations the expectations of organizational stakeholders will be set by their perceptions of the value to them of the research you are proposing to carry out. Gaining formal approval goes beyond choice of the research design, so we return to this important aspect of research planning at the end of this chapter. Note that as well as setting explicit requirements for your project, stakeholders may also have expectations and preferences regarding what they believe are suitable research methods based on their own experiences, professional background and so on. It is important

Table 8.1 Mapping research questions to research designs

Type of research question	Quantitative methods		Qualitative methods	
	Possible research focus	Possible research design(s)	Possible research focus	Possible research design(s)
What? (*descriptive questions*)	• Measurement and frequency distribution of key variables of a population or phenomenon • Description of aggregate properties of a population or phenomenon	• Descriptive surveys • Content analysis (for text)	• In-depth, thick description of a phenomenon and its context • Lived experience and perspectives of those involved in a particular situation • Understanding of the diversity of a phenomenon	• Interview study • Ethnography • Case study • Qualitative content analysis (for text)
Why? (*explanatory questions*)	• Testing of explanatory theory • Measurement of the impact of one variable on another • Prediction of a dependent variable from the value of one or more independent variables	• Experiments and quasi-experiments • Non-experimental explanatory designs (e.g. natural experiment, analytic survey) • Content analysis (for testing the impact of message content)	• Building explanatory theory • Identification of causal mechanisms, process and context • Understanding of actors' reasoning, values and beliefs from their perspective	• Case study • Grounded theory • Action research • Interview study • Ethnography
How? (*process questions*)	• Testing of process theory • Modelling of development of phenomena over time	• Analytic survey (for testing causal models) • Simulations	• Building process theory • Identification of process of change and development • Analysis of social construction of phenomena through social processes and language	• Grounded theory • Case study • Ethnography • Conversation analysis • Critical discourse analysis

to be aware of these when considering your choice of design. In some cases, considerable negotiation may be needed to reach agreement on what is acceptable as an approach. Remember, however, that you must always ensure that your research design is able to answer the research questions you have set.

8.2.4 Resources

Researchers rarely enjoy unlimited availability of resources such as time, money, people or technology. Lack of resources can significantly constrain the scale and scope of a research project. In some circumstances, resource limitations can actually prevent the desired research approach being carried out. The selection of a research design must therefore take into account practical resource constraints. Do you have sufficient time or travel budget, for example, to conduct a face-to-face interview study with respondents in different countries? Do you have sufficient funds to acquire specialized software for a computer simulation design? Thus, whilst resource constraints should not determine the research design, you will have to be aware of their potential impact and find ways of managing them at the design and planning stage. In particular, be aware of any time limits, especially with regard to submission dates for qualification programmes and deadlines for commercial projects.

8.2.5 Access

As researchers we may be able to think of many interesting research problems and ways of investigating them but the ultimate feasibility of many research projects is constrained by the availability of, and access to, appropriate sources of data. This may be access to a sufficient number of suitable respondents who will agree to be interviewed or to take part in a survey for primary research, or it may be access to relevant documents or databases for secondary analysis. Access to data is therefore an important consideration when choosing your research design because different research designs place different demands on data collection. Accessibility may not be an easy issue to assess at the start of a project and problems are often recognized or experienced only part way through a project (sometimes with disastrous consequences). It is therefore important to develop a good strategy for gaining and maintaining access early in your project, a topic we return to in Chapter 9 when we discuss sampling for data collection in more detail.

8.2.6 Ethical factors

It is essential that your research design take account of appropriate ethical standards and practices as discussed in Chapter 7. Ethical issues must be considered right from the start of the project, as these can affect your design decisions, especially when the research involves respondents from potentially vulnerable groups or involves some form of researcher intervention such as in an experiment. In addition, as we highlighted in Chapter 7, many research projects require that formal ethical approval is obtained before you begin data collection. Ensure that you think through the ethical implications of your proposed research design at an early stage, allow enough time to obtain ethical approval and consider alternative design options should approval be denied.

8.2.7 Researcher preferences

Your own philosophical orientation, interests, preferences, experiences and skills will all influence your choice of research design, just as they will influence your choice of research topic. You may instinctively be more comfortable with some research methods and techniques than others. Alternatively, you may wish to gain new research skills or to build on particular skills you have already developed. The role of personal preference in design choice is a contentious subject because, as Buchanan and Bryman (2007: 495) note, 'novice researchers are typically instructed not to allow personal preference and bias to intrude on "technical" decisions concerning research methods'. However, they go on to ask, 'should researchers be encouraged to experience guilt with respect to personal beliefs and passions, with respect to the skills that they have acquired, practised, and honed?' The answer is probably 'no', but the influence of personal preferences on the choice of research design should nevertheless be the subject of reflection by the researcher, as we have discussed in Chapter 1. In addition, a research project can be a great opportunity to build your skills and competencies in research and in a new topic area by moving beyond your comfort zone. Ultimately, however, you will still have to be able to complete the project successfully, so give careful thought to the feasibility of a project in terms of your current levels of knowledge and personal circumstances.

8.3 Planning your research project

Having chosen your overall research design, you should turn your attention to planning how you will carry out the project itself. Whether you are researching in an academic or organizational setting, effective planning will be an important factor in achieving a successful outcome. Planning a research project does not have to be enormously complex. With the exception of large-scale research projects with multiple researchers, you will usually need to use only some basic techniques of project management with which you are probably already familiar. You should aim to produce a project plan that identifies the following elements:

- project activities and deliverables
- project time schedule
- project risks.

If there is a larger research team involved, a resource schedule showing who is carrying out the various tasks is also useful. The resulting plan can then feed into your research proposal and be used as your guide during your project. Table 8.2 outlines the steps in generating a plan for a simple project.

8.3.1 Project activities

The precise activities that you will need to carry out depend on the details of the project. We can, however, identify some typical activities based on our five-stage research model and the generic elements of research design. We summarize these activities for a typical student research project in Table 8.3, to help you start your planning. You should adjust the content to match the format of your particular project.

Table 8.2 Developing a plan for your research project

Step	Task
1	Identify the key activities and deliverables in the project.
2	Estimate how long each activity will take and what resources you will need.
3	Work out the relationships and dependencies between the different activities. For example, do some activities (such as data collection) have to be carried out before others (such as data analysis) or can some be worked on in parallel?
4	Identify any schedule constraints such as deadlines, public holidays, resource availability, turnaround times for feedback and so on.
5	Develop a schedule for time and (where needed) for resources.
6	Identify and develop a plan for managing risks in the project.

Table 8.3 Typical activities in a student research project

Action	Typical activities	Typical outputs
Research design and planning	• Choose research design • Develop research project plan	• Research proposal • Ethical approval submission
Literature review	• Search, capture, synthesize and present critical review of relevant literature	• Draft of literature review section for final report
Data collection	• Finalize sampling plan • Develop, pre-test and pilot data collection instruments (e.g. questionnaire or interview guide) • Carry out data collection plan	• Sampling plan • Data collection instruments • Raw data • Draft of research design section for final report
Data analysis	• Prepare data for analysis • Analyse data • Draw conclusions	• Draft of analysis and findings section for final report
Writing up	• Final draft of report • Review of draft with supervisor • Final editing • Printing, binding and submission	• Final draft • Final submission of report

Note that we have included interim outputs in the form of draft work, on which you may have the opportunity to get feedback from your supervisor if you have one.

8.3.2 Developing a time schedule

One of the biggest challenges in planning a research project is working out how long you will need for the various activities. This is partly because doing research can be highly dependent upon the availability of others, for example, interview respondents, whose availability may be unknown at the start of the project. In addition, it can be hard to gauge how long certain activities will take you without prior experience (for example, doing data analysis for the first time). Unfortunately it is very difficult to give firm guidance here because it depends so much on the nature of the project, the willingness of others to participate, scheduling arrangements and your own circumstances and experience as a researcher (especially if you are researching for your studies while working full time). We therefore provide the following tips which may help you avoid drawing up an over-optimistic time schedule.

- Allow sufficient time for your literature review. Students often underestimate the time this will take. Becoming familiar with the search process, locating and reading articles and capturing the right information will take a significant amount of time.
- Be realistic about how long it will take you to arrange access to respondents and for them to be available to participate. This is particularly important when organizing appointments for face-to-face interviews. The more senior the person or the busier their lifestyle, the more difficult it will be to schedule appointments. Do not expect your research participants to be available to see you at short notice, so start planning this part of your research early if you are doing an interview study.
- Always factor in turnaround times for any forms of response to correspondence or contact from you (including return of questionnaires, review of drafts by a supervisor, requests for access and so on), whether it is electronic or not.
- Allow time for pre-testing and piloting any data collection instrument (such as a questionnaire) that you plan to use.
- Do not underestimate the time it takes to carry out data analysis, particularly if you are doing it for the first time.
- Allow sufficient time for writing up. We recommend that you write your research report as your project progresses. This should reduce the time it takes you to complete the final report but you will still need time to collate, review and edit the final version.
- Finally, allow enough time for printing, binding and submission if you have to produce a hard copy of your report.

Once you have identified the activities and their dependencies and estimated how long each will take you can draw up the time schedule for your project. This can be done as a table but is probably most easily communicated to others using a Gantt chart as shown in Figure 8.2 for a research project for a part-time student.

8.3.3 Assessing risk

A research risk is any uncertain event or condition that, if it occurs, has an effect upon the project. Therefore identifying risks is an important step when planning your research. We are primarily concerned with those risks that would have a negative effect and in Table 8.4 have listed some of the risks that we see commonly encountered during student research projects. Similar risks can arise in other research projects but an important additional risk factor for research projects that are done for a commercial or other client face is the problem of scope creep as we discussed in Chapter 2. Do not let your project get out of hand as a result.

ID	Task Name	Start	Finish	Duration	Nov 2013 3/11	10/11	17/11	24/11	1/12	Dec 2013 8/12	15/12	22/12	29/12	5/1	12/1	Jan 2014 19/1	26/1	2/2	9/2	Feb 2014 16/2	23/2	2/3	Mar 2014 9/3
1	Prepare and submit proposal	01/11/2013	11/11/2013	7d																			
2	Literature review	12/11/2013	10/12/2013	21d																			
3	Finalize sampling plan	11/12/2013	16/12/2013	4d																			
4	Questionnaire design	11/12/2013	19/12/2013	7d																			
5	Questionnaire pre-test and pilot	20/12/2013	26/12/2013	5d																			
6	Administer the questionnaire	27/12/2013	15/01/2014	14d																			
7	Draft method section of report	27/12/2013	01/01/2014	4d																			
8	Data preparation	16/01/2014	17/01/2014	2d																			
9	Data analysis	20/01/2014	31/01/2014	10d																			
10	Draft analysis and findings	03/02/2014	06/02/2014	4d																			
11	Draft final report	07/02/2014	25/02/2014	14d																			
12	Final editing	27/02/2014	05/03/2014	5d																			
13	Printing, binding and submission	06/03/2014	11/03/2014	4d																			

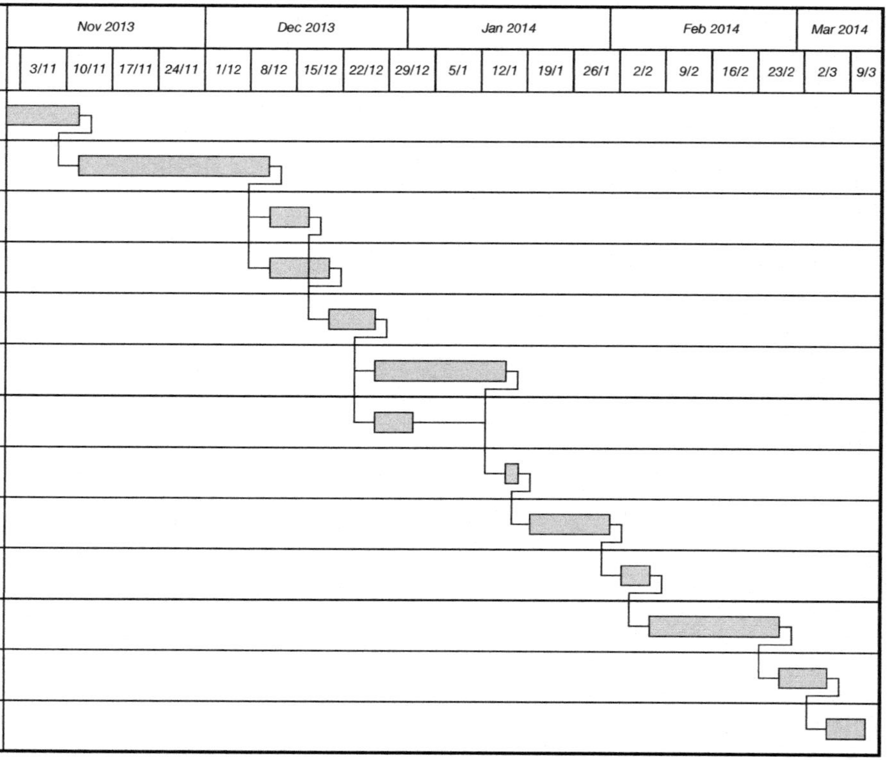

Figure 8.2 Example Gantt chart time schedule

PART II

Table 8.4 Example risks in a student research project

Action	Example risks	Example avoidance or mitigation strategies
Research design and planning	• Research proposal rejected • Ethical approval rejected	• Ensure you understand and adhere to the proposal guidelines • Discuss your ideas with potential supervisor or other tutors before submitting • Ensure that you understand and follow ethical guidelines; seek advice if unsure. • Be prepared to make changes and resubmit
Literature review	• Unable to access suitable sources	• Read around the literature prior to starting the topic to confirm availability of and access to suitable literature
Data collection	• Unable to access research site, required sample and/or achieve required sample size • Loss or corruption of data	• Negotiate and agree access to research site at the planning stage • Identify target population and sampling frame early in the project • Pre-test and pilot questionnaire or other data collection instrument to test access levels • Ensure you store data securely and have more than one secure back-up copy
Data analysis	• Missing/poor-quality data • Unable to analyse the data as planned, due to lack of skills • Data do not provide useful insights	• Pre-test and pilot questionnaire or other data collection instrument to reduce missing data problems and ensure data quality • Ensure that you have or can build the necessary analysis skills when deciding your research design • Choose research questions and a research design that will generate useful insights even if the results are not what was expected
Writing up	• Lack of information on procedures followed during data collection and analysis • Lack of time to write up before submission deadline	• Use a research diary to capture relevant details during your project • Begin drafting your report early during the project

Once you have identified possible risks you can prioritize them using a simple low/medium/high classification and develop strategies for avoiding or mitigating them as we have shown in Table 8.4. Make sure that you monitor risks as the project unfolds.

8.4 Managing your research project

Like any other project, research requires active management as well as careful planning. In particular you will have to pay careful attention to the management of time, risks, key stakeholders and your data once your project is underway.

8.4.1 Keeping to time

Once you have started your project you will need to monitor its progress according to your project plan. If you are the only researcher conducting your own project, then keeping the project to the time schedule is really down to your own time management skills and your ability to motivate other stakeholders to participate and support you as necessary. You may have to adjust your time schedule as the study progresses in the light of any changes that occur. Remain alert to any potentially serious disruptions to your schedule. If you are conducting the project for academic study, you should ensure that your assigned supervisor, as well as any sponsor you may be working with, is kept up to date with the progress of your study and any potential disruptions.

If you are working as part of a project team, then more formal project monitoring and reporting will be needed. You should provide regular updates of completion of elements of the study and identify any potential changes to the original schedule. Remember that managing expectations is an important aspect of a successful research project. Whichever type of project you are undertaking, use your Gantt chart to track progress, identify upcoming problems when they start to arise and communicate with key stakeholders clearly and appropriately. Be prepared to take action if something is obviously going off track.

8.4.2 Managing risk

If you have carried out a risk assessment as part of your project plan, then you will be aware of the potential difficulties that may arise. Once the project has commenced you should regularly refer to your risk assessment and consider the level of threat that each item continues to pose to the success of your project. As the project progresses you should be able to remove or downgrade the threat posed by different risks. Nevertheless you may encounter a situation where a risk to your project, such as the failure to collect sufficient data, actually occurs. As soon as you are aware of such a problem you should inform relevant stakeholder(s), such as your academic supervisor. Decisions will then need to be made in terms of alternative courses of action or, in the worst-case scenario, to halt the project pending more radical review of the problems and potential solutions. Whatever the case, ensure that you actively manage risk and do not just wait for things to go wrong.

8.4.3 Managing stakeholders

Throughout your project, you must ensure that you manage your relationships with key stakeholders. Engaging with stakeholders during your research is about fully understanding their expectations and managing these throughout your project. This is primarily done through close and accurate communication at both the planning and implementation stages. The level of contact will vary, depending on the type of project and your own status as student researcher or insider researcher.

Managing your project as a student researcher

When managing a research project that forms part of an academic qualification you will have one or more stakeholder(s) within the academic institution, such as your supervisor and perhaps other tutors or programme management, with whom you will interact. Your supervisor in particular will play a key role in your project. The relationship that you develop with your supervisor is therefore crucial to both the success of your research and your enjoyment of the process. The role and responsibilities of supervisors may vary from institution to institution, so we recommend that you make sure you familiarize yourself with any guidelines from your institution about the role of the supervisor. You should view your supervisor as a core resource in terms of knowledge and advice, who can become a close mentor and supporter during your research project. Take time to get to know your supervisor, and agree at the outset how you wish to work together. Establishing a few ground rules at the start can ensure that you gain the maximum benefit from this important relationship.

When carrying out a project as a student researcher it is essential that you make yourself familiar with all the academic requirements and institutional processes to which you must adhere. It is likely that the institution will provide you with this information in the guidance documents, which you should consult regularly during the project. Key aspects of this guidance will be the research proposal, required format for reporting, criteria for assessment and the time deadline for delivery. Failure to adhere to any such guidance may lead to failure to meet the requirements for your degree.

Managing your project as an insider researcher

If you are an insider researcher, doing research in or on behalf of your own organization, you will need to take into account the potential challenges that can arise as a result of being both a researcher and an organizational member. These have been categorized as 'organizational, professional and personal' by Costley et al. (2010: 1), who recognize the effects that they can have on your role as a researcher as well as on the outcome of your project. From an organizational perspective, being on the inside as an employee of the organization means that you will have pre-existing relationships with others with whom you may have close working contact. This position will have advantages. It will mean that you have deeper knowledge of the organization (for example its personnel, structure and products) and perhaps direct experience of the research problem itself. At the same time, as a researcher you will draw from your professional and personal life in terms of your past experiences, knowledge, skills and personal values.

As a researcher on the inside of an organization there will be other organizational members that you work with in your regular role and with whom you will interact and whose expectations you have to manage during the research project. In some cases, internal politics and power plays can create difficulties for the insider researcher. One way to avoid being caught up in all of this is to maintain an open and relatively neutral stance in relation to the viewpoints of others. This will in part be achieved by maintaining good communication and providing regular progress updates with relevant stakeholders. Even so, being an insider researcher can require strong interpersonal and communication skills to manage the ambiguities and tensions that your dual role as a researcher and organizational member can throw up. We give an example of a chief executive conducting insider research as a student researcher in Research in Practice 8.1.

RESEARCH IN PRACTICE 8.1

CEO as insider researcher

Many organizations in the non-profit sector rely on the support of volunteers who work for them. For her MBA final project Beverley Pass, CEO of a small charity, wanted to learn more about managing a volunteer workforce because her own organization relies heavily on the commitment and support of a team of volunteers.[1] She would therefore be taking the role of 'insider researcher' when running focus groups with her own volunteers. This threw up two key challenges.

First, the invitation to participate in the research would come directly from the CEO, so volunteers might feel obliged to attend, raising concerns about informed consent. Beverley therefore went out of her way to stress in her invitation to participate that there was no obligation to take part in the focus groups. She was also aware that her role as CEO might influence the data collected if participants were reluctant to talk about certain issues. She therefore explained that she was looking more broadly at the management of volunteers in the charity sector. This allowed participants to draw on other volunteer work they had done and not just on their experiences of the current organization and therefore, by implication, of Beverley and her management team.

Second, whilst facilitating focus groups of volunteers, Beverley became aware of the dynamics at play in managing the discussions. As CEO Beverley was very well informed about the topic and had an interest in the subject in terms of her research, but also in her role as CEO. As Beverley explained to one of the authors: 'sometimes, as the conversation progressed, I found it difficult to determine what to ask them. As issues arose that I found interesting I wanted to pursue them in my role as the CEO but they weren't necessarily part of my research. I had to keep asking myself, am I interested because it is part of my research or am I interested because I am the CEO?' This example underlines the difficulty for the insider researcher of separating their organizational role from their research role.

Managing a research project client or sponsor

Many management research projects involve working closely in conjunction with an organization, institution or professional body that either acts as the client for your research or facilitates it, for example, by allowing access and providing practical support. In either case you will need to manage the relationships with the key stakeholders in that organization. If the organization is acting as the client for your research, ensure that you agree the research objectives and deliverables, how you will carry out the investigation and what support you require from the organization. If you are doing the research as part of an academic qualification, be aware that the client organization's expectations in terms of the format of any output may be quite different. It may, for example, prefer a shorter, consultancy-style report or an oral presentation to a lengthy academic dissertation. When the organization is acting in a sponsorship role by granting you access to its site, personnel and data, you will need to agree ground rules in terms of how the research will be carried out and any specific issues regarding confidentiality, access and so on. No matter what your research situation is, ensure that you work to agreed rules and deadlines. Document your research activities and keep in regular communication with key stakeholders as the project unfolds.

8.4.4 *Managing your data*

A research project generates a huge amount of data in both digital and hard-copy format. Some of this will be the result of your literature review, much of it gathered as part of your data collection for your own research, and still more of it generated by you in the form of notes, analysis and so on. At the outset of your project you should think carefully about how you plan to capture, store and manage all of this. Set up a suitable secure filing system for both digital and paper documents. As the project unfolds, make sure that you can identify different versions of documents that you produce, as it is very easy to lose track of what you are doing. Finally, make sure that you have secure back-up of your data, kept separately from your working copies. Loss of data or of a draft of the final report due to computer failure or fire will require you to repeat many hours of hard work.

8.5 Keeping a research diary

One of the most valuable tools available to a researcher is a research diary or research journal. This is not an appointments calendar but a working document in which you record relevant information as you proceed through your project. As well as factual information such as dates of interviews or notes from discussions with your supervisor, it should include the thinking behind your decisions, such as why you chose a particular research design and your personal observations and reflections on your research and your role in it. As Hughes (2000) puts it, the focus of the diary is 'information about the researcher, what the researcher does, and the process of research'. Some of the aims of a research diary are (Jankowicz 2005):

- to generate a history of the research project by recording a summary of all of the decisions and activities you undertake and the outcomes of those activities

- to record your thinking about the research process as it happens
- to act as a place to record ideas as they occur to you and your thoughts as to future directions for the research
- to act as a record of people, places, or documents that you encounter during the research process
- to provide a place for reflecting on your own practices as a researcher and your research skills
- to provide a record on which you can base a reflective account of the project and your participation in it.

There are several different ways you can keep a research diary. Some researchers prefer a conventional notebook, others use a loose-leaf binder. If you use the latter you may want to use pre-prepared forms as we show in Research in Practice 8.2.

PART II

RESEARCH IN PRACTICE 8.2

Example research diary format

Although there is no standardized pre-set format for a research diary, it useful to think about the sort of information that you will want to record. The example here shows a possible layout for a diary using pre-prepared forms to be kept in a loose-leaf binder. This version makes it easy to track activities and record them for future reference.

Date	Activity	People involved	Aim	Outcome	Personal observations and reflections
6 March 2013	First meeting with client	Client, self	Agree expectations and deliverables; agree access and timescale	Draft terms of reference agreed with client. Outline project plan prepared. Follow-up meeting booked for 5 April 11	An exciting project. Client seems genuinely committed to finding a solution but I am worried that the scope of the project might creep as we get further down the road. Timings look a bit tight – need to ensure that access is arranged quickly
10 March 2013	Begin literature review	Self	Become familiar with online literature searching. Begin locating sources of relevant literature	Much more confident with using online journals. Located ten relevant literature sources	I have realized that my next action must be to set up a data storage system and build more time into my schedule for the literature stage. There is a lot out there and it's going to take some time!
15 March 2013	...	...	...	...	...

Alternatively, you may prefer to record your ideas electronically on a laptop, tablet or smartphone. The increased availability of note-taking software programs and apps makes this a very attractive option for those who like working in a digital environment. Regardless of the medium you use, do not feel constrained just to use plain text in your diary. Mind maps, sketches, diagrams or voice recordings can be equally valuable. Hughes (2000) suggests that the researcher use a diary every day. As you work on your project write an entry at regular intervals, even during periods when you are not actively working on the project. Your research diary will act as a mechanism for maintaining momentum in your project but will also be a valuable resource when you come to write up your project and reflect on your own performance as a researcher.

8.6 Preparing a research proposal

The research proposal is a document that provides an overview of the intended research. It sets out the purpose of the research and a plan for how it will be carried out. The proposal should contain a clear statement of your proposed design and the selection that you have made, with supporting rationale. Proposals are used in a variety of research situations, including:

- *Research as part of a qualification*, where the research proposal must usually be approved by the academic institution before the candidate can proceed with the research. Here approval requires meeting the terms of reference and academic judgement of a supervisor or reviewing committee.
- *Commercial research*, where the proposal serves as a formal statement of the intended research. The proposal may be in response to an invitation to tender from a potential client and the researcher or research team may well be in competition with other potential providers.
- *Funded research*, where the research proposal is used in the application for funding support. As with commercial research, the researcher is likely to be in competition with other researchers for available funds.

Whether you are looking to win business, access a research grant or get approval for a proposed dissertation, your proposal is an important document. As Maxwell (2013: 140, emphasis in original) points out, '*the purpose of your proposal is to explain and justify your proposed study to an audience of non-experts.*' Especially in competitive bidding situations, it is also a statement of your own or your research team's abilities to carry out the research (Gray 2009). The process of developing your research proposal also provides you with the chance to think about, develop and refine your proposed research and to get formal feedback. The latter is particularly relevant in student research projects, where you should take every opportunity to present and discuss your emerging ideas with those more experienced in research practice. We illustrate the process of generating a research proposal in Research in Practice 8.3.

8.6.1 The structure of a proposal

The exact content of a proposal will vary according to its purpose. However, Table 8.5 summarizes typical components of a proposal and their contents, again

RESEARCH IN PRACTICE 8.3

Preparing a research proposal: Trickle Out

Trickle Out Africa is a research project funded by the Economic and Social Research Council (ESRC) First Grant Scheme and launched in February 2011. It examines social and environmental enterprises in Eastern and Southern Africa and their role in sustainable development and poverty alleviation. However, the process of applying for and winning the grant began over two years earlier. In November 2009 an outline proposal was submitted by the project principal investigator, followed by submission of the full funding proposal in February 2010. The grant was awarded in November 2010.

When developing the grant proposal for the Trickle Out project the researcher recognized the need to demonstrate five outcomes from the research. These were: (1) innovation in research design, approach and methodologies; (2) relevance to policy and practice; (3) methodological rigour; (4) relevance to the funder's research priorities, in this instance the ERSC, and also to the specific focus of the call; (5) the potential for impact across academic, practitioner and policy spaces. The researcher particularly emphasized her experience of working in adverse conditions, her previous research in the field of social and environmental entrepreneurship, her access to relevant networks and contacts and her track record of success in relation to other research grants, to demonstrate that her skills, knowledge and experience made her the best person to undertake this research.

The potential impacts of the research were clearly stated and highlighted throughout the grant proposal for Trickle Out. This included: practitioner impacts through the creation of a web-based directory of social and environmental enterprises covering 19 countries across Eastern and Southern Africa; impacts on local research capacity through academic workshops with staff invited from regional institutions; and academic impact in terms of adding to knowledge and discussions in an emerging field, through the production of journal publications, conference participation and project reports. However, it was also imperative that the proposal should demonstrate the appropriateness and robustness of the methodology and provide justification, supported with evidence, for the research approach. Finally, it was important that the proposal should conform with the instructions from ESRC for submission with all required components included, and that it be completed with meticulous attention to detail, i.e. in-depth costing, avoiding typos and following stylistic instructions.

To learn more about the Trickle Out Africa Project please visit the website www.trickleout.net.

with the relevant chapter in this book for further reading. Before writing your proposal, ensure that you are fully conversant with any specific format or template you are required to use, including any word-count restrictions. For some student projects, it may be possible to discuss your proposal with a supervisor or other tutor before writing it (this will be made clear in guidance documents provided). In other situations, you may have the opportunity to clarify any questions with a representative of the reviewing body or those in the organization.

If possible, review other proposals and talk to those who have previously submitted proposals to the same body. Proposals that have been successful are likely to be most helpful, but unsuccessful ones can also be useful, especially if the writer has received feedback on why the proposal was rejected. As well as the formal requirements, a proposal writer 'needs a feel for the unspoken customs, norms, and needs that govern the selection process itself' (Przeworski and Salomon 1995: 1). This can be particularly important in competitive environments, where you should try to familiarize yourself with the types of project, the priorities and other requirements of the funding or buying organization. Finally, be aware that whilst your proposal documents your intended research design at the outset, your research project may adapt or change as you progress and therefore the final study may vary slightly from the original proposal. However, only if your study changes significantly in terms of the research problem and/or method are you likely to need to revisit your proposal, for example, if this is a formal requirement of any academic, funding or commercial body with which you are working.

Table 8.5 Typical structure and components of a research proposal

Component	Indicative contents	Relevant chapters in this book
Abstract or executive summary (if required)	A succinct summary of the proposed research	Chapter 15
Introduction	Explain the background to the research problem	Chapter 2
Purpose of the research	What the research aims to achieve	Chapters 1 and 2
Review of literature (if required)	Locate the proposed research in relevant literature	Chapter 3
Research objectives and questions	Identify the research questions that the project will answer (in some proposals, these might be stated as research objectives or hypotheses)	Chapter 2
Research design	Proposed research design, including proposed data collection, sampling strategy and data analysis	Chapters 4–6 (design) Chapters 9–12 (sampling and data collection) Chapters 13–14 (data analysis)
Deliverables	Format and method of dissemination of the results	Chapter 15
Ethical considerations	Identify and address any ethical considerations involved in the research	Chapter 7
Time frame, resources and budget	The overall plan for administering the project, including outline time-frame, resource requirements and, where appropriate, budget breakdown.	Chapter 8
Reference list (if required)	Correctly formatted in line with the proposal requirements and identifying all references used	Chapter 3

8.6.2 Developing a working title

As Saunders et al. (2012: 541) observe, the title 'is the part of the project report on which most of us spend the least time. Yet it is the only knowledge that many people have of the project.' The title is not just the main way of communicating to others what your project is about, it can also influence whether your research is located in online searches once you have completed it. Formulating your title also forces you to think carefully about how you will describe your research. For this reason it is worth developing a working title early so as to identify the real core of your project so that you can sum it up clearly and in a few words. In addition, you will often need to give your project a provisional title in the research proposal. You should revisit and refine your title as the work progresses to ensure that it still accurately captures the essence of the project. A good title has the following characteristics:

- conveys an accurate description of the research to the reader
- is not too long (as a guide, not more than 10–15 words)
- contains no abbreviations, jargon or acronyms
- is grammatically correct.

Opinions differ as to the use of humour or catchy phrasing in a title. As with other aspects of writing, it is important to know your target audience. Probably the best advice is to avoid doing so unless you are writing for a forum in which such usage is common. Even then, for the working title, keep it serious and focused on the contents of the study.

8.6.3 Developing an effective proposal

The process of developing a proposal is an iterative one. Where practical, we recommend that you seek feedback on drafts from colleagues or tutors or through seminars, meetings or other discussions. As you craft your proposal, keep in mind the following characteristics of a good proposal (Przeworski and Salomon 1995, ESRC 2012, Maxwell 2013).

- *Impact.* Your proposal should capture the reader's attention and sustain it throughout by demonstrating the significance and impact of the proposed research.
- *Coherence.* Whilst the structure of the proposal is usually fixed, it is still essential that the components are coherent in terms both of the underlying logic and of the way in which that logic is communicated through a consistent narrative.
- *Scope and scale.* The proposal should clearly indicate the scope and boundaries of your project. It should show what will, and what will not, be included in the project. At the same time it should enable the reader to assess the size or scale of the project and assess its feasibility.
- *Clarity.* Use plain language that communicates clearly. Many research proposals will be seen by people who are not specialists in the subject and your main argument should be accessible to them, even if some technical language is required to explain finer details. Ensure you check grammar and spelling before submission.

- *Credibility.* Your proposed research must be credible in terms of its ability to address your chosen research questions. It must also be feasible in terms of the time and resources available. Ensure that any timescales and budget data are credible and accurate.
- *Consistency with the brief.* As we have explained, research proposal requirements vary. Ensure that your proposal reflects the requirements of the brief.

On top of this, it is worth noting the advice offered by the Economic and Science Research Council, a UK research funding body:

Convey . . . your genuine interest, understanding and enthusiasm for the work. Keep the following questions in mind as you plan:

- What is the story you are telling?
- What is the audience?
- Why does it matter?
- Why now?
- Why you?

ESRC (2012)

CRITICAL COMMENTARY 8.1

How much planning is too much?

The purpose of this chapter has been to emphasize how important it is to plan and manage your process in a structured and rigorous way. The research proposal document captures much of this thinking in advance of actually starting the project itself. Forward thinking and attention to detail are of course important to the prevention of error and reduction of risk in any activity in life. However, we can ask ourselves as researchers whether over-emphasis upon pre-specification and planning may constrain our thinking. Furthermore, certain research designs, such as ethnography, are intrinsically less open to detailed planning than others, such as experiments, where pre-specification is seen as an important part of the rigour of the design.

Nevertheless, the reality of many research projects is that they are done with a limited set of resources, to a defined timescale and with clear expectations regarding the size and scope of the project deliverables. You should therefore aim to balance the competing needs of the requirements of your research problem with the degree of flexibility of your chosen research design and the need to apply sound planning and management. As in all walks of life, researchers become proficient at their craft by trial and error, success and failure. This is often achieved by being willing to step outside of narrowly defined models of the research process and engage in more creative thinking at the research design stage.

KEY LEARNING POINTS

- A research design lays out the way in which you are going to go about doing your research project. Your research questions are the bridge between your research problem and your research design. It is possible to map research questions to appropriate research designs.
- A number of factors should be considered at the selection of a research design. These include prior research and thinking, ethical factors, stakeholder expectations, access, resource availability and researcher preferences and skills.
- At the planning stage a researcher should consider all potential risk factors and, ideally, develop a risk assessment log which is consulted periodically as the project progresses.
- A research proposal is a document that provides an overview of the intended research. It is often the basis for subsequent approval of a project. The structure and content should make clear the purpose of the research, the intended design, data collection, analysis and deliverables of the project.
- A research diary can be a valuable mechanism for capturing relevant information as well as your thinking as you progress through your project.

PART II

NEXT STEPS

8.1 **Selecting a research design**. As a next step you need to finalize your research design in sufficient detail to provide a good basis for writing your proposal. Think about the research questions you have set and then look at Table 8.1 and decide on a specific research design that is appropriate for your project. Sum up your thinking by completing the following statements.

- I will adopt the following research design to investigate my research question . . .
- This research design is appropriate because . . .

8.2 **Identifying key stakeholders**. Identify the key people and/or organizations whose support will be important to the success of your project. Think here about how you are going to gain access to key stakeholders and keep their support.

8.3 **Identifying key resources**. Identify any key resources, such as software or access to a particular database, and make the necessary arrangements to ensure that they are available when you need them.

8.4 **Risks**. Look back at Table 8.4. Review the risks that you may encounter during your project and the degree of risk, taking into account how likely they are to happen and their potential impact, and decide how you intend to manage them. Record your assessment in writing and review it regularly as the project proceeds.

8.5 **Record keeping**. Decide on a format for your research diary/log. If you are setting out on a research project, begin a research diary now. Note how you will keep information on your progress and your reflections on your experiences.

8.6   Key activities and outline project plan. At this point you should be able to identify key activities needed to complete your research and so prepare a project plan. You will need to make an estimate of how long each activity will take. Use the table below (or other format if you prefer) to develop an outline project plan, making due allowance for any turnaround times for drafts or review.

Project planning table

Activity ID number	Activity	Estimated duration	Start date	Finish date	Notes
1					
2					
3					
. . . *n*					

8.7   Time schedule. Using the data from the table above, develop a graphical version of your time schedule for your project plan in the form of a Gantt chart for inclusion in your research proposal and to help you manage your project and communicate its progress to yourself and others.

Further reading

For further reading, please see the companion website.

References

Buchanan, D. A. and Bryman, A. (2007). 'Contextualizing methods choice in organizational research', *Organizational Research Methods*, 10(3), 483–501.

Costley, C., Elliott, G. C. and Gibbs, P. (2010). *Doing work based research: Approaches to enquiry for insider-researchers*. London: Sage.

ESRC (2012). *Writing a good proposal* [online]. Economic and Social Research Council. Available from: www.esrc.ac.uk/funding-and-guidance/guidance/applicants/application2.aspx [Accessed 24 August 2012].

Gray, D. (2009). *Doing research in the real world*. 2nd edn. London: Sage.

Hughes, I. (2000). *How to keep a research diary*. Action research e-reports, 5 [online]. Available from: www2.fhs.usyd.edu.au/arow/arer/pdf%20e-Report%20version/005.pdf [Accessed 1 December 2008].

Jankowicz, A. (2005). *Business research projects*. 4th edn. London: Thomson.

Maxwell, J. A. (2013). *Qualitative research design: An interactive approach*. 3rd edn. Los Angeles, CA: Sage.

Przeworski, A. and Salomon, F. (1995). *On the art of writing proposals*. Brooklyn, NY: Social Science Research Council.

Saunders, M., Lewis, P. and Thornhill, A. (2012). *Research methods for business students*. 6th edn. Harlow: Prentice Hall.

Note

1   Pass, B. (2013). *An investigation into key organisational factors, as identified by long term volunteers in UK charities that aid motivation and retention and thereby influence longevity of contribution*. MBA dissertation submission. Henley Business School, University of Reading.

Part III
Collect

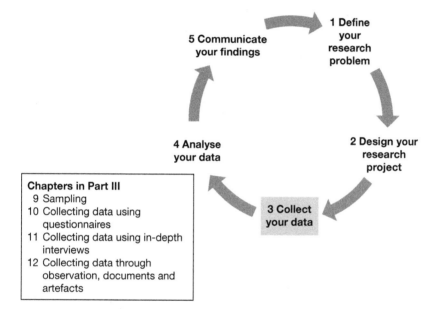

5 Communicate
your findings

1 Define
your
research
problem

4 Analyse
your data

2 Design your
research
project

3 Collect
your data

Chapters in Part III
 9 Sampling
10 Collecting data using
    questionnaires
11 Collecting data using in-depth
    interviews
12 Collecting data through
    observation, documents and
    artefacts

The ability to collect good quality data is essential in a research project. In Part III we therefore take a close look at data collection. We start in Chapter 9 by examining sampling, the process of deciding where you will collect your data and how much you will need to collect. The remaining three chapters look at specific methods for data collection. Chapter 10 reviews questionnaire design and administration, while Chapter 11 examines in-depth individual and group interviews. Chapter 12 looks at a range of other techniques for data collection including observation, documents and artefacts.

9 Sampling

CHAPTER SUMMARY

The key topics covered in this chapter are:

- defining sampling and the sampling process
- sampling methods
- sampling in qualitative and quantitative research
- deciding your sample size
- sampling and the Internet
- gaining and maintaining access.

9.1 Introduction

A key step in the data collection stage of your research project is deciding where you will collect your data and how much you will need to collect. This is the process of **sampling** and it has important implications for the quality and feasibility of your research. Firstly, selecting an inappropriate or inadequate sample of data can reduce the quality of your research to the point where your findings are meaningless. Secondly, gaining access to a suitable sample has major practical implications for your choice of research design and even whether or not a particular project is researchable. In this chapter we therefore take an in-depth look at the sampling process. We begin by defining what is meant by sampling, before looking at different sampling methods. We then discuss how sampling procedures are applied in qualitative and quantitative research, before looking at the important topic of sample size. Following a review of the implications of the Internet for sampling methods, we conclude the chapter with a look at the problems of gaining and maintaining access.

9.2 What is a sample?

The starting point for thinking about sampling is the idea of a **target population**. In research, the term 'population' refers to the totality of elements that are of interest to the researcher as a source of data. These elements may be individuals (such as customers, employees or managers), organizations (such as charities, schools or retailers), events (such as hospital operations or product recalls), documents (such as customer records within a database or online blog posts) or artefacts (such as pieces of equipment or technology). Depending on the nature of your research problem, your target population may be exceptionally large, very small or anywhere in between. If you were researching Internet users in the USA, for example, you would have a potential target population of around 243 million users (Internet World Stats 2013). By way of contrast, if you were investigating the experiences of current US Supreme Court justices, the target population would be precisely nine named individuals (Supreme Court 2013). If your research interest was in thoracic (chest) surgeons in the US, your target population would be 4,682 active physicians (AAMC 2012). Each population varies in terms of size, how well it is defined in terms of membership and how easy it is likely to be to access.

Factors such as these all influence whether or not it is possible to carry out a **census** of the entire population. For some situations, such as small populations that are easily accessible, for example, employees in a small company, a census may be the best approach. In others, even if it is theoretically feasible, it may not be desirable from a cost, time or efficiency point of view to collect data from everyone. In addition, if the population is very large, the amount of data may be overwhelming: imagine trying to process 243 million survey responses on your laptop or analysing hundreds of hours of interview data. For all these reasons, researchers typically take a smaller sub-group, known as a **sample**, from their target population. The individual elements that make up the sample are referred to as **cases** or **observations** (Figure 9.1). For example, if you were carrying out a survey study amongst employees and had a sample of 500 who completed your questionnaire, each respondent would be a case or observation within your research sample. (Note that the word case is being used here

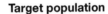

Target population

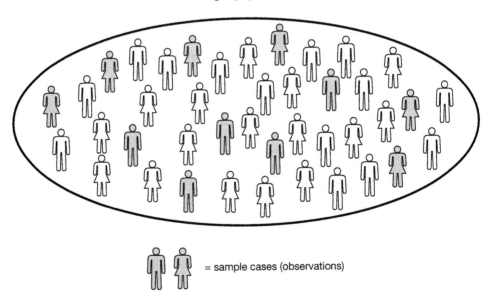

= sample cases (observations)

Figure 9.1 Target population and sample

differently from the way it is used in the context of a case study research design as in Chapter 6.)

9.2.1 The sampling process

The precise details of the sampling process depend on the type of research you are carrying out and, in particular, whether you are using quantitative or qualitative methods. Nevertheless, we can identify a series of steps that guide the sampling process. We show these in Figure 9.2 to set the scene for a more detailed discussion of particular aspects of sampling in the rest of the chapter.

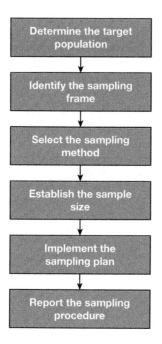

Figure 9.2 Generic sampling process

Step 1: Determine the target population

The first step is to determine your target population. Here you should refer back to your original research problem to identify the people, documents or other elements that are relevant to your investigation. At this stage it can be useful to use secondary data sources such as industry reports or government statistics to help you estimate the nature and size of the population and identify other relevant information that assists you in drawing up a population profile. Such information may also help you to assess how a sample within the population can be accessed.

Step 2: Identify the sampling frame

Next you need to identify the **sampling frame**, which is a listing of all the elements of your target population from which the sample can be drawn. So, for example, if your target population was all employees, a suitable sampling frame would be a list of all employees and their contact details. In reality, a sampling frame may not be complete, either because records are not accurate or because no full listing is available. As a result the sampling frame can be a source of bias in your sample, as we discuss when we look at selection bias.

Step 3: Select the sampling method

Step three involves selecting a suitable sampling method. The selection depends on the research design you are using and is a key area of difference between quantitative and qualitative research methods. As a general rule, quantitative researchers look to use sampling methods that will generate a sample that is statistically representative, whilst qualitative researchers use methods that generate a sample that is theoretically relevant but without being representative in a statistical sense.

Step 4: Establish the sample size

The next step is to determine how big a sample you need. Here again we see some significant differences between quantitative and qualitative research in terms both of the sample size and how it is determined. As well as impacting on the quality of your findings, sample size has significant practical implications for data collection, so we discuss it in more detail in Section 9.5.

Step 5: Implement the sampling plan

Implementation of the sampling plan can take place only once all of the previous steps have been addressed. This is where sampling as a planning activity merges with data collection itself. At this stage you should be monitoring progress to make sure that your sampling plan is working and that you are getting a sample of sufficient quality and size. You will also need to make sure that you can establish and maintain access during data collection.

Step 6: Report the sampling procedure

The sampling process used in your study must be fully reported within your final research report in the section where you describe your research design. This should include reporting of the target population, the sampling frame, the calculation of the sample size and response rate and details of the sampling method used. Any particular difficulties or anomalies encountered should be discussed in terms of how they were addressed and the potential impact they may have had on your findings.

9.2.2 Selection bias

In the process of obtaining your sample it is important that you do not introduce bias in your selection which will impact the subsequent quality of your research. Sampling or selection bias is the term used when certain members of the total population have a greater chance of being included, often as a result of the way in which the sampling process has been conducted. As a result, the sample may not be statistically representative in a quantitative project and this can affect any statistical generalizations made from the data. Selection bias is a key concern for quantitative research but may also occur in qualitative studies, where it can prevent a thorough exploration of a topic or introduce distortions by, for example, unintentionally excluding particular respondents from the sample. Recognizing sources of selection bias can help you to prevent this from adversely affecting your research.

There are three main sources of selection bias. Firstly, it can occur when only part of the target population have the opportunity to be in the sample because we have somehow systematically excluded particular individuals via our sampling frame or access method. For example, if you use the Internet to access a group such as 'public transport users' and some are not Internet users, then your sample will be biased towards 'public transport users who use the Internet' rather than public transport users as a whole.

Secondly, we may unintentionally include people in our sample who do not meet the sample criteria. For example, in order to determine whether someone should be included, we may use filter questions in a questionnaire or whilst arranging interviews. If such filter questions are not sufficiently precise we may include respondents who do not meet the criteria for the sample. Incentivization schemes in which people are rewarded for participation may also create bias in the sample, as we noted in Chapter 7.

Thirdly, problems may arise as a result of people declining to participate. The term **non-response bias** is used to refer to bias created because those who decline to take part are systematically different from those who do take part. Aspects of your research design (for example, the length or wording of a questionnaire) may deter certain people from wanting to take part. These people may have different features, such as being employed or unemployed or having different levels of education, and this may be relevant to your research project. Of course, being able to identify who does not take part can be difficult. Techniques such as comparison of early versus late responders (who are assumed to be similar to non-responders) can be used to help to identify potential non-response bias (see Armstrong and Overton 1977).

9.3 Sampling methods

A range of methods are available for choosing your sample. As we show in Figure 9.3, these fall into two groups, probability and non-probability methods, each with a number of different techniques. We will discuss each in turn before looking at how they are used in different research situations in the next section.

9.3.1 Probability sampling

Probability sampling methods use randomization or chance to select the sample, based on each member of the population having a known, although not necessarily equal, probability of being selected. Probability sampling methods are the preferred approach for quantitative research because they generate samples which can be analysed using appropriate statistical techniques to make inferences about the population from which the sample was drawn. For example, based on data from a probability sample of customers' spending habits, we could draw conclusions about the spending habits of the overall customer population. A number of different probability sampling

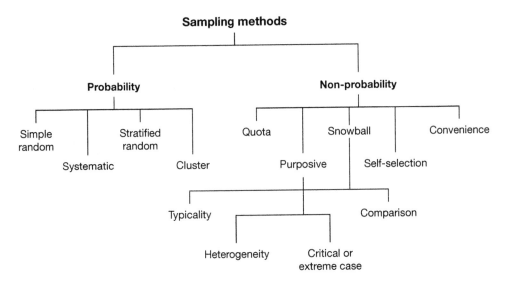

Figure 9.3 Probability and non-probability sampling methods

techniques can be used, depending on the target population and the research aims. These include the following.

Simple random sampling

In **simple random sampling** the required number of elements is simply drawn at random from the population so that there is a known and equal chance of selecting each one. This type of sampling relies on a complete and accurate sampling frame being available and assumes a degree of homogeneity within the target population. A workable procedure for randomized selection must also be available, for example, by assigning each individual in the population a unique identification (ID) number, writing each ID number on a piece of paper, mixing them up in a container and then drawing numbers at random until the required sample size is reached. The individuals whose ID numbers have been drawn then form the sample. For a large population computer assistance may be required. (Technically, what we have described is referred to as sampling without replacement; removing one individual ID changes reduces the remaining population and therefore changes the probability of selection. If the population is large, this change can usually be ignored.)

Systematic random sampling

Systematic random sampling is a variation of simple random sampling. It starts by placing all the elements of the population in a list, picking a start point at random and then moving down the list, selecting every *n*th individual as you go. The size of *n* is known as the sampling interval. It is calculated by dividing the total number in the population by the desired sample size. For example if we have 5,000 branches of a retail organization in our population and require a sample size of 200 branches, then the sample interval will be 25 (5,000/200). The start point is then selected randomly and we will select every 25th organization on our list. Supposing, therefore, that the start point chosen was 15, we would then select the 40th, 65th, 90th branch in the list and so on. Systematic random sampling is not really truly random but it can be easier to do manually and can still generate a representative sample.

Stratified random sampling

Sometimes the target population in our research contains a number of distinctly different sub-groups or 'strata' within it and we want to make sure that each sub-group is adequately represented in our sample. For example, a retail organization may have different types of outlet (hypermarket, supermarket, convenience store, petrol station etc.). Particularly if one of the sub-groups is quite small, random sampling might result in one group not being adequately covered or even being omitted altogether. In this situation we can apply **stratified random sampling**, in which the population is divided (stratified) into separate sub-groups and sample sizes are calculated for each one. This may be done by proportionate stratified sampling, in which the sample for each sub-group is proportionate to its size within the total population. Alternatively, it may be disproportionate stratified sampling, in which case the size of each sub-group may be determined by other factors (for example, choosing equal group size). Disproportionate stratified sampling can ensure that each group is adequately represented but the resulting overall sample will not usually be representative of the population as a whole.

Cluster sampling

Cluster sampling is often used in very large populations and where it may be difficult to accurately identify a sampling frame. This may happen due to the geographic spread of the target population. Suppose, for example, that a research study was investigating healthcare delivery in hospitals within a particular country and needed to gain access to a representative sample of 1,000 patients. Given the size and geographic spread of patients within the hospital network, it might be extremely difficult and costly to collect a sample based on the total population. Instead of selecting individual patients you could randomly select ten hospitals and then randomly select 100 patients from each to make up the sample of 1,000. This is the basis of cluster sampling. It can facilitate data collection (collecting data from patients in five hospitals, for example, may be much easier than collecting data from 1,000 patients spread across the country) but the resulting sample may be less representative than with other probability sampling methods.

9.3.2 Non-probability sampling

Non-probability sampling methods, as the term implies, do not use random selection for choosing a sample. Instead, the researcher uses alternative criteria such as theoretical relevance or convenience to choose the sample. Non-probability methods are particularly important in qualitative research but they are also employed in quantitative research, especially where probability methods cannot be applied. As a result they are very widely encountered in research, so it is important to understand the options available and their relative advantages and disadvantages.

Convenience sampling

A **convenience sample** is one in which the elements from the population are accessed through some point of contact that is convenient and practical to the researcher. This is often done through personal contacts such as work colleagues, fellow students, neighbours or may be by accessing large groups such as student cohorts within a college or university. Today it is also possible to contact a convenience sample through online communities or groups often found on social media platforms. Convenience sampling can provide a quick and cost-effective option but it can lead to bias in the selection process and therefore an unrepresentative sample. Care therefore needs to be taken to check the representativeness of the final sample and to discuss any resulting limitations when reporting your research.

Quota sampling

Quota sampling is a non-probability variant of stratified sampling in that the researcher sets out sample quotas for inclusion of specific sub-groups within the population. For example, if you were investigating customer responses to a new store layout in a hypermarket you might wish to know the views of different customer groups. You would then identify the relevant customer sub-groups (such as male and female) and calculate the desired quota (sample size) for each. Sample size could be proportionate to the size of each in the total population or based on some other factor, such as ensuring that each sub-group is adequately represented. Data are then collected using, for example, convenience or self-selection sampling, until the desired quotas are reached. Quota sampling gives some control over the final composition of the sample but, like convenience sampling, may not lead to a representative sample.

Purposive sampling

Purposive or **theoretical sampling** is an important form of non-probability sampling, widely used in qualitative research methods in which the researcher selects cases for the sample based on their theoretical relevance to the aims of the research. We will look at purposive sampling in more detail when we discuss sampling in qualitative research later in the chapter (9.4.2).

Snowballing

The **snowballing** approach to sampling is useful to researchers when a complete sampling frame is difficult to identify or access. The researcher starts with a few known members of the population who meet the sample characteristics and these are approached to participate and also to identify others they know who also meet the desired sample characteristics. For example, research amongst people who attend music festivals could be conducted by approaching known festival goers who then put the researcher in contact with other festival goers or pass on a research questionnaire for other festival goers to complete. As with other non-probability sampling methods, careful thought needs to be given with respect to selection bias in the resulting sample, but snowballing may be a particularly useful sampling approach when researching hard-to-access, relatively closed communities or groups.

Self-selection

Finally, if no prior sampling frame or access to potential participants exists, the researcher can use techniques to encourage relevant people to self-select for inclusion in a study. This can be done by placing advertisements in relevant newspapers or publications or placing posters in relevant positions. For example, a research study into children's behaviour could place posters in locations such as doctors' surgeries or 'mother and baby' clinics to ask for parents to volunteer to participate in research. Self-selection does raise concern about bias. It may be, for example, that parents who volunteer to discuss their child's behaviour may differ in terms of their attitudes or beliefs, in some systematic way, when compared to those who do not volunteer. As we discuss later in the chapter (9.6), self-selection is becoming an increasingly common method of sampling, particularly with the advent of the Internet, where researchers can place an announcement about their project online and ask for volunteers.

9.4 Sampling in quantitative and qualitative research

Sampling is an important consideration in both quantitative and qualitative research but the objectives and methods of each vary considerably. In particular, they differ with respect to their preference for probability and non-probability sampling techniques and the extent to which the sampling plan is fully specified in advance of data collection or responds to emerging findings as the research proceeds. Table 9.1 summarizes these differences, which we then discuss in more detail.

9.4.1 Sampling in quantitative research

Sampling procedures in quantitative research typically emphasize the importance of being able to use the resulting sample data to make statistical inferences about the target population. This, in turn, is a reflection of the interest in aggregate properties of populations and phenomena and the generalizability of any findings that characterizes

Table 9.1 Quantitative and qualitative sampling compared (adapted from Flick 2009: 119)

Sampling for quantitative research	Sampling for qualitative research
Selection on the basis of statistical representativeness of a wider population	Selection on the basis of theoretical relevance to the research question
One-shot collection of a sample following a plan defined in advance	Sampling plan responds to emergent findings during analysis
Sample size is defined in advance	Sample size may not be defined in advance
Sampling, data collection and data analysis are sequential	Sampling, data collection and data analysis may be iterative
Sampling is finished when the pre-determined sample size has been reached	Sampling is finished when theoretical saturation has been reached
Preference for probability sampling methods	Preference for non-probability, purposive (theoretical) sampling methods

PART III

much quantitative research. Consequently, a central aim of quantitative research sampling is to generate a sample that is statistically representative of the target population. Probability sampling methods are therefore the preferred approach because of their advantages in this respect. If non-probability methods are used, as they sometimes are in practice, care has to be taken regarding the generalizability of the findings and the extent to which they can be said to represent the target population.

In terms of sampling procedures, quantitative sampling is typically a sequential process in which the sample plan is decided in full in advance of data collection. Although, in practice, some adjustments may be made in response to problems in data collection, such changes should be avoided where possible and, if not, the consequences for sample quality should be assessed and reported in your findings. Particular concern is likely to be raised regarding possible selection bias and the sampling plan and the resulting sample should be carefully designed to minimize these, as we discuss at the end of this chapter. At the end of your report you should provide explicit, detailed and critical coverage of your sampling procedures and their implications for your findings.

9.4.2 Sampling in qualitative research

Sampling in qualitative research typically follows a very different logic to that in quantitative research, reflecting the different interests, such as investigation in depth and from the perspective of those involved, that characterize much qualitative research. In particular, qualitative research does not usually seek to make statistical general-izations, so is less concerned with the need to achieve statistical representativeness in sampling. Instead, sampling focuses on choosing a sample that is able to offer rich and in-depth insights into the phenomenon under investigation and to help the researcher build a theoretical understanding of it. In fact writers such as Maxwell (2013: 97) go so far as to suggest that the term sampling itself is problematic for qualitative research due to the assumptions in which it is rooted. Instead he proposes that the term 'purposeful selection' is more appropriate to the way in which qualitative research proceeds. Not surprisingly, qualitative research typically uses non-probability sampling methods, particularly purposive or theoretical sampling techniques. Table 9.2 summarizes different approaches to purposive sampling that may be used in qualitative research. Other non-probability sampling techniques may also be used in qualitative research. Maxwell (2013: 99), for example, points out the value of selecting on the basis of being able to develop 'the most productive relationships' that can help you gain access to the best data for your study. As with any non-probability sampling method, you should be careful about the extent to which your sampling approach may be introducing an element of selection bias into your research.

The sampling process used in qualitative research can also differ from those used in quantitative designs. Some projects may adhere to a sequential process similar to that in Figure 9.2, in which a sample is fully decided in advance by identifying the target population, developing a sampling frame and then choosing the sample members. Other qualitative research projects, however, take a more emergent approach to sampling, reflecting the developmental nature of some qualitative research designs. Here, sample membership and sample size are not fixed in advance of the project but instead respond to developments during data collection and analysis to allow the

Table 9.2 Approaches to purposive sampling in qualitative research (based on Maxwell 2013: 98)

Approach	Characteristic	Purpose
Typicality	Ensuring that the sample incorporates typical examples which represent the phenomenon under investigation	Sampling amongst typical cases provides confidence to the researcher of the relevance of the data derived and that it is representative of the population
Heterogeneity or maximum variation	Ensuring that the sample captures a range of variation and differences within the population	Provides the researcher with less data from each case but provides maximum variation across sampling cases for capturing diversity and the range of the phenomenon
Critical or extreme cases	Sampling includes cases that are an extreme example of the phenomenon being investigated	Provides a critical test of a theory under development or provides more insights than would be achieved from a 'typical' case
Comparison	Sampling captures cases that can be compared across different settings or individuals	Used in multi-case designs to enable the researcher to make comparisons that help to show the reasons for the differences between settings or individuals

researcher to follow up new lines of inquiry, to probe more deeply into a particular topic area and to test the adequacy of emerging theory. To use the term from grounded theory, sampling continues until the point where **theoretical saturation** is reached, that is to say, no new insights are emerging from the data or, as Woolcott (quoted in Baker and Edwards 2012: 4) puts it, 'you keep asking as long as you are getting different answers'. We illustrate the application of purposive sampling to a small qualitative research project in Research in Practice 9.1.

Some qualitative research designs, such as case study and ethnography, can also feature multi-stage sampling, in which the researcher first has to begin by identifying one or more research sites where the research will take place and then has to develop a sampling plan for use within that site. If you were conducting an organizational ethnography, for example, you would first have to select a suitable organization and then identify your sample within that organization using appropriate sampling techniques. This has some parallels to cluster sampling in quantitative research, although it uses purposive rather than probability sampling techniques.

9.5 Sample size

A question asked at the outset of most research projects is 'how big does my sample need to be?' It is sometimes assumed that the larger the sample size, the better the quality of the findings. In practice, as we have already explained, issues such as selection of the population and sampling frame, the sampling methods used and so on also affect the quality of your data. Nevertheless, sample size is important not only in terms of the implications for your analysis but also in terms of the cost, time

RESEARCH IN PRACTICE 9.1

Theoretical sampling: researching supplier–client relationships in outsourcing

A study conducted by Dibley and Clark (2009) set out to explore practitioner views of best practice in managing outsourcing relationships Specifically, the project aimed to investigate supplier organizations offering a range of outsourcing services. Sample selection began with the identification of four outsource supplier organizations offering a range of different expertise. These included HR solutions, customer management processes, IT solutions and general business process outsourcing. The researchers held discussions with each organization regarding the general objectives of the research, including the aim of identifying best practice and investigating what made their relationships with clients successful. Together, the researchers and each supplier organization identified suitable client organizations. These were where the relationship between the client and supplier could be defined as 'successful' and 'valuable'; where there was evidence of best practice and which allowed the project to cover a range of different sectors. Interviews were conducted with the supplier and client of each partnering relationship. The sample size was decided as the project evolved and at the point where a degree of theoretical saturation had been reached. In total, sixteen 60–90 minute interviews were conducted: six interviews with senior managers from the four outsource suppliers, and ten interviews with senior managers from six client organizations.

and effort required to reach a particular sample size. In this section we will take a look at the question of sample size for both quantitative and qualitative research.

9.5.1 Sample size in quantitative research

Sample size in a quantitative study, such as a survey, typically depends on three key factors.

1   The level of precision required. This refers to the maximum difference the researcher is prepared to tolerate between the estimated sample value obtained and the actual value that would be obtained in the population. In effect, this factor refers to the amount of error that will be accepted between the sample and population values. In general, the greater the precision required, the larger the sample that will be needed.
2   The homogeneity of the population. Different populations vary in terms of their homogeneity, that is, the degree to which members of the population share particular characteristics. The less homogenous (i.e. the more varied) the population, the larger the sample required.
3   The degree of confidence that you want in the accuracy of any generalizations you make about your population from your sample data. We explain this concept more fully in Chapter 13, but for now we will note that, everything else being equal, the higher the degree of confidence you want, the bigger the sample you will need to collect.

One thing that might surprise you is that population size is not mentioned. It is the size of the sample, not the size of the population from which it is drawn, that matters in most situations. Only when the sample represents a significant proportion of the population is an adjustment necessary.

Deciding on your sample size

Several formulae are available for calculating sample size and these are provided on the companion website to help you decide on an appropriate sample size for your project. Although such formulae can help you to decide on your sample size, in practice the decision is often influenced by other factors. Some of these factors relate to practical issues of cost, time and access mentioned earlier. Sample size may also be influenced by the type of analysis that is planned. Cohen (1992) provides guidance on sample sizes for different statistical techniques. Further guidance can also be had by looking at previous studies in your topic area to see what sample sizes have been used in the past.

9.5.2 Sample size in qualitative research

As we have seen, the logic of sampling in much qualitative research is different to that motivating quantitative research sampling, and the same applies to criteria for determining sample size, particularly if using theoretical saturation to guide your decision. An obvious difficulty with this approach, however, is that it is hard to know in advance when theoretical saturation will be reached. This makes it difficult to use as a basis for determining sample size in advance of the study. Whilst this is consistent with the flexible, emergent nature of much qualitative research, it does not help much with planning or budgeting for your project, especially if you have to declare your intended sample size in a proposal to a review board or supervisor.

So how big should your sample be? One option is to look at what other writers have done. In a study of 560 UK and Irish PhDs that used a qualitative approach, Mason (2010) found an average of 31 participants. Guest et al. (2006) looked at when saturation was reached in terms of identifying new codes in their data analysis. They found that saturation was reached after 12 interviews, although, as they point out, it is hard to know how generalizable their findings are. Another option is to seek the advice and experiences of other qualitative researchers. Adler and Adler (in Baker and Edwards 2012) suggest between 12 and 60, with a mean of 30, while Ragin (in Baker and Edwards 2012) proposes 20 for a Master's thesis and 50 for a PhD. Our own guidance as a planning figure for final projects on Master's programmes has been 12–15 in-depth interviews or 3–5 case studies using multiple sources of data. If you are doing an academic research project, your supervisor may also be able to offer advice on sample size.

In addition, we can identify a number of factors to take into account when deciding on a likely sample size for a qualitative project (Morse 2000, Baker and Edwards 2012).

- *Scope and complexity of the topic.* The broader the scope and the greater the complexity of the topic, the bigger the sample that is likely to be needed to ensure that the topic is adequately explored.

PART III

- *Population heterogeneity*. As with quantitative research, the more variation there is in the population of interest, the bigger your sample should be. Sample size may also need to be higher if you want to compare the experiences of different groups.
- *Quality of data*. The depth and richness of data that you gather in qualitative interviews may vary greatly between respondents. Such differences can influence the sample size needed.
- *Stakeholder expectations*. Although the research requirements should determine the decision on sample size, other stakeholders' expectations influence the final decision. In particular, those more familiar with the logic of quantitative sampling may find it difficult to accommodate the different requirements of qualitative research. Make sure that you are aware of the expectations of others when planning your sample size.

Remember that in qualitative research you will also need to allow for time to transcribe, analyse and report your data. An hour-long interview can generate anything up to 10,000 words; if you are not careful you may find yourself with more data than you can analyse thoroughly. Ultimately, as with quantitative research, the final sample size will be a balance between theoretical desirability and practical feasibility.

9.5.3 Response rates

Finally, you will need to take into account likely response rates when setting your sample size. The response rate is the percentage of those contacted who respond and take part in your research. This can be relatively low, depending on the subject of the research, the data collection technique used and the characteristics of the target population. A review of survey response rates reported in articles in leading organization and management journals between 2000 and 2005, for example, showed considerable variation depending on the distribution method used (Baruch and Holtom 2008). We show some of the findings in Table 9.3 to illustrate this variation.

In consumer studies the response rate can come down to single figures. A study of online shopping by Rose and Samouel (2009), for example, achieved a response rate of 3 per cent (3 in every 100 contacted) from online shoppers. This may seem very low but is in fact typical of consumer research studies. In many cases it is possible to estimate the response rate in advance, either based on reporting in prior studies (found in the literature) or from your own experience in the relevant field. Estimation

Table 9.3 Reported survey response rates by distribution method (based on Baruch and Holtom 2008)

Distribution method	Number of studies	% Response rates			
		Minimum	Maximum	Mean	Standard deviation
Web	6	10.6	69.5	38.5	15.1
Email	11	23.7	89.0	54.7	23.9
In person/drop in	31	30.0	83.0	62.4	16.9
Phone	10	10.0	86.2	49.1	24.1

of the anticipated response rate is crucial because it enables you to calculate the level of overall selection from the sampling frame required in order to achieve your intended sample size. In the online shopping study, for example, an anticipated response rate of 3 per cent meant that a total of 4,800 online shoppers had to be contacted to achieve the desired sample of 144. Response rates must always be presented in your final report.

9.6 Sampling and the Internet

The rise in the reach and usage of the Internet has made it a popular medium for researchers to use in order to collect data. It is estimated that in 2012 approximately 43 per cent of all research spending in the USA was conducted online, which in value terms equated to over US$1.8 billion (Terhanian and Bremer 2012). As a data collection channel, the Internet offers the benefit of efficiency in terms of both time and money. Obtaining relevant samples in short time frames can be very attractive to researchers, whether in a commercial or academic context. Additionally, the Internet can enable us to identify and access hard-to-reach populations who may otherwise be difficult to find and approach. For example, we can now identify and contact communities of interest through discussion forums and other channels that may give us access to people who have relevant insights into our research problem.

Despite these attractions, we must be aware of the limitations of the Internet from a sampling point of view. Firstly the extent of Internet usage penetration amongst the general population varies from country to country and many groups are still excluded from the Internet, due to income, age, technological access or preference. We therefore cannot automatically assume that Internet users reflect the full population in all research situations. Moreover, although it is a matter of some debate, sampling via the Internet should probably be considered as a form of non-probability sampling (Terhanian and Bremer 2012), so care needs to be given when assessing the statistical representativeness of any resulting sample.

9.6.1 Internet sampling in quantitative research

The online medium is perhaps particularly attractive to quantitative researchers because of its potential to facilitate quick and easy access to a large number of people at low cost. It is extensively used for data collection for survey studies, as we discuss in Chapter 10. From a sampling point of view, we can identify three main ways in which the Internet can be used in quantitative research for survey studies.

Conventional sampling

The first option is to generate the sample in the normal way and just to use the Internet as a channel for administering your questionnaire using an online survey tool. In this case the original sampling frame exists outside of the online environment, such as a customer database or employee listing that is held by an organization. The online questionnaire is made available to the sample by providing an online link to the survey, for example, by email. Participants can then follow the link to complete the questionnaire. Provided that the sampling frame adequately represents the target population and that all respond, it is possible to use probability sampling methods to generate the sample.

Direct access

A second approach to sampling is to access online groups or forums and to invite members to take part by following a link to an online survey site where the questionnaire is hosted. This is a form of self-selection sampling but can also be combined with snowballing by asking participants to pass the survey link on to others who fit the sample criteria. Alternatively, the Internet can be used for convenience sampling, where the survey is relayed to individuals within the researcher's own network of contacts. These sampling approaches are, of course, non-probability and so you need to be aware of the effect upon the representativeness of your sample and therefore potential selection bias.

Online panels

The third option is to use an online panel. An online panel is composed of a large group of people who have previously agreed to take part in online surveys. Panels are typically compiled by market research agencies that then use them to complete online surveys for clients. An online panel is therefore a set of pre-recruited members of a population from which a sample can be drawn for online research. The panel will be recruited according to a set of characteristics, most often relating to demographics such as age, gender, income or location. Additionally, a panel may reflect certain behavioural characteristics such as working in a particular industry, belonging to a particular interest group or using particular products or services.

Online panels have become a very popular way to obtain quantitative samples with minimal effort on the part of the researcher, passing a lot of the detailed problems of sampling onto the agency running the panel. Nevertheless, if you are considering using an online (or offline) panel you need to:

- Verify that the panel is representative of your target population. If you are dealing with a reputable market research agency it will be able to provide details of the panel demographics and how the panel is recruited and maintained.
- Verify that the actual respondents are representative of your target population. Again, the agency responsible for the panel should be able to provide details.

In addition, you should be aware that an online panel is a form of non-probability self-selection sampling because certain members of the population self-select to participate in the panel. Self-selection can in itself bias a sample because we do not know if those who select to participate share the same characteristics as those who do not. We discuss the role of panels in sampling and research in more detail in Critical Commentary 9.1.

9.6.2 Internet sampling in qualitative research

The Internet has also become an important part of qualitative research, for example, investigating online communities or exploring the content of social media commentary. From a sampling point of view it provides a valuable route for the researcher to access a sample directly through email or contact on a social media site such as Facebook. Alternatively, the researcher may identify a sample by becoming part of

---

CRITICAL COMMENTARY 9.1

The use of research panels

The motivations of people who take part in research panels is an important consideration for researchers when selecting this method for sampling. With the move to online panels it becomes even harder to confirm the appropriateness of people taking part. You will now find information online and in books guiding people to take part as respondents as a source of income (for example, Moore 2013). Knowing that panel members do match the characteristics of the population is crucial to the validity of the data and the quality of the research output. Members of an online panel may be rewarded with financial payments, donations or participation in lotteries. Incentives may introduce bias by encouraging people to participate only for the incentive. Brüggen et al. (2011) refer to professional respondents who may be regularly completing surveys only for the reward. The accuracy and honesty of such responses may be questionable as the respondent is motivated by the incentive, but also because repeated membership in a panel will make an individual highly familiar with questionnaire completion. Campbell et al. (2011) point out the practice of repeated completion where panel respondents complete multiple versions of a questionnaire in the same sample in order to gain financially. This practice is clearly damaging to the research community. Estimates of the prevalence of this activity range from 8 per cent (Lipner 2007) to 40 per cent (Walker et al. 2009). However, financial motivation may not be the only incentive to take part. Brüggen et al. (2011) suggest this type of motivation is not high in online panels but, rather, that other motivations may exist such as interest, obligation, desire to give an opinion, need for recognition, enjoyment or curiosity. No matter the actual motivation, as researchers we must be aware of the motivations that influence panel participants and consider how this form of sampling may introduce bias into our research.

PART III

an online community. As we discussed in Chapter 7, however, online research of this kind does raise some particular ethical issues regarding transparency and the consent of participants, so it is important to take these into account when considering this type of research. In Research in Practice 9.2 we give an example of sample access for an online participant observation study.

RESEARCH IN PRACTICE 9.2

Sample access for participant observation within an online firm-hosted brand community

A research study undertaken by a PhD student (Shapiro 2013) aimed to investigate what motivates an individual to participate actively in a firm-hosted online brand community. The research focused on the business to business (B2B) sector in the

United States and specifically aimed to understand the individual-level consequences and personal values that are satisfied through such active participation. An ethnographic method was used in the study which involved the researcher in collecting data via participant observation within an online community in order to gain access into the collective identity of the community.

Selection of the community for the study was based on four characteristics that would make the sample relevant to the research questions. These characteristics were:

1 An active community: the community had to be active with regular and daily postings by the community members.
2 A community centred on a strong, globally known brand with most discussion being focused on brand issues and brand development.
3 Firm-hosted: the community to be hosted and managed by a B2B brand.
4 A community that had a distinct group of very active, 'evangelical' members. The involvement of these individuals was so significant that the host firm personally acknowledged them.

Contact was made with community managers and online consumer experience teams at various companies to explain the details of the study. However, during this process of searching for a relevant community an approach was made to the researcher by a leading US firm in the software field that had become aware of the study and that had an online community that fitted all of the outlined requirements. The firm showed enthusiasm for the objectives of the research and how it could eventually be aligned with its own goals. Once access into the community has been negotiated, the researcher assessed the community through unobtrusive observation, which allowed the general culture and language of the community to be understood. During this phase, community activity and natural behaviour was not interrupted. The community was entered regularly by the researcher to look at salient activity and behaviour in the discussion forum. Field notes were recorded in a journal which gave an understanding of the history, nature and people of the community. Participant observation commenced after the unobtrusive observation had provided the researcher with a general understanding of the community and its characteristics. The researcher signed up as an official member of the community and posted an introductory letter to the community announcing the purpose of the research. Participant observation continued until such time as data saturation occurred.

9.7 Gaining and maintaining access

Sampling must take account of practical as well as theoretical aspects of your research, in the sense that you must be able to access your intended sample. If you cannot do so, you will need to rethink your intended sampling plan, and possibly your research design or even your entire research project. Sadly, some research problems remain unresearchable, due to access difficulties, so it is important to identify any potential access problems with your own project at the outset and to formulate strategies for dealing with them.

9.7.1 Access in quantitative research

Quantitative research typically requires fairly large samples made up of respondents with particular characteristics. As you develop your sampling plan following the process in Figure 9.2, you need to work out how you will identify your sampling frame and how you will make contact with members of your sample, if they are human respondents, or access documents or data stored on databases. Options include:

- Engaging the support of a sponsoring or client organization to gain access to a suitable target population and sampling frame, for example, a listing of organizational members, employees or customers. Depending on data protection and other confidentiality issues, you may not be able to get access to contact details directly and may instead have to ask the organization to distribute the data collection instrument on your behalf. In other cases you may be able to include your questions in an existing survey being done by the organization or to have it invite participation through other channels such as employee newsletters, websites and so on.
- Using online panels or other suitable samples organized by a market research agency. Since these are normally commercial organizations, their suitability will also depend on whether or not you have funding available.
- Using non-probability sampling methods via the Internet, as discussed earlier. The suitability and feasibility of this route is very much dependent on the nature of the topic.
- Using your own personal and professional contacts through a combination of convenience and snowball sampling. You will have to pay particular attention to the problem of selection bias if you use this route.

One of the challenges facing quantitative researchers is that, because of the sequential nature of the research, they do not know the viability of their sampling plan until data collection is underway, at which point it may be difficult or impossible to make changes. For that reason it is important to learn as much as you can about the target population and its likely response rates before starting. Reviewing prior research, talking to subject experts and other researchers and a small pilot study can all be used to learn more about potential access problems and thereby reduce the risk of failure.

9.7.2 Access in qualitative research

Similar options are available for qualitative researchers but somewhat different considerations apply in gaining and maintaining access. Smaller sample sizes, direct contact with participants and the emergent nature of sampling processes offer some advantages for qualitative researchers in that it is possible to monitor the progress of the sampling plan as it unfolds and to take actions to address any problems. Nevertheless, qualitative researchers do face other challenges in gaining the appropriate depth of access and time commitment from participants. This can be a particular problem if the researcher is an 'outsider' in terms of the community under investigation. In such situations, it can be very useful to identify and secure the cooperation of a gatekeeper who is a member of the group being studied or who has insider status and can facilitate access. Gatekeepers may occupy a formal position (such as a senior manager) or an informal one (such as an influential individual in a group). Depending on their interest and role, gatekeepers will require information about the study, the rationale for choosing the site or individuals that you want to research, how disruptive the data collection is likely to be and how the findings will be disseminated (including how the gatekeeper will benefit from the study). In other situations, the researcher will have to establish contacts directly with potential participants. Your personal and professional network, or those of colleagues or others interested in the project, are very valuable here. The Internet also offers routes to contact potential participants through social media sites, professional forums and other contact points.

9.7.3 Factors affecting access

Regardless of the type of research you are doing, there are a number of factors that may influence your ability to gain access or to get individuals to participate in your research. These include:

- Participant effort. If participants (whether individually or at an organizational level) are expected to put considerable time and effort into the research, they are unlikely to agree to take part unless they can see a good reason for doing so. Such a reason may be in terms of some direct benefit to them or because they see the research as valuable in other ways, for example, in terms of solving a shared problem. Good explanation of the purpose and relevance of the research can help provide this.
- Sensitivity. A particularly sensitive topic may deter participation, especially in some contexts where people may be nervous about consequences or repercussions if they participate. Good briefing, including appropriate commitments, taking time to build up trust amongst potential participants and the professionalism displayed by the researcher can help to overcome this barrier.
- Confidentiality. Topics vary in their degree of confidentiality, but in some business and management research projects commercial confidentiality may be a particular concern for potential participants. This can be a particular deterrent in research that is highly sensitive (e.g. an employee satisfaction survey) or where the research is taking place in a very tightly bounded population in which a respondent may be identifiable (e.g. a business-to-business qualitative research study within a small industry sector with limited numbers of competitor firms). In such cases, researchers may have to provide additional assurances regarding confidentiality. As a student researcher, for example, you may need to provide a copy of the confidentiality policy of your academic institution in addition to any other briefing documents. In some cases, particularly commercial research, it may be necessary to sign a non-disclosure agreement. In other cases, it may be preferable to adjust the research focus so that the level of confidential disclosure required is reduced.

Gaining and maintaining access is likely to be one of the toughest practical challenges in any research project. Your ultimate success will very much depend on the appeal of your research topic, your negotiation skills and your ability to build trust and credibility amongst stakeholders. Research in Practice 9.3 provides an example of sampling and data collection in a sensitive situation.

RESEARCH IN PRACTICE 9.3

Accessing a sample in a sensitive research topic

There are approximately 330,000 problem drug users in the UK, who are estimated to cost society over £15 billion a year, £13.9 billion of which is due to drug-related crime (Resnick et al. 2011). Many of these individuals currently access publicly funded substance-misuse services, which collectively provide a comprehensive array of treatments for adults with drug- and alcohol-related problems. These services are complex and include a range of interventions such as advice and information, community prescribing and dispensing, psychological assessments and virus screening and immunization. A research project was undertaken by a team of academics and practitioners who were interested to know about the quality of service provision from the perspective of the users of the service. The research project took place at a drug clinic providing substance-misuse services.

Given that the user perspective required the researchers to draw data from problem drug users who were patients of the clinic, this posed a difficulty of access for the team. Whilst it would be possible to identify users via the clinic management, the researchers needed to be able to access the drug users without deterring their involvement. They also needed to respect ethical considerations of privacy, anonymity and confidentiality of the clinic users. It was felt that if the researchers approached the drug users and collected the data it might not only deter involvement but also affect the accuracy of their responses. A survey using a paper-based questionnaire was used as the data collection method. The clinic had a 'service user forum' whose members included patients who had recovered or were in recovery from problem drug use. Two members of this forum who were recovering drug-user patients of the clinic were approached to distribute the questionnaire and collect the data either by face-to-face interviews or as a self-completed response by the users while in the clinic. Using this method of accessing the drug users via two recovering drug users who would have empathy and understanding of their situation, the survey resulted in 97 usable responses for the research team.

KEY LEARNING POINTS

- The target population is the totality of elements of interest to the researcher.
- As it is often difficult to access the total population, data from a sample, which is a sub-group drawn from the total population, is used for analysis. Sampling is the process by which we identify and access our sample data from the total population.
- The generic sampling process consists of six steps: determining the target population, identifying the sampling frame, selecting the sampling method, establishing the sample size, implementing the sampling plan and reporting the sampling procedure.

- Selection bias occurs when the sample is not representative of the population. Researchers should be aware of the sources of selection bias when designing their sampling and data collection.
- There are two families of sampling method: probability and non-probability. Probability methods use some element of randomization in order to generate a statistically representative sample. Non-probability methods select on the basis of other criteria.
- Sampling in quantitative research aims to produce a statistically representative sample, with a preference for probability sampling methods to allow statistical generalization. Sampling in qualitative research aims to produce a theoretically relevant sampling, with a preference for purposive non-probability sampling methods to support theory building.
- Sample size in quantitative research can be predetermined on the basis of the level of precision required, the homogeneity of the population and the confidence level required by the researcher. Sample size in qualitative research is often determined by the need to achieve theoretical saturation. When calculating sample size, it is important to take account of likely response rates.
- The Internet is now widely used for gaining access to samples through direct contact, via online communities or other groups or commercial online panels.
- Gaining and maintaining access is an important practical task in a research project and should be considered at the planning stage.

NEXT STEPS

9.1   Choosing a sampling method. Identify your sampling method using the following questions as a guide:

What is the population from which my sample will be taken?

For quantitative research:

a) What is my target population?
b) What sampling method (e.g. probability sampling, non-probability sampling) do I need to use? If probability, how will I conduct randomized selection?
c) What specific sampling method will I use?
d) What sample size will I need? Do I need to set any quotas?
e) For survey studies: what response rate do I expect and therefore how many questionnaires will I need to send out?

For qualitative research:

a) What sources of data are relevant to my inquiry?
b) Where will I find them?
c) What sampling method will I use?
d) What sample size should I use for planning purposes?

9.2   Gaining access. How will you gain access to your intended sample? What potential barriers might you encounter and how will you overcome them?

9.3 **Describing your sampling plan**. Use the following prompts to describe your sampling plan:

a) The proposed sampling method will be:
b) This is appropriate because:
c) The intended sample size is, or the following method will be used to determine the sample size:
d) This is appropriate because:
e) The limitations of my sampling plan are:

Further reading

For further reading, please see the companion website.

References

AAMC (2012). *2012 physician specialty data book*. Washington DC: Association of American Medical Colleges.

Armstrong, J. S. and Overton, T. S. (1977). 'Estimating nonresponse bias in mail surveys', *Journal of Marketing Research*, 14(3), 396–402.

Baker, S. E. and Edwards, R. (2012). How many qualitative interviews is enough? ESRC National Centre for Research Methods. Available from: http://eprints.ncrm.ac.uk/2273/.

Baruch, Y. and Holtom, B. C. (2008). 'Survey response rate levels and trends in organizational research', *Human Relations*, 61(8), 1139–60.

Brüggen, E., Wetzels, M., de Ruyter, K. and Schillewaert, N. (2011). 'Individual differences in motivation to participate in online panels: The effect on reponse rate and reponse quality perceptions', *International Journal of Market Reseach*, 53(3), 369–90.

Campbell, C., Parent, M., Plangger, K. and Fulgoni, G. M. (2011). 'Instant innovation: From zero to full speed in fifteen years – how online offerings have reshaped marketing research', *Journal of Advertising Research*, 51(1) (50th Anniversary Supplement), 72–86.

Cohen, J. (1992). 'A power primer', *Psychological Bulletin*, 112(1), 155–9.

Dibley, A. and Clark, M. (2009). *Best practice in managing relationships with outsource partners: An outsource supplier and client perspective*. Reading: The Henley Centre for Customer Management, Henley Business School.

Flick, U. (2009). *An introduction to qualitative research*. 4th edn. Los Angeles, CA: Sage.

Guest, G., Bunce, A. and Johnson, L. (2006). 'How many interviews are enough? An experiment with data saturation and variability', *Field Methods*, 18(1), 59–82.

Internet World Stats (2013). *Internet users in America June 30, 2012* [online]. Internet World Stats. Available from: www.internetworldstats.com/stats2.htm [accessed 25 April 2014].

Lipner, W. E. (2007). 'The future of online market research', *Journal of Advertising Research*, 47(2), 142–6.

Mason, M. (2010). 'Sample size and saturation in PhD studies using qualitative interviews', *Forum Qualitative Sozialforschung /Forum: Qualitative Social Research*, 11(3). Available from: www.qualitative-research.net/index.php/fqs/article/view/1428/3028 [accessed 25 April 2014].

Maxwell, J. A. (2013). *Qualitative research design: An interactive approach*. 3rd edn. Los Angeles, CA: Sage.

Moore, A. (2013). *Get paid to take genuine surveys online: 150 companies who pay for your opinion*. Cyberwave Media. Kindle publication, via Amazon.com (Amazon Digital Services, Inc.).

PART III

Morse, J. M. (2000). 'Determining sample size', *Qualitative Health Research*, 10(1), 3–5.

Resnick, S., Cassidy, K. and Fox, C. (2011). A perspective on relationship quality in drug treatment services using patient to patient research. *19th International Colloquium in Relationship Marketing*. New York: Rochester Institute of Technology.

Rose, S. and Samouel, P. (2009). 'Internal psychological versus external market-driven determinants of the amount of consumer information search amongst online shoppers', *Journal of Marketing Management*, 25(1–2), 171–90.

Shapiro, M. (2013). An exploration of active participation in a firm-hosted online brand community. PhD submission. Reading: Henley Business School, The University of Reading.

Supreme Court (2013). *A brief overview of the Supreme Court* [online]. Supreme Court of the United States. Available from: www.supremecourt.gov/about/briefoverview.aspx [Accessed 2 November 2013].

Terhanian, G. and Bremer, J. (2012). 'A smarter way to select respondents for surveys?', *International Journal of Market Research*, 54(6), 751–80.

Walker, R., Pettit, R. and Rubinson, J. (2009). 'A special report from the Advertising Research Foundation – the Foundations of Quality Initiative: A five-part immersion into the quality of online research', *Journal of Advertising Research*, 49(4), 464–85.

PART III

10 Collecting data using questionnaires

10.1 Introduction

Almost everyone has some experience of questionnaires, whether in the form of employee feedback, customer satisfaction surveys or as part of a formal research project. Perhaps because we are so familiar with them it is tempting to assume that they are an easy option for collecting data. In fact designing and administering a questionnaire requires careful thought and hard work if the resulting data are to be of any use in answering your research questions. This chapter therefore takes a structured approach to using questionnaires for data collection. We begin by looking at situations in which it might be appropriate to use a questionnaire and review some strengths and weaknesses of questionnaires as data collection tools. Next we introduce a simple process to follow when designing and using them. We look at each step in turn, with particular emphasis on how to formulate appropriate questions and lay out the questionnaire itself. We conclude with a discussion of pre-testing and piloting and a review of the options for distributing your questionnaire.

10.2 Why and when to use a questionnaire

A **questionnaire** is a particular type of **data collection instrument** that uses a standardized, structured set of questions to measure variables, such as respondent attitudes, that are of interest to the researcher. Depending on the research, a questionnaire may be designed either for self-completion by the respondents themselves or for completion by the researcher on the basis of oral answers from participants

Table 10.1 How questionnaires may be used in different research designs

Research design	Role of questionnaires in data collection
Survey study	Main or sole method used to measure relevant variables
Experiment and quasi-experiment	Used alongside other methods, such as observation, to measure relevant variables before, during and after the experiment
Non-experimental explanatory research	Used alongside other methods, such as secondary data, to measure relevant variables
Case study	May be used alongside other data collection methods, for example, for triangulation purposes
Action research	May be used alongside other data collection methods

given, for example, over the telephone. The data gathered by questionnaire are typically quantitative or easily quantifiable that can then be analysed to answer our research questions.

Questionnaires are most obviously associated with survey research designs in which they are likely to form the primary, and often the only, data collection method, but in practice their use is much more widespread, as we show in Table 10.1.

10.2.1 Advantages and disadvantages of using questionnaires

Questionnaires are such a widely used method of data collection because they offer a number of advantages. Specific advantages include:

- *Low cost.* Questionnaires can enable us to reach a large sample at a relatively low cost in time and money, particularly if an online survey tool can be used for distribution.
- *Speed of collection.* Responses to questionnaires can be obtained in a relatively short period of time. Data preparation can also be relatively fast if data are collected electronically and can be transferred directly into a software program such as a spreadsheet package for further analysis
- *Flexibility.* Questionnaires can be used to measure a wide variety of variables and can be administered in a variety of ways.
- *Anonymity.* Questionnaire distribution can be separated from subsequent data handling, so helping to ensure respondent anonymity and data confidentiality.
- *Reduced interviewer effects.* In self-completed questionnaires the role of the researcher in the data collection process is minimized, thus reducing the influence on the responses generated. If a questionnaire is administered face to face or by telephone, researcher training and standardized procedures are used to reduce interviewer effects.

Many of these advantages have been intensified with the introduction of online survey tools which permit distribution and collection of questionnaires via the Internet, as we discuss later in this chapter.

There are, however, some disadvantages to using questionnaires of which you should be aware. These include:

- *Variable response rates.* Given the ubiquity of questionnaires, potential partici-pants may be suffering from survey fatigue, leading to low response rates. Aspects of the questionnaire itself may also contribute to low response, such as its length, how interesting it is to respondents or the relevance of the topic. Response rates can be improved by careful design and administration of the questionnaire (see also Chapter 9 for a discussion of response rates).
- *Partial completion.* Respondents may fail to complete questions appropriately or fail to answer them in full. There may be no opportunity to identify and clarify poorly completed responses until they are detected at the analysis stage, when they may have to be removed, leading to reduced sample size and potential bias as a result of the pattern of non-completed items.
- *Limited range of responses for participants.* Questionnaires are fixed in terms of the structure and format of the questions. Respondents are required to answer in a way that matches how the researcher has framed the questions. There is little opportunity for respondents to provide feedback, for example, where they feel that the response options offered do not fit their preferred response.
- *Respondent literacy level.* Completion of a questionnaire can often require good levels of literacy, which may be a problem for some groups of respondents such as young children. Use of questionnaires across different language groups can also be challenging and requires careful thought by the researcher in terms of translation.

These disadvantages are inherent in questionnaire design, but their impact can be minimized by good questionnaire design and by a well thought-through process for administering the questionnaire.

10.3 The questionnaire design process

Your questionnaire must be able to generate valid and reliable data about the variables relevant to your investigation. At the same time it must be structured and laid out in a way that encourages participation and thereby a high response rate. It also needs to be in line with ethical requirements in terms of informed consent. Before it is sent out, it needs to be pre-tested and piloted. Finally, you will need to give careful thought to how you will distribute it to your sample. If you send out a poor-quality question-naire you will get poor-quality data back. If it is a really poor questionnaire, you may get no data back at all. Good questionnaire design is therefore fundamental to the success of your data collection.

To help you achieve this we recommend following a structured design process that we show in Figure 10.1. The remainder of the chapter is dedicated to examining each stage in turn to identify key points to consider and key decisions to be taken when using questionnaires for data collection.

10.4 Identify relevant concepts/variables

Once you have confirmed that a questionnaire is an appropriate data collection technique for your research, the first, and crucial, step is to identify the relevant concepts that you wish to measure as variables in your questionnaire. They should relate to your research question and any theory that you wish to test in your research.

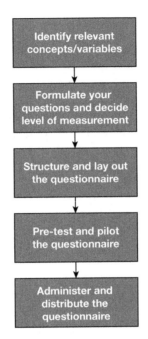

Figure 10.1 The questionnaire design process

RESEARCH IN PRACTICE 10.1

Dimensions of service quality

In a well-known article, Parasuraman et al. (1988) reported their development of the SERVQUAL instrument, a questionnaire used to measure service quality. Prior exploratory research had identified ten dimensions used by customers in assessing service quality. These dimensions were tangibility, reliability, responsiveness, communication, credibility, security, competence, courtesy, understanding/knowing the customer and access. These fed into the next stage of the research project, which resulted in the SERVQUAL instrument, which consists of five dimensions, defined by Parasuraman et al. (1988: 23) as follows:

1 tangibility: physical facilities, equipment and appearance of personnel
2 reliability: ability to perform the promised service dependably and accurately
3 responsibility: willingness to help the customer and provide prompt service
4 assurance: knowledge and courtesy of employees and their ability to inspire trust and confidence
5 empathy: caring, individualized attention that the firm provides to its customers.

Each of these dimensions is measured in the SERVQUAL instrument, allowing the researcher to gain an understanding of the different dimensions of service quality in the research situation.

In descriptive surveys, for example, relevant concepts will be those aspects of the phenomenon or population that you wish to be able to measure, for example, customers' satisfaction levels or their shopping frequency. In analytical surveys, the concepts will be derived from the theory you wish to test and are included in your conceptual model and hypotheses.

Once you have identified the relevant concepts you will need to define them. Based on your knowledge of the topic area and your review of relevant literature, you should define your concepts and the dimensions of them that you wish to measure in your questionnaire. The dimensions can be derived from a range of sources, including previous studies, theoretical literature on the topic or by carrying out exploratory research, for example, a qualitative interview study. Research in Practice 10.1 gives an example of the dimensions of a complex concept: service quality.

10.5 Formulate your questions and decide the level of measurement

The next step is to decide how you will measure the concepts you have identified as relevant to your research. To do this you will have to develop what are known as **indicators** that can be used as measures of those concepts. If, for example, you wanted to measure the concept of success in the context of a project, one possible indicator might be whether or not the project was completed on time. In questionnaires, of course, indicators will take the form of questions.

10.5.1 Formulating your questions

Formulating your questions is probably the hardest part of questionnaire design, at least for those new to research. It is our experience as tutors and supervisors that the weakest feature of most questionnaire-based student research projects is the questions they use to collect their data. So, how do you formulate suitable questions? There are, in principle, two options.

First, you can use or adapt well-established measures from prior research. Suitable measures can be found in academic journal articles or practitioner publications. Alternatively, handbooks such as Bearden et al. (2011), Price (1997) and Roth et al. (2008) provide listings of previously used questions. It is likely that you will need to adapt or tailor existing questions to fit the context of your own research. Aside from saving you the time of developing your own measures, the big advantage of using existing measures is that information regarding their validity and reliability will be available in the referenced work. Note, however, that just because a set of questions appears in print does not automatically mean that they are a good measure of your chosen concept. Ensure that you check the source for information on the quality of the proposed measure. Be aware also that some measures may be subject to commercial or other restrictions, so you should check before using them. Wherever existing measures are used their source should be fully acknowledged and referenced in your final report.

If no previous measures are available to use you will need to develop your own questions to collect your data. Pay close attention to the definitions and dimensions of the concepts you are intending to measure. Designing your own questions is a demanding task if you are trying to measure a complex construct, so ensure that you are thoroughly familiar with your topic, consult more specialist texts on question development and seek advice from your supervisor or other expert if possible.

In practice, many questionnaires contain a mix of both existing and new measures. Whatever you do, try to make sure the questions you include in your questionnaire represent the best possible measures of your research variables.

10.5.2 Levels of measurement

As you develop your questions you will need to decide what level of measurement to use for each of your variables. Measurement, as we are using the term here, is the process of assigning a number to an observation to facilitate analysis. In management research we often need to measure many different types of variable, including things like nationality, gender, employee satisfaction and share price. It is fairly obvious that using a number to 'measure' gender is not the same thing as using a number to measure share price. Therefore we need to be able to recognize different levels of measurement that we can use in our research. Conventionally we do this by distinguishing between **nominal, ordinal, interval** and **ratio** measurement levels.

Nominal data

The nominal level of data is the lowest level of measurement and is used when numbers are applied to distinguish different categories such as gender (i.e. male/female) or geographic location (e.g. different office sites). Membership of the categories must be mutually exclusive and categories have no natural rank order.

Ordinal data

Ordinal data can be placed in rank order from highest to lowest but do not allow us to measure how much difference there is between the categories. For example, measuring how often people drive, using the categories 'every day', 'at least 3 times per week', '1–2 times per week' and 'less than once per week' allows us to place respondents in rank order but we cannot specify exactly the difference between them in terms of the number of times they drive their car.

Interval data

Interval data can be placed in rank order but it is also possible to measure the size of the difference between the values. Interval data do not have a naturally occurring zero point, so whilst we can add or subtract values, it makes no sense to multiply or divide them. Temperature, measured in degrees Celsius, is an example of an interval scale. We can calculate the difference between 24°C and 12°C but cannot say that one is twice as warm as the other. Similarly, 0°C does not represent an absence of temperature.

One of the most commonly encountered rating scales in management research is the **Likert scales**. In response to a statement such as 'statistics is fun', for example, a Likert scale requires the respondent to indicate their degree of agreement or disagreement. Such an agreement scale usually ranges from 'strongly agree' to 'strongly

CRITICAL COMMENTARY 10.1

Likert scale data: interval or ordinal?

The Likert-type scale has become an established technique for measuring responses to statement items in social science questionnaires. Typically these will be statements regarding attitudes, perceptions or feelings to which the respondent indicates their level of agreement or disagreement. The output generated by Likert scales is treated as interval data and analysed using the techniques appropriate to that measurement level.

Despite this, there is debate over whether or not Likert scale data can really be considered as interval level. The alternative view is that Likert scale data should be treated as ordinal: responses can be placed in rank order but the intervals between the values cannot be assumed to be constant (Jamieson 2004). As a result, only those analysis techniques suitable for ordinal data should be used.

In management research it has become accepted practice to assume that 'people treat the intervals between points on such scales as being equal in magnitude' (Hair et al. 2007: 227) and therefore to treat Likert scale data as interval data. We follow that approach in this book. Nevertheless, this remains a contentious issue and it is important to be aware of the debate and to decide how you will treat Likert scale data in your project.

PART III

disagree' and, conventionally, a 5- or 7-point scale is provided. The data generated by Likert-type rating scales are often treated as interval data for analysis in managerial research but this use is contentious, as we discuss in Critical Commentary 10.1.

Ratio data

Finally, ratio data is the same as interval data, with equal distance between measurement intervals, but this time with a meaningful zero point. Length and age are two examples of ratio scales. Ratio data is the highest level of measurement

Implications of the different measurement levels

The level of measurement which you choose has implications for your subsequent data analysis because certain statistical techniques require a particular level of management. Decisions that you make at the questionnaire design stage therefore have serious implications for later stages of your research and so, as part of your research design, you should identify your intended analysis techniques to ensure that you collect appropriate data. We discuss the selection of statistical techniques by data type in Chapter 13 but, as a general rule, the higher the level of measurement, the more options you have from an analysis point of view. We summarize levels of measurement and their features in Table 10.2.

Table 10.2 Levels of measurement

	Allowable operations				
Level of measurement	Frequency counts	Place in rank order	Quantify difference between each value and add and subtract values	Multiply and divide values	Level of measurement
Nominal	✓				Lowest
Ordinal	✓	✓			↑
Interval	✓	✓	✓		↕
Ratio	✓	✓	✓	✓	Highest

10.5.3 Question format

Alongside deciding on your measurement level you will also have to decide on what question format to use. We now present a range of options from which to choose. As we explain, different formats generate data at different levels of measurement, so it is important to consider your choice of question format alongside your required measurement level.

Checklist

In checklist-format questions the respondent is presented with a list of options from which they select as many as apply (Figure 10.2). This generates nominal data but, as respondents may select multiple options, it does not result in each respondent being in one, and only one, category. This may complicate analysis because it is less easy to categorize respondents, so it is important to decide how the data will be analysed if you are intending to use this question format.

For what purpose do you use the Internet? (please select as many as applicable)

    a) Work/business   ☐

    b) Leisure   ☐

    c) Search for information about products and services   ☐

    d) Buying products and services   ☐

Figure 10.2 Example checklist question

Categorical scale

In this question format the respondent is presented with a list of options from which they select one, and only one, category. The categories chosen must be meaningful to the respondents, mutually exclusive and exhaustive (i.e. cover all options). For some questions it may be necessary to provide an 'other' category, sometimes with the option of an open question for the respondent to provide additional details. The data from such open questions may be hard to analyse, however, and if the 'other' option is heavily used it may also indicate poor choice of categories.

This is an important question format for gathering demographic data on your respondents. Variants include:

- *Binary choice* (Figure 10.3a). The respondent has two options, such as yes/no or male/female and must choose one. This type of question generates nominal data.
- *Multiple choice* (Figure 10.3b and c). The respondent has multiple options and must select only one. The categories can be nominal (such as marital status) or ordinal (such as age groups).

(a) What gender are you?

☐ Male
☐ Female

(b) What is your age?

☐ under 18
☐ 18–24
☐ 25–34
☐ 35–44
☐ 45–54
☐ 55+

(c) What is your marital status?

☐ Married

☐ Single (never married or never registered a civil partnership)

☐ Divorced or formerly in a civil partnership which is now legally dissolved

☐ Widowed or surviving partner from a civil partnership

☐ Separated (but still legally married or still legally in a civil partnership)

☐ In a registered civil partnership

Figure 10.3 Example categorical scale questions

Rank preference scale

In this question format, respondents are presented with a list of items and must arrange them in rank preference (Figure 10.4). This produces ordinal-level data for the items that have been ranked. Note that because the resulting data are ordinal there are constraints on using this type of data to calculate an overall ranking for each of the options. As a result the data generated may not be easy to interpret in practice. Respondents may also find it hard to rank a large number of items and may be unable or unwilling to differentiate between items. In our experience, rank preference scales are popular with novice researchers but can create problems later in the project if the analysis options have not been properly considered.

Please rank the following forms of exercise in terms of your preference where 1 = lowest and 5 = highest

        Jogging   ☐
        Cycling   ☐
        Swimming   ☐
        Squash   ☐
        Yoga   ☐

Figure 10.4 Example rank preference question

Numeric rating Likert-type scale

The Likert-type rating scale is often used to measure the strength of attitudes, feelings or opinions. Typically, respondents are presented with a 5- or 7-point scale on which they express the intensity of their views about a statement, as we show in Figure 10.5. The more scale points, the greater the potential to discriminate between respondents' opinions, but this has to be balanced against their ability to answer to that level of precision. Data are treated as either interval or ordinal (see Critical Commentary 10.1).

Please indicate below the degree to which you agree or disagree with the following statement:

'The Internet is an easy way to find out about products'

   Strongly   Neither   Strongly
   disagree   agree nor   agree
                disagree

   ☐   ☐   ☐   ☐   ☐   ☐   ☐

Figure 10.5 Example single-item Likert-type scale

Semantic differential scale

Semantic differential scales are another type of numeric rating scale that can be used to measure attitudes or feelings, and again can utilize a 5- or 7-point scale. The key feature of this type of scale is that it utilizes statements at each end of the scale that describe the attitude or feeling using opposite adjectives such as good/bad or happy/sad. Respondents circle numbers or place a mark along a continuum to indicate their own position. The example in Figure 10.6 is taken from an investigation into the various emotions generated during online shopping and shows eight different items (Rose and Samouel 2009). Numbers are assigned to each opposite emotion. The data generated are assumed to be interval.

Using the rating scale below please indicate the feelings you had following your most recent online shopping experience:

1 UNHAPPY	1	2	3	4	5	6	7	HAPPY
2 ANNOYED	1	2	3	4	5	6	7	PLEASED
3 CALM	1	2	3	4	5	6	7	EXCITED
4 RELAXED	1	2	3	4	5	6	7	STIMULATED
5 GUIDED	1	2	3	4	5	6	7	AUTONOMOUS
6 INFLUENCED	1	2	3	4	5	6	7	INFLUENTIAL

Figure 10.6 Example semantic differential scale (based on Rose and Samouel 2009)

Summated rating scale

The scale in Figure 10.6 is a single-item scale because it uses one question (item) to measure the underlying variable. An alternative approach is to use what is known as a summated scale or **multi-item scale**. As the names suggest, this is a scale which consists of several questions (items) that are combined (summated) in some way to produce a single measure for the chosen variable. Summated scales can capture more of the complexity of a concept and provide greater measurement precision, thereby giving a more valid measure than a single-item scale. Summated scales are very common in business and management research for measuring complex constructs and for developing new measures. Single-item scales may be used where a well-established measure exists or when measuring self-reported intentional behaviour (such as intention to repeat purchase). Examination of prior research in your topic area can help you to decide what type of scale is appropriate for your project.

The number of items in a summated scale and how they are combined can vary. In Research in Practice 10.2 we show an example of a summated scale used to measure affective commitment. In this case there are six items that would be included as six Likert-style rating questions in the questionnaire. Determining the level of affective commitment for a respondent involves calculating the arithmetic mean (average) score of the six responses by that particular respondent to give a single figure which can then be incorporated into further analysis. In addition, it would be standard practice

RESEARCH IN PRACTICE 10.2

Measuring affective commitment

The extent to which employees are committed to their organizations is of interest to both academics and practitioners. One dimension of commitment is what Meyer et al. (1993: 539) refer to as 'affective commitment'. 'Employees with a strong affective commitment', they suggest, 'remain with the organization because they want to' (Meyer et al. 1993: 539). In order to measure this dimension of commitment, Meyer et al. have developed and tested a multi-item scale. The scale consists of six items shown below. Each item is measured on a 1–7 rating scale (where 1 = strongly disagree; 7 = strongly agree). Those items marked (R) are negatively worded and need to be reverse-coded (i.e. 1 becomes 7, 2 becomes 6, etc.) before analysis (see Chapter 13). The final measure of affective commitment is calculated by taking the arithmetic mean (average) of the six items.

1 I would be very happy to spend the rest of my career with this organization.
2 I really feel as if this organization's problems are my own.
3 I do not feel a strong sense of 'belonging' to my organization. (R)
4 I do not feel 'emotionally attached' to this organization. (R)
5 I do not feel like 'part of the family' at my organization. (R)
6 This organization has a great deal of personal meaning for me.

when using multi-item scales to check the reliability of the scale, which we discuss in Chapter 13.

Developing valid and reliable summated scales is a demanding task and can easily form a research project in its own right. This is one of the reasons why we strongly encourage you to use existing scales, suitably adapted if necessary, where possible.

Open questions

The formats we have been looking at so far are examples of **closed questions**, in which the respondent is provided with a set of predefined responses from which they must choose one or more options. Closed questions are the most common format in questionnaires. The limited number of response options and their structured nature makes it easier to analyse the answers using quantitative analysis techniques. On the other hand, while the answer format provides structure for the respondents, it also constrains their responses to the researcher's view of the topic. The alternative is to adopt an open question format. **Open questions** do not have a fixed set of optional answers but invite the respondent to answer in their own words. You might, for example, ask respondents to explain in their own words their reasons for answering a closed question in a particular way. Open questions enable the capture of fairly rich and detailed data that may provide insights or responses beyond the researcher's initial framing of the research problem.

Open questions can vary in their complexity and degree of 'openness'. The simplest format is that of a single item response in which the respondent is asked to provide a single response to a specific question. This might be numeric (such as age or length of time in the organization) or textual (such as favourite colour or city of residence). In Figure 10.7 we show an example requiring a numeric response in the form of the respondents' annual household income. Although this type of question offers the possibility of eliciting an exact answer, in some cases, for example a sensitive subject like income, respondents may be unwilling or unable to provide the required degree of precision. In such situations a category scale offering a set of broader categories (e.g. of different household income levels) may be more suitable.

Alternatively, the question may be phrased more openly to invite a longer answer from the respondent. Figure 10.8 gives an example of open questions adapted from a workshop evaluation form that provides delegates the opportunity to make suggestions to the tutor for future workshops.

We recommend caution when using open questions in questionnaires. Response rates are likely to be much lower than for closed questions and responses can vary greatly in terms of the amount of information provided by each respondent. Perhaps most importantly, open-ended questions create additional complexity when it comes to analysis. Even an apparently simple question such as 'what is your job role?' can elicit many different sorts of answer, as the question may be understood in different ways by respondents and, with variations in spelling, language and local practice regarding how jobs are described, the resulting data can be very difficult to analyse. If you are really interested in capturing the respondents' own perspectives in their own words, you should perhaps consider a different research design such as a qualitative interview study.

PART III

> **What was your net household income during the last tax year?**
>
> £ [   ]

Figure 10.7 Example single item response question

> **In future workshops, what should the tutor:**
> **(a) Continue doing?**
> _____
> _____
> _____
>
> **(b) Do differently?**
> _____
> _____
> _____

Figure 10.8 Example open question

10.5.4 Evaluating the quality of your questions

It is important that the data collected by your questionnaire are valid and reliable, and good questions are central to this. In Chapter 4 we reviewed a range of criteria for judging quality in quantitative research and you should review them to help you assess the quality of your questions. Less technically, McGivern (2006: 351) offers the following checklist for the wording of any question to help to ensure reliability and validity.

- It measures what it claims to measure.
- It is relevant and meaningful to the respondent.
- It is acceptable to the respondent.
- It is understood by the respondent (and the interviewer).
- It is interpreted in the way in which you intended.
- It is interpreted in the same way by all respondents.
- It elicits an accurate and meaningful response.
- The meaning of the response is clear and unambiguous.

This means paying careful attention to how you word your questions. We give some examples of common mistakes in questionnaire wording in Table 10.3 to help you avoid basic errors. Ultimately, however, the most important thing is to ensure that the questions make sense to your respondents. This is something that requires a sound knowledge of your target population in terms of their level of literacy or degree of understanding of the research topic, along with careful pre-testing and piloting, as we discuss later in the chapter.

Table 10.3 Common mistakes in questionnaire wording

Mistake	Example	Possible remedy
Double-barrelled questions or statements	'I enjoy watching football and rugby on television'	Split into two questions.
Double negatives	'The project was not unsuccessful'	Change the wording so the statement is worded positively, combined with a rating scale.
Leading questions	'We should spend more money on welfare to ensure that no child goes hungry'	Adopt neutral wording; in this case if the researcher is interested in a possible link between attitudes to welfare spending and attitudes to child poverty, they could be measured separately and then the relationship investigated statistically.
Technical language or jargon	(a) 'Do you make use of Voice over Internet Protocol technology at home?' (b) 'Do you have a strong sense of affective commitment to my organization'	Ensure question wording is appropriate to your audience. In example (a) everyday language description plus an example could be offered. Example (b) is more difficult. Here the researcher is trying to measure a complex abstract concept (affective commitment) directly. A multi-item rating scale is likely to be more suitable as a measure.

10.5.5 Using a data collection matrix to manage your questions

Most questionnaires will contain numerous questions measuring several variables. To help you manage these and to make sure that you do not leave any vital questions out of your final questionnaire, we suggest that you set up a data collection matrix. This is a simple table as shown in Table 10.4 that you can use to keep track of the measures that are needed in your questionnaire. It provides a way of systematically linking research question, variables to be measured, details of the questions you will use to measure the variable, and where the questions appear in the questionnaire. As well as helping you to prepare your questionnaire, the data collection matrix provides a very useful guide during your analysis. It can also be included in your final report when describing your questionnaire. In Research in Practice 10.3 we illustrate a data collection matrix in use as part of a student project.

RESEARCH IN PRACTICE 10.3

Developing questions to measure variables in a conceptual model

For his final MBA project on factors influencing mobile shopping by smartphone, Davin Mac Ananey, whose study we first introduced in Research in Practice 4.1, developed a conceptual model that identified several variables that existing theory suggested could be relevant influential factors.[1] To test the model, it was decided to use an analytic survey study, with data being gathered by questionnaire. Designing the questionnaire involved identifying the relevant variables in the model and formulating suitable scales to measure them. Davin did this by building on previous work that had looked at factors influencing technology adoption all the way back to Davis' (1989) work in the area. Below we present a simplified version of the model, containing only two of the independent variables that were used in the final study, along with examples of the questions used to measure the variables captured in a data collection matrix similar to that in Table 10.4.

Simplified conceptual model

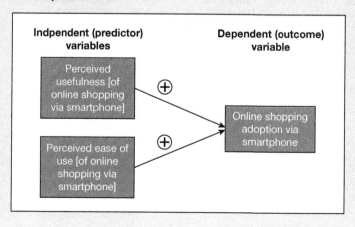

EXAMPLE DATA MATRIX

Variable	Number of items in the scale	Questions to measure variable	Sources	Question numbers in questionnaire
Perceived usefulness (PU) (independent variable)	5	1 Shopping online through my smartphone would improve my efficiency in my ability to shop. 2 Shopping online through my smartphone would enable me to do my shopping conveniently. 3 Shopping online through my smartphone would enhance my effectiveness in my ability to shop. 4 Shopping online through my smartphone would save me time. 5 In general, I believe shopping online through my smartphone would be useful.	Taylor and Todd (1995), Khalifa and Cheng (2002), Wang and Barnes (2007), Kurnia et al. (2006) and Wong and Hiew (2005)	Q 6–10
Perceived ease of use (PEOU) (independent variable)	3	1 It is easy to learn to shop online through your smartphone. 2 Shopping online through your smartphone is understandable and clear. 3 Shopping online through your smartphone is/might be easy to use.	Wang and Barnes (2007), Luarn and Lin (2005), Chew (2007) and Lin and Wang (2005)	Q 11–13
Online shopping adoption via smartphone (SSA) (dependent variable)	3	1 I have adopted online shopping through my smartphone. 2 I believe I will continue to shop online through my smartphone in the future. 3 I believe my interest towards online shopping through my smartphone will increase in the future.	Davis (1989), Bhattacherjee (2001), Mallat et al. (2006), Kurnia et al. (2006), Luarn and Lin (2005), Liao et al. (2007), Khalifa and Shen (2008), Moon and Kim (2001) and Shin (2007)	Q 31–33

Note: The responses above are examples only and are not included in our reference list.

Table 10.4 Example data collection matrix

Research question(s)	Concept/ variable to be measured	Questions to be included in the questionnaire	Number of items in the scale	Source(s) of questions	Question numbers in questionnaire

10.6 Structure and lay out the questionnaire

Even the best questions will not produce the desired results if your questionnaire is compromised by poor layout or a confusing structure. As part of the questionnaire design process you will also need to decide on the structure and layout of your questionnaire. You should order your questions so that respondents find the questionnaire structure both logical and easy to follow. This will improve the potential response rate by encouraging respondents to feel involved and engaged in the process of completing the questionnaire. Figure 10.9 provides a suggested structure for your questionnaire.

PART III

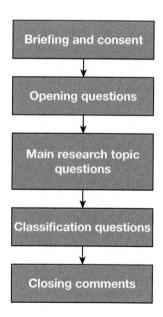

Figure 10.9 Suggested questionnaire structure

10.6.1 Briefing and consent

The questionnaire should begin by briefing the respondent about the nature of the research and requesting their informed consent in line with the ethics guidelines discussed in Chapter 7. The briefing information should start with a short statement informing the respondent of the purpose of the research and what it is seeking to investigate. It should confirm procedures regarding respondent anonymity and data confidentiality and include an informed consent disclaimer along the lines of:

> By completing and returning this questionnaire it will be understood that you give consent for your responses to be used for the purposes of this research project.

10.6.2 Opening questions

Your opening questions should get the attention of the respondent and help to build rapport. They should be uncomplicated and immediately relevant to the respondents, thereby building their confidence and interest in participating. Leave more complex or probing questions until later in the questionnaire. Opening questions can also be used as filter questions to screen respondents to establish that they do meet required sample characteristics. For instance, in consumer experiences with a particular product a filter question might be included to confirm that respondents have used that product. Filtering will, however, impact on the ultimate sample size and is not a substitute for a properly targeted sampling plan. Research in Practice 10.4 gives an example of filter questions from a study of online search behaviour.

10.6.3 Main research topic questions

The main body of your questionnaire contains the majority of the questions that you have identified in your data collection matrix and that will provide the bulk of the data needed to answer your research questions. Questions should be grouped together by general topic and should build logically in terms of the sequence of the questioning. The order of the questions should be such that you begin broadly and slowly to funnel into more specific questions. This gives the respondent a general understanding of the topic being investigated before moving on to more detailed questioning. In sequencing the questions you should also be aware that answers to earlier questions may influence responses to later ones. For example, questions about a respondent's attitude to risk-taking by others might influence their answers to subsequent questions about their own risk-taking behaviours.

A number of aspects of the structure and layout will contribute to an effective response rate. Firstly, think about the relative importance of your questions. If there are questions that are not compulsory or critical to the analysis, put them at the end so that if the respondents give up you still have some potentially usable data. Secondly, think about the ways in which respondents are asked to indicate their answers. Consistency is helpful for respondents, so try to keep questions with similar response formats together (e.g. all Likert scale questions) and use the same response mechanism (such as ticking a box, circling an option or entering a number) as much as possible. Thirdly, consider the visual aspects such as the amount of space between questions, size of the typeface, or use of colour. These decisions should always be made with

RESEARCH IN PRACTICE 10.4

Example filter questions

For a study on online search (Rose and Samouel 2009) the sample consisted of frequent online shoppers who were using the Internet to search for product information related to small electrical goods. Below we show some of the filter questions used at the start of the questionnaire to identify relevant respondents for the sample.

Q1: How frequently do you use the Internet? (please select one only)

a) Daily ☐

b) Weekly ☐

c) Monthly ☐

d) Less than once a month ☐

If you have selected c) or d), please *do not* complete the questionnaire

Q2: For what purpose do you use the Internet? (please select as many as applicable)

a) Work/business ☐

b) Leisure ☐

c) Search for information about products and services ☐

d) Buying products and services ☐

If you have selected a) and/or b) only, please *do not* complete the questionnaire

Q3: Please indicate if you have ever searched for information online for any of the following items:

a) Small electronic goods (e.g. MP3 player, CD-player, audio-recorder)   Yes ☐ No ☐

b) Electrical white goods (e.g. washing machine, microwave, refrigerator)   Yes ☐ No ☐

c) Larger electronic goods (e.g. PC, printer, television, games console)   Yes ☐ No ☐

d) Computer accesories (e.g. software, hardware accessories, upgrades)   Yes ☐ No ☐

If you have answered No to all, please *do not* complete the questionnaire

regard to the characteristics of your respondents and then tested in the pre-test and pilot stage. Finally, make sure that you proofread your questionnaire. Spelling errors and grammatical mistakes are unlikely to impress potential respondents.

'Don't know' and conditional routing questions

In some questionnaires not all questions will be relevant to all respondents. For example, respondents will not be able to answer questions about their experiences of a product they have never used and it would make no sense to force them to give a response. Indeed, if they did, it would potentially distort the findings.

One solution is to include a 'don't know', 'not applicable' or similar option as part of the question response choices (note that 'don't know' is not the same as 'neither agree nor disagree' as the mid-point of an odd-numbered Likert-type scale). Inclusion of a 'don't know' option creates the risk that respondents will choose it because they are too lazy to fill in the questionnaire correctly. To some extent this can be assessed, along with the need to include the 'don't know' option, during the pre-test and piloting of the questionnaire.

Another option which is useful if there is a large section of questions that do not apply to certain respondents is to use conditional routing questions. These allow you to direct people to relevant areas of the questionnaire. Conditional routing questions take the general form: 'if you have answered *X* then go to question *A*, if not go to question *B*'. If they are included they should be clearly signposted throughout the questionnaire to aid accurate completion. Most online survey tools contain routines to support routing questions, but for other forms of self-completed questionnaires conditional routing adds complexity and needs to be carefully tested. In addition, any form of routing question will affect the sample size for the questions within the questionnaire. If responses that are critical to your research project are given by only a small proportion of respondents, you may find yourself without enough data. Like filter questions, routing questions are not a substitute for a well-executed sampling plan. Nevertheless, used appropriately, they can help to ensure that respondents are required only to answer questions within their experience, and thereby they support completion rates and reduce the risk of spurious data as a result of inappropriately answered questions. Figure 10.10 gives an example of conditional routing questions.

Question 9 Have you heard or seen any advertisements for a mobile telephone service in the past ten days?

☐ Yes
☐ No

If you answered No, please go to Question 13

If you answered Yes, were the advertisements on TV, radio or both?

If TV, go to **Question 10**
If radio, go to **Question 11**
If both, go to **Question 12**

Figure 10.10 Example of conditional routing

10.6.4 Classification questions

In most research projects you will need to collect demographic and socio-economic information, such as age, gender or income. Classification questions are used to collect this kind of data. In some projects this information will be central to your research question, for instance, if you were investigating the impact of age on smartphone use or the difference in satisfaction levels between male and female customers. In others it is needed so that you can describe the sample from which your data has been obtained and compare it to the target population. To develop your classification questions you should first draw up a list of the relevant classification variables, based on your research questions and the characteristics of the target population. To do this you may need to look at secondary data, such as organizational records or government statistics, that give more details on the characteristics of your target population.

You should be aware of the personal nature of some classification data, such as salary, and, therefore, how the sensitivities of respondents may affect their willingness and ability to provide a response. In order to overcome this, consider using categorical scales with a range of options (as shown in Figure 10.3 for age) rather than asking for exact numbers. Willingness to provide classification data can be strongly linked to the respondent's belief in the anonymity of the questionnaire and therefore the ability of the researcher to link specific data to specific respondents. A clearly worded briefing and informed consent statement will help in this regard. It is also common practice to place classification questions at the end of your questionnaire, by which time the respondent should be more comfortable about the nature of the research and providing personal data.

10.6.5 Closing comments

Closing comments can include any instructions for return and submission if these have not already been dealt with, along with any courtesies such as thanking respondents for their time.

10.7 Pre-test and pilot the questionnaire

Before sending out your questionnaire it is essential that you test it to identify any problems while there is still time to correct them. We recommend a two-stage approach. Firstly, carry out a pre-test of your questionnaire with a small group of people (ideally similar to, or familiar with, your intended sample) in order to check that the questions are clear and they understand them. Ask them to complete the questionnaire. Time how long it takes and ask for feedback on their experience of completing it. Do the questions make sense? Is the language and wording appropriate? Is the structure and layout clear and easy to follow? You can also include subject matter experts in your pre-test, as they can give more detailed insight into the questions themselves. If you are a student researcher we strongly recommend that you get feedback from your supervisor as well. The pre-test stage provides you with guidance and feedback for improvements and changes during the early design stage.

Secondly, you should conduct a full test of the questionnaire by carrying out what is called a pilot study. A pilot study is conducted amongst a small sub-group of the target population and using the same administration method as the full survey will use. The purpose is to identify any problems or difficulties with the questionnaire and to test the administration of the questionnaire under operational conditions. In addition, if a sufficient sample is acquired it may be possible to run preliminary data analysis, although this will depend on the sample size required for the test(s) being used. In some cases, it may be possible to ask some respondents for feedback on how they experienced completion of the questionnaire. A pilot study should happen at a point where it is still feasible to make meaningful changes prior to full data collection and analysis. While pre-testing and piloting can be time consuming, they will help to ensure that your questionnaire is fit for purpose.

10.8 Administrate and distribute the questionnaire

The design process should also consider the administration method that you use for your questionnaire, for example, whether it will be distributed on paper or via the Internet. When deciding on how to distribute your questionnaire you have a range of options, including:

- Face-to-face interview, where the respondents is asked questions by the interviewer, who completes the questionnaire either on paper or via an electronic device such as a tablet.
- Telephone interview, where the interviewer contacts the respondent by telephone and administers the questionnaire via a pre-prepared script.
- Researcher delivery and collection, where the researcher (or assistant) delivers a hard copy of the questionnaire to respondents, who fill it in for later collection by the researcher. A variant of this can be used in studies such as experiments where a participant may be asked to complete a questionnaire prior to, during or after the experiment.
- Post or internal mail, where the researcher distributes the questionnaire in hard copy and it is self-completed by the respondent, who returns it in a similar way. Note that if a public postal service is used, consideration needs to be given to how to manage return postage using pre-paid envelopes or a similar arrangement.
- Email distribution, where an electronic version of the questionnaire is delivered to the sample using an existing email distribution list. Respondents complete the questionnaire and return it via email (or in some cases, print out, complete and return the questionnaire by other means such as internal mail).
- Online, where access to the questionnaire is via a URL link that is distributed to the sample by post, email or other electronic means, or alternatively by posting it on a website such as a social media site or online community.

10.8.1 Choosing a distribution method

The method selected for questionnaire distribution is in part dictated by the nature of the sampling frame being used and the type of contact details you have (e.g. whether you have access to email, telephone or other contact details) as well as the sampling method (e.g. some form of probability sampling method versus self-selection, snowballing, etc.). Other considerations in the choice of questionnaire distribution will be the characteristics of the sample and the method to which they are most likely to respond. A further consideration is the nature of the research topic and the degree of sensitivity or complexity involved. In some instances there may be value in having an interviewer present in person who can ensure that the respondent both understands and is comfortable with the questions. In others, the greater anonymity of self-completion may be preferred. Where a questionnaire is administered by a team of field workers, it is important to provide clear briefing to them regarding their role and involvement in the questioning of respondents. Finally, consider likely response rates for your chosen sample, given your intended distribution method as discussed in Chapter 9.

10.8.2 *Online questionnaires*

The Internet has become a very important channel for questionnaire administration. Electronic distribution can reduce turnaround times and costs and allow the researcher to involve participants who would be difficult or impossible to reach using more traditional distribution methods such as post or telephone. Online questionnaires can also reduce data collection and entry errors that can arise through manual data entry error. This also saves time. Working online can also enable you to enhance the format for layout, appearance and usability of the questionnaire. In addition, an online questionnaire may appeal to particular groups of respondents, thanks to their familiarity with the online environment, speed of access and ease of completion and return.

The popularity of online questionnaires, at least amongst student researchers, is partly due to the widespread availability of dedicated but user-friendly proprietary online survey tools. These support the researcher in creating, distributing and collecting the questionnaire. If you are considering using an online survey tool we suggest that you review the different options available. Based on our own experiences we recommend that you confirm the following points before making a decision.

- Does the survey tool support the question formats and any special requirements (such as conditional routing) that are needed?
- How easy is the design interface to use and is support available if there is a problem?
- What policy does the site have regarding data security and is this adequate for the project?
- What file formats are available for exporting data on completion of the project? (For analysis you will need to be able to export the raw response data in a suitable format such as a Microsoft Excel-readable file.)
- Are there any limitations regarding, for example, the number of questions or the number of respondents?

In many cases the answers to these questions will depend on the package purchased. Often the free or trial options place restrictions on the options available, number of respondents/questions, output file formats and so on, so make sure that you understand these when evaluating different providers' offerings. You should also check whether you have access to a suitable online survey tool via your academic institution or organization.

KEY LEARNING POINTS

- Questionnaires use standardized, structured questions to gather quantitative or quantifiable data on variables of interest to the researcher. As a data collection technique they can offer low cost, speed of collection, flexibility, anonymity and reduced interview effects. Potential disadvantages include variable response rates, partial completion, the limited range of responses offered and requirement for respondent literacy.

- A structured approach should be taken to questionnaire design, including: identification of relevant concepts, formulation of appropriate questions, structuring the questionnaire, pre-testing and piloting and questionnaire administration.
- The choice of concepts to be measured as variables in the questionnaire should be driven by the research question, prior theory and research and any conceptual model/hypotheses to be tested.
- Question formulation involves selecting appropriate question wording, deciding a suitable level of measurement (nominal, ordinal, interval or ratio) and choosing an appropriate question format. For measuring more complex concepts, a multi-item, summated scale is often used. Questions should be evaluated against appropriate quality criteria.
- Structure and layout of the questionnaire are also important. Questionnaire structure may include the following elements: briefing and consent, opening questions, main research topic questions, classification questions and closing comments.
- Questionnaires should be pre-tested and piloted before being distributed. Distribution options depend on the target population, sampling frame and nature of the characteristics of the sample. Administration methods include face to face, telephone, post, email or online. Online is an increasingly important distribution channel.

NEXT STEPS

10.1 Identifying relevant concepts/variables. Draw up a data matrix (see Table 10.4). Return to your research questions and any conceptual model/hypotheses you are using. Identify the key concepts that you are investigating in your research project and list them in your data matrix. How are the concepts defined in the literature you have studied?

10.2 Questionnaire administration. Decide how you will administer your questionnaire so that you can make arrangements regarding distribution and return and, if using online survey, design your survey using an appropriate online survey tool.

10.3 Formulating your questions. Review your literature; identify any scales or questions that already exist from prior research that can be used for the measurement of your own variables. Ensure that the prior variables do match the definition of your own variables. Note the wording of the questions and consider any adaptation you will need to make. Note the references in your data collection matrix. If no existing measures are available, decide how you will develop your own measures. Select an appropriate measurement level and question format for each question and record them in your data collection matrix.

10.4 Preparing your questionnaire. Begin to draft your questionnaire by using the structure provided at Figure 10.9. Use each of the five boxed headings to create five sections for your questionnaire and use your data collection matrix to populate each section. Once you have done that, review your questions and the overall questionnaire for completeness and accuracy.

10.5 Pre-testing and piloting. Carry out a pre-test and pilot of your questionnaire. Incorporate any required changes, recording what was done and the reasons for doing so in your research diary or journal.

Further reading

For further reading, please see the companion website.

References

Bearden, W. O., Netemeyer, R. G. and Hawks, K. (2011). *Handbook of marketing scales: Multi-item measures for marketing and consumer behavior research*. 3rd edn. Thousand Oaks, CA: Sage.

Davis, F. (1989). 'Perceived usefulness, perceived ease of use, and user acceptance of information technology', *MIS Quarterly*, 13(3), 318–40.

Hair, J. F. J., Money, A. H., Samouel, P. and Page, M. (2007). *Research methods for business*. Chichester: Wiley.

Jamieson, S. (2004). 'Likert scales: How to (ab)use them', *Medical Education*, 38(12), 1217–18.

McGivern, Y. (2006). *The practice of market and social research: An introduction*. Harlow: Prentice Hall.

Meyer, J. P., Allen, N. J. and Smith, C. A. (1993). 'Commitment to organizations and occupations: Extension and test of a three-component conceptualization', *Journal of Applied Psychology*, 78(4), 538–551.

Parasuraman, A., Zeitmahl, V. A. and Berry, L. L. (1988). 'SEVQUAL: A multiple-item scale for measuring customer perceptions of service quality', *Journal of Retailing*, 64(1), 12–40.

Price, J. L. (1997). 'Handbook of organizational measurement', *International Journal of Manpower*, 18(4/5/6), 305–558.

Rose, S. and Samouel, P. (2009). 'Internal psychological versus external market-driven determinants of the amount of consumer information search amongst online shoppers', *Journal of Marketing Management*, 25(1–2), 171–90.

Roth, A. V., Schroeder, R., Huang, X. and Kristal, M. (2008). *Handbook of metrics for research in operations management: Multi-item measurement scales and objective items*. London: Sage.

Note

1 Mac Ananey, D. (2013). *An investigation into the factors that drive online shopping adoption through smartphones in the United Kingdom*. MBA dissertation submission. Henley Business School, University of Reading.

PART III

11 Collecting data using in-depth interviews

CHAPTER SUMMARY

The key topics covered in this chapter are:

- using in-depth interviews to collect data
- interviewing individuals
- interviewing groups
- using technology in interviewing
- capturing and storing your interview data.

11.1 Introduction

In this chapter we look at how to gather qualitative data by interviewing research participants. We can obtain verbal accounts of behaviours, events, preferences, thoughts or emotions by interviewing research participants one by one using individual interviews, or in a group setting, for instance through **focus groups**. Although interviews have traditionally been done face to face, there is currently much interest in the potential of the Internet, and social media in particular, as a data collection medium in qualitative research. We therefore include a discussion of the issues emerging from using technology to conduct both individual and group interviews. Interviews can generate a lot of data, so you also need to develop protocols for recording and storing the data that you collect. We discuss how to do this in the final section of the chapter.

Interviews are a very widely used data collection method in qualitative research. Table 11.1 lists some research designs discussed in Chapter 6 and identifies the possible role of individual and group interviews as data collection methods in each.

11.2 Individual interviews

An interview consists of the researcher talking directly to research participants. This may take various forms. Fully **structured interviews** with closed-ended questions are characteristic of interviewer-administered surveys, as discussed in Chapter 10. In this chapter we focus on **in-depth interviews,** which are generally semi-structured or even

Table 11.1 The role of interviews in different research designs

Research design	Role of interviews in data collection
Interview study	Primary data collection method
Ethnography	Used alongside observational methods
Case study	Used alongside any other method
Grounded theory	Main method, alongside observations. May be complemented by analysis of documents
Action research	Main method, alongside analysis of documents. May be complemented with observations
Experiment	May be used as a supplementary method to gather insights into participants' experiences during the experiment

completely unstructured. In-depth interviews are useful for deriving detailed information or to get insights into the lived experience of participants.

Features of in-depth interviews include (Legard et al. 2003: 141–2):

- combination of structure and flexibility, allowing both the coverage of desired topics and the follow-up of emergent issues during the interview
- generation of data through interaction between the researcher and the participant
- employment of a range of techniques by the researcher to achieve depth in the responses
- opportunity to generate new understandings of issues raised in the interview
- sensitivity to the participant's own language as a way of understanding meaning.

Denzin and Lincoln (2000: 633) describe the in-depth interview as 'a conversation, the art of asking questions and listening'. Simply launching into questions because you happen to have access to someone is likely to result in irrelevant data, along with a lost opportunity to address topics that later turn out to be central to your research question. This means that careful planning is essential to increase the level of insight and the credibility of your study. The following sections will help you to plan your interviews.

11.2.1 Choosing your interviewees and scheduling your interviews

When choosing whom to interview you should follow the guidelines on sampling that we set out in Chapter 9. As interviews typically form part of a qualitative study, non-probability methods are generally preferred, particularly purposive or theoretical sampling. Likewise, the general guidance given in Chapter 9 should be used to help you decide on your intended sample size. The decision as to how many interviews are needed should also take into account the type of research design adopted, the philosophical orientation of the research and what other data sources are being used. One approach, as we noted in Chapter 9, is to continue interviewing until you reach theoretical saturation. This requires that you reflect on the insights generated during the data collection process, so that you are able to identify when you have reached theoretical saturation and do not need to conduct additional interviews.

PART III

Elite interviewing

One particular type of interview that is common in business research is elite interviewing. According to Marshall and Rossman (2006: 105), '"elite" individuals are those considered to be influential, prominent and/or well-informed people in an organization or community; they are selected for interview on the basis of their expertise in areas relevant to the research'. Examples can include chief executives and senior managers, the leaders of employer or labour organizations, or industry analysts and commentators.

Elite interviewing with subject matter experts can be useful in exploratory research, as it taps into the experiences and expertise of a diverse range of individuals and groups. However, you should always consider carefully whether such potentially partial, privileged accounts provide the insight that you need for your research questions. Table 11.2 presents some of the potential benefits and problems of this method.

Table 11.2 Potential benefits and problems of elite interviewing

Potential benefits	*Potential problems*
• Extra knowledge, due to the informant's position and experience	• Establishing the expertise of the informant
• Broad overview of issues	• Gaining access and follow-up
• Retrospective accounts	• Control of the interview process
• Draw upon informant's tacit knowledge	• Partial perspective
• Explanation of complex situations – 'why' and 'how' questions	• Philosophical concerns about privileged accounts
	• Ensuring confidentiality and anonymity may be more difficult when reporting findings

Scheduling your interviews

When scheduling your interviews, you need to take into consideration that data collection may take much longer than anticipated. This is particularly likely to occur if you are interviewing people with busy schedules or who are geographically dispersed. You should therefore start arranging your interviews as early as you can. Make sure that you allow sufficient time for each interview. In addition to the time that you need to spend on site interviewing you need to take into account travelling time to and from the site. You will also need time to organize the logistics of the meeting (e.g. prepare the room for the interview) and to follow up with research participants, for example to request clarification of points raised in the interview.

Interviewing not only takes time, but also requires considerable energy and mental focus. Avoid scheduling too many interviews for the same day, or without intervals between each, as you will be too tired to get the best out of each one. If you are new to interviewing, allow yourself plenty of time between sessions so that you can reflect not only on the content of the interview but also on your own interviewing skills.

11.2.2 *How much structure?*

Adding structure to your interview requires a more direct style of questioning and may reduce the opportunities to follow up and explore emerging topics. On the other hand, very unstructured interviews can be hard to relate to the underlying research question and, therefore, difficult to analyse. Adding structure also facilitates comparisons between different interviewees. In most cases you are likely to be using a semi-structured approach, with a limited number of key questions or discussion topics, but with scope to probe each topic area. Easterby-Smith et al. (2012) warn against the assumption that less intervention from the interviewer will lead to more insight into the interviewee's perspective. They argue that lack of structure may lead to misunderstandings about what is being discussed or about the meaning of what is being said. The result of too little intervention, they argue, is poor-quality data being gathered.

11.2.3 *The interview guide*

Of vital importance is the **interview guide** (also known as an **interview schedule** or **interview protocol**), which is the list of topics to explore during the interview and, if relevant, the set of questions that you are going to ask. The open-ended questions in a semi-structured interview, however, will be more like discussion topics than the sort of closed-ended questions that you see in the typical quantitative survey described in Chapter 10. Remember that the aim of a qualitative interview is not to measure a set of predefined variables but to investigate the experiences and understandings of participants. Nevertheless you need to ensure that your interviews gather data relevant to your research questions, so designing the interview guide is an important part of carrying out interview-based data collection. Keep your research questions in mind as you do so. The choice of specific topics for discussion will also be informed by the results of your literature review, your own prior knowledge and experience of the topic area, or preliminary discussions with those knowledgeable in the area.

As you develop your interview schedule, you should be careful with the wording of the questions so as to avoid technical or ambiguous language, which may lead to misunderstandings. Be aware that relatively few topics can be covered in a semi-structured interview. In an hour-long interview you can expect to address between six and ten main topics, if any time is to be allowed to probe and explore emerging issues. Even covering this many topics may be challenging with some interviewees. As you design your interview schedule it can be helpful to create a simple table in which you list your research questions and your proposed discussion topics to make sure that nothing is left out and (sometimes even more importantly) that the schedule is not crowded with questions that are not relevant and will simply take up interview time, to the detriment of core themes.

A feature of in-depth interviewing is that it is not unusual to refine topics/questions, or to include new ones, as the research proceeds:

> The development of the interview guide does not end at the start of the first interview. It may be modified through use: adding probes or even whole topics which had originally not been included but have emerged spontaneously in interviews; dropping or re-formulating those which are incomprehensible to

participants or consistently fail to elicit responses in any way relevant to the research question(s).

King (2004: 15)

Be aware, however, that the more changes you make during the data gathering process, the more difficult it will be to compare between interviews and, hence, analyse the resulting data. In other words, you should be ready to amend the interview schedule, but do not do so without sound reasons.

11.2.4 Types of interview question

Specific techniques can be applied within the interview setting in order to improve the quality of the output. It can be difficult to elicit opinions, perceptions or feelings that are deeply held by the individual. It may be difficult for the respondent to discuss these issues, either because of social sensitivity or because of lack of internal awareness of them or their relevance. There are different types of question to encourage certain types of answer (Table 11.3).

You can see from the examples in Table 11.3 that there are likely to be points of sensitivity of which the researcher would need to be aware when formulating interview

Table 11.3 Types of interview question

Type of question	Example question
Background/demographic	• What is your role in the organization? • What were your experiences of volunteer work before joining the organization? • Tell me about your career prior to joining the organization
Descriptive (more directive and may be more factual; responses are likely to be more constrained by the question)	• What new development projects are currently in progress? • What activities are you undertaking in social media? • How is the department organized?
Open (give greater opportunity for exploring the topic and more scope for the participant to develop their own views)	• Tell me about your experience of the firm's employee retention policies. • How do you go about preparing for a new overseas assignment? • How do you feel when you are doing a coaching session? • What does sustainability mean to you?
Probing (follow up earlier questions to gain a fuller understanding, clarify points that are unclear, obtain additional details or examples, understand the respondent's reasoning and own explanations etc.)	• What do you mean? • Can you give me an example of that? • Why do you think this is the case? • What was the result of that? • What makes you say that? • What did you mean by it being a typical example of . . . ? • How was that different from other situations you have experienced? • How did you feel about that?

questions. In some situations even simple requests for information about background experience may make interviewees feel that the researcher is questioning their suitability for their job if they are not handled sensitively by the researcher. In some cases you may find that participants struggle to answer some questions, particularly those relating to deep feelings and motivations or to topics that they have not really articulated before. In such circumstances, researchers can use projective techniques. These involve the use of stimulus material such as pre-prepared pictures, cartoons, examples of products or simple self-complete activities such as asking someone to place a list of items in their order of preference. Questions can then be built around the stimulus items. You can also use photographs (for instance, ask participants to bring some along to the interview) as a way of helping participants to talk about complex issues that they may be reluctant or unable to explore through direct questioning (Boddy 2005).

Another useful interview approach is the **critical incident technique** (CIT). This technique, which was introduced by Flanagan (1954), has been used in variety of ways within qualitative interviews (Chell 2004). CIT can be used to investigate significant happenings, such as a particular event, intervention, process or problem, identified by the interviewee and how they were managed, why they happened, who was involved, what the consequences were and so on. In the interview, the researcher asks the respondent to think of a particular incident or example that is relevant to the topic. For instance, if the subject was 'effective project meetings', the researcher might ask the participant to think of a project meeting that was particularly effective (or ineffective) in which they had been involved. This incident then forms the basis for probing questions such as (Chell 2004: 49):

- What happened?
- What happened next?
- Why did it happen?
- Who was involved?
- What were the outcomes?
- What tactics were used to deal with the situation?

CIT can help participants to focus on their own experiences and generate a rich dataset based on experiences and perceptions, thereby supporting an inductive approach.

There are some question styles that should generally be avoided because of their potential to influence the answer in particular ways or because they close down rather than open up the topic. Examples include (Smith et al. 2009, King and Horrocks 2010):

- Leading questions such as 'so you would agree that leadership is important in projects?'
- Questions that make presumptions about the topic or the participants' view of it, such as 'what discriminatory behaviour have you seen in your time in the organization?' (This question presumes that the respondent has seen such behaviour; a more open style would be preferred.)

- Closed questions such as 'do you believe that current recruitment policies are effective?', which may put participants under pressure to choose a particular position, whereas they may not see the issue in such terms.
- Manipulative questions such as 'given all of the poverty in the world, do you think that bonuses should be cut for senior managers?', which can create a situation where a particular type of answer is likely.
- Overly complex, multiple questions such as 'can you tell me a bit about your background, educational qualifications, job experiences and how you came to be here?' These can be confusing for the interviewee, who may answer only one part of the question, and also for the interviewer because it can be hard to keep track of what has been said during the course of the interview.

When formulating your questions, you should be aware of the potential problem of **social desirability bias**. This refers to the tendency of respondents to give answers that protect the respondent's ego or that are deemed to be correct or socially acceptable (Fisher 1993). For example, in market research respondents might exaggerate their ownership and use of designer products because it is socially desirable to be associated with certain brands.

King and Horrocks (2010) suggest that when you are preparing your interview guide, writing out your questions in full makes you focus on how you have worded them and can help to avoid the problems we have identified here. As you develop your questions, make sure that the language is appropriate for your interviewees. Generally it is sensible to avoid jargon or technical language unless it is a highly specialized topic and your interviewee is comfortable with the terminology being used.

11.2.5 Sequencing the interview

Careful thought needs to be given to the sequencing of the interview. At the start briefly describe the research, indicate the aims of the interview and explain why the interviewee has been asked to take part. You should also assure the participant of confidentiality and obtain their agreement to the interview being recorded, if relevant. This is the point at which you would ask the participant to sign an appropriately worded informed consent form (see Chapter 7 for an example).

It is usually best to open the interview with an 'ice breaker' question on a topic that engages the participant but is not too challenging. The background/demographic questions in Table 11.3 are typical examples. They can generate information that is relevant to the research but are likely to be an easy and comfortable topic for the interviewee. More complex or controversial topics should be raised later in the interview.

As you come towards the end of the time agreed for the interview, you can signal that you are reaching the final topic so as to allow the interviewee time to return to a more conversational mode (Legard et al. 2003). If possible, avoid ending the interview on a negative or stressful note (King 2004). Also, it is good practice to invite the interviewee to add any comments or to address issues that they feel are important before concluding. Finally, you should thank the participant for their time, confirm any arrangements regarding confidentiality and, if appropriate, their willingness to take part in a follow-up interview or answer further questions (which could be by telephone or email).

11.2.6 Interviewing skills

Kvale outlines the characteristics of a good interviewer:

> A good interviewer knows the topic of the interview, masters conversational skills and is proficient in language, with an ear for his or her subjects' linguistic style. The interviewer must continually make on-the-spot decisions about what to ask and how; which aspects of a subject's answer to follow up, and which not; which answers to comment and interpret, and which not. The interviewer should have a sense for good stories and be able to assist the subjects in the unfolding of their narratives.
>
> Kvale (2007: 81)

There are several skills you should concentrate on developing.

- Practise 'active' listening. This means that you really listen to what the person is saying and respond with a question that is useful to you. It is all too easy to focus on the next question and not really listen to the person at all.
- Try to put the respondent at ease by opening with simple, ice-breaking questions, or even by spending a few minutes just chatting before you start recording or taking notes.
- Phrase questions sensitively so that your interviewee is not put on the defensive.
- Practise your observation skills, and note particular voice tones, body language, silences or obvious discomfort.
- Check your understanding throughout the interview by summarizing what has been said and seeking clarification.
- Avoid judgemental responses to interviewee comments, such as 'that's very interesting' or 'that must have been annoying', that may be interpreted by the interviewee as indicating what kind of answers you are expecting to hear.

It is difficult to acquire all these skills at once, especially when you are trying to take notes as well. It takes practice. So, before embarking on your data collection, you should conduct a pilot interview. The pilot interview is an excellent opportunity to practise your skills. It also allows you to check whether the interview guide works as you intended and how long the interview is likely to take. For the pilot, try to select a participant who is likely to be easier to interview, perhaps one whom you already know. After the pilot interview, you should reflect on your interviewing skills, the type of data generated and the appropriateness of the interview guide. In some cases it may even be possible to discuss how the interview went with the participant, which provides additional useful feedback.

11.2.7 Technology-mediated interviews

Traditionally, there has been a strong preference for face-to-face interviews. However, there is growing awareness of the benefits of technology-mediated in-depth interviewing. Options include telephone, including Internet telephony, and both synchronous and asynchronous text-based interviewing.

Telephone-based interviewing

Conducting interviews over the telephone, including Internet telephony services such as Skype, can speed up and reduce the cost of data collection – e.g. travelling time and expenses. It can even be the only feasible way to reach participants in a broad geographic region and it facilitates the accommodation of different diary schedules. Some respondents may feel more at ease discussing sensitive matters over the phone rather than face to face. Some participants may actually prefer telephone interviews, as they offer more flexibility, are easier to reschedule in case of an emergency and do not require the interviewee to host the interviewer. Telephone interviews are particularly useful for extended projects or those aiming to capture the participants' views in real time, as the researcher can check the participants' thoughts and experiences at particular points in time or stages in a process.

However, there are disadvantages, too. Telephone interviews work only where a reasonable level of trust can be established between interviewer and interviewee, which may be difficult if the interviewee is not used to being interviewed in this way. As it is more difficult to establish rapport over the telephone, opportunities to probe topics in depth can be restricted. Extra thought needs to be given to how to record the interview (Section 11.4), and even so there may be some loss or distortion of what is being said, due to technical difficulties or background noise. Furthermore, the quality of the interpretation of the data collected may be compromised because the interviewer does not have access to non-verbal data such as gestures or facial expressions. The absence of visual cues also makes it difficult to control the discussion topics, as there are limited opportunities for the interviewer to interject without disrupting the flow of conversation and questions may need to be repeated to improve clarity. Nevertheless, telephone interviewing can be an effective form of data collection in qualitative research. Stephens (2007: 213), for example, reporting on his experiences conducting elite interviews with Nobel laureates by telephone concluded that it was a 'valid and useful' tool for geographically dispersed samples.

Text-based interviewing

Traditional interviewing, even if done remotely, is based on a synchronous, verbal exchange between the interviewer and the participant. An alternative is to use text-based interviews in which the exchange between interviewer and participant is in written form, although still following a question–answer structure. One version of this is the asynchronous email interview. Morgan and Symon describe the process:

> In electronic interviews, a number of e-mails would be exchanged over an extended time period. Initially, a small number of questions are asked or a topic is raised and the participant will reply, offering their thoughts and opinions. The researcher will then need to respond specifically to those ideas, asking further questions or for clarification, raising linked issues, and generally 'opening up' the discussion. These communications may last for some weeks until the topic is exhausted or the participant shows sign of losing interest.
>
> Morgan and Symon (2004: 23)

More recently, researchers have been using social media as a channel for conducting text-based interviews. In this case, a question is posted in writing via the selected

RESEARCH IN PRACTICE 11.1

Interviewing using social media

Ana Canhoto reflects on the use of social media to collect data for the paper 'Customer service 140 characters at a time – the users' perspective', which she co-authored with Moira Clark (Canhoto and Clark 2013):

Our objective was to investigate how organisations should respond to brand-related comments on social media platforms. Our research questions were: (1) What types of online relationships are most valued by social media users? and (2) What support do social network users perceive they derive from interacting with organisations online?

Potential interviewees were approached through the popular social media platforms Facebook, LinkedIn and Twitter, because we wanted to study existing social media users.

First, we posted a generic message on the selected networks, inviting users to provide examples of companies who handled interactions with customers on social media particularly well. We probed for details about the interaction – e.g. whether it was an isolated accident, or a recurring one. Once the factual information was collected, we moved on to interviewees' perceptions, asking what aspects of the interaction the respondents had appreciated the most, and why these were important for them. If the interviewees were still engaged, we would ask for additional examples. In practice, interviewees rarely responded to more than three sets of questions.

The vast majority of the replies came through Twitter. As the use of social media platforms in data collection is such a nascent practice, we did not really know what response rates to expect from each platform. We think that the relative popularity of Twitter over the other platforms could be because Twitter is mostly used as a conversation platform, often between people who have never met. In contrast, on Facebook or LinkedIn, users interact mostly with people that they know already.

PART III

social network or micro-blogging platform. The participant replies and the researcher then asks further questions until the topic is fully explored. In Research in Practice 11.1 one of the authors of this book reflects on her experiences of interviewing via social media.

Collecting textual data electronically offers several advantages. It gives access to users in dispersed geographic locations and bypasses problems of the cost and accuracy of interview recording and transcribing. The ability to 'time shift' participation in asynchronous communication can make it easier for potential interviewees to take part (Anderson and Kanuka 2003).

However, it also presents challenges. As with telephone interviews, there is loss of visual data and it is difficult to establish rapport with the participants. Moreover, using public platforms means that interviewees can be offered neither confidentiality nor anonymity, which are two important factors in gaining access to individuals. It may be difficult to confirm the identity of the respondents. Furthermore, using the electronic medium may result in lower levels of interactivity (Mann 2000), with users typically responding to fewer questions than in a face-to-face context. In addition, the use of micro-blogging platforms such as Twitter may lead to very short replies.

Ultimately, whether or not it is advisable to use technology to conduct text-based in-depth interviews depends on your research questions, the study's participants and your skills.

11.3 Group interviews

Group interviews are used for research topics that benefit from exploration within a social group setting. Group interviews should not be seen as a way of conducting several individual interviews at the same time. Instead, they should be used when you want to benefit from the interaction between participants as a result of which the group dynamic generates more insight than would have been the case with individual interviews. A key role in this process is played by the moderator or facilitator, 'who promotes an interaction and ensures that the discussion remains on the topic of interest' (Stewart and Shamdasani 1998: 505).

Group interviewing can take a variety of forms, including completely informal unstructured 'conversations' with groups of people during field research. Group discussions may also be used in conjunction with other forms of data collection. The best-known variant of group discussions is, perhaps, the focus group, although the terms 'group interview' and 'focus group' are often used synonymously and the distinction is not always clear. This section concentrates on the focus group type of group discussion.

A focus group brings together a number of participants to discuss a focal topic and is particularly suitable to explore emergent issues from the perspective of the participants. They are often associated with market research, although their application is very broad and can include:

- obtaining general background information on the research topic of interest
- learning how respondents talk (i.e. in their own words) about the phenomenon under investigation
- stimulating new and creative ideas and concepts for further research
- eliciting latent opinions on selected topics
- exploring, checking and explaining research conclusions.

Focus groups can be a time-effective approach to the collection of qualitative data and the group dynamics should help the generation of new thinking and insights. They are an important method with some respondents, such as children, who may be more comfortable in a group setting. However, it is not suitable to explore issues that require individual introspection, or for topics where privacy or commercial confidentiality are likely to inhibit open discussion in the group. It is also possible that social pressure limits the expression of views that diverge from the majority, a phenomenon known as compliance. In turn, this can lead the group to reach a consensus decision that results from the desire for group harmony and acceptance, rather than the critical consideration of alternative perspectives. More introverted or less confident members may also find it difficult to express their views in front of others in the group, while in certain cultural or organizational settings it may be deemed impolite or unwise to disagree publicly with others, particularly if they are more senior. Focus groups may also be of limited value with elite interviewees, as it may be impractical to bring together several executives in the same room at the same time.

11.3.1 Composing the focus group

Who takes part in a focus group is important both to group dynamics and to the credibility and usefulness of your findings. Clearly one criterion is the participants' knowledge of the topic itself. You also need to consider the homogeneity of participants. People from similar backgrounds may find it easier to discuss some topics, but lack of diversity may reduce fresh thinking. The presence of people from different positions in the organizational hierarchy may be a particular issue here. A balance is probably needed, although you may convene groups with different members precisely to compare those differences.

Another issue to decide is whether to bring together complete strangers or to use people who already form a natural group (e.g. an existing project team). The former may require more socialization time at the start of the meeting, taking time away from discussion. However, the latter may give problems if the group works with hidden assumptions of which you, the researcher, are not aware.

Researchers will sometimes use intermediaries to recruit focus group participants in specific locations or close-knit communities, and where there are language barriers. However, using intermediaries means that the researcher cannot control the recruitment process. Parker and Tritter report the following problems arising from using intermediaries to recruit participants for a study of diabetes in South Asian women:

> [T]oo little was known about those who attended the focus group in relation to those who might have attended and little, if anything, was known about those who were actually approached but refused to attend [. . .] recruitment can drift into a process of 'convenience' sampling, whereby people whom we know little about are selected simply because of their accessibility.
>
> Parker and Tritter (2006: 29)

Recommendations as to the size of a focus group vary. Some writers (e.g. Sayre 2001) recommend larger groups (10–12 is often cited), but if you do not have experience of facilitating group discussions, you should start with fewer participants. A big group is difficult to manage and also does not allow individuals much input time (with 10 participants, each would contribute only an average of six minutes' input in a one-hour meeting). Barbour (2007) suggests that even smaller numbers might be appropriate in some situations. A focus group of subject matter experts is an example where a smaller group (perhaps 4–6 participants) might be suitable. The authors' own experience is that 7–8 is a manageable number for most topics.

In terms of how many focus groups to hold, Krueger and Casey (2000) advise conducting three or four focus group interviews with each type of participant. This number should be enough to reach theoretical saturation.

11.3.2 Planning the focus group

Running a focus group can be very challenging, so good preparation is essential. You should conduct a pilot focus group, particularly if this is your first time interviewing in a group setting. In terms of scheduling, it is advisable not to conduct more than one focus group per day, particularly if you lack experience. Other points to consider when planning a focus group include the following.

Timing and recording

Plan on 1½ to 2 hours for the session, which should give you about 1 to 11/2 hours' actual discussion time. During this time, there will be a multitude of ideas discussed and interventions to manage, so it will be very difficult to take notes at the same time. We therefore recommend audio or video recording the meeting, if you have informed consent from all participants. Video recording has the added advantage of allowing you to record body language and other aspects of group interaction that an audio recording would miss.

Choosing the setting

The setting of the group interview can influence the quality of the data generated. You should therefore take into account the nature of the location (for example, whether it is 'home' territory for the participants or outside their normal environment), the level of formality, lighting, seating, the ambient noise level and the level of security and privacy. You may also need to arrange refreshments, car parking, access for those with special needs and so on.

Choosing the location

The location should allow for the non-obtrusive observation and recording of the participants and the discussion. So, for instance, recording equipment or note-takers or a representative of the client may be beyond a one-way mirror, or in another room. There are commercial service providers that offer facilities that meet all these requirements, which you may prefer to use, depending on your requirements and your budget.

Selecting the topics

The actual topics to be discussed will depend upon the purpose of the focus group. Do not overestimate the number of topics you can cover in a single session. Just as with individual interviews, you should prepare an interview guide based on the research questions and containing a checklist of the points that ought to be covered in the discussion, and in which order. Table 11.4 provides an outline for a focus group conducted for concept testing for a new brand of diet breakfast cereals.

11.3.3 Conducting the focus group

Running a focus group can be a real challenge for the novice researcher. Below are some issues to keep in mind for each of the five stages of the focus group meeting, as identified by Finch and Lewis (2003).

The first stage is about scene setting and clarification of ground rules. At this stage it is vital to put people at their ease. You introduce the topic in non-technical language,

Table 11.4 Example of a discussion outline for a focus group

Stage	Topics
Welcome and ground rules	Welcome
	• Purpose of meeting • Recording of interview • Expectations regarding confidentiality • Informed consent • Discussion rules
	Introductions
Ice breaker	The perfect breakfast cereal
	• Characteristics • Associations
Discussion	General attitudes towards breakfast cereals
	General purchase and consumption of breakfast cereals
	• Probe for specific types and brands of cereals
	Purchase and consumption of breakfast cereals when trying to lose weight
	Attitudes towards diet breakfast cereals
	• Probe for specific brands
	• Specific experiences and satisfaction
	• Brand perceptions
Testing and conclusions	Show and discuss packaging concepts
	Show and discuss advertising concepts
	Reactions to sample product

indicate the aims and objectives of the focus group and outline the ground rules for the meeting. You also need to ensure that you have the fully informed consent of all participants, including permission for any recording, and ask participants to confirm this by signing a suitably worded consent form (see Chapter 7).

The second stage is to introduce each participant. The aim here is to get people thinking of themselves as a group so as to encourage discussion and interaction. Invite participants to introduce themselves, briefly. Take this opportunity to note down the location by name of each participant to help you in the meeting, or use name cards if appropriate.

In the third stage, you should introduce the opening topic. The opening topic is often a general one, to get everyone engaged and to act as a scene setter for later topics. Try to encourage full participation, and also interaction within the group. If someone seems to be dominating the discussion, you should bring others in. You can try a general approach, such as 'What do other people think about this?' Alternatively, depending on the participants, you may address specific members by name: 'What does [name] think about this suggestion?'

Once the rules and scope are clear, and everybody feels relaxed and reassured, we can move on to the fourth stage, the discussion of the main topic areas for the focus group. It is at this stage that your skills as a moderator will be most tested. You must find the right balance between intervening to keep the group on topic and allowing flexibility to explore interesting areas. You also need to keep everyone involved, probe for fuller responses on key topics and prevent the group discussion dissolving into simultaneous dialogue. Moreover, you must ensure that the actions of the focus group participants do not run against the ethical principles we discussed in Chapter 7, for example, bullying or embarrassing other members of the group.

The fifth and last stage is to conclude the discussion. You should select the final topic in advance and signal the ending of the meeting by introducing it as the final topic. At the end, offer people the chance to raise any issues they feel have been left out. Finally, close with the normal courtesies.

11.3.4 Technology-mediated focus groups

As with individual interviews, there is a growing interest in, and use of, technology-mediated focus groups that bring together geographically dispersed participants. Again, these can be synchronous or asynchronous, using audio/video or text.

Particular advantages of technology-mediated focus groups are ease of participation and reduction in cost. They are easier to organize than physical meetings and therefore can be conducted at shorter notice than traditional focus groups. They are particularly effective for participants who are hard to reach, for instance, frequent travellers or people with mobility problems. It is possible that participants give more honest answers, as they do not feel inhibited by the close presence of the moderator and the other participants. In the case of text-based focus groups, for example, via discussion forums or instant messaging, there is the advantage of not needing to transcribe the responses, which saves time and money, and reduces mistakes.

However, there is a loss of visual data and other non-verbal inputs, such as body language. It may be difficult to take full advantage of the benefits of group interviewing if there is limited interactivity. It is also difficult to expose the participants to external stimuli such as a product sample or material for a new staff uniform, unless these are sent ahead of the group interview (which is not always possible for logistical, cost or commercial-sensitivity reasons).

A synchronous, i.e. real-time, text-based focus group will really put your moderating skills to the test. It is very difficult to keep the momentum going, as you will have to read and react to the various comments, while typing probing questions or prompts to move the discussion along. A good tip is to have a number of pre-typed standard sentences such as 'thank you for that contribution; could you elaborate on that point?' which you can then copy and paste into the discussion platform. This type of online focus group is recommended for projects covering simple, straightforward issues, for instance, following up a previous meeting or experience. Research in Practice 11.2 gives an example of using Skype for a text-based synchronous focus group.

Asynchronous text-based focus groups may run over several days. Participants are asked to log in a certain number of times per day and register their responses to particular questions or prompts. The moderator reads the comments and probes on specific issues or asks the next question on the discussion guide. This type of focus group tends to generate more content than the synchronous focus group, be it face to face or technology mediated. It also allows time for deeper reflection by each

RESEARCH IN PRACTICE 11.2

Using Skype to conduct a text-based focus group

Doctoral researcher Silvia Lang reflects on the use of Skype to conduct focus groups for her research into electronic word of mouth.

> Online focus groups worked well for me because my participants were familiar with Skype. It was cost-effective and I could include participants from a broad geographical area.
>
> To ensure privacy, I set up accounts specifically for the project, changing passwords and deleting the conversation history between sessions.
>
> When I posted a question, they all replied at the same time. So, typing skills were important. I had sentences prepared for the welcome, the introduction, the questions and the end. And I had an assistant checking that I replied to all comments and alerting me if someone was silent for too long. I used two computers simultaneously. If someone was silent or dropped out, I used the second computer to reach out to them, by email or on their private Skype accounts.
>
> I had the content of the discussions right there, with no need for transcriptions. But the answers tended to be short because that's how people chat on Skype. And they used smiley faces and emoticons, so I had to keep asking people to explain what they meant by those. I could not check their body language, so I lost that dimension. Also, people kept jumping to other topics that they thought were related, for instance online shopping, and I had to redirect the conversation.
>
> I felt that the participants were more relaxed than in a traditional setting. They were not concerned with language issues because no one heard their accents, and many were joining in from their sofas, a café or other relaxed place.

PART III

participant and for the researcher to introduce a variety of online or offline prompts, such as asking the participants to visit a website, try a product sample or reflect on comments made earlier in the process. However, in this format there is a heightened risk of participants dropping out between interactions. There may also be an expectation on the part of the participants that the researcher will react promptly to their comments and engage with them when they are online. This is simply not possible for the majority of research projects, as they do not have moderation 24 hours in the day, for several consecutive days. There are commercial service providers that offer platforms for conducting online focus groups.

11.4 Capturing and storing your interview data

Whether you are interviewing the research participants individually or in a group, you need to ensure that you record and store all the data. You also need to make notes of the context of the data collection, such as if there were any interruptions, or there was loss of eye contact after a particular question. In this section, we discuss general principles of data collection in interviews.

11.4.1 Recording the data and your notes

The traditional way of recording fieldwork data and contextual information was to take notes. The field notebook has been the favoured means of capturing notes such as descriptions of people whom the researcher met, events related to the fieldwork or key conversations, as well as the researcher's own actions, feelings and working hypotheses. A useful alternative is to create paper copies of your interview guide with plenty of blank space in which to note down participants' answers and your notes.

However, capturing everything in writing is not ideal, as your attention is divided between what is being said, what should happen next and what you are trying to write. It is particularly difficult to keep accurate notes in a group setting. Moreover, it is often difficult to capture in a few words the complexity of what is being discussed or the context of the data collection. For instance, if you are conducting a focus group with six users of a particular product, you may wish to record what is being said and by whom and with what effect, in addition to reflections on how the use of product samples impacts on the interactions between individuals.

In many situations the preferred data capture option is to use audio recorders and/or video cameras. Using such devices allows you to focus on what is being said or what is happening rather than taking notes. Recording also allows you to capture more data. Often, when you go back to your recordings you will notice subtle elements such as shifts in the vocabulary or changes in tone that you may have missed during the actual interview; you can also use your recording to clarify exactly what happened, in what order and in reaction to what. Video recording also helps you to capture non-verbal aspects of communication, which are such an important source of qualitative insight.

Digital audio recording devices are particularly useful, as the resulting files can easily be transferred (e.g., by email), backed up and edited. In addition to specialist recorders, most smartphones and MP3 players offer a recording facility which may be suitable. Points to consider when selecting a recording device include the following.

- Test the recording quality in a real-life interview situation. Check that your recorder can cope with a reasonable level of background noise and with the layout of the room. This can be a particular problem with focus groups where more specialized equipment may be needed.
- Check that the device has adequate battery life and storage space (i.e. memory) and that recording will not be interrupted or terminated by incoming calls or messages if you are using a smartphone or similar device.
- Ensure that the file is easily exportable to other platforms for playback, storage and analysis.

Always test the equipment before you use it to make sure that you know how to operate it and to check for sound quality. Where possible, use some sort of back-up during the interview, for example, by taking notes as well as recording or by having more than one recorder.

It is also possible to record telephone interviews but the options depend on the technology. For traditional landline telephones, adapters are available that plug into the telephone handset jack and a digital recorder. Recording software is available to use with Internet telephony such as Skype. Mobile phones vary, but a number of recording apps are available, depending on your phone's operating system. Lastly, there are a number of commercial call services that offer recording services.

Whatever recording method you use, always ask for permission from the research participant when the interview is scheduled, and remind them again when it comes to the actual interview. In addition to gaining their consent to be recorded, you also should offer to stop the recorder at any time if the research participant wishes.

11.4.2 Storing the data and your notes

You will need to file your data and notes thoroughly and systematically to ensure that you can access them at a later stage, but you can also make them accessible to other members of your research team. It also provides an evidence trail to show that your work was completed legitimately. Detailed records also help with micro-level analysis and understanding of your data, because they allow you to review all of the issues that were raised during the data collection, to look for discussion on topics the salience of which only becomes evident in later stages of the project and to study details such as hesitations or the specific vocabulary used in particular exchanges. Above all, keeping extensive records allows you to extract quotations in the respondents' own words, which can be used when presenting your findings to illustrate participants' views.

Immediately after the session, take time to organize your records: save them, back them up, give them a name and description and store them safely. We also recommend creating a master list of all the information collected, its source and where it is stored.

You need to make sure that you adhere to any ethical or legal requirements regarding data protection, both general (e.g. masking the identity of the respondents) and specific to your institution (e.g. regarding saving documents in the cloud). Finally, you need to consider how you are going to destroy the data collected, namely, when you are going to do so and whether you need to use specialist services to handle the destruction of confidential data.

PART III

CRITICAL COMMENTARY 11.1

The nature of interview data

One area of debate among qualitative researchers is the nature and status of the data generated by interviews. Interview data fall into the category of researcher-instigated data: they are created in the interactions between the interviewer and the interviewee. Taking this position to an extreme, it can be argued that what is said and how it is said is a product of the social context of the interview and the interactions within it and does not reflect some underlying external reality. This view, which is particularly associated with some forms of social constructionism, challenges the notion that we can treat interviews simply as a 'pipeline for transmitting truthful knowledge' (Holstein and Gubrium 2011: 151). From this perspective, the interview changes from being a 'resource' for finding out about the world outside the interview to a 'topic' where the research focus is on investigating the ways in which meaning is actively constructed during the interview by the participants.

So where does this leave the interview study? Silverman (2010) suggests that you can treat interviews as a resource or as a topic, but the position adopted will have to be explained and justified. Miller and Glassner (2011) argue that rigorous analysis of interview data reveals evidence about both the world outside the interview and the world as it is constructed inside the interview. 'Combined', they suggest, the two perspectives 'offer important insights for theoretical understanding' (Miller and Glassner 2011: 137). However you decide to treat your interview data, this discussion should caution against a naïve approach to assuming that interview or any other form of researcher-instigated data give unproblematic access to the world 'out there.'

KEY LEARNING POINTS

- In-depth interviews may be conducted individually or in a group setting, either face to face or mediated by technology. They can incorporate varying degrees of structure, but a semi-structured approach offers some advantages for analysis.
- Preparing for an individual interview involves developing a suitable interview guide including relevant questions in an appropriate sequence. Careful thought needs to be given to the number of topics that can be adequately covered in the time available.
- Focus groups are a form of group interview. Preparation for a focus group involves deciding on the group composition, the venue and the topics to be discussed.
- Technology can be used for both individual and group interviews. Applications include telephone and Internet telephone services for verbal interviews and email and Internet for text-based interviews.
- Data capture and storage need careful planning. Audio and video recording are recommended, but the researcher should always gain participant agreement. Written field notes provide an opportunity to capture additional details, including the thoughts of the researcher. Storage needs to be well organized and secure.

NEXT STEPS

11.1 The role of interviews in the research design. Revisit the key research articles from the literature that you have reviewed and identify how they use individual and/or group interviews to collect qualitative data. For instance, is it the only tool to collect data, or is it used in conjunction with other tools? Reflect on how the use of interviews helped the authors to answer their research questions.

11.2 Assessing the advantages and disadvantages of interviews as a data collection approach. List the advantages and disadvantages of individual interviews and focus groups as a data collection approach for your project. Consider a broad range of factors, including the likely cost or time required for data collection.

11.3 Addressing limitations. Identify the limitations arising from using interviews in your study.

11.4 Technology-mediated data collection. Decide if you are going to use some form of technology interface, as opposed to face to face, to conduct your interviews. Ensure that you know how to use the technology interface and deal with technical problems. Check that participants are comfortable with the technology, as well.

11.5 Set up your data collection. Negotiate access and clarify expectations regarding how long you can stay on the site, what you can access and what you will be providing in return. Decide the type of instructions and the level of structure that you need to provide to the research participants. Construct the interview guide and prepare appropriate briefing and informed consent documents (Chapter 7). Organize logistical aspects such as booking rooms or creating online discussion forums. If relevant, set up anonymized online accounts and passwords. Carry out a pilot interview to confirm your arrangements.

11.6 Recording your data. Decide how you are going to record and store the data, and your notes. Obtain authorization to record the interviews, as relevant.

Further reading

For further reading, please see the companion website.

References

Anderson, T. and Kanuka, H. (2003). *E-research: Methods, strategies and issues*. Boston, MA: Pearson Education.

Barbour, R. (2007). *Doing focus groups*. London: Sage.

Boddy, C. (2005). 'Projective techniques in market research: Valueless subjectivity or insightful reality?', *International Journal of Market Research*, 47(3), 239–54.

Canhoto, A. I. and Clark, M. (2013). 'Customer service 140 characters at a time: The users' perspective', *Journal of Marketing Management*, 29(5–6), 522–44.

Chell, E. (2004). Critical incident technique. *In*: Cassell, C. and Symon, G. (eds) *Essential guide to qualitative methods in organizational research*. London: Sage.

Denzin, N. K. and Lincoln, Y. S. (eds) (2000). *Handbook of qualitative research*. 2nd edn. Thousand Oaks, CA: Sage.

Easterby-Smith, M., Thorpe, R. and Jackson, P. R. (2012). *Management research*. 4th edn. London: Sage Publications.

Finch, H. and Lewis, J. (2003). Focus groups. *In*: Ritchie, J. and Lewis, J. (eds) *Qualitative research practice*. London: Sage Publications Ltd.

Fisher, R. J. (1993). 'Social desirability bias and the validity of indirect questioning', *Journal of Consumer Research*, 20(2), 303–15.

Flanagan, J. C. (1954). 'The critical incident technique', *Psychological Bulletin*, 51(4), 327–358.

Holstein, J. A. and Gubrium, J. F. (2011). Animating interview narratives. In: Silverman, D. (ed.) *Qualitative research*. 3rd edn. London: Sage.

King, N. (2004). Using interviews in qualitative research. *In:* Cassell, C. and Symon, G. (eds) *Essential guide to qualitative methods in organizational research*. London: Sage.

King, N. and Horrocks, C. (2010). *Interviews in qualitative research*. London: Sage.

Krueger, R. A. and Casey, M. (2000). *Focus groups: A practical guide for applied research*. 3rd edn. Thousand Oaks, CA: Sage.

Kvale, S. (2007). *Doing interviews*. London: Sage.

Lang, S. (2014). *Antecedents of travellers' eWOM communication. PhD thesis submission*. Oxford Brookes University.

Legard, R., Keegan, J. and Ward, K. (2003). In-depth interviews. *In:* Ritchie, J. and Lewis, J. (eds) *Qualitative research practice*. London: Sage Publications Ltd.

Mann, C. (2000). *Internet communication and qualitative research: A handbook for researching online*. London: Sage.

Marshall, C. and Rossman, G. B. (2006). *Designing qualitative research*. 4th edn. Thousand Oaks, CA: Sage Publications.

Miller, J. and Glassner, B. (2011). The 'inside' and the 'outside': Finding realities in interviews. In: Silverman, D. (ed.) *Qualitative research*. 3rd edn. London: Sage.

Morgan, S. J. and Symon, G. (2004). Electronic interviews in organizational research. *In:* Cassell, C. and Symon, G. (eds) *Essential guide to qualitative methods in organizational research*. London: Sage.

Parker, A. and Tritter, J. (2006). 'Focus group method and methodology: Current practice and recent debate', *International Journal of Research and Method in Education*, 29(1), 23–37.

Sayre, S. (2001). *Qualitative methods for marketplace research*. Thousand Oaks, CA: Sage.

Silverman, D. (2010). *Doing qualitative research. A practical handbook*. 3rd edn. London: Sage Publications.

Smith, J. A., Flowers, P. and Larkin, M. (2009). *Interpretive phenomenological analysis*. London: Sage.

Stephens, N. (2007). 'Collecting data from elites and ultra elites: Telephone and face-to-face interviews with macroeconomists', *Qualitative Research*, 7(2), 203–16.

Stewart, D. W. and Shamdasani, P. N. (1998). Focus group research: Exploration and discovery. *In:* Bickman, L. and Rog, D. J. (eds) *Handbook of applied social research methods*. Thousand Oaks, CA: Sage.

PART III

12 Collecting data through observation, documents and artefacts

---

CHAPTER SUMMARY

The key topics covered in this chapter are:

- collecting data by using observation
- collecting documents and other records as sources of data
- collecting data through diaries
- using artefacts as a source of data.

12.1 Introduction

Collecting data by questionnaire or interview involves asking participants about a phenomenon of interest. In this chapter we look at other methods of gathering data. The first is observation in which, rather than ask people what they do, we instead observe their actual behaviours. The second method is to collect documents or other records that can be used to shed light on our research topic. The third method also involves collecting documents, but this time instigated by the researcher asking participants to create diaries or other records. The fourth method is the collection of artefacts: objects such as pieces of technology, clothing or products that people use in their everyday or organizational lives and that might inform our research.

12.2 Collecting data by observation

Observation of what people do can be a very rich source of data. Observation can help us to understand both individual behaviours and how people interact with each other and with their environment. As a data collection method, it involves the purposeful observation, recording and analysis of behaviours in an organized way. Observation in different forms has many possible applications in both quantitative and qualitative research designs, as shown in Table 12.1.

Table 12.1 The role of observation in different research designs

Research design	Role of observation as a data source
Ethnography	Primary data collection method
Case study	May be used alongside any other method
Grounded theory	May be used alongside interviews and other data collection methods
Action research	May used alongside other data collection methods, either as part of the action research project cycle or for the researcher's thesis cycle
Conversation analysis	Primary data collection method (in the form of recording naturally occurring conversations)
Experiment	Used alongside other methods, such as questionnaires, to measure relevant variables before, during and after the experiment
Non-experimental explanatory research (quantitative)	May be used alongside other methods, such as questionnaires, to measure relevant variables

12.2.1 Advantages and disadvantages of observation as a data collection method

The key advantage of observation is its potential to generate first-hand data about people's behaviour instead of relying on their memory and descriptions of it. In doing so it can avoid some of the problems associated with self-report, such as social desirability bias. Observation can be particularly useful when you cannot ask questions of the research participants or they cannot explain their behaviour, for instance, if you were studying how young children react to a new toy. Market researchers have also employed observational techniques to learn, for example, how customers use products or shop for items in a retail store. Observation may also be the only way of capturing some types of interaction or very transient behaviours in sufficient detail to allow further access, for example, in conversation analysis. Finally, observation can be carried out in different ways and for different purposes, which gives it the wide range of applications identified in Table 12.1.

Although observation may appear to be an ideal way to record actual behaviour, it does have a number of drawbacks. Firstly, observation tends to be a relatively slow way of collecting data, because we can collect data only at the pace at which the phenomenon occurs. This, and the attendant costs, imposes practical limitations on its application. Although there have been many examples of lengthy observational studies, such as Schouten and McAlexander's (1995) three-year ethnographic study of Harley-Davidson motorcycle owners, discussed in Chapter 6, it can also concentrate on behaviours of relatively short duration. For example, where researcher time is limited, observing how business partners behave in a negotiation process may be more practical than observing how the partnership relationship evolves over time. Secondly, observation has very limited application in the study of private behaviours, such as personal habits or certain types of interactions to which the researcher is unlikely to have access. Thirdly, observation is feasible only if the phenomenon that you are studying is actually observable or inferable from exhibited behaviour.

Consequently, it does not allow the study of underlying motives or thought processes leading up to the behaviour. For example, observation may be useful to capture consumer queuing behaviour in a bank but it does not help us to understand the motivations or experiences of those involved. Observation on its own may therefore help us to understand what takes place, but not why. Fourthly, although observation may help to address some aspects of social desirability bias, it is still vulnerable to observer effects (particularly if the observation is overt), whereby the presence of the observer influences the behaviour of those being observed. Lastly, as we shall discuss later, observation can raise some challenging ethical questions regarding, for example, the degree of consent required or the responsibilities of the researcher if they observe illegal behaviours.

12.2.2 Forms of observation

Observation can take several different forms according to the requirements of the research project and the preferences of the researcher. The options available can usefully be described in terms of four dimensions.

Researcher role

The first dimension the role of the researcher. Gold (1958), in a well-known article, identified four roles that the researcher can adopt in an observational study, depending on the degree of participation in the setting being studied. We use that framework here, with some differences of interpretation.

1   Complete observer. In this role, the researcher simply acts as a spectator to events as they happen. Observation can be covert or overt.
2   Participant-as-observer. In this role, classically the one adopted in a long-term ethnographic study, the researcher participates in the social setting whilst simultaneously adopting the role of observer.
3   Observer-as-participant. In this role, the researcher enters the social setting primarily as an observer but participates to a limited extent. Such a role might be suitable if spending a short time in the field, for example, observing a small number of senior management team meetings.
4   Complete participant. In this role the researcher acts as a full participant (for example, by becoming a group member); the observational role is not revealed to others and is therefore a covert one. This role has been used in some ethnographic studies but clearly raises ethical concerns regarding informed consent, since a measure of deception is involved.

Covert versus overt observation

Closely linked to the researcher role is whether to make your presence known or, instead, to observe the participants covertly. This decision is often influenced by the concern that knowledge of being observed, and what the researcher is interested in, will influence the behaviours of those whom you are observing, leading to bias as a result of such observer effects. For instance, employees may want to present a particular image of the company or how they conduct daily tasks if they think they are being observed. However, there are serious ethical issues to consider when making the decision between covert and overt observation, as discussed in Chapter 7. A possible solution is to disclose the fact of observation but not the specific area of interest. For instance, you may tell a recruitment panel that you are observing them in order to understand the dynamics of a job interview, but do not mention that you are particularly interested in how the interaction between recruiters and interviewees varies with gender. Alternatively, if you are able to spend a prolonged period in the social setting your presence as an observer may become accepted to the point where it is no longer a factor in people's behaviour, although this can still raise ethical issue in cases of extreme or illegal behaviour.

Natural versus artificial settings

A further decision to make is whether you are going to observe participants in a natural setting or a contrived one. In a natural setting you observe the behaviour as it occurs in an everyday or organizational context. For example, you might observe project teams working on a project in their ordinary office environment. In a contrived setting, on the other hand, you manipulate the conditions under which the behaviour takes place. This manipulation can be as limited as changing product layout in a retail store to observe customer reactions or go as far as conducting observation in a laboratory setting. Using a contrived approach may speed up the data gathering process or allow control of extraneous variables in an experiment, but there is the risk that the behaviour observed differs from what would occur in a natural setting.

Structured versus unstructured observation

Finally, you need to decide how structured your observation should be. Here you have two options. You can approach the research setting with a prior list of characteristics and behaviours that you want to observe. This approach, known as structured observation, is associated with quantitative research designs such as experiments. Alternatively you can respond to and record events as they unfold without deciding the focus of your observations beforehand. This approach, referred to as unstructured observation, is typical of qualitative observational studies such as ethnography. We will now look at using observation in qualitative and quantitative research.

12.2.3 Qualitative approaches to observation

The qualitative approach to observation has its roots in social anthropology and ethnography. The goal is typically to understand the meanings that the research participants attach to their actions by observing them in order to generate a thick description of the situation being investigated. The researcher may adopt a variety of roles, and even change role during the study, but some degree of participation is common, particularly in ethnographic studies. Observation may be covert or overt, depending on the context and ethical issues, but will generally be done in a natural setting, such as the workplace. In keeping with the inductive orientation of much

RESEARCH IN PRACTICE 12.1

An observational study of customer-profiling practices at a UK-based financial institution

The research design was a case study undertaken in a financial institution and data collection took place over a period of 14 months (Canhoto 2007). In order to obtain a comprehensive view of the phenomenon under study, a combination of data collection methods was used, namely in-depth interviews, analysis of electronic and paper-based documents, and observations. For the observation, the researcher opted for an 'observer-as-participant' approach, where the respondents were aware that they were being observed and were told of the purpose of the study. She used recording devices, also with the knowledge and consent of the participants. The researcher felt that such an approach was not only more ethical than adopting either a complete participant or complete observer role but also allowed the researcher more freedom to take notes than would otherwise be possible.

Access was negotiated with the head of the department, who obtained permission from the chief executive officer. The head of the department introduced the researcher to team leaders and explained that it was an academic research project and empha-sized that participation was entirely voluntary. The team leaders then introduced the researcher to the members of their teams and repeated the message regarding the scope and participation. No one declined to take part in the study.

Over the period of 14 months, the researcher visited the organization on various occasions, at intervals ranging between one and four weeks, observing staff in the back office as well as in three of the financial institution's commercial branches. Her field notes particularly focused on collecting data regarding the tasks performed, what sources of information were used to complete the tasks, patterns of communication within the team and across departments and whether the behaviours matched those prescribed in the organization's policy documents and training manuals. Once the observations within each unit or brand were concluded, the researcher presented her written account to the participants for them to comment on the conclusions being drawn.

PART III

qualitative work, observation is likely to be relatively unstructured, with the researcher deciding on what to record as events unfold rather than beforehand. An example of the use of observation as part of a case study is given in Research in Practice 12.1.

Observation requires attention to detail if it is to be productive of useful data. Creswell (2007: 134–5) identifies the following steps in collecting data by observation.

- Choose the site for the observations; this includes securing access and getting the necessary permission to the site and to individuals. You may need to identify a formal or informal gatekeeper who can help you with this process.
- Decide on your role as observer, as discussed above. Your role may change over time, for example, moving from a peripheral position to more complete member-ship of the group being studied.

- Identify who or what to observe, for how long and when. The support of a gatekeeper who can introduce you to participants may be helpful at this stage.
- Decide how you will capture your observations and your reflections on them.
- Start with limited objectives. In the first few sessions you may not be able to get much insight into behaviours. Focus on observing rather than taking notes.
- Withdraw slowly from the site once the observation is finished, ensuring that you thank participants and confirm how the data will be used and the findings disseminated.

Whatever type of observational data you are collecting, you need to make sure that you capture and store all the data. As with qualitative in-depth interviews, the simplest way of recording your data is to make notes in your field notebook. Although they may be complemented with audio or video recordings or photography, field notes remain an important way of capturing observational data. However, as Hammersley and Atkinson (2007: 142, emphasis in original) point out, this raises the questions of '*what* to write down, *how* to write it down and *when* to write it down'. The final answers depend, of course, on the requirements of your particular study, the role you have taken as researcher and the circumstances in which you are carrying out the observation. In the context of writing ethnographic field notes Emerson et al. (1995), however, offer the following useful advice.

- Start off by noting your initial impressions of the situation, then start to focus on key events of incidents. As observation proceeds, try to move beyond your personal reactions as the researcher to develop an understanding of what is important or significant from the perspective of those involved in the situation.
- Start broadly, then focus your observations as your own knowledge of the situation develops. Be alert to patterns or regularities in what is happening, and also to exceptions that can deepen your theoretical understanding of the phenomenon.
- Use 'jottings' (Emerson et al. 1995: 17), brief written notes, to capture points of interest for later write-up as a fuller set of field notes for subsequent analysis.

In some situations it may not be possible to make any notes during observation, in which case you should try to record your thoughts as soon as possible afterwards. Not only will this aid recall but it can avoid the writing task becoming too much of a burden.

12.2.4 *Quantitative approaches to observation*

Quantitative approaches to observation typically take a more structured approach, with the aim of producing quantified or quantifiable data for subsequent numerical analysis. Structured observation has a long tradition in management practice, for example, when carrying out detailed work studies of job tasks in production management. It has also been used in management research. In a well-known study on the nature of managerial work, for example, Henry Mintzberg (1973) carried out structured observation of five chief executives to find out what they actually did. Structured observation can be used in a variety of research designs, including experiments, and may be carried out in natural or artificial settings. The researcher role must allow adequate time and scope for detailed recording, so a complete observer role may be most suitable.

Structured observation involves the coding of the observed behaviour according to a defined observation or **coding schedule.** This specifies in advance which actions or behaviours are to be recorded and how they will be categorized. The contents of your coding schedule are determined by the research questions you are trying to answer. For example, if you were investigating factors causing high levels of customer complaint in a supermarket, your coding schedule would seek to capture behaviours that might be relevant to the in-store experience, such as store cleanliness, how long customers are required to wait at the counter or the behaviour of sales staff towards them. The format in which you capture data can vary. You might, for instance, decide to record the frequency of each behaviour over a particular time period such as one day, or to capture the duration (start and finish times) of particular activities. In Research in Practice 12.2 we give an example of coding schedules for structured observation.

For your own project you may be able to use or adapt an existing coding schedule that has been used in prior studies. If not, you will need to develop your own. If this is the case, you should consider the following.

- Begin by identifying the focus of your observation, based on what is relevant for your research questions. As with developing a questionnaire, you need to be clear on what it is you want to measure in your observation. Prior theory will be useful at this point in helping you to define and develop your coding scheme.
- Determine the elements such as behaviours or activities that you wish to observe during your study. Define each one so that it can be understood by the coder or explained to the reader in the final report.
- Formulate a code for each element and decide what format you will use for recording, for example, in terms of event frequency, time sampling or duration of activity.
- Develop your coding schedule document so that it is easy to understand and use in the conditions under which the observation will be carried out.

When collecting observation data using a coding schedule you should be aware of a number of issues that can affect data quality. Firstly, as with other forms of observation, there may be observer effects that influence participants' natural behaviour. This may be overcome by covert observation if that is possible and ethically acceptable, or reduced by making observer behaviours less intrusive. Secondly, there can be selectivity or inconsistencies in either the sampling or the coding process, leading to bias. Sampling problems can be reduced by careful thought about the timing of the observations, selection of who is observed and location of the observations to generate a representative sample. Problems in coding can arise due to inattention by the coder or misinterpretation of the coding schedule or inconsistencies in coding if more than one observer is used. A clear coding schedule and appropriate briefing and training of the observers can reduce these risks. Measures of inter-rater reliability can be used to assess the consistency of multiple observers/coders. Finally, as with other forms of observation, structured observation does not inform us of the reasons why people do what they do. This may require further investigation regarding the motivating factors behind their behaviour.

RESEARCH IN PRACTICE 12.2

Examples of structured observation coding schedules

If we were undertaking observation in a supermarket in order to understand the underlying causes of customer complaints regarding checkout service we could create an observation schedule that included factors believed to influence satisfaction levels. These could then be recorded in different ways. In Example 1 we show a simple coding schedule to capture the frequency of events. In Example 2 we show a coding schedule used to record each occurrence that is observed during an interval of time. The latter technique, referred to as time sampling, has the advantage of preserving the sequence of events.

Example 1: Event frequency

Observed behaviour	Number of observations Date/hour: . . .
One or more checkout tills not staffed	////
Sales staff talking to one another	/////////
Sales staff ignoring customers	///////
Queue of more than two customers at a checkout till	///////////////
Untidy checkout till	//

Example 2: Time sampling

Observed behaviour	1st (10 mins)	2nd (10 mins)	3rd (10 mins)	4th (10 mins)	5th (10 mins)	6th (10 mins)	Date _____ Hour observed _____
One or more checkout tills not staffed	/	/				//	
Sales staff talking to one another		/	/			/	
Sales staff ignoring customers	/	/	/			/	
Queue of more than two customers at a checkout till			/				
Untidy checkout till	/	/					

PART III

12.2.5 Technology-mediated observation

As with other forms of data collection, it is possible to use technology to collect observational data. Researchers have long used video to study behaviours in the physical world, for instance, in consumer research, to record private behaviours in the home. This has the advantage of making the presence of the observer less obvious, particularly if the cameras are positioned in a non-intrusive way. It also has the potential of speeding up data collection, as various individuals, groups or sites can be 'observed' simultaneously. Furthermore, it facilitates the observation of the behaviour of participants across diverse geographic locations. Video data also provides a permanent record that can be studied more closely and revisited as required during analysis. Audio recording can also be used to collect 'observational' data in the form of naturally occurring conversations. Audio recordings may be easier to make than video in some situations and are a particularly important source of data for conversation analysis. Some of the first work in conversation analysis was actually done using data from taped telephone calls (Wooffitt 2003). Any recording requires appropriate permissions and ethical clearance.

More recently, researchers have been seeing the Internet as an important environment in which to conduct observational research. This can take the form of monitoring discussion forums, following the participants' social media presence or observing their browsing behaviour, among others. It is important to distinguish here between observing online behaviours and capturing online content. Observing online behaviour, sometimes described as netnography, goes beyond recording what people write, and focuses on behaviours or actions (Kozinets 2002). Areas of interest include how often users interact with each other, what social norms guide those interactions, whether there is a formal or informal hierarchy, among others. As with traditional ethnography, the researcher can adopt different roles from complete (passive) observer to active participant. Research in Practice 9.2 (in Chapter 9) gives an example of participant observation in an online community, and in Chapter 7 we discuss ethical issues that can arise in online research.

12.2.6 Choosing your approach to observation

If you are thinking of using observation as a data collection method, you will need to decide what type of observation is appropriate. In making that decision, you should consider the following.

- Purpose of the research and intended research design. Consider how observation will support your research, answer the research question and how it will be integrated into your intended research design.
- Access. A key consideration is where the research setting will be for the observation and how you will gain access to it. This may take some time to organize and to negotiate access. During this process you will need to agree whether the observation will be covert or overt and how you will address any ethical concerns.
- Comfort in the role. Think about the skills that you have to carry out the observation and how you feel about the role, such as participant-observer, that you will adopt.

- Time available. When reviewing your project time schedule at the outset of your research, ensure that you have sufficient time available for the planned observation.
- Cost implications. Consider any likely costs in accessing and participating in the observation, as compared to alternative data collection methods.

12.3 Collecting documents and other records

So far we have looked at the ways of collecting data by asking people or watching how they behave. We now turn our attention to another important source of data in management research: documents and other written or electronic records. Insights into the behaviours, attitudes or activities of people and organizations can be drawn from the documents and other records they create in daily life. We may also be able to use secondary data such as administrative records or data from prior research that has been collected for other purposes by organizations, institutions and researchers and that we can re-analyse for our own research. Documents and records can therefore be used in research to help us find out about something external to the document itself. They can also be the object of research in their own right, however, for example, in content analysis or critical discourse analysis.

The term 'document' as we are using it here covers a very broad range of written, printed or electronic matter and can include textual, visual and even audio formats. The data contained may be verbal, such as meeting notes; numeric, such as sales statistics; or non-verbal, such as images from advertisements. This is a very broad definition but, in our view, provides a fairer description of the ways individuals and organizations today use documents to express themselves or to achieve particular goals. The growth in popularity and importance of the Internet and the emergence of social media and similar sites has further blurred the boundaries of what constitutes a document, whilst at the same time providing researchers with potential data sources and objects of inquiry. In addition, there are other types of written or electronic record such as organizational databases, government statistics and data from previous research projects that can be important sources of secondary data for research projects. This diversity and richness means that documents and other records have many potential applications in different research designs, as we show in Table 12.2. Note that these data sources can also be relevant at other points in your research project (for example, for background information or as part of the literature review), but in this chapter we are focusing on their use in the empirical stage of your research.

12.3.1 Advantages and disadvantages of documents as data sources

Documents offer a number of potential advantages as a data source. One of the most important is that they are a form of naturally occurring data. They exist independently of the researcher and represent an unobtrusive, non-reactive form of data collection (Webb et al. 1966), avoiding some of the problems that can arise as a result of social desirability bias. Documents, and other records, can also be very useful in retrospective longitudinal research, since they can provide a contemporary record of events that can be reviewed by the researcher. You might, for example, use customer complaint letters and emails to trace how the nature of customer complaints has changed over time. More generally, documents can be an important source of data for triangulation

Table 12.2 The role of documents and other records in different research designs

Research design	Role of documents and other records
Ethnography	May be used as a supporting data source
Case study	May be used alongside other methods; may be particularly useful in retrospective studies
Grounded theory	May be used as a supporting data source
Action research	May used alongside other data collection methods, either as part of the action research project cycle or for the researcher's thesis cycle
Content analysis (both quantitative and qualitative)	Primary data source; may be in the form of text, pictures, video or other visual media
Critical discourse analysis	Primary data source; may be in the form of text, pictures, video or other visual media
Experiment and quasi experiment	Secondary data may be used alongside other methods to measure relevant variables before, during and after the experiment
Non-experimental explanatory research (quantitative)	Secondary data may be the primary data source or be used alongside other data collection methods, such as questionnaires, to measure relevant variables

PART III

in research designs such as case studies to complement other sources such as interview accounts or as part of a mixed methods research project. In some situations documents and other records may offer a lower-cost and quicker data collection method than alternative methods, depending on the type of documents and their accessibility. Lastly, because of their characteristics, documents and other records can allow us to research topics that might not otherwise be researchable, for example, events for which there are no respondents available or accessible.

There are, of course, potential disadvantages to using documentary data sources. Coverage of a topic, as with any other source, is likely to be partial, leaving gaps that may have to be filled by other data collection methods, since it is rarely possible to go back to the author to ask for more details. Partial coverage may be worsened by problems in locating or getting access to particular documents or other records. Such problems can arise from a combination of practical, ethical and legal reasons, as would be the case if you wanted, for example, to access an organizational database containing confidential and/or personal data. The quality of documents and other records as data sources can also vary and, in some cases, be difficult to ascertain. Documents are created for a purpose, and reflect that purpose, rather than the needs of the research. Neither are they necessarily an accurate representation of their subject. For instance, newspapers may represent a sensationalist view of an event from a particular editorial viewpoint, whilst company policy guidelines may not reflect what is done in practice. Archived collections of documents, such as the files that have been kept on a particular project, can also represent a partial viewpoint, depending on the criteria used to decide what documents were kept and what were destroyed. Similar concerns arise when looking at secondary data such as government and organizational statistics or previous research projects.

12.3.2 *Finding and obtaining documents*

The process of collecting documents and other records involves two steps: finding and obtaining. Several factors will influence the way you go about doing so.

Sampling plan

The requirements of your sampling plan will influence how you approach collecting your documents, depending on whether your research question requires you to address the whole population of a particular type of document or just those documents relevant to a specific event or organization (Lee 2012). For instance, a study of changes over time in the way public companies have discussed environmental sustainability in their annual reports could use the complete set of annual reports for the target population or take a random sample from a predefined sampling frame.

Either way, you will have to define your target population, identify a suitable sampling frame and decide a sampling approach. In some cases, such as the annual report example, this may be relatively straightforward. In others, such as television or online advertisements, it can be more difficult, since no suitable listings may be available and you will have to develop your own or, if possible, use an existing archive such as library catalogue or electronic bibliographic database (see Chapter 3) to help you identify relevant documents. If your focus is on specific events or organizations, for instance, studying environmental reporting by a specific company in the light of a particular incident, such as an oil spill, you would have to identify and obtain documents that relate to that scenario. Online searching will be helpful for public records or open access documents, but non-public documents will be more difficult to identify and obtain.

Are the documents in the public or private domain?

A second important factor in document collection is therefore whether the documents are in the public domain or held privately by an individual or organization. Documents in the public domain are available to any member of the public to view. They may be accessible via the Internet or located in a library, public or government institution. If they are online, they may also be in downloadable versions, which will make collection and storage easier. There are also a growing number of archives or other repositories of documents and secondary data that are available online. In Table 12.3 we identify a range of different data sources and the types of data available. Other institutions or organizations, such as commercial research firms, also make documents or other data records available online. Such data may or may not require some form of payment or subscription to gain full access. Locating public domain documents will require similar techniques, such as online searching, to those you will have used for your literature review. You should revisit Chapter 3 for further guidance as well as other sources of online documents that may be useful in your research.

Privately held documents and records will not be so easy to identify or obtain. In business and management research, documents held internally by organizations fall into this category and are likely to be a potentially very valuable data source. For example, if you were researching a particular strategic decision, access to internal documents such as records of meetings or strategic analysis reports could offer

Table 12.3 Example sources of online secondary data

Type of data	Example sources
National census data	– UK National Census by the Office of National Statistics (www.ons.gov.uk/ons/index.html) – US Census Bureau (www.census.gov/)
Government surveys and statistics	– UK Office of National Statistics (www.statistics.gov.uk) – National Archives and Records Administration of the United States (NARA) (www.nara.gov) – Eurostat (http://epp.eurostat.ec.europa.eu/)
Large-scale surveys	– OECD statistics (http://stats.oecd.org/) – Euromonitor (www.euromonitor.com/)
Longitudinal studies	– British Household Panel Survey (https://www.iser.essex.ac.uk/bhps) – UK Millennium Cohort Study (www.cls.ioe.ac.uk/)
Qualitative secondary data archives	– UK Data Archive (also includes quantitative data) (www.data-archive.ac.uk)

significant insights into what went on. At this point it is useful to distinguish between the formal 'official' documents and records in an organization and the less official, 'grey materials'. Examples of official documents include human resource records, company reports, customer satisfaction surveys or employee handbooks. These are the documents that are created and acknowledged by the activities of an organization. As a researcher you will need to make contact with the respective owner of these documents to negotiate access. Less official 'grey' documents include emails, memoranda, notes from team meetings and personal working notes. These may reside with individuals within the organization, often in their own laptops or files and not stored centrally. Such data may be difficult to locate and the researcher may not even be aware of its existence unless it is mentioned by the holder. Additionally, although such documents may generate important insights, their ownership status may be unclear and they may be easily lost, for example, if an individual leaves the organization. Gaining access to organizational documents is likely to be easier if you are an insider researcher. Whatever your status, you should ensure that you have permission to access and use any documents or records and that you respect your ethical obligations as a researcher as well as any legal or other restrictions relating to their use. Similar considerations apply to documents or other records held by private individuals.

Location

Although many documents can be accessed via the Internet, physical location has not disappeared as a factor when collecting documents. In some cases it will still be necessary to visit an archive such as a library or record office in person either to negotiate access or to view the documents themselves, even if they are open to public access. The same applies to private documents which may not exist in digital format or may be held in electronically or physically secured areas that cannot be accessed from outside. When planning your document collection you will need to take these factors into account, as they can have both time and cost implications for your project, since you may have to travel and spend time on site studying documents.

Document format

Documents and other records come in different formats, which can affect how you collect and store them. Whilst many will be in electronic format, some may be printed or even handwritten. If you are collecting documents in electronic format, make sure that you have the technology to read them. If you are planning to use computer software to support your analysis, it is also helpful to obtain the document in a format that can be read directly by your chosen program. If downloading data, check what formats are available and choose the most useful; if obtaining electronic data from an organization, ask for it to be provided in a suitable format. In the case of documents that are available only in printed or written format, you may be allowed to copy, scan or photograph the document. If not, you will have to rely on field notes. If original documents are loaned to you, you will need to arrange for their safe return on completion of the project.

Particular issues arise when the documents of interest are in the form of online content such as organizations' websites or user-generated content such as blogs and discussion forum postings. In some cases it may be possible to search such material directly using conventional online search techniques. This is likely to be easiest if your search is relatively focused, for example, in terms of particular forums or other websites. In a study of user requirements for mobile technology, for instance, Gebauer

RESEARCH IN PRACTICE 12.3

Capturing social media comments

A research study was undertaken by Volker Krön, an MSc student, to investigate the impact of social media on marketing activities, focusing on one particular service that had recently been launched in the market.[1] The objective of the research was to identify, analyse and understand the nature of user-generated content (UGC) about the new offering that was being created in social media and to understand how this contributed to its marketing.

To do this the researcher used a research design involving content analysis of social media UGC in relation to the service. To identify relevant UGC content an automated crawler technology was used that trawled popular social media websites as well as predefined discussion forums entered into the search. Using the crawler software a total of 5,411 pieces of relevant UGC content were identified and captured covering a six-month period during 2012.

The search detected only text content. Other media such as photo or video content was not included in the research. The pieces of UGC included short messages on social media sites and text comments on video platforms, in blogs and discussion forums. The proposed research was subject to ethical review and approval before being allowed to proceed.

et al. (2008) collected user reviews of four products from a single online media website. In other cases, however, you may want to capture everything that has been written about a particular organization or issue across a range of different locations. Manual searching is likely to be difficult, given the size of the potential dataset. One option is to use technology to help data collection. In Research in Practice 12.3 we give an example of a research study using crawler software to collect data relating to social media postings. Note that such technology can still require extensive researcher input to set up the search and to filter the results. In addition, it raises some complex ethical issues regarding the use and reporting of such online material, as we discuss in Chapter 7. You should give very careful consideration to these before carrying out your research and seek further advice if necessary.

12.4 Diaries and other researcher-instigated documents

An alternative to using pre-existing documents and records is for the researcher to ask participants to keep records at particular points in time or following certain events by creating and maintaining a diary. This could be a simple journal entry or a record of events, for instance, about time spent on different activities during the working day. In other situations, researchers want to capture personal reflections such as the participants' views of the progress of a new product development, as well as notes on their feelings and attitudes. Participants may be asked to keep data concurrently with particular events that they are involved in, for instance, a food diary in which they record what they eat and how they feel at the time. Alternatively, they may be asked to enter the data retrospectively, for example, at the end of the day or at the end of a specific event, such as a meeting. The former offers enhanced spontaneity and detail, but the latter may be more practical, less taxing and make it easier to ensure confidentiality (for instance, where diaries focus on aspects of the work day or workplace).

Diaries may be written by hand into a notebook but nowadays such records may be captured through blogs, status updates on social networks or even via mobile phone. For instance, you might give each participant a private blog where they can create their online journal for the project. Using personal accounts in this way can give you access to 'personal experience unknowable to anyone else' (Stern 2004: 72). You will also have to decide the degree of structure that you provide to respondents when asking them to keep a diary. In some cases, you may want to keep instructions to a minimum, allowing participants maximum creativity in terms of the content and the form of what they write. Alternatively, you may wish to specify what elements to include, how often to write and so on. A more structured approach can help to ensure that you collect data on all aspects of your research questions and the output may be easier to analyse. Against this, a structured format generates data that is less open ended, exploratory and idiosyncratic than the non-directive approach. In designing your own diary study, it is worth taking into account Bowey and Thorpe's (1986) advice based on their experiences of running a multiple diary study.

- Consider the participants' ability to express themselves well in writing.
- Assess the consequences of excluding certain participants from the study, for example, causing offence if they are excluded.

PART III

- Provide some structure to focus the participants' entries. At least, supply a list of general headings.
- To sustain interest and reduce drop-out, maintain regular contact with the participants, providing continuous encouragement and reassurance.
- Think about how best to ensure confidentially in the collection process; in particular, whether to ask for concurrent or retrospective entries.

Research in Practice 12.4 gives an example of a diary study.

We have concentrated here on diaries, but these are not the only format that researchers can ask participants to generate. Patterson (2012), for example, asked students who were Facebook users to write 'introspective essays' about their relationship with the Facebook brand which formed the basis for his research study. Photographs and drawings can also be a form of participant-generated data that has potential application in the study of organizations and management. An introduction to their use is given in Vince and Warren (2012).

RESEARCH IN PRACTICE 12.4

Using diaries for data collection

For her final-year research project whilst studying for an MSc in Coaching and Behavioural Change, Ann James investigated the impact of performance anxiety on the coach.[2] She was not interested in assessing or comparing individual coaches' propensity for anxiety. Rather, she wanted to focus on their subjective experience of anxiety and to understand whether anxiety levels can be influenced by deliberate participation in reflective activity before a coaching session.

The researcher decided to use diaries, as she felt that this medium supported the desired immediacy and spontaneity while providing participants with the opportunity to reflect. Research participants were asked to notice and capture their experiences of anxiety in live coaching situations for four coaching sessions each. Furthermore, they were asked to record those experiences in a template provided by the researcher (see template below). All instructions were issued by email, followed by one-to-one telephone conversations with each coach for clarification and confirmation of their understanding of the task.

For sessions one and two, coaches were instructed to prepare for and conduct their coaching sessions in their usual way. They were asked to complete a reflective diary for each session, writing up their material as soon as possible after the session had taken place. In each diary entry they were asked to:

- record the circumstances, events and their observations of their own state in the immediate run-up to the session
- notice and record the occurrence and evidence of any anxiety they experienced during the session
- notice and record any physical, physiological, cognitive and emotional responses that accompanied the experience
- include their reflections and insights.

Following receipt of their diaries for session two, coaches were sent an additional instruction for the next two sessions. Specifically, they were asked to engage in a planned, reflective activity before the coaching session. Furthermore, they were asked to conduct the coaching session in their usual way after the reflective activity, and to complete the diary as previously, thus allowing comparison between their experiences of coaching with and without the pre-session reflective activity.

Reflections record template

Reflections record   Page: ....

Initials of coach: ....   Session no.: .... of 4

Reflections	Actual and factual

12.5 Artefacts

Another source of data available to the researcher is the physical artefacts that people may use, for example, to carry out their work or to express their identity. Artefacts can include the tools that employees may use to perform a particular work task, or the clothes that job applicants may wear for an interview, or the products and their packaging that are produced by an organization. Artefacts are a potentially important source of insight in research because so much of our communication is done by means other than words and because aspects of the physical environment, such as pictures, tools and furniture, influence our behaviour through their material presence and their symbolic meaning. An ethnographic study by Clarke (2011), for example, showed how entrepreneurs used visual symbols, including settings (such as office furniture), props (such as prototypes) and dress (informal or formal) in different ways during their 'entrepreneurial performances'.

Despite their potential significance, however, artefacts have not received much attention as a source of insight in research. Consequently it is rare to see a management research project that relies exclusively on this type of data. Instead, it tends to be used as a complement to other data sources. For example, a study of new technology implementation could include investigation of the physical system and observation of how it is actually used by operators. Alternatively, a diary study of consumer shopping habits could be supported by the collection of shopping lists, carrier bags, till receipts and so on.

Artefacts are likely to belong to someone else. They may belong to an institution, an organization or an individual as their private property. They may be housed in a secure site such as a museum or library; alternatively they may be in the possession of private individuals. They may also be expensive items or have high sentimental value for their owners. If they cannot be moved or are stored in a secure site you may gain access to them for only a specific period of time and will have to rely on your field notes, along with photographs or video if permitted. If you are asking research participants to gather artefacts as input to your research, you may wish to restrict the type of objects that participants can produce. Otherwise, you risk ending up with a list of material that is cumbersome to store or difficult to compare. You will also need to consider the safe keeping of any items that are loaned to you and the arrangements to return them to respondents following the research, if necessary. These factors should be taken into account if you are intending to include the study of artefacts as part of your data collection.

CRITICAL COMMENTARY 12.1

Observer effects and unobtrusive measures

In this chapter we have mentioned observer effects and their potential influence on research data. Observer effects arise when participants' awareness that they are being researched influences their behaviour. Webb et al. (1966) suggested four dimensions of what they called 'reactive effects':

1 awareness of being tested or 'the guinea pig effect', as a result of which participants behave in ways other than normal, for instance to create a particular impression
2 role selection, in which the participant tries to adopt a particular role within the research, for example, in response to their expectations about what the researcher is looking for
3 measurement as a change agent, in which the mere fact of being part of the research project induces change
4 response sets in self-report measures such as questionnaires in which respondents' answers exhibit a pattern that is clearly unrelated to the questions actually asked, for example, consistently choosing one position on a scale, irrespective of the question.

Webb et al. (1966) propose what they call unobtrusive measures as a counter to these problems. Naturally occurring data, covert observation and artefacts are examples of such measures.

KEY LEARNING POINTS

- Observation as a data collection method involves the purposeful observation, recording and analysis of behaviours and other activities in an organized way.

- Designing an observation study requires decisions about the researcher's role, whether the observation will be covert or overt, whether the setting should be natural or artificial and the degree of structure required.
- Qualitative observation is typically unstructured, with data collection by means of field notes in order to generate thick description of the situation. Quantitative observation generally uses a predefined, structured coding schedule with a view to generating quantitative or quantifiable data. Observation can also be carried out in online environments, for example, during netnography.
- Documents are written, printed or electronic materials that contain verbal, numeric or non-verbal data. Along with other records, such as company operating data, they are an important source of data in research.
- The collection of documents and other records for a research project is influenced by the sampling plan, whether or not the documents are in the public domain, their location and the format they are in. Access to organizational documents will have to be negotiated with document holders and appropriate permission and ethical clearance gained.
- Diaries and other researcher-instigated documents, such as drawings and photographs, provide another useful source of data. The degree of structure and the guidance given on the content of diary entries should take into account the focus of the research.
- Study of physical artefacts and their use can offer valuable insights into the ways in which material things are used and into the meanings they hold for people.

PART III

NEXT STEPS

12.1 The role of non-verbal accounts in your research design. Revisit the key research articles from the literature that you have reviewed and identify any that have collected data by means other than survey or interviewing the research participants. What collection methods have been used?

12.2 Assessing the advantages and disadvantages of the selected data collection tools. With reference to your specific research project, list the advantages and disadvantages of the data collection approaches discussed in this chapter. Consider a broad range of factors, including the likely cost or time required for data collection.

12.3 Addressing limitations. Identify the limitations arising from using the selected data collection tools for your study.

12.4 Technology-mediated data collection. Decide if you are going to use some form of technology interface to collect your data. Ensure that you know how to use the technology interface and deal with technical problems.

12.5 Set up the empirical exercise. Think about how you will negotiate access to the research site and clarify expectations regarding how long you can collect data, what you can access and what you will be providing in return. Decide the type of instructions and the level of structure that you need to provide to the research participants, if relevant. Construct the coding schedule, if relevant.

12.6 Capturing your data. Decide how you are going to capture and store the data, and your notes.

Further reading

For further reading, please see the companion website.

References

Bowey, A. M. and Thorpe, R. (1986). *Payment systems and productivity*. Basingstoke: Macmillan.

Canhoto, A. I. (2007). Profiling behaviour: The social construction of categories in the detection of financial crime. (PhD). London School of Economics.

Clarke, J. (2011). 'Revitalizing entrepreneurship: How visual symbols are used in entrepreneurial performances', *Journal of Management Studies*, 48(6), 1365–91.

Creswell, J. W. (2007). *Qualitative inquiry and research design: Choosing among five traditions*. 2nd edn. Thousand Oaks, CA: Sage.

Easterby-Smith, M., Thorpe, R. and Jackson, P. R. (2012). *Management research*. 4th edn. London: Sage Publications.

Emerson, R. M., Fretz, R. I. and Shaw, L. L. (1995). *Writing ethnographic fieldnotes*. Chicago, IL: The University of Chicago Press.

Gebauer, J., Tang, Y. and Baimai, C. (2008). 'User requirements of mobile technology: Results from a content analysis of user reviews', *Information Systems & e-Business Management*, 6(4), 361–84.

Gold, R. L. (1958). 'Roles in sociological field observations', *Social Forces*, 36(3), 217–23.

Hammersley, M. and Atkinson, P. (2007). *Ethnography, principles in practice*. 3rd edn. London: Routledge.

Kozinets, R. V. (2002). 'The field behind the screen: Using netnography for marketing research in online communities', *Journal of Marketing Research (JMR)*, 39(1), 61–72.

Lee, B. (2012). Documents in organizational research. *In*: Symon, G. and Cassell, C. (eds) *Qualitative organizational research*. London: Sage.

Mintzberg, H. (1973). *The nature of managerial work*. New York: Harper and Row.

Patterson, A. (2012). 'Social-networkers of the world, unite and take over: A meta-introspective perspective on the Facebook brand', *Journal of Business Research*, 65(4), 527–34.

Schouten, J. W. and McAlexander, J. H. (1995). 'Subcultures of consumption: An ethnography of the new bikers', *Journal of Consumer Research*, 22(1), 43–61.

Stern, B. B. (2004). *Representing consumers: Voices, views and visions*. London: Routledge.

Vince, R. and Warren, S. (2012). Participatory visual methods. *In*: Symon, G. and Cassell, C. (eds) *Qualitative organizational research*. London: Sage.

Webb, E. J., Campbell, D. T., Schwartz, R. D. and Sechrest, L. (1966). *Unobtrusive measures: Nonreactive research in the social sciences*. Chicago, IL: Rand McNally.

Wooffitt, R. (2003). *Conversation analysis and discourse analysis*. London: Sage.

Notes

1　Krön, V. (2013). *The power of listening: Analysing consumer generated social media content concerning the product "Entertain" to identify related fields of actions in marketing*. MSc Strategic Marketing Leadership dissertation submission. Henley Business School, University of Reading.

2　James, A. (2012). *Performance anxiety in the coach: An exploration of the brain mechanisms and processes that affect the quality of thinking available to the coach in challenging coaching situations*. MSc in Coaching and Behavioural Change dissertation submission. Henley Business School, University of Reading.

Part IV

Analyse

The purpose of data analysis in research is to move from a set of raw data, such as the responses to a questionnaire or recordings of in-depth interviews, to knowledge that helps you to answer your research question. In the process you need to turn the raw data into something that provides meaning in relation to the research questions that you are trying to answer. In doing so you want to be confident that any conclusions you reach are justified by your data. You will also need to be able to communicate your findings, so an important aspect of data analysis is preparing output that is meaningful to others.

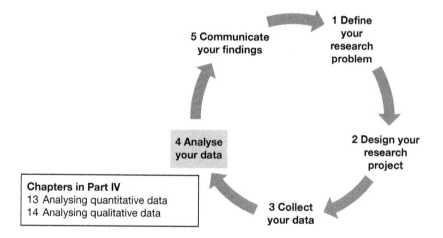

Chapters in Part IV
13 Analysing quantitative data
14 Analysing qualitative data

These activities are the focus of Part IV. In Chapter 13 we take a look at quantitative data analysis, including the use of descriptive and inferential statistics. In Chapter 14 we review qualitative data, introducing the coding process and the use of visual display techniques to help your analysis. Both chapters are supported in the companion website by guides, including video, on how to use software to support the analysis process.

13 Analysing quantitative data

```
CHAPTER SUMMARY

The key topics covered in this chapter are:

• introducing quantitative data analysis
• entering your data
• preparing your data
• exploring your data
• answering your research questions
• presenting your findings.
```

13.1 Introduction

The focus of this chapter is quantitative data analysis. We begin by setting out a simple process to follow when carrying out quantitative data analysis. We then look at how to get your data ready for analysis before introducing techniques for exploring and describing your data using tables, summary statistics and graphs. Next, we introduce some more advanced analysis techniques, including how to use inferential statistics to test hypotheses and estimate population parameters. We conclude with a brief look at presenting your findings.

This chapter is designed to be used in conjunction with the book's companion website, which covers analysis techniques introduced here in more detail and shows how to carry them out using popular software packages.

Note: unless otherwise stated, the data used in this chapter are fictitious.

13.1.1 Using a computer

Quantitative data analysis is going to involve using statistics. Fortunately, quantitative data analysis software packages are widely available, which largely removes the need for you to be able to perform statistical calculations yourself. These programs range from basic statistical functions within spreadsheet packages to bespoke statistical analysis software. Choice of program depends on the analysis you are doing. Whilst spreadsheet-based software will be adequate for many simple projects, a specialized statistics package will be needed for more advanced analysis. In this chapter and on the companion website we refer to two programs that represent different ends of the spectrum in terms of specialization:

- Microsoft Excel (hereafter Excel) as an example of a popular spreadsheet package
- IBM SPSS Statistics (hereafter SPSS) as an example of a specialist statistics program that is widely used in social science research.

The companion website gives further information on using these two packages for the analysis techniques introduced in this chapter.

13.1.2 *The analysis process*

Figure 13.1 presents the key steps in quantitative data analysis. It is essential to begin with careful data entry and thorough preparation prior to analysis. The next step is data exploration, during which you get a feel for your sample data. This provides the platform from which to answer your research questions. Throughout the process you need to think about how you will present your findings, so it is important to save your output as you work and keep a record of the decisions that you make and actions that you take.

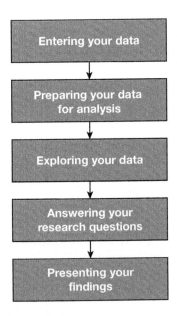

Figure 13.1 The quantitative data analysis process

13.2 Entering your data

The first step in the analysis process is to get your data into a format that can be analysed by your chosen software program.

13.2.1 *Creating a data matrix*

A standard format for preparing quantitative data is to set up a case-by-variable data matrix. Figure 13.2 shows a typical example that was created in Excel and is laid out as follows.

- The first column contains a unique numerical identifier (ID) for each case. This allows you to refer to individual cases and, if required, recover the original layout if it is changed during the analysis process.
- Columns after the first one represent individual variables. In a data matrix for a questionnaire, for example, each question would have its own column.
- Rows contain the data for a particular case or observation, such as an individual respondent to a questionnaire.

An individual cell in the grid therefore represents the unique data for a particular variable for a particular case. In Figure 13.2, for example, cell C3 represents case number 2's age in years (46).

	A	B	C	D	E
1	Respondent ID	Gender	Age (years)	Customer satisfaction	Affective commitment
2	1	0	38	2	3
3	2	1	46	4	5
4	3	0	36	6	6
5	4	1	53	3	4

Figure 13.2 Example data matrix created in Excel

If your data were captured electronically (e.g. using an online survey tool) data entry should be a straightforward process of exporting the file in an appropriate format and then opening it in your chosen software. If you have collected your data on paper, you will probably have to enter your data by typing it directly into your analysis software.

13.2.2 *Coding*

Data that are already in numerical form can usually be entered directly into your data matrix. Other data will need coding prior to entry. In the context of quantitative data analysis, **coding** is the process of assigning meaningful numerical values to responses to facilitate analysis. The most common coding task is the allocation of numbers to categories of nominal variables (such as gender or occupation) so that they can be analysed using appropriate statistical techniques. For example, rather than entering the words 'male' or 'female' in the data matrix for a gender variable, you would allocate each response category a number (e.g. male = 0, female = 1) and enter the number instead, as shown in column B of the data grid in Figure 13.2.

Table 13.1 Example codebook entry for a single question in a questionnaire

Question number	15
Variable name	Licence
Question wording	What type of driving licence do you hold?
Categories and codes	Full driving licence = 1 Provisional driving licence = 2 Do not hold a driving licence = 3
Special instructions	Leave missing values blank

For variables where there are more than two categories each category is similarly allocated its own unique number. The resulting coding scheme should be carefully recorded by building up a codebook that contains the question number, question wording, the variable to which it refers and the coding structure used, as shown in Table 13.1.

Where data are captured using Likert-type scales, the responses should be coded and entered as numerical values rather than statements. A 5-point response scale, for example, labelled 'strongly disagree' to 'strongly agree' could be coded 'strongly disagree' = 1 to 'strongly agree' = 5, with the mid-point 'neither agree nor disagree' being coded 3.

Guidance on coding other types of data, including multi-answer and open-ended questions, can be found on the companion website.

13.2.3 Managing your data

Good data management is essential in any research project to guard against potential data loss and to maintain data security, so make sure that you:

- create a back-up of your master data, stored in a secure environment separately from your working copy of the data on your laptop or PC
- save your work regularly, making back-ups of your working files
- record any changes you make to your master dataset and store a fresh back-up copy in a secure environment
- store and/or destroy the data securely at the end of the project in accordance with relevant data protection rules and any agreements made with respondents or other stakeholders.

If you are carrying out a project for an academic qualification you will probably be required to keep a copy of your data until your award is confirmed. Make sure that you understand the requirements of your institution regarding data handling, storage and disposal.

13.3 Preparing your data for analysis

Once your data have been entered, you can start final preparation for analysis. This involves the following steps:

- checking for errors
- dealing with missing values
- transforming your data to facilitate analysis
- checking scale reliability.

13.3.1 Checking for errors

Errors can occur during data collection or data entry. Error checking takes time and is boring but needs to be done; it is also better to do it early rather than wasting time analysing faulty data. Actions to take include the following.

- Check that the responses fall within the valid range for the variable. A score of 55 on a 5-point Likert scale, for example, is obviously wrong.
- If filter questions have been used in a questionnaire, confirm that the rules have been applied correctly. For example, if someone indicates in response to a filter question that they have not used a particular service, they should not then go on to rate the quality of that service.
- Look for logical inconsistencies in responses. A person who responds that they are 20 years old in one question should not report that they have 30 years' work experience in another.
- Confirm that respondents fall within the target population.

Correct errors where possible; errors that cannot be corrected should be removed from the dataset. Where a case should not have been included in the sample it should be removed. Note any changes and the reasons for them in your research log.

13.3.2 Dealing with missing values

For some observations in your data matrix there may be no data to be entered in a particular cell. This might be because the question did not apply to that particular case, because the respondent failed to answer or because the data could not otherwise be obtained. These cells represent **missing values**. It can be useful to code such missing values in a consistent way to distinguish, for example, between failure to respond, non-applicability or other data problems. SPSS allows you to predefine a number of missing values. (If using Excel, you can leave the cell blank and use the comments function to record the reason for the missing value.)

Missing values in a data matrix are a fact of life in many research projects and need to be dealt with, as they can affect your analysis by reducing sample size, distorting summary statistics and, potentially, introducing **bias** if there is a systematic pattern to the missing data. One option is deletion. Hair et al. (2007) suggest exclusion of a case or variable if the missing data points exceed 10 per cent of the total. Alternatively, cases with missing values may be excluded on a variable-by-variable basis; otherwise they remain in the dataset. A third option is substitution, in which another value (such as the sample mean) is substituted for the missing value. Whatever decisions you make regarding missing values should be reported in your final write-up.

13.3.3 Transforming your data to facilitate analysis

Data transformation is the process of changing your original data to a new format to facilitate analysis or reporting. This can include recoding data into new categories, such as recoding nominal data into a smaller number of groups. For example, information about a respondent's town or city of residence might be recoded according to the county, state or province in which the town or city is located in order to reduce the number of categories. Recoded data may be easier to report, or recoding may be needed if the number of cases in each category is too small for analysis. If recoding, always ensure that the original data are kept for checking or further analysis.

Another common data transformation task is **reverse coding** any questions with negatively worded statements (see Chapter 10). This is often needed if you are intending to combine both positively and negatively worded questions in a summated scale but it can also be useful if you are comparing results from both negatively and positively worded questions. For a 5-point Likert-type scale, for example, reverse coding involves changing a rating of 5 to a rating of 1, 4 to 2, 2 to 4 and 5 to 1 (3 does not need to be changed). Specialist software such as SPSS includes routines to facilitate recoding.

If your research involves using multi-item scales to measure certain concepts you will need to calculate the combined scale. Table 13.2 shows an example of a summated scale where the mean of the responses to five questions (PU1 to PU5) is calculated to give an overall measure of Perceived Usefulness (PU) for each respondent. If you are using existing scales you should check to see what summation method is appropriate for your chosen scale.

Table 13.2 Example summated scale (PU = perceived usefulness)

Respondent ID	PU1	PU2	PU3	PU4	PU5	PU
1	3	2	3	3	3	2.8
2	5	5	5	5	3	4.6
3	3	3	5	4	3	3.6
4	3	3	2	3	2	2.6
5	4	4	5	5	4	4.4

13.3.4 Checking scale reliability

If you are using multi-item scales to measure a concept you need to ensure that respondents' answers to the items (questions) are consistent. If they are not, it may indicate that the scale is not a reliable measure. A common test of scale reliability is Cronbach's coefficient alpha (or just **Cronbach's alpha**), which returns a score between 0 and 1. The higher the score, the higher the reliability of the scale. A common rule of thumb is that an alpha of 0.7 is an appropriate threshold to indicate a reliable scale, although scores between 0.6 and 0.7 may also be accepted (Hair et al. 2010). Cronbach's alpha can be calculated using SPSS. See the companion website for more details.

13.4 Exploring your data

Once your data are ready for analysis, the next stage is data exploration using summary statistics and graphical display techniques. The initial goal is to get a feel for your dataset and what it is telling you about your sample. Throughout the data exploration stage you should be alert to anomalies or other interesting or unexpected features of your data that warrant further investigation, whilst also keeping your research questions in mind. Ensure that you record what you have done by saving appropriate output and noting your emerging thoughts in your log.

Begin by exploring each variable individually, a process known as **univariate analysis**. Once you have a sound understanding at the univariate level, you can then investigate any differences or associations between variables or groups. Is there, for example, an association between customer satisfaction and loyalty? Do full-time employees differ from part-time employees in their level of engagement? Analysis of two variables simultaneously is known as **bivariate analysis**; analysis of more than two is known as **multivariate analysis**. When you reach this point you are likely to be ready to start working on the next level of analysis: answering your research question. Working examples of these analyses can be found on the companion website.

13.4.1 Univariate data exploration techniques

Univariate analysis techniques can be used to describe and summarize each variable in your sample, typically in terms of four main characteristics:

- frequency distribution
- central tendency
- dispersion
- shape of the distribution.

Choosing an analysis technique

The choice of analysis technique is strongly influenced by the measurement level of your data (i.e. nominal, ordinal, interval or metric). Table 13.3 lists techniques for exploring and summarizing data, along with the measurement level with which they are most compatible. For some analysis techniques data may need recoding into a smaller number of categories if the number of categories is too large to be handled easily.

13.4.2 What is the frequency distribution of a variable?

One of the first things you will want to know is how much of your sample falls within different categories or ranges of values for each variable. This is referred to as the variable's **frequency distribution**. Tabular and graphical techniques can be used to explore and present this information.

Frequency tables

Frequency tables provide a very useful way of investigating the frequency distribution of nominal and ordinal variables, as shown in Figure 13.3. **Metric data,** which means

Table 13.3 Univariate descriptive statistics and graphical presentation techniques

Category	Typical applications	Summary statistic/technique	Measurement level of data		
			Nominal	Ordinal	Metric (interval/ratio)
Frequency distribution	Examine and report the frequency distribution of responses	Frequency tables	Yes	Yes	Yes (may need recoding)
Measures of central tendency	Identify and report a typical response value for the variable	Mode		Yes	Yes (may need recoding)
		Median		Yes	Yes
		Mean			Yes
Measures of dispersion	Measure and report the extent to which the responses are spread out	Variation ratio	Yes		
		Range		Yes	Yes
		Interquartile range		Yes	Yes
		Variance/standard deviation			Yes
		Coefficient of variation			Yes
Shape of the distribution	Measure and report the extent to which the variable conforms to a normal distribution	Skewness			Yes
		Kurtosis			Yes
Graphical techniques	Examine and report the distribution of responses graphically	Pie chart	Yes	Yes	Yes (may need recoding)
		Bar chart	Yes	Yes	Yes (may need recoding)
		Histogram			Yes
		Box plot			Yes

Gender

		Frequency	Percent	Valid Percent	Cumulative Percent
Valid	Male	20	60.6	62.5	62.5
	Female	12	36.4	37.5	100.0
	Total	32	97.0	100.0	
Missing	System	1	3.0		
Total		33	100.0		

Figure 13.3 Frequency table of respondent gender ($n = 33$) (created in SPSS)

interval or ratio data, will often need to be recoded into a smaller number of range bands, in which case they can be treated as ordinal data. Where there are missing values in the dataset, as here, an additional column can be included to report valid per cent. This is the percentage of the total of non-missing values for each category in the sample. This is the fourth column in Figure 13.3. Rows represent categories, with the last row providing totals for the columns. Note the use of the letter *n* in the caption, to indicate sample size.

Frequency tables allow you to see whether responses are fairly evenly distributed across the categories by checking whether the percentages for each category are similar. When presenting frequency tables in reports, a simplified format is often used. These contain only the category frequency counts and valid per cent information, as shown in Table 13.4.

Table 13.4 Simplified frequency table showing frequency of car driving ($n = 1220$)

		Frequency	*Per cent*
Valid	Every day	783	64.2
	At least 3 times per week	264	21.6
	1–2 times per week	127	10.4
	Less than once per week	46	3.8
	Total	1220	100.0

Exploring and presenting frequency distributions graphically

Bar charts can be used to depict the data in frequency tables and to explore the frequency distribution of nominal and ordinal variables in a more visual way. Each bar represents a particular category or value of the variable and the height or length of the bar represents the frequency count or valid per cent of the observations in that category. Example horizontal and vertical bar charts are shown in Figure 13.4 using the data in Table 13.4.

Bar charts can be used with any level of measurement, but **histograms** are commonly used for showing the frequency distribution of a metric variable and for spotting potential extreme values. They are normally drawn vertically as a series of bars with no gaps in between, as shown in Figure 13.5. When creating a histogram,

PART IV

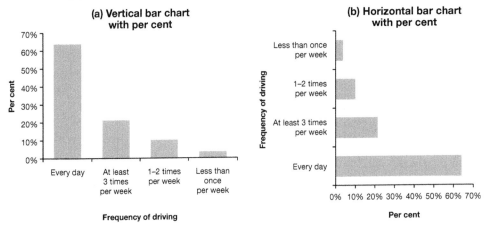

Figure 13.4 Bar charts showing frequency of car driving (*n* = 1220)

the range of observed values in the variable is divided into class intervals or bins. These intervals, which are usually equal, are known as the bin range and are shown on the horizontal axis. In the example in Figure 13.5 the intervals are set at two years. The height of the bar represents the frequency of cases in the class interval.

Pie charts can be used to depict the data in a frequency table in a more visual way by representing each category as a slice of a pie. The relative size of each slice indicates the proportion of the whole represented by each category. Pie charts can be used with any measurement level but are primarily useful where the aim is to show differences in proportions. Figure 13.6 shows different examples of pie charts based on the same dataset.

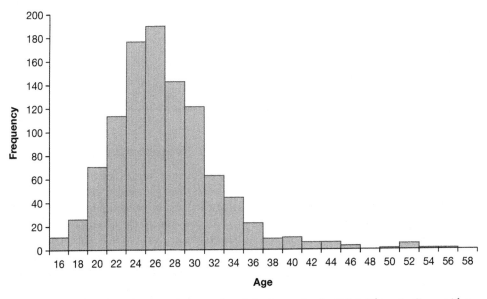

Figure 13.5 Histogram showing the age of medal winners in the 2012 Olympic Games (data from *The Guardian* 2012)

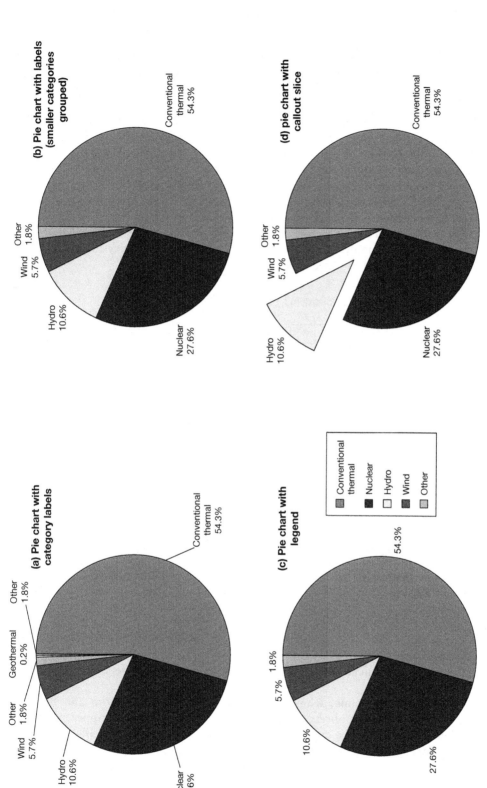

Figure 13.6 Example pie charts showing European Union EU27 electricity production by source, 2011 (Eurostat 2012)

PART IV

What is a typical value for a variable?

Measures of central tendency (or location) can be used to identify a typical value or average response for a variable. The three most commonly encountered are:

1   The **mode**, which is the most frequently occurring value for the variable. It can be used for any level of measurement (metric data may need to be grouped) but is the only measure of central tendency applicable to nominal data.

2   The **median**, which is the value that is in the middle of the distribution, i.e. has 50 per cent of the observed values lying below it and 50 per cent above it (Figure 13.7). It can be used for ordinal and metric data. An advantage of the median is that it is relatively insensitive to extreme values.

3   The arithmetic **mean**, which is the arithmetic average of the dataset. The mean is the most commonly encountered measure of central tendency for metric data but it is influenced by extreme values.

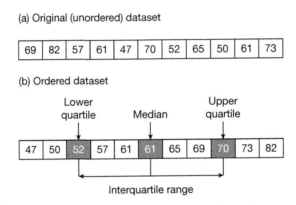

Figure 13.7 Calculating the median and interquartile range for a dataset

13.4.3 How spread out are the responses?

Measures of dispersion (or spread) provide a way of summarizing the level of agreement between cases for a particular variable and indicate how well your chosen measure of central tendency typifies the variable. Common measures include:

•   The **range**, which is the spread of data from the minimum to the maximum value for the variable. Range is a simple measure of spread, applicable to ordinal and metric data. The maximum and minimum values can also be reported along with the range.

•   The **interquartile range**, which is the range between the bottom and the top 25 per cent of the observations, known as the lower and upper quartiles (Figure 13.7). It can be applied to ordinal or metric data. The smaller the interquartile range, the better the median is as a summary of the data. The interquartile range can be shown graphically on box plots.

•   The **variance** and **standard deviation**, which are both measures of how far the distribution is spread out from the mean. Although variance is an important measure we often report the standard deviation (which is the square root of the variance), since this is measured in the same units as the mean, which makes it easier to interpret. The lower the standard deviation, the better the mean is as a summary of the data. Both are applicable to metric data only.

13.4.4 Exploring the shape of a variable's distribution

Examining the shape of the frequency distribution of your ordinal and metric variables will give you a better understanding of how well your summary statistics capture relevant features of the data. It will also help you to identify any outliers that may need special handling in your analysis and to check whether or not your data meet any assumptions required by statistical tests that you plan to use later. In particular, you may need to check whether or not your data conform to a normal distribution.

Looking for outliers or extreme values

An **outlier** is an observation with characteristics that are distinctly different from other observations in the sample, such as a very high or very low value for a particular variable. Outliers may arise as the result of data collection or data entry errors that have not been detected during data cleansing; these should be corrected as described earlier. Others may be accurate observations for which you have an explanation but which still strongly influence the findings. Outliers may also be observations for which you have no explanation; these may indicate some aspect of the population of which you were not aware and warrant further investigation.

Outliers can exert a strong influence on some statistical measures such as the arithmetic mean, as we show in Research in Practice 13.1. Frequency tables and graphical displays can be used to help identify potential outliers, following which they should be thoroughly investigated before you decide what action to take. One

PART IV

RESEARCH IN PRACTICE 13.1

Outlier or not?

To illustrate the potential problem that outliers can cause, Hair et al. (2007) cite the example of the impact of US businessman Bill Gates' personal net worth on calculations of the average (mean) net worth of households in Medina, Washington. According to their calculations, the average net worth of Medina households including Bill Gates was just over US$44 million in 2003. Removing Gates (net worth US$46 billion at that time) from the calculation brought the average net worth of the remaining households down to just over US$6 million. Removing two other very wealthy individuals with a combined net worth of over US$7 million brought the average household net worth down to US$224,189. But what figure provides the most representative picture of household net worth in Medina? Should Gates be excluded from the analysis? Should a different analysis technique be selected, one that is less sensitive to extreme values? 'The answer', as Hair et al. (2007: 323) put it, 'depends on the research objectives'.

approach is to employ analysis techniques that are less sensitive to outliers (such as using the median rather than the mean). In extreme cases you may need to remove outliers from your analysis but this should be a last resort. Any action that you take regarding outliers should be discussed and justified in your final report.

Is a variable normally distributed?

Some statistical tests require that your data are normally distributed. The **normal distribution** (also known as a Gaussian distribution) can be identified by its characteristic bell shape (Figure 13.8). It is symmetrical about a single central peak which represents the most frequently occurring value of the distribution (i.e. the mode), with the mode, median and mean all being identical. Another interesting property of the normal distribution is that almost all of the distribution (99.73 per cent) lies within ± 3 standard deviations (σ) of the mean (μ).

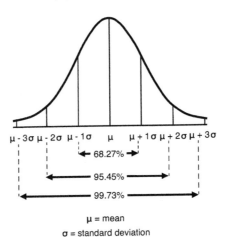

Figure 13.8 Normal distribution

A variable may differ from a normal distribution in one of three main ways:

1   The number of peaks (modes). The normal distribution has a single peak and is therefore **unimodal** (i.e. it has one mode). Data with more than one peak is described as **bimodal** (two peaks) or **multimodal** (more than two peaks) and may suggest subgroups within the data that are worth further investigation (Figure 13.9).
2   Lack of symmetry. Asymmetrical data are said to be skewed (Figure 13.10), and **skewness** can be identified visually by the longer 'tail' of values to one side or the other. If the tail runs in the direction of the higher values, it is right tailed or positively skewed. In the opposite direction it is left tailed or negatively skewed. The mean of skewed data will tend to be pulled in the direction of the skew. Extreme skewness may indicate the existence of outliers.
3   Relative 'peakiness'. **Kurtosis** is the term used to describe the extent to which a distribution is peaked or flat (Figure 13.11). A 'flat' distribution exhibits negative kurtosis and is said to be platykurtic. A 'peaked' distribution shows positive kurtosis and is described as leptokurtic. Extreme kurtosis is an indication that the distribution of the data is non-normal.

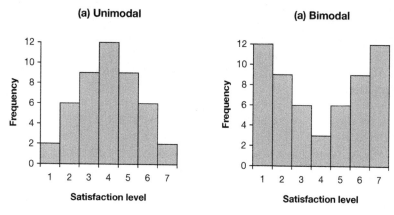

Figure 13.9 Unimodal and bimodal data

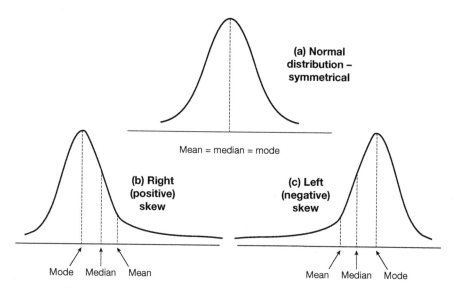

Figure 13.10 Skewness

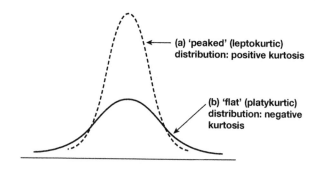

Figure 13.11 Kurtosis

Histograms are the starting point for investigating whether or not a metric variable is normally distributed. Some software packages, including SPSS, offer the option of superimposing a normal distribution curve over a histogram to aid visual inspection. In addition, you can calculate summary statistics that measure skewness and kurtosis. For both measures, a perfectly normal distribution should return a score of 0. Otherwise:

- A positive skewness value indicates positive (right) skew; a negative value indicates negative (left) skew. The higher the absolute value, the greater the skew.
- Similarly, a positive kurtosis value indicates positive kurtosis; a negative one indicates negative kurtosis. The higher the absolute value, the greater the kurtosis.

Further details on interpreting skewness and kurtosis statistics can be found on the companion website, along with a discussion of the **Kolmogorov-Smirnov** and the **Shapiro-Wilk statistical tests** that can be used to test the assumption that your sample data are drawn from a normally distributed population.

A **box plot** can be used to identify potential outliers and to explore the shape of the variable's distribution. A box plot (also known a box-and-whisker plot) consists of a box-shaped area that shows the interquartile range and contains a bar indicating the median. Attached to the box are two 'whiskers' which represent more extreme values. Conventions vary regarding the whiskers. In SPSS, for example, the box plot whiskers extend to the smallest and largest values that are within one and a half lengths of each end of the box. Values beyond that are individually flagged. Figure 13.12 shows the components of a typical box plot.

Figure 13.13 gives an example box plot created in SPSS using the Olympic medal winner age dataset shown in the histogram in Figure 13.5. Note the potential outliers. Each one has been individually numbered to make it easier to identify in the dataset for further checking. SPSS also highlights observations with values more than three times the height of a box with an asterisk or star (*).

13.4.5 Exploring more than one variable

Many interesting problems in quantitative analysis can be addressed only by combining data from two or move variables simultaneously. For instance:

- to investigate whether or not there are differences between groups with respect to their scores on variables of interest
- to investigate whether or not two or more variables are associated.

This is the domain of bivariate and multivariate analysis and in Table 13.5 we summarize a range of techniques that can be used for exploring your data.

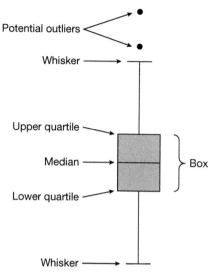

Figure 13.12 Components of a typical box plot

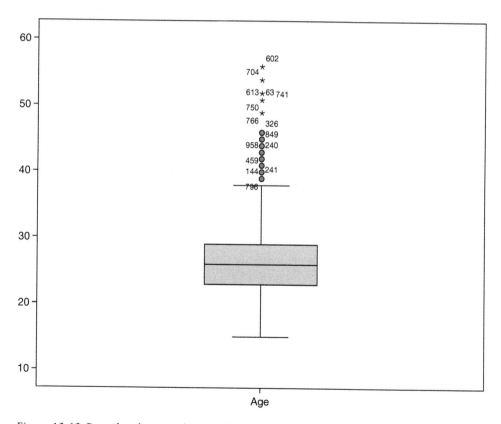

Figure 13.13 Box plot showing the age of medal winners in the 2012 Olympic Games (data from *The Guardian* 2012)

Table 13.5 Techniques for exploring more than one variable

Purpose	Statistic/ technique	Measurement level		
		Nominal	Ordinal	Metric (interval/ ratio)
Compare different groups or different variables with respect to their scores on metric variables of interest	Tables of means	Yes (as a grouping variable)	Yes (as a grouping variable)	Yes
	Bar chart of means	Yes (as a grouping variable)	Yes (as a grouping variable)	Yes
	Box plot	Yes (as a grouping variable)	Yes	Yes
Explore the association between two nominal or ordinal variables	Contingency tables	Yes	Yes	
	Clustered bar chart	Yes	Yes	
	Stacked bar chart	Yes	Yes	
Explore the association between two metric variables	Scatterplot			Yes

Exploring differences between groups

Tables offer a simple way of comparing the means of different groups in your sample, as shown in Table 13.6. In addition, if the categories are ordinal, the table can be inspected to see if there is any direction to the relationship. In Table 13.6, for example, you can see that the mean level of satisfaction decreases with age; this suggests that there is a negative association between customer age and customer satisfaction levels in the sample data.

Group means can also be presented visually using bar charts. Each bar represents a category within the categorical variable and the height or length of the bar represents the mean of the metric variable. as shown in Figure 13.14a. Where the values of the metric variable fall within a very narrow range it may be desirable to truncate the scale used for the metric variable rather than show the full range of the scale (Figure 13.14b). Truncating the scale will tend to emphasize visually any differences between the groups but can also be misleading, so always ensure that you clearly indicate the axis scale.

If you have ordinal or metric data as one variable and categorical data as the other, multiple box plots can be used to compare different categories, with each box plot representing the scores for one group of the categorical variable as shown in Figure 13.15. Note how the box plot, by combining information about dispersion and central tendency, reveals that there is considerable overlap between adjacent age groups. Multiple box plots can also be used to compare two or more metric or ordinal variables.

Table 13.6 Table of mean satisfaction levels by customer age group (*n* = 175)

Age group	Mean (1 = highly dissatisfied, 7 = highly satisfied)	Standard deviation	Min.	Max.	Range	n
18–29	5.10	.898	3	7	4	30
30–39	4.72	1.108	2	7	5	35
40–49	4.19	1.055	2	6	4	38
50–59	3.91	.969	2	6	4	41
60 and over	3.70	.961	2	6	4	31
Total	4.30	1.111	2	7	5	175

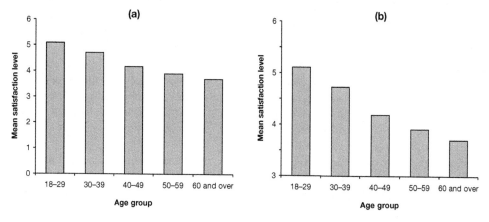

Figure 13.14 Bar charts of mean satisfaction levels by customer age group (data from Table 13.6)

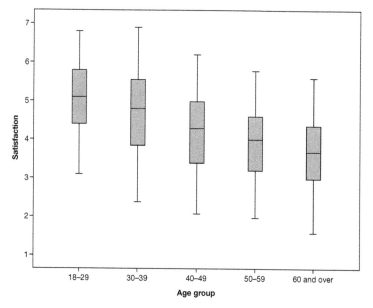

Figure 13.15 Multiple box plots of mean satisfaction levels by customer age group (data from Table 13.6)

Exploring associations between categorical variables

Researchers are often interested in exploring associations between categorical variables. Is there, for example, an association between how often people drive and their level of income? **Contingency tables** provide a starting point for answering such questions. The basic layout is illustrated in Table 13.7, which shows a contingency table created using data relating to frequency of driving and household income. Contingency table layouts can be described using the format: number of rows × number of columns (r × c), so this is a 3 × 4 contingency table. The numbers in the cells are frequency counts, showing how many observations fall into each. Totals are also given for each row and each column. These are referred to as marginal totals. In addition there is a grand total (i.e. the total sample size) in the bottom right-hand corner of the table.

Frequency counts are not always easy to interpret, especially if the group sizes are different, so it is common practice to convert them to percentages. If one of the variables is thought to be the independent variable it is conventional to use the total number of observations in each category of that variable to calculate the percentages. In Table 13.8 we have selected household income as the independent variable because we believe that it may affect driving frequency. Percentages are therefore calculated as row percentages (if column totals had been used, then the percentages of each column would have summed to 100).

From the percentages for each income category for each driving frequency category, you can see that there appears to be an association between income and driving frequency. Looking at the first column of the table, you can also see that the proportion of those driving every day increases with household income, suggesting a positive association between household income and driving frequency (73% > 65% > 52%): driving frequency increases as household income rises. Note how much easier it is to interpret the percentages as compared to the simple counts, given the unequal group sizes and larger number of cells.

Clustered bar charts can be used to display the data from contingency tables graphically. Figure 13.16 shows the data from Table 13.8 presented in this way. Driving frequency is used for the horizontal axis and the bars in each cluster represent the percentage of observations for each category of the household income variable. Notice how the chart underlines the association in the sample data between income and driving frequency and that inspection of the two outside driving frequency groups confirms that the relation is positive.

Another way of presenting contingency tables is to use a **stacked bar chart** as shown in Figure 13.17. This time the observations from the household income category groups are stacked in a single bar rather than clustered side by side. Each section of the bar represents the proportion of the household income category for that driving frequency group. The overall height of each bar indicates the relative total size of each group.

A variant of the stacked bar chart is one in which each stacked bar represents 100 per cent of the observations for that bar (Excel calls this a 100 per cent stacked bar chart). As shown in Figure 13.18, each bar represents a category of household income and each section within the bar represents the per cent of each driving category in that bar. This layout is particularly useful for showing the proportion of each driving frequency category for each income group but loses any indication of the relative size of each income group.

Table 13.7 Contingency table showing frequency of driving by driving licence holders aged 17 and household income, showing counts (*n* = 1220)

		Driving frequency				
		Every day	At least 3 times per week	1–2 times per week	Less than once per week	Totals
Annual household income						
Up to £15,000	Count	205	110	55	23	393
£15,000 to £25,000	Count	228	72	36	13	349
Over £25,000	Count	350	82	36	10	478
Totals	Count	783	264	127	46	1220

13.4.6 Exploring associations between metric variables

When both variables are metric, you can use a **scatterplot** to examine the relationship between them. If they have been specified, the independent (predictor) variable should be plotted on the *x*-axis and the dependent (outcome) variable on the *y*-axis. Figure 13.19 shows a scatterplot of data on 14 book titles, showing the number of hits on the seller's website and for each title the number of copies sold on the website.

Scatterplots are especially useful for examining four features of the association between two metric variables.

1 *Whether the association is positive or negative.* If the association between two variables is positive, a high score on one variable is associated with a high score on the other; in a scatter plot this is shown when the line of points run upwards from left to right (Figure 13.20a). A negative association, on the other hand, is indicated when the slope runs downwards from left to right (Figure 13.20b).

2 *Whether or not the relationship is linear.* A linear relationship is characterized by the data points lying in roughly a straight line. Departures from linearity can take many different forms. One possibility is a curvilinear relationship, as shown in Figure 13.20c. Some statistical measures of association (such as the Pearson correlation coefficient) make the assumption that the relationship is linear; this can be checked using scatterplots.

3 *The strength of the relationship.* The more concentrated the points, the stronger the relationship between the variables; conversely, the more scattered they are, the weaker the relationship. Summary statistics of relationship strength are available, but visual inspection of a scatterplot is the starting point.

4 *Identifying outliers.* Observations with unusual combinations of values may constitute outliers from the overall pattern, as we show in Figure 13.20d, where two points in the lower right corner are distinctly different from the general pattern. Such outliers can affect the assumption of linearity and exert a strong influence on some analysis techniques. They should be examined closely and, if appropriate, removed from the analysis.

PART IV

Table 13.8 Contingency table showing frequency of driving by driving licence holders aged 17 and household income, showing per cent of row totals (*n* = 1220)

	Driving frequency				
	Every day (%)	At least 3 times per week (%)	1–2 times per week (%)	Less than once per week (%)	Totals (%)
Annual household income					
Up to £15,000	52	28	14	6	100
£15,000 to £25,000	65	21	10	4	100
Over £25,000	73	17	8	2	100
Totals	64	22	10	4	100

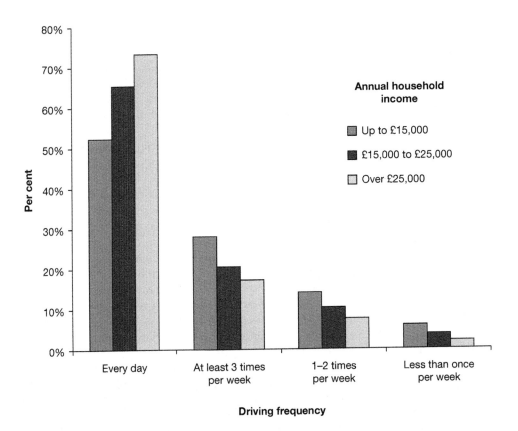

Figure 13.16 Clustered bar charts of driving frequency by annual household income (*n* = 1220)

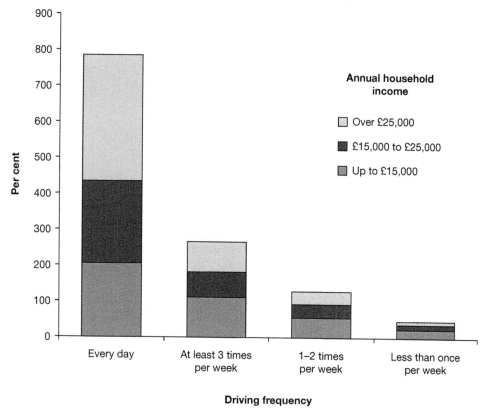

Figure 13.17 Stacked bar chart of driving frequency by household income (*n* = 1220)

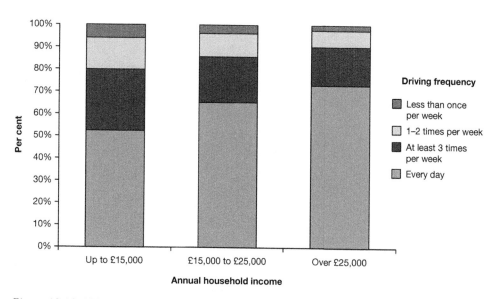

Figure 13.18 100 per cent stacked bar chart of driving frequency by household income (*n* = 1220)

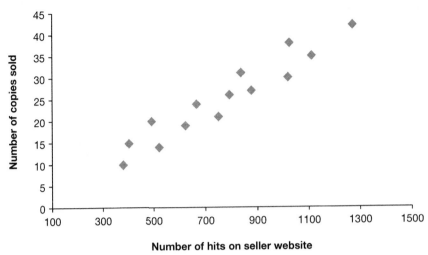

Figure 13.19 Scatterplot of number of hits on seller website and number of copies sold online for 14 different book titles

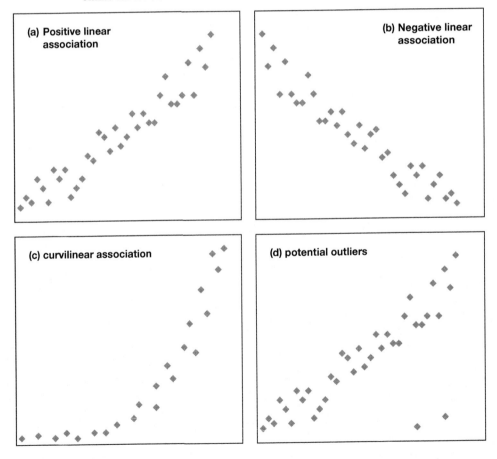

Figure 13.20 Example scatterplots

13.4.7 Exploring time series data

A **time series** is a form of longitudinal data that consists of a sequence of observations over time. Usually the observations are of a single entity (such as a firm, industry or country) at regular intervals (such as monthly or yearly) over a fairly long period. Time series are very common in business and management, whether dealing with aspects of the organization such as its sales, staffing levels and numbers of customers, or of the broader economy such as national income, unemployment or retail sales. Visual inspection is important for analysing time series, so one of the first things that you should do is plot your time series as a line chart. Time is plotted along the horizontal x-axis, the values for the variable on the vertical y-axis. Figure 13.21 shows two plots of the same time series. The visual difference is due to the differences in the scaling of the vertical axis. Figure 13.21b chart has a much higher resolution which emphasizes the change over time; in Figure 13.21a the change is barely discernible. As with any other graph, care needs to be taken both when drawing and interpreting time series plots.

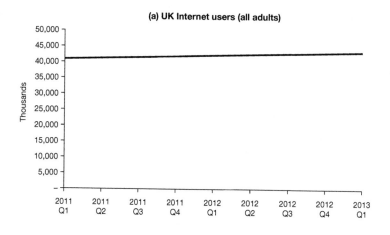

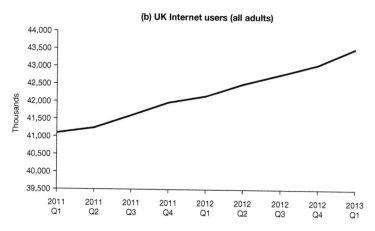

Figure 13.21 UK Internet users, thousands (all adults) (ONS 2013)

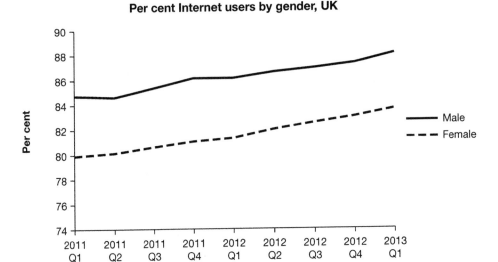

Figure 13.22 Time series plot showing per cent Internet users by gender, UK (all adults) (ONS 2013)

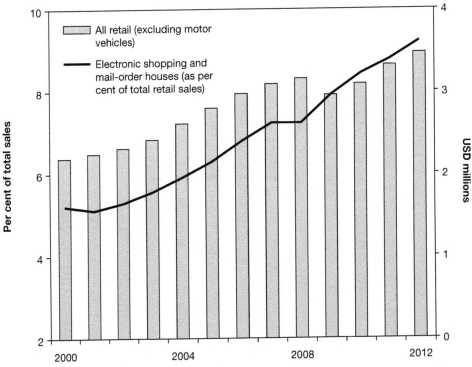

Figure 13.23 Time series plot showing total retail sales (excluding motor vehicles) and electronic shopping and mail-order house sales as per cent of total retail sales, USA 2000–2012 (US Census Bureau 2013)

PART IV

Two or more sets of time series data can be plotted for comparison of trend and other features. Figure 13.22, for example, compares the use of the Internet by gender over a two-year period.

If the time series are measured in different units, it can be useful to use index numbers. Alternatively, different scales can be used on the vertical axes. In some cases it is clearer to use a different chart type (such as a bar chart) to emphasize differences in scale. Figure 13.23 shows this by presenting changes in total US retail sales between 2000 and 2012, plotted as a bar chart with the scale on the right, and the per cent of total sales represented by electronic shopping and mail-order houses, plotted as a line graph with the scale on the left.

Further details on time series analysis can be found on the companion website.

13.5 Answering your research questions

We have called the next step in the analysis process 'answering your research questions', to stress the need to focus your analysis on achieving your research objectives. This stage involves applying appropriate analysis techniques to your data and interpreting the results. Choice of technique depends upon your research questions. It is also heavily influenced by the level of measurement used and how many variables are being analysed at once.

13.5.1 Descriptive and inferential statistics

Before looking at specific statistical techniques, we need to explain the crucial difference between descriptive and inferential statistics. **Descriptive statistics**, such as the sample mean or standard deviation, are used to analyse, summarize and simplify your sample data. **Inferential statistics**, on the other hand, are used to make inferences about the population based on the sample data. To illustrate this distinction and the reason we need to make use of inferential statistics, suppose that you were investigating whether or not there is a difference between full-time and part-time employees in terms of their level of engagement. You use descriptive statistics to explore your sample data and find that the mean engagement level is higher for full-time employees than it is for part-time employees. But does this difference hold for the population of all company employees or only for those in your sample? Here you run into a problem: **sampling error**.

Sampling error refers to the naturally occurring difference between a sample statistic and the true measure for the population. The difference between the engagement levels of the two groups in your sample may be due to sampling error rather than to an underlying difference between full-time and part-time employees. This is where inferential statistics come in. You could use a suitable inferential statistical test to see whether it is likely that the difference in engagement levels found in your sample reflects an underlying difference in the overall population or has come about as a result of sampling error. Note that because of sampling error even inferential statistics do not allow us to be absolutely certain, but they do give us an indication of how confident we can be in our findings in relation to the population.

Inferential statistics have two critical applications in quantitative research projects:

1   to estimate population parameters
2   to test hypotheses.

We will begin by looking at how to use inferential statistics to estimate population parameters, before examining hypothesis testing in more detail.

13.5.2 Estimating population parameters

The characteristics of the sample are known as **sample statistics**; the characteristics of the population are known as **population parameters**. For example, the mean of the sample data is a sample statistic but the mean of the population from which the sample came is a population parameter. Sample statistics, such as the sample mean, provide a **point estimate** of the corresponding population parameter (i.e. the population mean), but in practice a point estimate cannot be expected to provide an exact value of a given population parameter, due to sampling error. You can, however, use inferential statistics to provide an estimated range of plausible values for the unknown population parameter. Such **interval estimates** are called **confidence intervals** and have the general form:

   Point estimate ± Margin of error

The point estimate is normally the relevant sample statistic (e.g. the sample mean) and the margin of error is calculated according to a desired confidence level. The result is two numbers which are the lower and upper boundaries for the confidence interval, either side of the point estimate, as we show in Figure 13.24.

It is common to calculate confidence intervals at the 95 per cent confidence level (although 90 per cent and 99 per cent intervals are also used). What this 95 per cent means is that if we took 100 samples at random from the population, 95 of them would fall within the boundaries of the confidence interval. The higher the confidence level, the wider the interval that will be calculated, so a 99 per cent confidence interval will be wider than a 95 per cent confidence interval for the same data. Interval width is also affected by the variability in the sample (higher variability increases interval width) and by sample size (higher sample size reduces interval width). Research in Practice 13.2 shows confidence intervals in use.

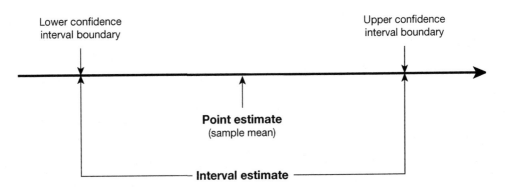

Figure 13.24 Point and interval estimates

RESEARCH IN PRACTICE 13.2

How satisfied are the customers?

You have been asked to investigate satisfaction levels among a company's customers. A survey of a random sample of customers shows a mean satisfaction level of 4.25, measured on a 7-point multi-item scale where 1 is highly unsatisfied and 7 is highly satisfied. Local managers are relieved. Maybe the score is not great – they hoped it would be closer to 6 – but at least it looks positive: the average is just the 'right' side of the scale's midpoint of 4. For your report, you decide to include not just a point estimate of the customer population mean but also confidence intervals, so as to give managers a better idea of the range of plausible values for the true population mean based on the sample data. The table below shows 95 per cent and 99 per cent confidence intervals for the population mean. The 95 per cent confidence interval shows that the lower confidence level is 3.80 and the upper confidence level is 4.70; for the 99 per cent confidence interval, the figures are 3.68 and 4.82, respectively. Note that the 99 per cent confidence interval is wider than the 95 per cent confidence interval. Note also that both confidence intervals include values below 4, indicating that the true population mean may plausibly be below the scale midpoint. Perhaps the local managers will not be so satisfied with their customers' satisfaction levels when they see the final report.

Table of confidence intervals for the mean

Confidence interval	Sample mean	Lower confidence level	Upper confidence level
95%	4.25	3.80	4.70
99%	4.25	3.68	4.82

PART IV

Confidence intervals are particularly useful for estimating and reporting parameters such as the population mean and we recommend that they are used and reported when describing a population on the basis of suitable sample data. They are not difficult to calculate using a computer and in SPSS are routinely included as part of the output from a number of different tests. Confidence intervals can also be used to compare the mean scores of different groups as shown in Table 13.9. If any of the groups' confidence intervals overlap, it cannot be assumed that their population means are different. Confidence intervals can also be plotted visually using a confidence interval chart as shown in Figure 13.25. The chart suggests a negative association between customer age and satisfaction levels but also shows that there is considerable overlap in the confidence intervals between adjacent groups. Further statistical tests can be used to confirm these findings.

Table 13.9 Customer satisfaction levels by age group showing confidence intervals for the mean (*n* = 175)

Age group	n	Mean	Standard deviation	95% confidence interval for mean	
				Lower bound	Upper bound
18–29	30	5.10	0.898	4.76	5.44
30–39	35	4.72	1.108	4.34	5.10
40–49	38	4.19	1.055	3.84	4.53
50–59	41	3.91	0.969	3.60	4.21
60 and over	31	3.70	0.961	3.35	4.06
Total	175	4.30	1.111	4.13	4.46

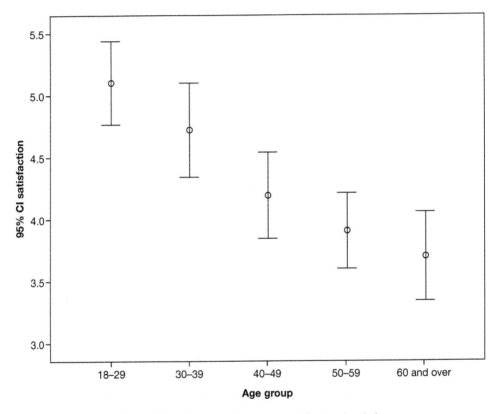

Figure 13.25 Chart of confidence intervals for mean satisfaction levels by customer age group (data from Table 13.9)

13.5.3 Testing hypotheses

In Chapter 4 we introduced deductive research designs that involve formal hypothesis testing. Although it is not always explicitly stated, hypotheses are normally statements about the population being examined, not just the sample. This is important, because if you have collected sample data you face the problem of sampling error. As a result you cannot simply take the sample statistics as reflecting the true picture for the population, so inferential statistics are used to carry out hypotheses tests. A general procedure for doing so is shown in Figure 13.26 and each step is described in more detail below.

Formulate null and alternative hypotheses

The starting point is to formulate clear, testable hypotheses. Although this is shown as part of the analysis process, your hypotheses are normally formulated much earlier, as discussed in Chapter 4. They should be closely linked to your research question and to existing theory or prior research. Formulating a hypothesis involves developing two statements, the research (or alternative) hypothesis and the null hypothesis. The **research hypothesis** (typically written as H_1) is a statement of what you expect to find in the data. The **null hypothesis** (written as H_0) is usually a statement that there is no difference or no association between the variables of interest. For example, if you were testing a research hypothesis that there is a difference between full-time and part-time employees' engagement levels, the null hypothesis would be that there is no difference between the two groups.

If you are new to hypothesis testing, the need for a null hypothesis may seem rather strange. It is important, however, because the hypothesis test is actually to see whether the evidence is sufficiently strong for you to be confident in rejecting the null hypothesis. If the null hypothesis is rejected, the research hypothesis is accepted

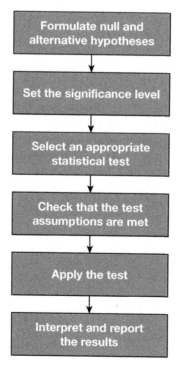

Figure 13.26 Hypothesis testing procedure

Table 13.10 Example hypothesis statements

Example 1	
H_1:	There is a difference between the mean level of engagement of full-time employees in Company A and the mean level of engagement of part-time employees in Company A.
H_0:	There is no difference between the mean level of engagement of full-time employees in Company A and the mean level of engagement of part-time employees in Company A.

Example 2	
H_1:	There is a positive association between the number of years working at Company A and level of engagement of employees at Company A.
H_0:	There is not a positive association between the number of years working at Company and level of engagement for employees at Company A.

in its place. For this reason, the research hypothesis is also commonly referred to as the **alternative** (or alternate) **hypothesis.**

Table 13.10 shows two examples. The first is about expected differences between two groups. It is what is known as a **non-directional hypothesis** because it does not specify in which direction the difference should lie, just that they will not be the same. The second example concerns an expected association between two variables. In this case it is formulated as a **directional hypothesis** because the expected direction of the association (i.e. positive) is stated. Where there is more than one research hypothesis to be tested, it is common to number them consecutively (e.g. H_1, H_2, H_3, and so on).

Set the significance level

The next step is to decide on the criteria for rejecting or accepting the null hypothesis. This is done by setting what is called a **significance level**. Referred to by the Greek letter α (alpha, not to be confused with Cronbach's alpha), the significance level is expressed as a probability and specifies the level of risk of committing what is known as a **Type I error** (Figure 13.27). Type I errors occur when you reject the null hypothesis when it is in fact true. In business and management research, α is usually set at 0.05 (i.e. 5 per cent). What this means is that we are prepared to take a 5

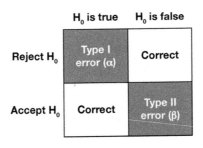

Figure 13.27 Type I and Type II errors

in 100 (i.e. 1 in 20 or 5 per cent) chance of rejecting a null hypothesis when it is actually true. If safety were at stake, for instance, in a drug trial, a higher significance level such as 0.01 (1 in 100 chance of a Type I error) might be preferred.

Another possible error is known as a **Type II error** (Figure 13.27). This occurs when the null hypothesis is accepted when it is actually false, so we fail to detect something that is really there. The probability of doing so is referred to as β (beta) error. There is a trade-off between the two types of error. Reducing the probability of a Type I error (by making α smaller) increases the probability of a Type II error.

A related concept is the statistical power of a test. Power refers to the probability of correctly rejecting the null hypothesis when it should be rejected and is equal to $1 - \beta$. In other words, power determines the probability of finding an effect if one is there. It is influenced by the chosen α, but also by the sample size (larger sample sizes give greater power), by the degree of variation in the population (the larger the variation in the population, the lower the power) and by the size of the effect (for example, the magnitude of difference) that you are trying to detect (the smaller the size of the effect, the lower the power).

Select an appropriate statistical test

Selection of an appropriate statistical test depends on what you are testing for and the type of data being analysed. A useful categorization of statistical tests distinguishes between parametric and non-parametric tests. **Parametric tests** can be used with interval or ratio data and make certain assumptions about the distributional properties of the data. Where those assumptions are not met, or where the data are nominal or ordinal, **non-parametric tests** may be used instead. In this chapter we indicate whether tests are parametric or non-parametric; other test assumptions are discussed in the relevant section for each test on the companion website.

Check that the test assumptions are met

Once you have selected your test, you need to check that your data meet any assumptions required by the test. These vary according to the particular test and we list them when discussing each test. In some cases further testing of assumptions is needed after the test has been run. If the assumptions of the test cannot be met, a different test may have to be applied.

Apply the test

Applying the test is the moment where computers come in really handy because they do all (or most) of the number crunching for you, so, rather than formulae and lots of calculations, you will usually be presented with the output from the test. A simplified example test output is shown in Table 13.11. It is taken from an independent 2-sample *t*-test, which tests for the difference in mean scores between two groups. The hypotheses being tested are:

H_1:   There is a difference between the mean level of engagement of full-time employees and the mean level of engagement of part-time employees.

Table 13.11 Example statistical test output (independent 2-sample *t*-test)

	Full-time employees	Part-time employees
Mean engagement level	4.8	2.9
Variance	1.84	1.60
Observations	30	30
Degrees of freedom (*df*)	58	
Test statistic (*t*)	5.584	
Significance (two-tailed) = *p*-value	0.000	

H$_0$: There is no difference between the mean level of engagement of full-time employees and the mean level of engagement of part-time employees.

The table shows that the mean engagement levels for full- and part-time workers are 4.8 and 2.9, respectively, and there are 30 respondents in each group. There are two key values that you need to check. The first is the **test statistic**, which is calculated as part of the test routine and used to determine the degree to which the sample data are consistent with the null hypothesis. The second is the **p-value** (probability value), which is the probability of observing a test statistic that is at least as extreme as the one that has been observed, assuming that the null hypothesis is true. You can think of the *p*-value as the probability that your null hypothesis is correct. It will take a value between 0 and 1. In this case the test statistic (*t*) is 5.584 and the *p*-value is 0.000.

The output also includes the **degrees of freedom** (*df*) for the test. Simplifying somewhat, this number represents the number of values that are free to vary when calculating some common test statistics (such as the *t*-test). Where relevant, it is normally included in the test output and it is standard practice to report the degrees of freedom in your write-up.

Interpret and report the results

You now compare the *p*-value from your test results against your pre-specified significance level (α). If the *p*-value is less than your chosen significance level, you can reject the null hypothesis (H$_0$) and accept the research (or alternative) hypothesis (H$_1$). The test result, as shown in Table 13.11, gives *p* = 0.000. Since 0.000 is less than 0.05 (i.e. *p* is less than α) you reject the null hypothesis (H$_0$) and accept the research (alternate) hypothesis (H$_1$). You conclude that there is a statistically significant difference in the mean level of engagement of full- and part-time employees.

If *p* had been greater than 0.05 you would have accepted the null hypothesis (H$_0$) and rejected the research (alternate) hypothesis (H$_1$). You would have concluded instead that the there is no difference in the mean level of engagement of full- and part-time employees.

To sum up the procedure:

- if $p < \alpha$ then reject H_0 and accept H_1
- if $p \geqslant \alpha$ then accept H_0 and reject H_1.

Testing directional hypotheses

In the example just given, the research hypothesis (H_1) was non-directional: it did not specify whether full-timers' level of engagement was more or less than that of part-timers, merely that they were different. The required test therefore just looks for difference, regardless of the direction of that difference. Such tests are known as **two-tailed tests**. Had the research hypothesis been directional (e.g. that part-timers' engagement levels were higher), a **one-tailed test** would have been required. The basic procedure remains the same but you may need to adjust the p-value if the statistical software you are using reports only the p-value appropriate for a two-tailed test. Further details on running one-tailed tests are given on the companion website.

How significant is significant?

The output of a hypothesis test tells us whether our results are statistically significant but does not tell us much about the practical implications. Remember that the power of a statistical test is influenced by sample size, so a very small difference might turn out to be statistically significant if a large sample is used. When interpreting your results you should evaluate their practical significance as well as their statistical significance. Reporting relevant descriptive statistics, confidence intervals, sample sizes and full p-values can also help you to communicate the practical significance of your research to readers. In addition, there are a number of standard measures of **effect size** that can be reported to indicate the magnitude of any observed effect. Further details can be found in Cohen (1992).

13.5.4 Significance tests (1): tests of difference

A very wide range of significance tests are available. We introduce some common ones in this section, grouped into two categories, starting with techniques used for tests of difference, for example, between two or more groups. Tests of this type are important in experimental designs (for example, in comparing pre- and post-test results), for comparing groups in natural experiments and in descriptive studies for testing for differences between demographic groups. These are summarized in Table 13.12.

Is the sample mean different from a known population mean?

A **one-sample *t*-test** is used to test whether the population mean from which your sample is drawn is the same as a comparison mean specified as part of the test. You could use it, for example, to test whether the level of customer satisfaction in one particular retail store is different from the company's target customer satisfaction

Table 13.12 Significance tests (1): tests of difference

Purpose	Name	Measurement level of variables
Significance test of whether the sample comes from a population with a specified mean (parametric)	One-sample *t*-test	Interval or ratio
Significance test of the difference between the means of two paired samples (parametric)	Paired two-sample *t*-test	Metric (dependent)/ categorical with two paired groups (independent)
Significance test of the difference between the means of two independent (not related) samples (parametric)	Independent two-sample *t*-test	Metric (dependent)/ categorical with two non-paired groups (independent)
Significance test of the difference between the means of three or more groups (parametric)	One-way, independent analysis of variance (ANOVA)	Metric (dependent)/ categorical with more than two groups (independent)
Significance test for difference between two groups (non-parametric)	Mann-Whitney test	Ordinal or metric (dependent)/categorical with two non-paired groups (independent)

level. The one-sample *t*-test requires interval or ratio data from a single probability sample. The data should be normally distributed, although the test is reasonably robust provided the data are unimodal and fairly symmetrical. The test can be run in SPSS.

Differences in means between two related groups: paired 2-sample t-test

The **paired (or dependent) 2-sample *t*-test** is appropriate where the groups are related or paired. A typical example is an experimental design where the same individuals are measured pre- and post-treatment and the researcher wishes to test for differences in the mean of the two scores. The test assumes that the differences between the scores for the two samples are normally distributed. This can be checked by computing the differences (for example in Excel or SPSS) and examining for normality. The paired sample *t*-test can be run in Excel or SPSS.

Differences in means between two independent groups: independent 2-sample t-test

An **independent 2-sample *t*-test** can be used to compare the mean scores of two independent groups. You might wish to compare, for example, the male and female customers in your sample in terms of their average age to see whether any difference between them is likely to hold at the population level. The independent 2-sample *t*-test requires a categorical independent variable with two independent groups and an interval or ratio dependent variable. The dependent variable should be normally distributed and the variance of the two groups should be approximately equal. If the variances are not equal, a version of the test that adjusts for inequality of variance can be used. Both versions of the test can be run in Excel or SPSS; the latter also includes the option of testing the assumption of equal variance as part of the test and gives output for the *t*-test adjusted for unequal variance. An example is given in Research in Practice 13.3.

RESEARCH IN PRACTICE 13.3

Independent 2-sample *t*-test

An independent 2-sample *t*-test is being used to determine whether there is a statistically significant difference in levels of satisfaction (measured on a 7-point summated scale where 7 is 'highly satisfied') between customers of convenience stores and customers of megastores. The tables below show sample output from SPSS. The first table (Group Statistics) reports descriptive statistics for the two groups showing that the mean satisfaction level of convenience store shoppers in the sample is higher than that of megastore shoppers (4.84 > 3.44). The sample size (n) of each group is 25 (note that sample sizes do not need to be equal to run this test).

The second table (Independent Samples Test) contains the test results. The first two columns report the results of Levene's test for equality of variance. The null hypothesis for this test is that the variances of the two groups are equal. If the result of this test is significant (i.e. $p < 0.05$) we would conclude that variances are significantly different. In this case it is not significant (0.915 > 0.05), so we would accept the null hypothesis and conclude that the variances of the two groups are equal. This allows us to use the output in the row marked 'Equal variances assumed' when reporting the results of the test. (If the variances are not equal, the results from the row marked 'Equal variances not assumed' should be used instead.) The results of the *t*-test are shown in the columns headed '*t*-test for equality of means'. The test statistic (t) is 3.163 with 48 degrees of freedom (df). The *p*-value is 0.003 which is less than the significance level of 0.05; we would therefore conclude that the difference is statistically significant. The SPSS output also reports the difference between the two means which is 1.400 (i.e. 4.84 − 3.44) and includes a 95 per cent confidence interval for the difference. The latter does not include zero, which suggests that zero is not a plausible value for the mean difference at the 95 per cent confidence level, something confirmed by the results of the *t*-test.

Research in Practice 13.3 (Continued)

Independent 2-sample t-test (SPSS output)

Group Statistics

	Store format	N	Mean	St. Deviation	Std. Error Mean
Satisfaction level	Convenience store	25	4.84	1.546	.309
	Megastore	25	3.44	1.583	.317

Independent Samples Test

		Levene's Test for Equality of Variances		t-test for Equality of Means					95% Confidence Interval of the Difference	
		F	Sig.	t	df	Sig. (2-tailed)	Mean Difference	Std. Error Difference	Lower	Upper
Satisfaction level	Equal variances assumed	.011	.915	3.163	48	.003	1.400	.443	.510	2.290
	Equal variances not assumed			3.163	48.973	.003	1.400	.443	.510	2.290

Differences in means between three or more groups: one-way independent ANOVA

If you want to compare the means of more than two independent groups, you can use **one-way independent ANOVA** (analysis of variance). You might wish to compare, for example, the mean level of employee satisfaction at different locations to see whether any differences were statistically significant. One-way independent ANOVA requires a categorical independent variable with three or more independent groups and an interval or ratio dependent variable. The dependent variable should be normally distributed and the variance of the groups should be approximately equal. The test can be run in Excel or SPSS; the latter can also run a test for equality of variance.

Mann-Whitney test

If you wish to compare two independent groups but your data do not meet the assumptions of the independent *t*-test, for example, because the dependent variable is ordinal rather than metric, the **Mann-Whitney test** may be used instead. This is a non-parametric test that tests for differences in the ranked scores of two independent groups. The null hypothesis is one of no difference between the groups. The test can be run in SPSS.

13.5.5 Significance tests (2): measuring and testing association

Contingency tables and scatterplots are very useful for exploring potential associations between variables but, as with other findings from sample data, they should be subject to further examination and testing. Here we look at some widely used techniques for doing so for different levels of measurement (Table 13.13).

Nominal and ordinal variables: chi-squared test of association

If you have created a contingency table of two categorical variables, the **chi-squared test of association** (also referred to as chi-square or χ^2, using the Greek letter chi) can be used to test whether there is a statistically significant association between the two variables. The test works by comparing the observed frequencies of the cells in the contingency table with the frequencies that would be expected if there was no association between the variables, in order to calculate a test statistic that is compared to an appropriate chi-squared distribution for significance. The chi-squared test is a non-parametric test and is very flexible but it does require that the samples are independent (i.e. each case can appear in only one cell) and that the data are frequency counts, not percentages. If used for a 2 × 2 table the frequency of each cell in the expected frequency table should be at least 5. For larger tables, no more than 20 per cent of cells should have less than an expected frequency of 5 and none below 1. The test can be run in Excel (with some manipulation of the data) or in SPSS. An example is given in Research in Practice 13.4.

Table 13.13 Measures and tests of association

Purpose	Name	Measurement level of variables
Test of association between two categorical variables (non-parametric)	Chi-squared (χ^2) test of association	Nominal or ordinal
Test of association between two categorical variables (non-parametric)	Fisher's exact test	Nominal or ordinal (small samples and 2 × 2 contingency tables)
Measure the strength of association between two categorical variables (non-parametric)	Cramer's V	Nominal or ordinal (for two ordinal variables with a large number of categories, use Spearman's rho or Kendall's tau)
Measure the strength of association between two categorical variables (non-parametric)	Phi	Nominal or ordinal (2 × 2 contingency tables)
Measure the strength and direction of association between two metric variables (parametric)	Pearson's correlation coefficient (r)	Metric
Measure the strength and direction of association between two ordinal variables or between one ordinal and one metric variable (non-parametric)	Spearman's rho (ρ)	Ordinal or metric
Measure the strength and direction of association between two ordinal variables (non-parametric)	Kendall's tau (τ)	Ordinal or metric
Predict the value of a dependent variable from knowledge of the value of one or more independent variables	Linear regression	Metric (dependent), metric (independent)

PART IV

RESEARCH IN PRACTICE 13.4

Chi-squared test of association

The chi-squared test allows us to test whether or not the association between household income and driving frequency that we saw in Table 13.8 is statistically significant. The test output, generated in SPSS, is shown below. The first table (Case processing summary) provides a summary of the cases included in the analysis. The second table (Annual household income * Driving frequency crosstabulation) is the contingency table of the data, showing counts and per cent of row totals (this is the same data as in Table 13.8). The third table (Chi-square tests) contains the test result. The relevant one is marked Pearson chi-square and gives a test statistic of 43.685 with 6 degrees of freedom (df) and a *p*-value (labelled Assymp. sig.) of 0.000. This is below 0.05 so we would therefore conclude that the association between annual household income and driving frequency is statistically significant.

(Note that below the table SPSS advises you that the assumption regarding the number of cells with an expected frequency below five is satisfied by your data.)

Research in Practice 13.4 (Continued)

Chi-squared test of association (SPSS output)

Case Processing Summary

	Cases					
	Valid		Missing		Total	
	N	Percent	N	Percent	N	Percent
Annual household income *Driving frequency	1220	100.0	0	.0	1220	100.0

Annual household income *Driving frequency Crosstabulation

		Driving frequency				Total
		Every day	At least 3 times per week	1–2 times per week	Less than once per week	
Annual household income	Up to £15,000	Count	205	110	55	23	393
		% within annual household income	52.2	28.0	14.0	5.9	100.0%
	$15,000 to £25,000	Count	228	72	36	13	349
		% within annual household income	65.3	20.6	10.3	3.7	100.0%
	Over £25,000	Count	350	82	36	10	478
		% within annual household income	73.2	17.2	7.5	2.1	100.0%
Total		Count	783	264	127	46	1220
		% within annual household income	64.2	21.6	10.4	3.8	100.0%

Chi-Square Tests

	Value	df	Asymp. Sig. (2-sided)
Pearson Chi-Square	43.685[a]	6	.000
Likelihood Ratio	43.714	6	.000
Linear-by-Linear Association	38.408	1	.000
No Valid Cases	1220		

a. 0 cells (.0%) have expected count less than 5. The minimum expected count is 13.16.

Nominal and ordinal variables: Fisher's exact test

If you have a 2 × 2 contingency table with a small sample or cells with expected frequencies below 5, you can use **Fisher's exact test** instead of chi-squared. It can also be used for larger tables and bigger samples, but in such situations the chi-squared test is usually adequate. Fisher's exact test can be run in SPSS.

Nominal and ordinal variables: measures of association (Phi and Cramer's V)

Phi and **Cramer's V** can be used to provide a direct measure of the strength of the association between the variables in a contingency table. Phi is used for 2 × 2 contingency tables, whilst Cramer's V can be used for any size of contingency table (including 2 × 2). Both statistics take a value between 0 and 1, where 0 shows no association and 1 shows perfect association. They can be calculated in SPSS when carrying out chi-squared or Fisher's exact test and SPSS also reports the statistical significance for each test. Note that the value of Cramer's V cannot be compared reliably between different-sized tables (de Vaus 2002a). If both your variables are ordinal with a large number of categories you can use Spearman's rho or Kendall's tau as a measure of association instead of Cramer's V.

Metric variables: Pearson's correlation coefficient (Pearson's r)

Pearson's correlation coefficient or Pearson's r (also referred to as the Pearson product–moment correlation coefficient) is a measure of the strength of the linear association between two metric (interval or ratio) variables. It takes a value between -1 and 1, where -1 is perfect negative correlation and 1 is perfect positive correlation. In practice, perfect correlation is highly unlikely and the resulting value of r will lie somewhere between the two extremes, as shown in Figure 13.28.

To interpret Pearson's correlation coefficient first check whether the association is positive (positive values of r) or negative (negative values of r). Next assess the strength of the association. Table 13.14 offers rules of thumb for doing so on the basis of the value of r. In addition, Pearson's r can be tested for statistical significance where the null hypothesis is that there is no association (i.e. that $r = 0$).

Pearson's correlation coefficient should be used only if the association between the two variables is linear, so check this using a scatterplot. In addition, if you are testing for statistical significance, the data should come from normally distributed populations. Pearson's correlation coefficient can be calculated in Excel or SPSS; its statistical significance can be calculated in SPSS, as shown in Research in Practice 13.5.

Ordinal variables: Spearman's rho and Kendall's tau

Spearman's rank-order correlation coefficient, also known as **Spearman's rho**, is a non-parametric summary statistic for measuring the association between two ordinal variables. Like Pearson's r, Spearman's rho returns a value between -1 and 1. It can be run in SPSS, which can also perform a significance test of the null hypothesis of no association between the variables. An alternative to Spearman's rho is Kendall's rank correlation coefficient, more commonly known as **Kendall's tau**. You can use Kendall's tau in preference to Spearman's rho when there are many tied ranks, for instance as a result of having a low number of categories in the ordinal variables.

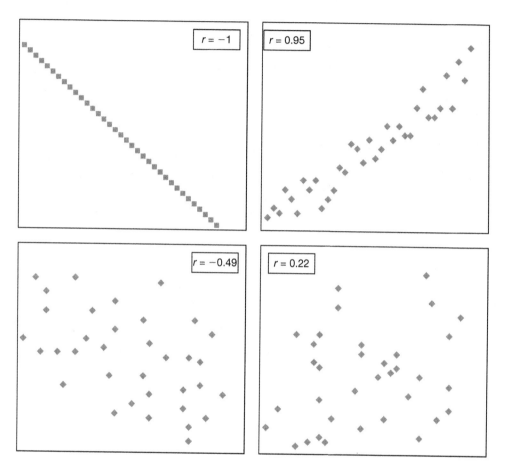

Figure 13.28 Scatterplots illustrating the strength of Pearson's correlation coefficient (*r*)

Table 13.14 Descriptors for correlation coefficient strength
(Cohen 1992: 157, de Vaus 2002b: 272)

Absolute value of correlation coefficient	Descriptor
0.10 to 0.29	Low
0.30 to 0.49	Medium
0.50 to 0.69	High
0.70 and above	Very high

RESEARCH IN PRACTICE 13.5

Pearson's correlation coefficient

In this example, SPSS is used to calculate Pearson's r for the book sales and seller website hit data from Figure 13.19. It is in the form of a correlation matrix which shows all possible combinations of correlations between the two variables. The cells in the leading diagonal running from top left to bottom right report the correlation between each variable and itself, hence the correlation coefficient (Pearson's correlation) of 1. The other cells give the correlation coefficient (r) between sales and hits on the seller website. The coefficient is 0.954, indicating a very strong positive correlation between the two variables. SPSS also reports the p-value (Sig. (2-tailed)) for the test of the null hypothesis that $r = 0$. Since $p = 0.000$ we can conclude that the result is statistically significant. Note that SPSS also marks the correlation coefficient with two asterisks (**) to show that this is significant at the 0.01 level. Overall, we would conclude that there is a very strong positive association between hits on the seller website and sales.

Pearson's r for the correlation between website hits and online sales (SPSS output)

Correlations

		Hits on seller website	Sales (copies)
Hits on seller website	Pearson's correlation	1	954**
	Sig. (2-tailed)		.000
	N	14	14
Sales (copies)	Pearson's correlation	.954**	1
	Sig. (2-tailed)	.000	
	N	14	14

**. Correlation is significant at the 0.001 level (2-tailed).

Predicting the value of one variable from another: linear regression

Regression analysis can be used to predict the value of a dependent (or outcome) variable from knowledge of the value of one or more independent (or predictor) variables. Regression analysis can therefore be used for forecasting based on the knowledge of independent variables. Regression analysis is also used for testing hypotheses about the expected relationship between independent and dependent variables in explanatory research. As a result, regression is a very important analysis technique in quantitative research. In this section we will introduce bivariate (or simple) linear regression applied where we have one metric dependent variable (Y) and one metric independent variable (X), using the example of book sales and website hits. The expected relationship is shown visually in Figure 13.29.

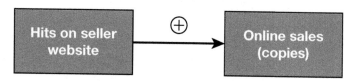

Figure 13.29 Conceptual model of the relationship between website hits and book sales

The data used are the number of hits on the seller's website and the number of copies sold on the website for 14 book titles, introduced earlier and used in Research in Practice 13.5. In bivariate **linear regression** the software will find a straight line that best summarizes or 'fits' the data points in the scatterplot, as shown in Figure 13.30. Rather than relying on guesswork, regression analysis of this kind uses a technique called least squares to generate the line. Any straight line such as this can be described by a simple formula, which you can think of as a mathematical model that summarizes the relationship between website hits and sales in the data. The basic formula is:

$$Y = b_0 + b_1 X_1$$

The two parameters (b_0 and b_1) are referred to as **regression coefficients** and are shown in the formula in Figure 13.30. The first, b_0, is the intercept ($b_0 = -0.36$) which is where the line crosses the y-axis where $X = 0$. It gives the value that the dependent variable (Y) will have when the independent variable (X_1) has a value of zero. The second coefficient, b_1, is the slope (gradient) of the line ($b_1 = 0.033$). It shows how much the dependent (Y) variable changes as the independent (X_1) variable changes: the higher the value of b, the steeper the slope and the bigger the change in Y for a given change in the value of X_1. The b_1 coefficient also tells you about the direction of the change: if it is positive, the slope is positive; if it is negative, the slope is negative.

We can use the equation to calculate an expected value of Y for a given value of X. Using the website hit data, for example, we can predict the number of copies sold (Y) if there are 1000 website hits (X_1) as follows:

Sales = $b_0 + b_1 \times$ website hits
   = 0.36 + (0.033 × 1000)
   = 32.64

Our regression model therefore predicts that if the book seller achieves 1000 website hits, it will sell approximately 33 copies of the book.

This regression line is a line of best fit but it is not a perfect fit; some of the points in the scatterplot lie above or below the line. We therefore need a measure of how good the fit is. This is provided by the **coefficient of determination**, known as R^2. By converting the value of R^2 into a percentage (multiply by 100) you get a measure of what per cent of the variability in the dependent variable is explained by the regression model. The unexplained variance is due to other variables not included in the model. The higher the R^2, the better the fit of the model. We have shown R^2 for the online

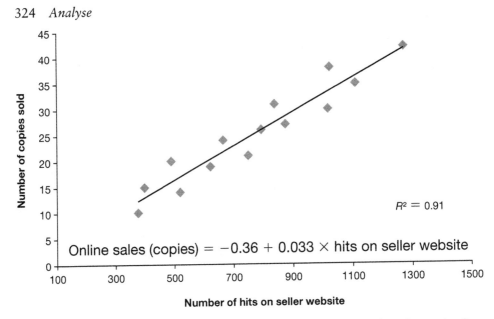

Figure 13.30 Scatterplot, regression line and regression equation for website hits and online book sales ($n = 14$)

book sales in Figure 13.30. It is 0.911, which indicates that 91 per cent of the variance in book sales is accounted for by the model.

Bivariate regression can be run in both Excel and SPSS. Figure 13.31 shows output from SPSS using the book sales and website hits data. To interpret this, start by identifying the R^2, which is contained in the box marked Model Summary. The R^2 (= 0.911) confirms that the model explains 91 per cent of the variability in the dependent variable. The statistical significance of R^2 is reported in the table labelled ANOVA. The test statistic is in the column marked F (= 122.641) and the resulting probability is given in the column marked Sig. (= 0.000). Since this is below 0.05, you would conclude that R^2 is statistically significant. Next look at the regression coefficients in the B column of the table labelled Coefficients. Here you see the intercept is −0.36 and the b_1 coefficient for Hits on seller website is 0.033. The statistical significance of the coefficients is given in the same table in the column marked Sig. and the test statistics for each in the column marked t. You can see that both are below 0.05, showing that the coefficients are significantly different from zero. The output also includes confidence intervals for the regression coefficients. These give an idea of their likely range.

Overall, on the basis of the output in Figure 13.31, you would conclude that there is a statistically significant relationship between website hits and book sales. As well as checking statistical significance, you should also consider the practical significance of your findings. For example, is the impact of website hits on sales large enough to make the information practically relevant and useful? Linear regression also requires some assumptions to be met for its use to be appropriate. We discuss these in more detail on the companion website. Despite these limitations, regression analysis offers us greater insights into a bivariate relationship than the correlation coefficient alone.

Model Summary

Model	R	R Square	Adjusted R Square	Std. Error of the Estimate
1	.954[a]	.911	.903	2.920

a. Predictors: (Constant), Hits on seller's website

ANOVA[b]

Model		Sum of Squares	df	Mean Square	F	Sig.
1	Regression	1045.423	1	1045.423	122.641	.000[a]
	Residual	102.291	12	8.524		
	Total	1147.714	13			

a. Predictors: (Constant), Hits on seller's website
b. Dependent Variable: Sales (copies)

Coefficients[a]

Model		Unstandardized Coefficients		Standardized Coefficients	t	Sig.	95.0% Confidence Interval for B	
		B	Std. Error	Beta			Lower Bound	Upper Bound
1	(Constant)	-.036	2.404		-.015	.988	-5.273	5.202
	Hits on seller's website	.033	.003	.954	11.074	.000	.026	.039

a. Dependent Variable: Sales (copies)

Figure 13.31 Regression analysis for book sales and website hits (selected SPSS output)

Bivariate regression can be extended to include more than one independent variable by using **multiple regression,** thereby allowing the testing of more complex conceptual models. Multiple regression analysis generates a value for R^2 for the overall model and a regression equation with a regression coefficient for each independent variable:

$$Y = b_0 + b_1X_1 + b_2X_2 + \ldots + b_nX_n$$

where b_0 is the intercept, b_1X_1 is the contribution of independent variable X_1, b_2X_2 is the contribution of independent variable X_2, and so on, holding the effects of the other variables constant. It also allows the researcher to assess the relative importance of each independent variable in predicting the dependent variable. This can help us to answer the question of which independent variable makes the greatest contribution in the prediction of the dependent variable, as shown in Research in Practice 13.6. We discuss multiple regression, including test assumptions, in more detail on the companion website.

PART IV

RESEARCH IN PRACTICE 13.6

Factors influencing smartphone shopping adoption

In this Research in Practice we revisit MBA student Davin Mac Ananey's study of factors influencing online shopping by smartphone.[1] Here we present a fuller version of his conceptual model, this time with three independent variables and one dependent variable. All variables are measured on a multi-item 7-point rating scale.

Conceptual model of factors influencing smartphone shopping adoption

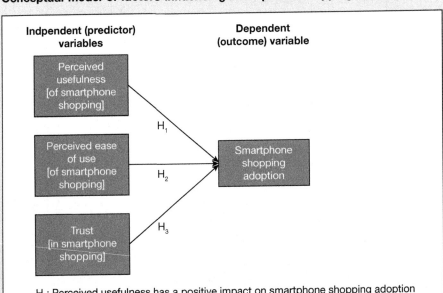

H_1: Perceived usefulness has a positive impact on smartphone shopping adoption
H_2: Perceived ease of use has a positive impact on smartphone shopping adoption
H_3: Trust has a positive impact on smartphone shopping adoption

Multiple regression analysis generates a value for R^2 for the overall model and a regression equation with a regression coefficient for each independent variable:

$$Y = b_0 + b_1X_1 + b_2X_2 + \ldots + b_nX_n$$

where b_0 is the intercept, b_1X_1 is the contribution of independent variable X_1, b_2X_2 is the contribution of independent variable X_2, and so on, holding the effects of the other variables constant.

The results of the regression showed that the R^2 was 69 per cent with a p-value of 0.000. The b coefficients for the independent variables were as shown in the table below.

Summary of *b*-coefficients for independent variables

	b-coefficient	p-value
Perceived usefulness	0.841	0.000
Perceived ease of use	0.103	0.067
Trust	0.323	0.000

As a result, H_1 and H_3 were accepted at the 5 per cent significance level whilst H_2 was rejected: perceived usefulness and trust both have a statistically significant impact on smartphone shopping adoption. Further inspection of the test output showed that perceived usefulness has a greater relative impact than trust. Perceived ease of use had a much lower relative impact and was not statistically significant. In his final report Davin went on to discuss the practical significance of his findings.

Inferring causality

Tests such as chi-squared, correlation and regression can help us to establish whether variables co-vary. As we explained in Chapter 5, however, you cannot infer causality on this basis alone, since other criteria need to be met as well. It is important, therefore, to be careful when interpreting the results of such tests.

13.5.6 Taking it further

There are many more multivariate analysis techniques available to the researcher. Hair et al. (2010) classify these into dependence and interdependence techniques:

- Dependence techniques, such as multiple regression, in which one or more variable is identified as a dependent variable to be explained or predicted by two or more independent variables.
- Interdependence techniques, such as cluster analysis and factor analysis, in which there is no dependent variable. Instead, the aim is to analyse the underlying pattern structure in the variables or cases being analysed.

The companion website gives guidance about where to learn more about multivariate analysis techniques.

CRITICAL COMMENTARY 13.1

The cult of statistical significance

The Cult of Statistical Significance is the title of a book by Ziliak and McCloskey (2008) that criticizes the emphasis placed on statistical significance testing in many branches of science.

Ziliak and McCloskey are not alone in their criticisms of the central role played by significance testing. We will pick up two concerns that relate to our discussions of significance testing in this chapter. The first is that, as we have noted, statistical significance is not the same as practical significance. With very large samples, tiny effects can be statistically significant. Whether such effects are of practical relevance depends on the context. That is why we have stressed the need to discuss effect sizes and practical significance along with statistical significance when reporting your results. The second is that significance testing can encourage what Field (2013: 76) calls 'all or nothing thinking', where researchers use a pre-specified significance level in a very dogmatic way, treating a result where $p < 0.05$ as significant and dismissing one where $p > 0.05$ as insignificant, even if the differences between the two observed p-values might be tiny and both be very close to 0.05. Avoiding such apparent arbitrariness is one of the reasons we have suggested that you report full p-values and use confidence intervals rather than simply mark some results as 'significant' and others 'non-significant'. Providing more information in this way allows the reader to make an informed judgement about your results.

13.6 Presenting your findings

Having completed your analysis, you will need to present your findings. You should use a combination of tables, charts and figures to present your findings, as well as text. Make sure that you integrate them into your text by applying the 'hamburger' or 'sandwich' technique of (1) introducing the material, (2) presenting it and (3) interpreting and commenting on it. Chapter 15 gives further guidance.

When reporting the results of your hypothesis tests, we recommend that you clearly indicate the hypotheses being tested, the relevant sample statistics, the appropriate test statistic and the exact p-value from the output. You should then interpret the result, commenting on both the statistical and practical significance of your findings. Reporting conventions vary, particularly when describing significance levels. One alternative is to report p-values as a range, for example $p < 0.05$ or $p < 0.01$, rather than give the exact p-value. Another method is to use asterisks (*) to indicate the level of significance. A common practice is to use one asterisk (*) to show that $p < 0.05$ and two asterisks (**) indicate that $p < 0.01$. Our view is that exact p-values convey more information and therefore are to be preferred, but in your reading you will see all three methods being used.

KEY LEARNING POINTS

- The aim in quantitative data analysis is to move from raw data to knowledge that will help you to answer your research questions.
- The process of quantitative data analysis involves data entry, data preparation, data exploration, using the data to answer your research question and presentation of your findings.
- In data entry you get your data into a format that can be analysed by your chosen software package.
- Data preparation includes checking for data entry or other errors, dealing with any missing values, carrying out any data transformation such as creating summated scales and checking scale reliability.
- Data exploration uses summary statistics and tabular and graphical analysis techniques to identify the main features of your sample data.
- Univariate exploratory analysis involves looking at variables individually, typically in terms of four characteristics: frequency distribution, central tendency, dispersion and the shape of the distribution.
- Bivariate exploratory analysis examines two variables simultaneously in order to answer more complex descriptive questions, to investigate differences between groups or to see whether or not two variables are associated.
- Time series are a form of longitudinal data that consists of a sequence of observations over time.
- Answering the research question in quantitative analysis involves the use of descriptive statistics to analyse, summarize and simplify your sample data and the use of inferential statistics to draw conclusions about the population from which the sample data were drawn.
- Inferential statistics can be used to generate confidence intervals which represent a range of plausible values for a population parameter such as the mean or population proportion.
- Inferential statistics can be used to carry out significance tests of hypotheses. Hypothesis testing entails formulating null and research (alternative) hypotheses, deciding on a significance level for acceptance of the test, selecting an appropriate test, checking assumptions, applying the test and interpreting the results.

PART IV

NEXT STEPS

13.1 Getting ready to start your analysis. Before you start your analysis, review your research questions and your conceptual model and hypotheses (if you are using them in your project). If you have not already done so, ensure you have access to your intended analysis software on a suitable laptop or PC.

13.2 Entering your data. Follow the guidance in Section 13.2 to enter your data into your chosen software package. Make sure that you create a secure back-up copy of your data.

13.3 Preparing your data. Follow the guidance in Section 13.3 to prepare your data for analysis. Make notes of all your actions, ensuring that you create new master and back-up copy of your data if you make any changes.

13.4 Exploring your data. Follow the guidance on data exploration in Section 13.4. The following sequence is suggested.

a) Calculate final sample size after all data preparation.
b) Describe your sample demographics.
c) Explore and describe other variables in your dataset.
d) Test any assumptions required by statistical tests you plan to run.

13.5 Answering your research questions. Now apply your proposed analysis techniques.

a) If you are carrying out hypothesis testing, are the results statistically significant?
b) Are your findings of practical significance?
c) What conclusions do you draw in relation to your research questions?

13.6 Presenting your findings. Review your analysis, your notes and your saved output. Decide which tables, charts etc. should be incorporated in your final report and/or presentation. Ensure that they are securely stored, ready for preparing your report.

13.7 Summary of chart types used in this chapter

Chart	Name	Description	Typical applications
	Pie chart	Plot of the proportion of the whole represented by each category or value of a variable	Showing the relative proportions of the categories within a nominal or ordinal variable. Best used with a smaller number of categories
	Bar chart	Plot of the frequency of each category or value of a variable	Comparing the frequency of each category within a nominal or ordinal variable. For ordinal data the categories can be arranged in rank order to make it easier to spot patterns
	Clustered bar chart	Plot of the frequency of each category or value of a variable for different groups placed side by side	Comparing the frequency of each category of a nominal or ordinal variable for each group in the grouping variable. If the grouping variable is ordinal, the groups can be arranged in rank order to make it easier to spot patterns
	Stacked bar chart	Plot of the frequency of each category or value of a variable for different groups stacked in a single bar	Comparing the total of each group in the grouping variable and the relative frequency of each category within each group. If the grouping variable is ordinal, the groups can be arranged in rank order to make it easier to spot patterns
	100 per cent stacked bar chart	Plot of the proportion of each category or value of a variable represented by each group stacked in a single bar representing 100 per cent of the observations	Comparing the relative proportions of each category of a normal or ordinal group between different groups in the grouping variable. If the grouping variable is ordinal, the groups can be arranged in rank order to make it easier to spot patterns
	Bar chart of means	Plot of the means of a variable for different groups	Comparing and showing differences in means between different groups. If the grouping variable is ordinal, the groups can be arranged in rank order to make it easier to spot patterns
	Histogram	Plot of the frequency distribution of a metric variable	Inspecting the shape of the distribution to check for multimodality, outliers, skewness and kurtosis

13.7 Summary of chart types used in this chapter (Continued)

Chart	Name	Description	Typical applications
	Box plot	Plot of summary statistical measures of an ordinal or metric variable	Inspecting the shape of the distribution. and particularly for identifying potential outliers
	Multiple box plot	Box plots for more than one variable or for the values for different groups in a single chart	Comparing the distribution of a variable for different groups or for different variables in a single chart
	Scatterplot	Plot of multiple observations of two variables set as the x- and y-axes	Visual inspection of the association between two variables to investigate the strength of the association, whether it is positive or negative, whether or not it is linear and identifying potential outliers
	Line chart	Plot of values for one or more variables over time	Visual inspection of time series data to identify trends and to compare variables over time
	Confidence interval chart	Plot of confidence intervals for groups or variables	Comparing the confidence intervals for different groups or for different variables in a single chart

13.8 Summary of statistical tests used in this chapter

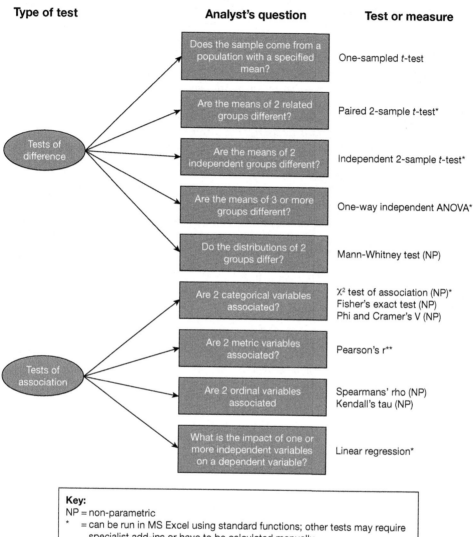

Type of test	Analyst's question	Test or measure

Tests of difference

- Does the sample come from a population with a specified mean? → One-sampled *t*-test
- Are the means of 2 related groups different? → Paired 2-sample *t*-test*
- Are the means of 2 independent groups different? → Independent 2-sample *t*-test*
- Are the means of 3 or more groups different? → One-way independent ANOVA*
- Do the distributions of 2 groups differ? → Mann-Whitney test (NP)

Tests of association

- Are 2 categorical variables associated? → X² test of association (NP)* / Fisher's exact test (NP) / Phi and Cramer's V (NP)
- Are 2 metric variables associated? → Pearson's r**
- Are 2 ordinal variables associated → Spearmans' rho (NP) / Kendall's tau (NP)
- What is the impact of one or more independent variables on a dependent variable? → Linear regression*

Key:
NP = non-parametric
*   = can be run in MS Excel using standard functions; other tests may require specialist add-ins or have to be calculated manually
** = can be calculated in MS Excel but significance test is not included

PART IV

Figure 13.32 Summary of statistical tests

Further reading

For further reading, please see the companion website.

References

Cohen, J. (1992). 'A power primer', *Psychological Bulletin*, 112(1), 155–9.

de Vaus, D. (2002a). *Surveys in social research*. 5th edn. Abingdon: Routledge.

de Vaus, D. (2002b). *Analyzing social science data*. London: Sage.

Eurostat (2012). *Electricity production and supply statistics*. Brussels: European Commission.

Field, A. (2013). *Discovering statistics using SPSS*. 4th edn. London: Sage.

The Guardian (2012). Olympics 2012: Full list of every medal winner – and how they break down [online]. Available from: www.theguardian.com/sport/datablog/2012/aug/10/olympics-2012-list-medal-winners#age.

Hair, J. F. J., Black, W. C., Babin, B. and Anderson, R. E. (2010). *Multivariate data analysis*. 7th edn. Upper Saddle River, NJ: Pearson.

Hair, J. F. J., Money, A. H., Samouel, P. and Page, M. (2007). *Research methods for business*. Chichester: Wiley.

ONS (2013). *Internet access quarterly update: Q1 2013*. London: Office of National Statistics.

US Census Bureau (2013). *Estimates of monthly retail and food services sales by kind of business*. Washington, DC: US Census Bureau.

Ziliak, S. T. and McCloskey, D. N. (2008). *The cult of statistical significance*. Ann Arbor, MI: University of Michigan Press.

Note

1 Mac Ananey, D. (2013). *An investigation into the factors that drive online shopping adoption through smartphones in the United Kingdom*. MBA dissertation submission. Henley Business School, University of Reading.

14 Analysing qualitative data

CHAPTER SUMMARY

The key topics covered in this chapter are:

- organizing, preparing and coding your data
- creating memos
- using software in qualitative data analysis
- making connections in your data with visualization techniques
- answering your research questions
- drawing and verifying conclusions from qualitative data
- presenting qualitative data in your report.

14.1 Introduction

In this chapter we introduce some key techniques for analysing qualitative data. We begin by looking at how to prepare your data for analysis. We explain how to use coding to identify the key themes in your data, including the role of software packages in qualitative analysis. We then present two types of visual display techniques, matrices and networks, and show how they can help you to describe and interpret your data in the context of different research questions. We then consider ways of verifying your findings so that you can be confident, and demonstrate to others, that they give a trustworthy account of the problem under analysis. The chapter concludes with guidance on how to present qualitative analysis in your final report.

14.2 The qualitative analysis of data

Qualitative data analysis is typically focused on interpreting non-numerical data such as recordings from an interview or notes from field observations. Its primary aim is not quantification and the analysis does not use techniques of statistical inference. There are few prescribed procedures, partly because many qualitative studies adopt an inductive, theory-building approach to analysis, but also because there are different approaches depending on the research design, the types of data and the philosophical orientation. In this chapter we introduce a set of analysis techniques that can be

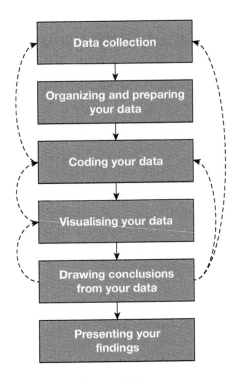

Figure 14.1 Steps in the qualitative analysis of data

applied in a wide variety of qualitative research projects built around the simple process depicted in Figure 14.1.

The steps in Figure 14.1 are consistent with an inductive approach to research, where the aim is to build theory from the data; although, as we shall see, it is also possible to incorporate a preliminary conceptual framework into this process. Although Figure 14.1 shows a relatively linear process, qualitative data analysis typically proceeds in an iterative rather than sequential manner. Because the size of your sample (e.g. the number of interviews) may be influenced by when you reach theoretical saturation, preliminary data analysis usually begins alongside data collection. Also, preliminary conclusions may point to the need for further data collection, which may in turn lead to those preliminary conclusions being modified.

Quantitative analysis methods can also be used to analyse qualitative data, using the techniques of (quantitative) content analysis as introduced in Chapter 6. We also discuss the use of numbers in qualitative data analysis later in the chapter.

14.3 Organizing and preparing your data report

In a qualitative study you may end up with a very large and unstructured dataset consisting of numerous pieces of papers and files, in addition to field notes, which you need to store and organize, so that you can easily find and access it when you need to. You also need to prepare this mix of materials for analysis, such as converting audio recordings into textual format.

14.3.1 Getting organized

As soon as data collection begins it is crucial to organize your data. Digital files such as text, video recordings or illustrations should be organized into computer folders. Physical objects need to be stored in suitable containers, such as a box file. Data such as handwritten notes or photographs that exist in physical format only may need to be copied or scanned.

You also need to spend some time developing a naming system that helps you to identify the content of each file. The key is to use names that are descriptive enough to help you quickly locate the materials needed. For instance, if you are interviewing in three locations and you wanted the file name to indicate the gender of the interviewee and the location, you could use L1M1, to indicate Location 1, male interviewee number 1.

Think about how your files should be categorized, which files should be kept together in a folder and which belong in a sub-folder. Files and folders should be organized in a way that best reflects your thinking about the project in question, and this can change as the process evolves. For instance, if you have collected data from more than one location, you may initially have a folder for each location but later you may prefer to organize the folders around themes from your analysis. Ensure that you store your data securely to prevent theft and unauthorized access and to protect against accidental loss or damage. Create a back-up copy of your master data and copies of your work as you proceed; store these securely, separately from your laptop or PC.

14.3.2 Preparing your data

Data preparation should begin while data collection is underway. We recommend that you type out your field notes while they are still fresh in your mind and store them alongside the raw data to which they refer. Practical tips for managing your notes include the following:

- Details of the data source. Ensure that you can identify the source of your data by including relevant details, such as the name and job position of the research participant and the time, date and location of data collection.
- Page layout. If you are working with paper copies, make one page margin extra wide, or use double spacing, for annotations.
- Page numbering. Ensure that each page is clearly numbered.
- Line numbers. Numbering each line of notes helps to record the location of key bits of data.

14.3.4 Transcribing your audio and video recordings

We recommend that you transcribe your recordings, if possible. The benefits of transcription, as compared to audio or digital recordings include:

- it is easier to analyse textual data
- it is quicker to review data already analysed
- it is easier to cross-reference and refer back to previous analysis
- it facilitates the use of verbatim quotations when writing up your final report.

You will have to decide whether you are going to do your own transcriptions or work with a professional transcriber. The advantages of doing your own transcriptions include saving money, being able to guarantee confidentiality and enabling you to immerse yourself in the data. Transcription, however, is time consuming. It can take between four and eight hours to transcribe a one-hour interview, depending on the number of people speaking, your skills and the quality of the recording. Moreover, the time that you invest in transcription is time that you cannot spend in collecting further data or analysing what you have collected already, delaying the conclusion of your project.

If you decide to do your own transcriptions, there are various tools available. Specialist transcription software, such as Express Scribe, www.nch.com.au is better for playing back and reviewing recordings than a conventional media player. Another option is voice recognition software (VRS). VRS tends to struggle with multiple voices in a typical interview but instead you can listen to the recording and then repeat the content in your own voice into the software. This can be faster than transcribing the interviews yourself if you are not a fast typist and cheaper than using a professional transcriber.

When transcribing, create a new paragraph every time a person starts speaking. If relevant, identify each speaker at the beginning of each paragraph, e.g., interviewer, participant 1 and so on. If you are using transcription software, you can bookmark sections of the file to mark important points for review. You can add notations to your transcript in order to signal pauses, noticeable changes in pitch and other details of the conversation Although most types of analysis do not require this level of detail, it is used in conversation analysis (see the examples in Table 14.1).

14.4 Coding your data

Within the dataset that you have collected, some data will have more significance for your study than others. Hence, you need to select and focus on the material that is relevant to your research questions. Miles and Huberman (1994) call this **data reduction**. It requires that you are thoroughly familiar with your data. To become so, you need to read through all the materials collected to get a sense of the whole dataset, before breaking it into parts and immersing yourself in the details. Moreover, the words, images and other data collected may have multiple meanings that can be fully understood only when analysed in context.

Once you have familiarized yourself with the data, you can begin **coding**. Coding in qualitative data analysis involves looking at the data, identifying relevant themes and marking them. You can think of coding as applying a selective filter to your material to funnel a mass of raw data into meaningful concepts or themes (Dey 1993).

14.4.1 What to code?

A code is 'a label attached to a section of text to index it as relating to a theme or issue in the data which the researcher has identified as important to his or her interpretation' (King 2004: 257). These sections might relate to events, statements, objects or actions/interactions in the data that appear to be significant to your research questions. The sections sharing common characteristics or with related meanings are grouped under a common code.

Table 14.1 Conversation analysis transcription symbols (based on Wooffitt 2005: 211–12 and ten Have 2007: 215–16)

Symbol	Meaning	Example
(0.0)	The number in brackets indicates a time gap in seconds	A: that was (0.5) interesting
(.)	A very short pause (less than two-tenths of a second)	A: that was (.) interesting
(( ))	Non-verbal activity	A: here we go ((hands over form))
(word)	Unclear fragment of talk: the word represents the transcriber's best guess	A: I got home really (late)
[ ]	Overlapping talk; the first bracket indicates where the overlapping talk begins, the second where it ends	A: I was planning to talk [to you] about this B: [I see]
[[	Two square brackets indicate that speakers start a turn simultaneously	A: [[right] then B: [[okay]
WORD	Upper case indicates a section of talk noticeably louder than those around it	A: that was NOT clever
↑ ↓	Higher (↑) or lower (↓) pitch in the talk immediately following the arrow	A: that was ↑ interesting
> <	The talk surrounded by the inequality signs is noticeably quicker than surrounding talk	A: that was an >ah ha< moment for me
word	Underlining indicates speaker emphasis	A: that was interesting
:::	Colons shows that a speaker has stretched out a sound or letter; the more colons, the more stretched	A: o::::kay
?	A rising intonation; it does not necessarily indicate a question	A: that was interesting?
–	A dash indicates a sharp cut-off to a word or sound	A: turn lef– no right
,	Continuing intonation	A: one, two, three
·hh	The hs indicate a breath. If prefixed with a dot, an in breath is meant; if there is no dot, an out breath is meant. The more hs the longer the breath	A: hhhh finished

What makes particular pieces of data interesting or significant will be determined by your research questions. For instance, if your research question related to individuals' motivations to help as volunteers, you would look for data that referred to reasons, beliefs, values and so on and that might provide insight into their motivations for volunteering.

In some situations, coding will be inductive, so the researcher does not have any codes in mind before starting the analysis. As relevant themes are identified in the data, the researcher decides upon a suitable code and allocates it to that particular section. In this approach, the researcher allows for intuition to guide the coding process. In other cases, the researcher adopts a deductive approach, starting data reduction with themes that serve as sensitizing concepts (Blumer 1954). These **a priori codes** may come from the literature or the research questions. In practice, researchers often adopt a mixed approach. They may start with an initial list of codes, but are prepared to revise, add to or reject initial ideas as the analysis proceeds.

14.4.2 *The coding process*

The example provided in Research in Practice 14.1 should help to make the process more concrete.

RESEARCH IN PRACTICE 14.1

Example of the coding process

In this extract from an interview transcript, a manager talks about a new role leading the start-up division of a large corporation. The researcher asked about obstacles faced in the new role, to which the interviewee replies:

	First of all we face the scepticism. I think when I took the job on, nine months ago now, the reaction of my peers was probably 'that's great, sounds very exciting – they'll never let you do it'. I think we've overcome that to a large extent. Then there is resistance, not because people don't like the idea but because inevitably it means we need resources, we need skills, we need cooperation from other business units and it's not necessarily at the moment been proved to them that by giving us those things it helps them towards their objectives at all.

Below, we see the same extract after coding has begun. The researcher has highlighted relevant parts of the text and allocated each a code, which is written in the margin.

Scepticism	First of all we face the scepticism. I think when I took the job on, nine months ago now, the reaction of my peers was probably 'that's great, sounds very exciting – they'll never let you do it'. I think we've overcome that to a large extent. Then there is resistance, not because people don't like the idea but because inevitably it means
Resources	we need resources, we need skills, we need cooperation from other
Conflicting objectives	business units and it's not necessarily at the moment been proved to them that by giving us those things it helps them towards their objectives at all.

The coding process can be done manually on paper copies. You work line by line, highlighting appropriate segments of data and noting the name of the code in the margin with pen or pencil. As you work through another transcript, you look for further occurrences of those codes. As you progress you are likely to encounter other codes. In the case of the study reported in Research in Practice 14.1, subsequent interviewees might identify issues not mentioned before, for instance, jealousy as a result of someone getting the new role. The additional obstacles need to be labelled using another appropriate code (jealousy, in this case).

Naming and defining your codes

You need to think carefully about how you will name and define your codes. Names may come from the language of the respondents, in which case they are called in vivo codes (e.g. 'scepticism' in Research in Practice 14.1), or from your own interpretation of what is happening (as in the case of 'conflicting objectives') or from theory. Whatever the source of the name, you need to be consistent in how you apply the code, so you will need to develop working definitions of your codes as you proceed. As coding is the start of the process of theorizing about your data, developing definitions for your codes is an important part of that process.

Managing your codes

As you proceed, you will need to keep a record of what you have coded and where, so that you can retrieve coded segments later. If you are coding on paper, you can keep an index system, noting down the source document and the line number of each section of text for each of your codes. The disadvantage of this method is that you have to look up the original source document if you want to re-read the text that you have coded.

Alternatively, you can create an index card for each code, noting the name and definition of the code at the top of the card. Then, using scissors and some glue or tape, cut the corresponding data from a copy of the original data source and paste

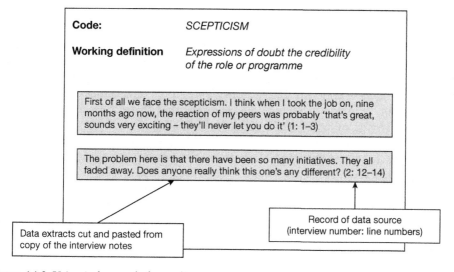

Figure 14.2 Using index cards for coding

Table 14.2 Using tables to manage coding

Code	Working definition	Interview 1	Interview 2
Scepticism	Expressions of doubt about the credibility of the role or programme	First of all we face the scepticism. I think when I took the job on, nine months ago now, the reaction of my peers was probably 'that's great, sounds very exciting – they'll never let you do it' (lines: 1–3)	The problem here is that there have been so many initiatives. They all faded away. Does anyone really think this one's any different? (lines: 12-14)
Resources	Potential or actual conflicts of resources arising as a result of the programme	Then there is resistance, not because people don't like the idea but because inevitably it means we need resources, we need skills, we need cooperation from other business units (lines: 4–6)	Data extracts cut and pasted from the copy of the interview notes
Conflicting objectives	Potential or actual conflicts of objectives arising as a result of the programme	It's not necessarily at the moment been proved to them that by giving us those things it helps them towards their objectives at all (line: 6–8)	

it onto the relevant card, recording where each extract came from, as illustrated in Figure 14.2. As you add codes, you can add index cards, and because each card is separate it is easy to rearrange them for later analysis. This traditional way of coding qualitative data allows you to look at all the data belonging to a particular code.

Another option is to create a table cross-tabulating your data sources with your codes, as illustrated in Table 14.2. As coding proceeds, add columns for each data source and rows for each code. This is also a simple form of data display matrix that allows you to compare responses.

14.4.3 Coding hierarchies

The codes generated in the first stage of data reduction are your initial or level 1 coding (Hahn 2008). If some of your level 1 codes share common features, you should group them under one theme. In our start-up example, the four codes identified could be grouped under the theme 'obstacles to success', as shown in Figure 14.3.

Furthermore, as 'scepticism' and 'jealousy' seem to be dimensions of the same type of phenomenon, you could create a label showing that these codes are related, as in Figure 14.4. This is called a level 2 code (Hahn 2008).

The process of creating levels of codes reduces the number of blocks you are working with. It can be thought of as a form of **hierarchical coding**, which has the following benefits:

> Hierarchical coding allows the researcher to analyse texts at varying levels of specificity. Broad higher-order codes can give a good overview of the general direction of the interview, detailed lower-order codes allow for very fine distinctions to be made, both within and between [interviews].
>
> King (2004: 258)

PART IV

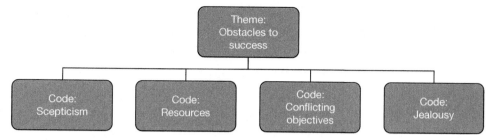

Figure 14.3 Emerging themes

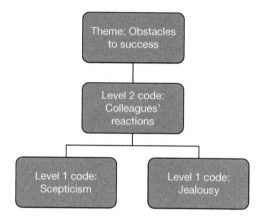

Figure 14.4 Level 1 and 2 codes

If you find that you have created a code that is too 'broad' and which needs detailed analysis, you would split the original code into sub-categories. For instance, you could unpack the code 'resources', as illustrated in Figure 14.5. Here, you are creating a hierarchy in reverse, starting with the broad, higher-order category and adding lower-order, fine-grained codes. When you create a new code in a later document you must revisit your earlier data to see whether there is any other case that should be relabelled with the new code.

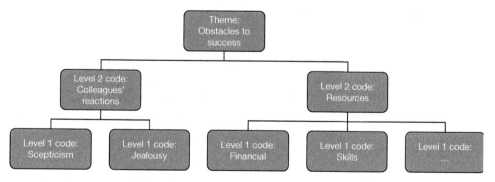

Figure 14.5 Creating sub-categories

PART IV

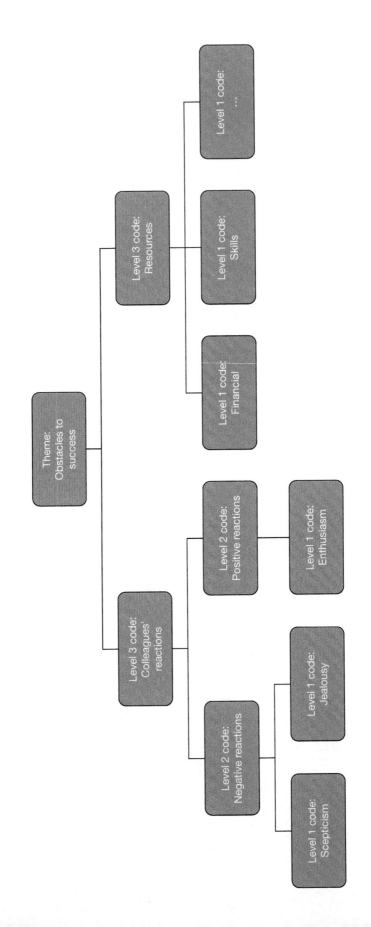

Figure 14.6 Examples of a revised coding scheme

As you progress, you may also find cases that actually contradict what you found earlier, for instance, the new role was met with enthusiasm, leading to unrealistic expectations and thus becoming an obstacle to success. If so, you need to create a new level 1 code. Moreover, because this reaction is so different from the others, you need to create a level 2 code that reflects this difference. You also need to create an even higher-level code, a level 3 code, to show how the existing level 2 codes are related. Figure 14.6 illustrates the expanded coding scheme.

As this example shows, codes relate to each other at increasing levels of abstraction. Multiple level 1 codes are aggregated into a level 2 code reflecting the interconnectedness of the codes under it. In turn, related level 2 codes are aggregated into a level 3 code, and so on, in an iterative process, until you reach a level that represents your results in a coherent manner, as illustrated in Figure 14.7.

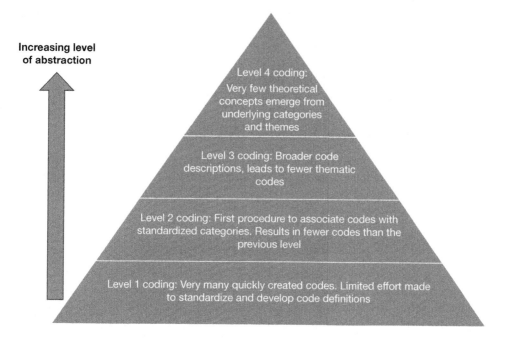

Increasing level of abstraction

Level 4 coding: Very few theoretical concepts emerge from underlying categories and themes

Level 3 coding: Broader code descriptions, leads to fewer thematic codes

Level 2 coding: First procedure to associate codes with standardized categories. Results in fewer codes than the previous level

Level 1 coding: Very many quickly created codes. Limited effort made to standardize and develop code definitions

Figure 14.7 Coding hierarchy (adapted from Hahn 2008: 172)

14.4.4 Memoing

As you re-read and code your materials, you will see how things fit together and how they relate to theory. In a research project spanning several weeks or, perhaps, months it is nearly impossible to remember all of those 'aha!' moments. So, you need to capture your thoughts before they are lost, using a technique known as **memoing**.

A **memo** may be a short phrase, a sentence or even a paragraph recording your ideas as they happen. You can capture them in your field notes, in a separate file or in your research diary, to help you draw conclusions and write up your analysis. Memos are also helpful to capture the factors in the setting that appear to explain your findings, for instance, an event that occurred in the organization or a demographic characteristic of the research participants. It is important to note such factors because they provide structure to the study and are important to describe its context.

Strauss and Corbin (1998) describe three types of memo: coding notes relating to the codes and categories that you created; theoretical notes capturing your thoughts about emerging theory; and operational notes covering the procedures that you followed or reminders for the future. They offer the following suggestions to help you to use memoing effectively:

- Give the memo a subject title, such as the name of the code to which it relates,
- Date each memo for filing and future reference.
- Note the type of memo (coding, theoretical or operational).
- Include extracts of raw data and details of the source, if relevant.
- Make your memos conceptual rather than just descriptive; capturing the ideas and insights emerging.

As with field notes, capture your thoughts as soon as they occur. You can return to them and expand on your original ideas as needed. You will find that the writing process itself helps to develop your analysis.

14.5 Using computers in qualitative data analysis

Although coding is a process of data reduction, it may generate a large number of codes and, in turn, a huge amount of coded data needing further interpretation and analysis. It requires a considerarble amount of data management, which is what computers are good at.

14.5.1 Using word processing and spreadsheet software

The coding process can be supported by using word processing or spreadsheet software. In MS Word, for example, the comment function can be used for your initial coding and to make short memos on particular sections of text. MS Word can also be used to create tables such as Table 14.2. Large datasets are more easily managed in a spreadsheet program, such as MS Excel, as shown in Figure 14.8. Additional columns can be added for each coding level, as you develop a hierarchy; use the sort functions to organize the lower-order codes. Software can also facilitate writing up, as it is easy to extract data or relevant sections from the table for inclusion in the final report.

14.5.2 Using CAQDAS programs

There are specialist software packages designed to support code-and-retrieve activities in qualitative analysis. They are known as computer aided qualitative data analysis software (**CAQDAS**) and include packages such as NVivo and Atlas.ti. CAQDAS packages can assist with various aspects of the coding and analysis process, as summarized in Table 14.3.

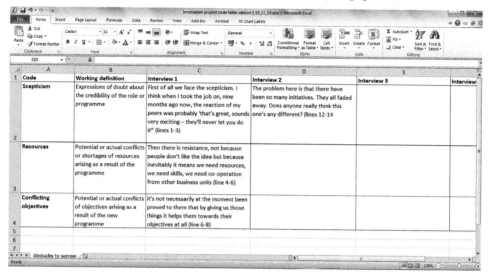

Figure 14.8 Coding table created using a spreadsheet (Excel)

Table 14.3 Some functions typically performed by CAQDAS programs (based on Lewins and Silver 2009)

Task	Example
Project management and data organization	Plan tasks, maintain a project diary and create memos Store documents of various types, including raw data, which can be tagged and annotated
Keeping close to the data	Almost instant access to the data
Coding and analysis	Thematic analysis of the data through the use of codes Generate and manage memos
Searching and visualization of data	Perform searches of the datasets, retrieve coded data and, where visualization tools are available, create models, charts and other diagrams
Outputs	Generate reports, charts and other outputs that help to visualize the data and the relationships being made, and share with other members of the research team

CAQDAS programs have several advantages and disadvantages, which we summarize in Table 14.4. CAQDAS, like other software packages, can help with the manipulation and management of the data, but there is no replacement for the researcher's skill and judgement in data exploration and interpretation.

You can learn more about using CAQDAS on the companion website for this book, which also contains an introduction to using NVivo for qualitative data analysis.

PART IV

Table 14.4 Advantages and disadvantages of CAQDAS programs

Advantages	Disadvantages
• Helps with project management, data organization, generation and manipulation of codes	• It encourages narrow range of analysis techniques (Coffey et al. 1996)
• Can accelerate the process of data analysis, particularly with large amounts of data	• Can give you a false sense of security
• Can produce reports and charts that assist visual analysis as well as reporting	• The tools have their own learning curve, and small projects may not justify the investment of time to acquaint yourself with the software
• Helps the sharing of data within the team	• May lead to an emphasis on frequency counts, to the detriment of understanding the underlying meaning
• Can improve the study's 'trustworthiness' because it enables you to show the coding and analysis processes	

14.6 Using visualization to make connections

During coding we start to see connections between data segments, building abstract and inclusive conceptual categories. But we still need to understand how emerging concepts are connected, before answering our research questions. For instance, you may want to compare the experiences of different participants, understand the chronological sequence of events in your data or the mechanisms influencing those events.

One option is to revisit your materials to draw conclusions and write up your findings. However, relying on text alone has several limitations, as Miles and Huberman point out:

> It is hard on analysts because it is *dispersed* over many pages and is not easy to see as a whole. It is *sequential* rather than simultaneous, making it difficult to look at two or three variables at once. It is usually *poorly ordered*, and it can get very *bulky*, monotonously overloading. Comparing several extended texts carefully is very difficult.
>
> Miles and Huberman (1994: 91, emphasis in original)

Plain text can also be a cumbersome way of presenting your findings, particularly when comparing several research participants or analytical units such as different groups in an organization. Moreover, text may not be a very effective way of communicating some aspects of your findings in a meaningful manner. Visual displays can on the other hand give a systematic, visual representation of the data. They can be used to depict differences, relationships and interconnections within the overall dataset, for example, how job roles changed over time and the impact those changes had on staff morale; or to depict the relationships between your codes and categories, for example, in a causal pathway.

Visualization techniques can be applied to a single unit of analysis such as one document or interview, or to several units at once to help in comparative analysis. In addition, they can be used both during the analysis process and, suitably edited, as a presentation device in the final report. Like other analysis techniques, of course, visual data displays have limitations; we review some of these in Critical Commentary 14.1.

14.7 Types of visual data display

Visual displays, which can take many forms, may be broadly classified into one of two types: data matrices and networks (Miles and Huberman 1994). We will look at each in turn.

14.7.1 Data matrices

A data matrix is basically a cross-tabulation. The data are displayed in rows and columns. The headings for the rows and the columns reflect the dimensions that you want to capture in your analysis and may come from a prior conceptual framework or emerge as coding gets underway. The data entered in each cell of the matrix is driven by the matrix headings and can vary in abstraction. You may start by entering all the relevant data in the corresponding cell. At a higher level of abstraction, you may enter selected quotes that illustrate the situation described by the specific row and column headings. At still higher levels of abstraction, you may select a word or phrase that captures the idea that you want to convey. You may also condense your findings into symbols which communicate the findings in a non-textual manner.

In Table 14.5 we show the extract of a data matrix that comes from an unpublished multiple case study of online banks. The researcher was interested in how banks differed in their patterns of interaction, internally as well as with outside stakeholders. This matrix helped the researcher to compare practices across the different cases that composed the study. The columns represent the concepts being analysed (internal versus external interactions) and the rows show the different companies studied (here, the original names have been replaced by fictitious ones). The cells display summaries of the data coded around the concepts studied.

Data matrices can help you spot patterns in the data. For example, do certain types of bank follow certain practices? Do certain practices occur together? Do types of banks differ in the practices they follow? In this way, data matrices can help you answer focused questions about your data. We show this in action in Research in Practice 14.2 which uses a data matrix to explore and summarise differences between two different types of bank in terms of their innovation routines.

Data matrices are not limited to cross-tabulating cases with concepts identified in the coding process. They are much more flexible. Figure 14.9 shows some possible column headers that could be used when developing data matrices. You might, for example, create a table using a dimension of time (such as months) as the column headers and different cases (which might be individual interviewees) as the row labels to display how they changed or developed over time. The cells contain relevant data extracts or summaries that relate to each case and time period. Alternatively, you might investigate the relationships between different concepts by using them as column headers and rows in your matrix, for example, by cross-tabulating dimensions

Table 14.5 Example of a data matrix

Company	Internal interactions	External interactions
Bargain Bank	• Open communication with direct access to top management • Relatively small number of employees located close together	• Frequent contact with customers emphasized as part of the company's culture
The People's Bank	• Cross-functional and cross-subsidiary project teams used to improve internal knowledge sharing and learning	• Use of partnerships to share expertise (e.g. Partner A) • Importance of using the Internet as an opportunity to connect more often with customers
Big Bank	• Open communication • Non-dictatorial management style • Need for feedback mechanisms	• Knowledge sharing across the company's network of business partners • Cooperation to develop new product offerings
Other bank	. . .	. . .

RESEARCH IN PRACTICE 14.2

Using a data matrix to display comparisons

When studying the data from the online banking project, the researcher noticed that start-up banks had a different approach to internal interactions than the more established institutions. The researcher decided to produce a version of the matrix that brought out the differences between types of bank, rather than between individual organizations. The table below shows an alternative way of organizing data. This time the banks have been grouped into two categories, start-ups vs established banks. Banks are now shown in the columns rather than in the rows. The researcher is investigating whether there is any difference in the way they use 'informal routines' as a means of developing and exchanging ideas.

Informal routines used by online banks

	Start-up banks	Established banks
Informal routines	• Small teams on a single site easily able to communicate • Open communication culture to bring forward new ideas • Use of new brand to communicate need for innovation to staff	• Long-established periods of idea mobilization characterized by informal networking • Ideas kept 'covert' until workable to avoid their being crowded out • Use of web fairs to generate support for new ideas

At this point, the researcher returned to the data to look for further evidence confirming or disconfirming the emerging findings.

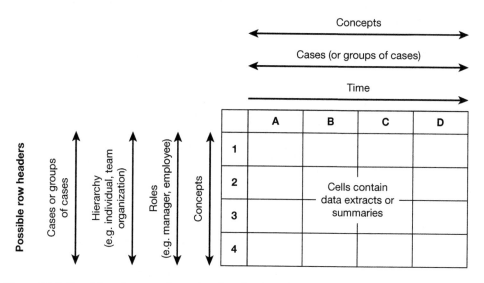

Figure 14.9 Possible column and row headers for data matrixes

of customer satisfaction with dimensions of service quality to investigate whether they are related. We will take a further look at different ways in which matrices can be used later in the chapter.

14.7.2 Networks

A network is a form of visual display using nodes (points) and lines linking the nodes together. The nodes can be concepts from your coding, events or entities such as organizations or people. The lines show connections between them. You can convey additional information about the links by using arrows to indicate directionality or effect (such as causal influence); symbols such as '+' or '−' to indicate whether an effect is positive or negative; and different line widths to reflect the intensity of the link. Further information can be incorporated by exploiting the vertical and horizontal dimensions of the network display. For example, if you are depicting a process, you can show the progression of time along the horizontal axis and the various actors involved on the vertical axis, as in Figure 14.10.

The focus of your network and what to use as nodes depend on the purpose of your display. A network display of communication patterns between members of a virtual project team, for example, might have individual team members as the nodes with the links representing the direction, strength and frequency of interaction. A network display of the development of a start-up business, on the other hand, might use critical events (such as an injection of capital) as the nodes and use the lines to represent the sequencing of those events.

A very practical application is to depict the relationships between the concepts that you have coded in your data. In using displays in this way, you are starting to

PART IV

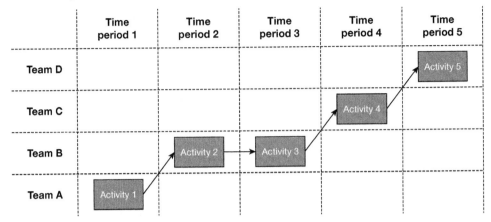

Figure 14.10 Example of a network display incorporating vertical and horizontal dimensions

depict your coded data in the form of a concept map or conceptual framework. We have already encountered this use of visual display in the form of conceptual models in Chapter 3. The concept map may draw on existing theory or be developed entirely from the data.

14.7.3 Choosing a visual display format

The choice of visual display format depends on what you are trying to understand or communicate. Regardless of the format or level of analysis, you will have to go through various iterations to create your display. Start with a simple display, and build it up as you progress. Developing the displays is also likely to raise further questions, requiring you to revisit your data to clarify meanings or steps in the process, or even collect more data to fill in the gaps, which is why it is essential to start analysing your data early in the research process. Give each display a meaningful title and date it, keeping a record of the criteria used to produce and populate your displays, for instance, why you chose particular nodes in a network. Use memos and your research diary to record your thoughts as you work, so as to support your final writing up.

14.8 Answering your research question

If you are new to qualitative data analysis, it can be difficult to see how coding and visual displays can be used in practice to answer specific research questions. In this section we look at the use of these tools to answer the 'what', 'why' and 'how' type research questions. We are not trying to provide an exhaustive blueprint or a set of recipes but, instead, to help you to develop your understanding of the tools themselves and thereby to make creative and effective use of them in your project.

CRITICAL COMMENTARY 14.1

Limitations to data display techniques in qualitative research

It is important to be aware of the limitations and pitfalls of using visual data displays in qualitative analysis. They include the following:

- Imposing an unsuitable display format onto your analysis. Miles and Huberman (1994) suggest that this is a particular risk early on in the analysis process and recommend that you experiment with different types of displays for the same data. Problems may also arise when using a prior framework that forces your analysis in a particular direction (Charmaz 2006).
- The approach may be too reductionist, oversimplifying what is a complex reality. A related risk is that the display becomes increasingly detached from the data as the analysis proceeds.
- The displays may be too large or complex to be practically useful. Displays can easily grow in size and complexity as the analysis unfolds, and can be difficult to share with others, particularly in written reports where physical space is limited. This requires careful thought and the redrawing of displays to make them suitable for sharing with others.
- Visual display techniques are not appropriate for all projects. Some projects may not require the analyst to go beyond hierarchical coding in order to answer the research questions. Also, visual displays may not be suitable for some research designs, such as conversation analysis.
- Visual display may appeal to some individuals more than others. Your own preferences should also be taken into account when choosing your analysis techniques.

PART IV

14.8.1 Answering 'what' questions

Qualitative answers to 'what' questions typically aim to give a detailed description of a phenomenon, its features and its context. The focus of coding will depend on what aspects of the phenomenon are interesting or relevant to the aims of the study, and these may not be clear at first. So, your initial coding may simply be aimed at identifying what is going on in your data. Further rounds of coding then start to focus on key aspects of the phenomenon and its context. If your research takes an emic perspective, with an emphasis on understanding and describing participants' views, you may use in vivo coding. On the other hand, if using a theory-led approach, you may draw on aspects of that theory to formulate a priori codes to start the data reduction process. Early in the coding process, it can also be helpful to apply what Saldaña (2013: 70) calls 'attribute coding', in which you use features about the sources such as demographics (gender, age etc.), the setting (location, organization etc.) or other aspects of the context. Attribute codes can help subsequent analysis by facilitating the comparison of groups or the description of different settings or contexts.

Data matrices can be useful in descriptive work because they allow you to display the various components of a phenomenon and explore the range of variations for each of these components within and between cases. A further use of matrices is to develop a descriptive taxonomy of your cases. Careful inspection of a data matrix cross-tabulating cases and relevant concepts from your coding may reveal that cases cluster together in different groups in terms of shared characteristics, as we saw in Research in Practice 14.2, where different types of bank were grouped on the basis of patterns of informal routines. The clusters may allow you to develop a taxonomy that reduces complexity but highlights important, shared features of the different groups.

Network displays can also be used to explore the answers to 'what' questions. One application is to depict the network of relationships in which individuals or social units (e.g. groups or organizations) are located. The nodes represent the members of the network and the lines the interactions between them. The result is a simplified form of social network diagram, as shown in Figure 14.11 showing key actors involved in the award of research grants. While members of the network interact with each other, not every node interacts with all the others. The specific pattern of relationships between nodes results in different network forms. Social networks are typically drawn from one of two perspectives: the whole network or person centred. Whole-network views depict the entire network within a defined boundary such as an organization; personal networks depict the network around the focal member (such as a particular individual). Simple network diagrams like Figure 14.11 can be useful to capture the context of the issue that you are studying, depicting not only the key actors but also the roles that they play, what is exchanged (e.g. applications, grant funding, reviews and so on), positive or negative attitudes and other contextual information.

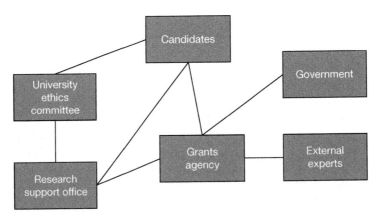

Figure 14.11 Example of a simple social network display

14.8.2 Answering 'why' questions

If your study focuses on 'why' questions your goal is to explain why something is happening. As explained in Chapter 5, this is a controversial area, but we can nevertheless suggest two key applications for qualitative research methods: investigating causal mechanisms and understanding actors' reasons and beliefs in a particular situation. One approach is to apply what Saldaña (2013: 163) calls 'causation coding', which attempts to identify the mental models people use to make sense of cause-and-effect questions, placing the emphasis on actors' reasoning in a particular situation. Saldaña (2013: 164) suggests that words and phrases in the data such as 'because', 'so', 'as a result of', 'and that's why' may indicate causal attribution by a respondent, though accounts of causal sequences may not be linear and require careful investigation. The search for potential links between the cause and effect is consistent with our emphasis on explanation in terms of causal mechanisms and identifying the pathway through which causes operate.

Data matrices can support qualitative causal analysis by helping us to deepen our understanding of the situation and, above all, to explore patterns of potential causes, causal mechanisms and outcomes. Miles and Huberman (1994: 148) suggest starting with what they call an 'explanatory effects matrix' to get an initial understanding of the situation by tracing out the short- and long-run effects. To illustrate this type of matrix, suppose that we were investigating the impact of an advertising campaign on customers' brand perceptions. During the coding process, the researcher classified respondents according to their status as customers, their overall assessment of the campaign, their views on the campaign and their resulting intentions. Subsequently, the researcher started to build an explanatory effects matrix as shown in Table 14.6 to bring together these different dimensions.

An explanatory effects matrix such as Table 14.6 is a starting point for identifying the 'emerging threads of causality' (Miles and Huberman 1994: 148) but further analysis is required if we are to get a deeper understanding of causal factors. One approach is to use cross-case comparison to investigate the relationship between influencing factors and outcomes of interest to the research. Data matrices can be

Table 14.6 Example of an explanatory effects matrix (numbers in brackets indicate interview number: line number)

Customer type	Overall assessment (0 = neutral, + = positive, − = negative)	Short-run effects (e.g. belief state of viewers)	Longer-run consequences (e.g. intentions of viewers)
Prospective customer	0	'Sounds great but would they really do that?' (4: 8)	No examples of intention to change current behaviour
		'All companies say that sort of thing' (6: 23)	. . .
Existing customers (satisfied)	+	'They go to the end of the world to help the customer' (1: 11)	. . .
Existing customers (dissatisfied)	−	'This never happens in reality. It is all a lie.' (3: 36)	. . .
		'It's not like that at all' (7: 12)	. . .

RESEARCH IN PRACTICE 14.3

Using a data matrix in an investigation of success factors

Wilson et al. (2002) investigated factors for success in customer relationship management systems, using a multiple case studies approach. The authors used a cross-case comparison data matrix to present the findings, an extract from which is shown here. Each factor is given a brief description along with a rating in terms of its presence and influence. Asterisks (*) are used to show the degree of presence, with three asterisks indicating the factor is fully present (DK means insufficient data to rate the factor for that case) and +/− symbols indicating degree of influence, with ++ showing that the factor appears to be 'influential in determining project success' (Wilson et al. 2002: 210). The criteria used to judge influence were (a) consistency of evidence and (b) whether the factor's presence or absence influenced the benefits gained and there was a plausible explanation linking the factor to the outcomes.

Example cross-case comparison (extracts from Wilson et al. 2002: 209, Table 3)

Factor	Case A Utility	Case B Electricity generator	Case C Paper manufacturer
Determine INTENT gain champion/ sponsor	***/++ New marketing board member crucial	***/+ Commerce director's board presence vital	**/+ Lack of board continuity unhelpful
Ensure market orientation	**/+ Clear desire to improve from top	*/+ Previously poor but improving	*/+ Tendency to production orientation
Define approval procedures which allow for uncertainty	DK	*/+ Inherently risk-averse organisation	**/++ A problem in one project

very helpful here, since they facilitate such comparisons, as exemplified in Research in Practice 14.3.

You can also depict causal relationships using network displays, which can take the form of the sort of causal diagrams typically associated with quantitative explanatory research. This format is particularly suitable if the subsequent model is to be further tested using quantitative methods, for instance, as part of a mixed methods study. In other situations, it may take the form of systems diagrams, incorporating feedback loops and other mechanisms.

Miles and Huberman (1994: 163) describe causal networks as 'the analyst's most ambitious attempt at an integrated understanding' of the data. They warn against trying to force order into loose-ended events, oversimplifying complex relationships and confusing plausible networks with accurate explanations of what happened. To counter these weaknesses, they recommend that we start by focusing on fragments

PART IV

of the cause–effect relationship, understanding them in detail, before trying to produce a condensed display of all the dependent and independent variables and their relationships. Even then, as we have repeatedly emphasized, the researcher should be cautious about making causal claims.

14.8.3 Answering 'how' questions

A study focusing on 'how' questions aims to explain what happens by taking a process view, such as the sequence of events or activities that lead to a particular outcome, such as the adoption of a new technology. Qualitative methods are particularly well suited to investigating process and building theory about change, as we pointed out in Chapter 5. Coding plays an important part in process research, even when subsequent analysis is done quantitatively, because of the need to identify events in the data that are relevant to the process being analysed. Event types can vary according to the purpose of the study. Poole et al. (2000), for example, suggest six different categories of events for coding in the context of innovation research:

1   Activity events, such as administrative reviews, strategy meetings and budgeting cycles
2   Idea events, when a significant change in ideas about the innovation occurs
3   People events, when there is a change in personnel or roles
4   Transaction events, when there is a change in the legal or social contracts linked to the innovation
5   Context events, when there is a change in the external or organizational environment of the innovation
6   Outcome events, when there is a change in the criteria by which the innovation is judged.

When coding participant accounts from a process perspective, Saldaña (2013: 98) suggests that expressions such as 'if', 'then', 'and so' may indicate a sequence or process.

A time-ordered visual display can be particularly useful for the study of processes. You can create a matrix in which you cross-tabulate events, arranged in time order, against other dimensions of your topic, such as who is involved. For a study of the spread of innovation, for example, you might use the column headers in the matrix to record the key stages (events) in the process, and the rows to represent hierarchical levels such as individual, team, organization, industry and so on. The cells are then populated with relevant data; for instance, details of what happened, why and so on. Again, you can add symbols or use formatting to emphasize aspects of the data, such as their relative importance or a change of direction. This type of matrix is called an events listing (Miles and Huberman 1994: 110) and we show an example in Research in Practice 14.4.

You can also produce an edited version of the event listings matrix called a critical incidents chart (Miles and Huberman 1994: 113). In a critical incidents chart you present the data organized by time and type of event, but you display information only for those events considered particularly important for the issue that you are studying, either by you as the researcher or from the perspective of the research participants, for example, a particular economic inducement, an educational initiative

PART IV

RESEARCH IN PRACTICE 14.4

Visualizing events and processes

The figures below were produced for a study of monitoring processes at a UK bank (referred to as BFI in the report), in order to detect financial crime (Canhoto 2007).

Records of observed banking behaviour are first scrutinized by two types of agents: customer-facing staff such as those working in branches, and the automated transaction monitoring system. When the pattern of behaviour does not match existing prototypes of 'legitimate behaviour' at the scrutiny stage it is categorized as 'unusual' and it is reported to an expert team, the MLRO unit. The analysts in this unit investigate the alert, alongside other input such as previous transaction history. This is the 'analysis' stage. If the analyst agrees that the behaviour is not legitimate, it is classified as 'suspicious' and referred to an external entity (the FIU) using a form known as 'SAR'.

The sequence of events is illustrated in matrix form in the table below. Time is shown on the left-hand side, from top to bottom, mirroring how text is read in the UK, where the work was published. Other variables deemed important for the analysis are captured in the table as column headers.

Events listing matrix for the detection of financial crime at BFI

Step	Agent	Activity	Input	Category	Output
#1	• BANK staff (e.g., branch) • ATMS • External sources (e.g., victim of fraud)	Scrutiny	Observed banking behaviour	Unusual behaviour	Referral to MLRO team: Alert
#2	• Analysis	Analysis	• Alert • Client history • Specific intelligence re: client or transaction	Suspicious behaviour	Referral to FIU: SAR

The display below shows the same monitoring process but in network format. Time is still represented on the vertical axis, from top to bottom, and agents are shown on the horizontal axis. The other elements of the process are captured within the network. Further symbolic elements are used to aid in the communication of the findings such as a box to represent an input, a diamond to represent a decision and a triangle to represent the possible outcomes of the decision.

Network display for the detection of financial crime at BFI

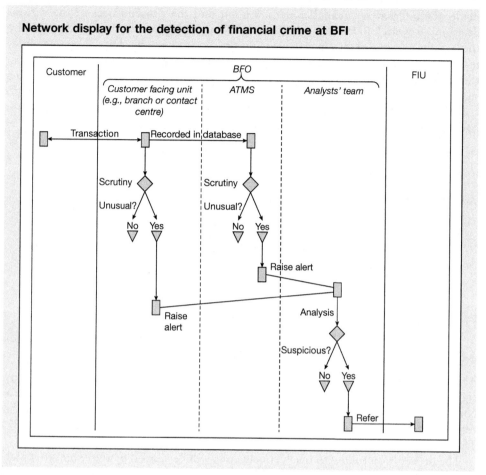

or a change in the environment. Critical incident charts can be produced at varying levels of detail. The focus on specific incidents helps us to gauge the chain of events that lead to a particular outcome and facilitates the comparison across research settings. However, it requires you to manipulate the data, making decisions on what to include and what to leave out. What seems important at one stage may seem less so later in the analysis. Conversely, information that seemed unimportant early in the analysis process may acquire heightened importance in the light of additional data or further analysis. Hence, it is important to keep an open mind when preparing this type of chart and revisit it as you collect and analyse more data. You should start with a full events listing chart before producing the summarized version that focuses on critical events only. Moreover, you should keep detailed notes about why you kept specific events in the chart or excluded them.

You can also use networks to visualize processes. Networks are better than matrices for communicating the idea of flow, capturing complex or long processes, representing recurring events and emphasizing how individual events reinforced each other, as illustrated in Figure 14.12. Networks are also very effective to represent decision processes. Flow charts, in particular, are very useful to depict key decisions to be made, the alternatives available at each point and the consequences of the various decisions. Research in Practice 14.4 shows a network display used in this way. Despite the benefits of network displays to visualize processes, they offer limited opportunities to provide detailed information about the events depicted, the agents involved and the outcomes of those events. To overcome this you can use additional visual elements such as the shape of the boxes, the width of lines, colours and various symbols to convey more information; for instance, events may be depicted by rectangular boxes and actions by circles.

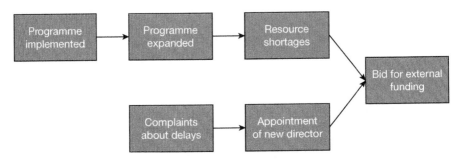

Figure 14.12 Example of an events network

14.9 Drawing and verifying conclusions

As you code your data, prepare memos and create visual displays, you begin to identify significant parts of the data, key themes and how they are related, and to draw conclusions. Miles and Huberman (1994) proposed a series of tactics to help the researcher make sense of data, and we summarize a number of these in Table 14.7. They should be used in conjunction with the tools we have introduced so far.

The process you follow to reach conclusions will be shaped by the extent to which you are taking an entirely inductive approach versus making use of initial sensitizing concepts or a prior theoretical framework. In the former, you seek to build theory directly from the data, identifying emerging themes and developing propositions about the relationships between them as analysis unfolds. In the latter, you use existing

Table 14.7 Tactics for getting meaning out of data (based on Miles and Huberman 1994: 360–1)

Tactic	Comments
Noticing patterns	Look for patterns of similarities and differences between categories and/or patterns of processes, involving connections in time and space
Clustering	You may be able to cluster coded concepts into larger categories, you may be able to cluster subjects (interviewees/cases, etc.) into meaningful groups and/or you may be able to cluster activities or events into useful sets
Making contrasts/ comparisons	How does X differ from Y? What is the practical significance of any difference?
Noting relations between concepts	What sort of relationships can you envisage between X and Y?

PART IV

theory to guide your analysis of the data by focusing on particular themes and their possible relationships. Either way, you should adopt an iterative approach to your analysis, alternating between data and (emerging) theory in a process of constant comparison between the two. Iteration can deepen our understanding and provide a basis for drawing robust and rigorous conclusions. In our experience this is the most difficult stage of any qualitative analysis project, demanding a combination of creative yet rigorous thinking.

14.9.1 Counting in qualitative research

Counting is a possible tactic for helping you to generate meaning from qualitative data. We are not referring here to the use of quantitative methods (such as quantitative content analysis) to analyse non-numeric data, or to the combination of qualitative and quantitative research in a mixed methods study, but to the use of counting (such as the number of times a code occurs in a particular source) within an otherwise qualitative study. Counting in such situations immediately raises two concerns. Firstly, neither the sample sizes nor the non-probability sampling methods typically employed in qualitative research would permit reliable statistical inference beyond the sample. Secondly, even if we do turn our back on statistical inference and simply count the sample data, there is still the risk that counting qualitative data leads to the situation where, perhaps subconsciously, numerical frequency displaces understanding and interpretation as the basis of the analysis.

For these and other reasons we suggest that counting should be used with caution in qualitative analysis. Nevertheless, there are situations in which counting may prove a helpful tactic for the qualitative data analyst. Counting can be used to check our own understandings of what is happening in the data. It can be used to help us check for negative evidence and to ensure that we are not relying on some informants, to the exclusion of others. Counting can help us identify patterns that provide inspiration for further (qualitative) investigation. Note that we are not drawing conclusions on the basis of the counts but using them to help us develop our analysis.

In addition, exact counts may be preferable to using vague expressions such as 'many interviewees', or 'the majority of respondents' when reporting results. Remember, however, that the basis of qualitative analysis is interpretation and the understanding of the diversity of a phenomenon, not its frequency. Something that occurs only once in your data may be analytically as important as something that occurs many times. If used with caution and not as the basis for drawing conclusions or making inferences beyond the sample, counting can have a supporting role in qualitative analysis.

14.9.2 Determining the trustworthiness of your findings

Rigorous and disciplined thinking must be carried through into the final stages of your analysis, in the way you determine the credibility of your findings. In Chapter 4 we discussed the question of quality in research and introduced Lincoln and Guba's (1985) suggestions for establishing the trustworthiness of a research study. We recommend that you re-read that section carefully, noting the methods suggested there. In addition, Table 14.8 offers a number of suggestions for testing or confirming your findings.

Table 14.8 Testing and confirming your findings (Lincoln and Guba 1985, Miles and Huberman 1994, Creswell and Miller 2000)

Tactic	Explanation
Triangulation	Triangulation is based on the idea that multiple perspectives on a research situation can be compared to see whether findings can be confirmed. Options include: • data triangulation, comparing multiple sources of evidence (such as different interview respondents or different types of data) • theory triangulation, comparing different theoretical perspectives of the same data • researcher triangulation (checking for agreement between evaluators; see inter-rater reliability on the companion website) • methodological triangulation, comparing findings using different research methods in a multi-method study
Respondent validation	You can use respondent validation (or member checking) at different points in the research, for example, to give respondents an opportunity to comment on interview transcripts or to gain feedback on emerging and/or final findings of your research. Feedback gained may be seen as a way of gathering additional insight into the research findings from the perspective of those involved in the situation rather than as a validation of the 'truth' status of the findings. In applied research projects, you may seek feedback from potential users of the output in terms of its practical relevance
Checking that we have not been biased in our selection of data or been over-influenced by particular sources	It is easy to be influenced by a particularly compelling account or be biased in our selection of data, for example, during coding. Common mistakes include: • overreliance on easily accessible informants • overweighting dramatic events • overweighting evidence that fits the researcher's emerging explanation rather than contradicting it
Weighing the evidence	In some situations we may need to weigh the evidence collected, for example, to resolve conflicting factual accounts. Factors to consider include: • nature of the informants/data sources – how well informed are they about a particular aspect of your topic? • circumstances of data collection – do these impact on the quality of your data? • can you validate the data in some way (e.g. through triangulation)?
Looking for negative (disconfirming) evidence	Be on the look out for evidence that contradicts emerging explanations (the term 'deviant case' is sometimes used to refer to such evidence). How does such evidence affect those explanations? What modifications are necessary to your emerging conclusions?
Checking out rival explanations	Think about rival explanations that may account for what you are finding in your data. Perhaps there is an alternative explanation that is stronger than the one you had developed initially. Here, looking for negative evidence can be helpful
Reflecting on our own role and on the influence on the research process	As discussed in Chapter 1, as researchers we are active agents in the research process, including the analysis and our final account. You can consider including a reflexive account as part of the final report, where you reflect on your role in the research process

14.10 Presenting qualitative data

In this final section of the chapter we look at aspects of presenting the results of your qualitative data analysis. Whilst, overall, you should follow the general guidelines and structure for a research report discussed in Chapter 15, there are some points to bear in mind when reporting qualitative research.

14.10.1 Preserving confidentiality and anonymity

In-depth analysis, small sample sizes and the use of direct quotations from sources can make it especially difficult to preserve the anonymity and confidentiality of respondents when writing up. A single data extract may be enough to reveal the identity of a respondent or an organization to the reader. Ensure that you carefully screen all direct quotations, paraphrases or summaries to guarantee that any identifying references are removed or changed so as to preserve anonymity. In addition, as discussed in Chapter 7, you should use pseudonyms (e.g. Big Bank, Pharmco, etc.) or other designators (such as letters of the alphabet) when referring to particular individuals or organizations. Alternatively, you can use generic descriptions, such as the job role. This requirement can make it difficult when describing your sample, since, both for the credibility of your research and to provide relevant contextual or demographic background, some level of detail may be needed. Table 14.9 gives an example of how respondent anonymity can be balanced with the inclusion of background and contextual details that are relevant to the study.

Table 14.9 Example table showing respondent details

Case	Type	Respondents
CONCO	Construction company	1 senior manager 3 project managers 1 project office staff member
SOFCO	Software engineering company	1 senior manager 4 project managers
DESCO	Design consultancy	2 senior managers 2 project managers 1 project office staff member

14.10.2 Presenting quotations

Verbatim quotations from interviews or other sources will play an important part in your write-up. They can be employed to show the language people use in connection with a particular topic, to illustrate the meanings they attach to what is going on, to indicate how they express their views and to portray the richness of individual accounts (White et al. 2003). Silverman (2010: 347) offers the following advice on presenting verbatim quotations:

- Make one point at a time.
- 'Top and tail' each extract to show how it fits into your analysis, in what we call the 'hamburger' technique.

- Acknowledge any limitations of your data and your analysis of them.
- Convince the reader of the soundness of your interpretation.

Silverman (2010) also suggests numbering your data extracts. This is not universal practice, but can be particularly useful if you are referring to an extract several times and at different points in your write-up.

Quotations should typically be no longer than two or three sentences for most qualitative data analysis (longer extracts may be used in specific techniques such as conversation analysis). Very short extracts can be incorporated into the body of the text; longer ones are best presented as separate blocks of text, indented to make their status as quotations clear to the reader.

14.10.3 Presenting data using visual data displays

Visual data displays can be a very effective way of presenting aspects of your findings to readers. It is important not to over-use them and to remember that they do not constitute analysis on their own. The 'hamburger' method described for presenting quotations should also be used to introduce visual displays and explain their significance. You will also need to make sure that they are clear and easy to follow.

KEY LEARNING POINTS

- The process of qualitative analysis of data begins with data collection and includes organizing, preparing, storing, coding and visualizing your data, as well as drawing conclusions and presenting your findings.
- Analysis can begin during the data collection to support sampling; qualitative data analysis is typically iterative in nature.
- Qualitative research can accumulate a large number of data sources in different formats that require systematic organization prior to analysis. Data must be prepared for analysis; this includes transcribing audio and video recordings.
- Coding helps you to reduce the data and move from raw data to meaningful themes. Hierarchical coding helps you to analyse data at varying but related levels of abstraction.
- Memoing provides a way of capturing your thoughts with respect to coding, emerging theory and operational issues in your analysis.
- Software can help you manipulate and visualize the data. For larger projects in particular, you may consider using a CAQDAS program, although you should be aware of the strengths and weaknesses of such software.
- It can be difficult to analyse and process large sections of text, and cumbersome to communicate your findings effectively using just text. Visual displays help to overcome the limitations of text during analysis and presentation.
- Matrices display data in the form of cross-tabulations, whereas networks display data using nodes and links. We can use additional dimensions to represent time and level of analysis, and we can use formatting and symbols to increase the amount of information conveyed through each display.

- Coding and visual displays can be used together to help you answer your research questions. Matrices and networks help you to identify and compare key concepts, actors and contextual factors when answering 'what' questions. Visual displays also help to explain the effects observed, or why things happened the way they did, to answer 'why' questions. Finally, matrices and networks are useful to capture the sequence of events and activities over time, when analysing process in response to 'how' questions.
- It is essential to verify our findings so as to reassure others of the trustworthiness of our study. Verification techniques include triangulation, respondent validation and looking for negative evidence.
- Presenting qualitative data involves careful attention to respecting commitments to anonymity and confidentiality. Data extracts and visual displays should be presented one at a time using the 'hamburger' technique of introducing, presenting and commenting on the material.

NEXT STEPS

14.1 Getting ready. Organize your data into files and folders, and give them descriptive names. Transcribe your audio and video recordings, if relevant. Type and save your field notes, using the same filing and naming system used for your data files. Decide whether you are going to use software to analyse your data and, if relevant, find out what training or advice is available.

14.2 Familiarizing yourself with your data. Read and re-read your data carefully. Use memos to capture your ideas and emerging themes. Ensure that your memos are cross-referenced with your data, such as a particular point in the transcript, so that you can easily locate and retrieve that piece of data later, if needed.

14.3 Coding your data. Start coding your data. Ensure that you keep an index of your codes and their definitions, including any hierarchical relationships between them. If you rename or change your codes, remember to revisit the coded material to assess whether the chosen label is still relevant.

14.4 Staying organized. Ensure that you save all relevant output. Make a note of preliminary findings in your memos, and of the implications of these findings for your research questions. As you work, keep a detailed log of what you do, to help you write up the final report.

14.5 Reviewing your analysis plan. Review your analysis plan to ensure that it is still appropriate in the light of your data exploration. Decide what changes, if any, need to be made (for example, collect more data). If appropriate, you should discuss these with your supervisor.

14.6 Answering your research questions. Develop visual displays for your data, depending on whether you are pursuing a what, why or how type of project.

a) Experiment with alternative matrices and networks.
b) Develop displays for various level of analysis.
c) Revisit previous displays as the analysis progresses and your understanding of the data improves.
d) Draw out and review the trustworthiness of your conclusions.
e) Keep a log of what you do and save relevant output for your report.

Further reading

For further reading, please see the companion website.

References

Blumer, H. (1954). 'What is wrong with social theory?', *American Sociological Review*, 19(1), 3–10.

Canhoto, A. I. (2007). Profiling behaviour: The social construction of categories in the detection of financial crime (unpublished PhD). London School of Economics.

Charmaz, K. (2006). *Constructing grounded theory*. London: Sage.

Coffey, A., Holbrook, B. and Atkinson, P. (1996). 'Qualitative data analysis: Technologies and representations'. *Sociological Research Online* [online], 1(1). Available from: http://www.socresonline.org.uk/1/1/4.html [accessed 28 April 2014].

Creswell, J. W. and Miller, D. L. (2000). 'Determining validity in qualitative inquiry', *Theory into Practice*, 39(3), 124–30.

Dey, I. (1993). *Qualitative data analysis*. London: Routledge.

Hahn, C. (2008). *Doing qualitative research using your computer: A practical guide*. London: Sage.

King, N. (2004). Using templates in the thematic analysis of text. *In*: Cassell, C. and Symon, G. (eds) *Essential guide to qualitative methods in organizational research*. London: Sage.

Lewins, A. and Silver, C. (2009). 'Choosing a CAQDAS package'. *NCRM Working Paper* [online]. Available from: http://eprints.ncrm.ac.uk/791/1/2009ChoosingaCAQDASPackage.pdf [accessed 7 November 2013].

Lincoln, Y. S. and Guba, E. G. (1985). *Naturalistic inquiry*. Beverly Hills, CA: Sage Publications.

Miles, M. B. and Huberman, M. A. (1994). *Qualitative data analysis*. 2nd edn. Thousand Oaks, CA: Sage.

Poole, M. S., Van de Ven, A. H., Dooley, K. and Holmes, M. E. (2000). *Organizational change and innovation processes*. Oxford: Oxford University Press.

Saldaña, J. (2013). *The coding manual for qualitative researchers*. 2nd edn. London: Sage.

Silverman, D. (2010). *Doing qualitative research: A practical handbook*. 3rd edn. London: Sage Publications.

Strauss, A. and Corbin, J. (1998). *Basics of qualitative research*. 2nd edn. Thousand Oaks, CA: Sage.

ten Have, P. (2007). *Doing conversation analysis*. 2nd edn. London: Sage.

White, C., Woodfield, K. and Ritchie, J. (2003). Reporting and presenting qualitative data. *In*: Ritchie, J. and Lewis, J. (eds) *Qualitative research practice*. London: Sage.

Wilson, H., Daniel, E. and McDonald, M. (2002). 'Factors for success in customer relationship management (CRM) systems', *Journal of Marketing Management*, 18(1–2), 193–219.

Wooffitt, R. (2005). *Conversation analysis and discourse analysis*. London: Sage.

Part V

Communicate

Part V addresses how to communicate the output of your research to interested audiences. As these audiences may vary we look at two specific types of research reporting: an academic report being submitted for assessment as part of an academic qualification, and a report for a practitioner audience. We provide guidance on the structure and content for each and identify the typical differences between them. This is supported by advice and tips on the process of writing and editing. We conclude the chapter with a look at alternative ways of communicating your results.

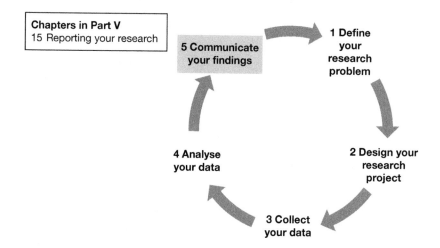

Chapters in Part V
15 Reporting your research

5 Communicate your findings

1 Define your research problem

2 Design your research project

3 Collect your data

4 Analyse your data

15 Reporting your research

CHAPTER SUMMARY

The key topics covered in this chapter are:

- writing for an academic qualification
- writing for a practitioner audience
- writing up your report
- using other ways of reporting your research.

15.1 Introduction

You are now reaching the final stage of your research project. You have collected and analysed your data and the task before you is to communicate your findings. If you cannot do so successfully, then it does not matter how well you have done or how hard you have worked up to this point: people either will never hear of your research or will ignore it if they do. Reporting your research is therefore a key stage in your project. It is also one that can be very demanding, especially if you are new to research. In essence, reporting will involve answering four questions about your research.

1 What? The topic of your research.
2 Why? The problem that your research addresses.
3 How? The research methods you used to carry out your research.
4 So what? The conclusions and recommendations from your findings.

How you communicate the answers to those questions and to what level of detail will depend on the purpose of your project and the audience you are trying to reach. In this chapter we therefore look at different ways of reporting your research, and for different audiences. We begin by looking at written reports, starting with writing for an academic qualification such as a dissertation or thesis. We then discuss what to think about when writing for a practitioner audience, before taking a more detailed look at the writing process itself. We end the chapter by introducing other ways of communicating your research results.

15.2 Writing for an academic qualification

If you are doing your research project as a student researcher you will almost certainly be expected to produce a written report which will form all or part of the assessment for your academic or professional qualification. Depending on the qualification, its level and where you are studying, the report may be referred to as a research project, dissertation or thesis. In the UK, the word dissertation is typically used at Master's-level and thesis at doctoral level; in the USA it is usually the other way around.

Regardless of the terminology, reports written for an academic qualification share a number of characteristics. Firstly, the primary audience for your report will be your supervisor and other academic tutors who will read it in order to assess whether it meets the required standard for your course of study. Make sure therefore that you understand the assessment process and the criteria against which your project will be marked. Secondly, particularly at Master's level and above, you will typically be expected to demonstrate an understanding of existing theory and prior research in your topic area and where your own research fits within that. This is usually assessed by requiring a critical review of the literature in the report. Thirdly, you will have to explain and justify the way you carried out your investigation, usually by way of a section of the report focused on the research design. Finally, you will be required to conform to the structure and format laid down by your academic institution for your particular degree, as we discuss next.

15.2.1 Structure and content of a report for an academic qualification

Although academic institutions and different qualifications vary in terms of their detailed requirements, there is a generic structure that is followed for many academic reports, which we outline in Table 15.1 before discussing key elements in more detail.

Title page

The detailed content of the title page will probably be specified by your academic institution. The one item that you will have freedom over, however, is the title of your report. In your research proposal you will have given your project a working title (Chapter 8) that captured the intention of the research at that point. Now is the time to review that provisional title. Does it still reflect the actual nature of the research undertaken and/or the outcomes? Does the wording convey the essence of what the research is about, including the key concepts or variables involved? Does it need to communicate the context of the research or the method used, so as to help the reader judge its relevance? If the answer to any of those is 'no', you should review and edit your title.

In Research in Practice 15.1 we list the titles of a selection of articles to show different ways in which the writers have presented their work. Note the use of two-part titles, with the parts separated by a colon. This can be used to separate a more general statement of the topic area from details about the specific subject, the research method or the context of the research. It is sometimes employed to separate an attention-grabbing or humorous headline from a more serious statement of the subject matter. As we noted in Chapter 8, however, humour or catchy phrasing should be

Table 15.1 Typical structure and components of a report for an academic qualification

Part	Component	Description
Front matter	Title page	Indicates the title, author and the qualification for which submission of the report forms all or part
	Abstract	A concise summary of the report for the reader
	Acknowledgements	Thanks or other acknowledgements for support or help during the research
	Table of contents	Section and sub-section headings and page numbers
	Lists of tables and figures	If required, lists of tables, figures or other numbered items, with page numbers
	List of abbreviations or technical glossary	If required (may be needed in some research projects, depending on the subject matter)
Body of report	Introduction	Background to the research problem, why it is significant, the overall purpose of your research and the structure of the report
	Literature review	A critical review of the literature in the topic, locating your own research within it and leading into your research questions
	Research questions/ hypotheses	Statement of the specific research questions and, if included, any research hypotheses (often supported by a conceptual model)
	Research design	An overview and justification of the research design used in the project
	Results	Presentation of the results of the analysis, supported by appropriate extracts from the data or output from the analysis. Sometimes combined with discussion into a single section
	Discussion	Discussion of the results of the analysis in the context, for example, of the literature. This section may include a discussion of research limitations
	Conclusions and recommendations	Conclusions of the research in relation to the research questions and recommendations for theory/practice as a result. This section often includes a discussion of research limitations, if not discussed earlier. Suggestions for further research are often made at this point
End matter	Reference list	List of all works cited in the report
	Appendices	Additional information that may be relevant to readers of the report but does not form part of the main body

PART V

RESEARCH IN PRACTICE 15.1

Research titles

Here is a selection of titles from research articles that illustrate different approaches. Consider how effectively the titles communicate to you the nature of the project and how it influences your expectations about the research.

- 'What information can relationship marketers obtain from customer evaluations of salespeople?' (Lambert et al. 1997)
- 'Online customer experience in e-retailing: An empirical model of antecedents and outcomes' (Rose et al. 2012)
- 'Shaken and stirred: A content analysis of women's portrayals in James Bond films' (Neuendorf et al. 2010)
- 'The "coping" capacity management strategy in services and the influence on quality performance' (Armistead and Clark 1994)
- 'Aesthetic labour in interactive service work: Some case study evidence from the "new" Glasgow' (Warhurst et al. 2000)
- 'Factors for success in customer relationship management (CRM) systems' (Wilson et al. 2002)
- 'E-business education at AACSB-affiliated business schools: A survey of programs and curricula' (Etheridge et al. 2001)
- 'Chocs away: Weight watching in the contemporary airline industry' (Tyler and Abbott 1998)
- 'Attitudinal, self-efficacy, and social norms determinants of young consumers' propensity to overspend on credit cards' (Sotiropoulos and d'Astous 2013)

used only if it is likely to be acceptable to the target audience. If you do use the colon method, you should still keep your title concise and to the point.

Abstract

The abstract appears at the start of an academic report or academic journal article. It provides a short, concise and accurate summary of the content of the report. It should allow the potential reader the opportunity to familiarize themselves with the content of your report and decide whether or not to read the full document. Typical content includes:

- the research topic
- the purpose of the research
- outline of the research design
- key findings and conclusions.

The length of the abstract varies. For a short report, a single page is sufficient, although your institution may give specific guidelines or word count. Craswell (2005) suggests that about two-thirds of the abstract should be devoted to the findings and conclusions, but again, you may be given more specific guidance. Abstracts do not normally include figures or references. Along with your title, the abstract is the first thing the reader will encounter, so it is important to get it right. Our suggestion is that you write it last, but not at the last minute: give yourself time to refine and edit it before submission.

Table of contents

This is an essential component of your report and should accurately show all chapters and sub-sections of chapters, along with their page numbers. If appropriate, include lists of tables and figures as well, and a list of abbreviations and technical glossary (as in Table 15.1).

Introduction

The introduction should review the background to the research problem, establish its significance, explain the overall purpose of your research and lead the reader into the report itself by setting out the structure of the document. At the end of the introduction you and your reader will have a shared understanding of what is to follow. Building on ideas by Booth et al. (2008) and Minto (2009), we suggest the following general structure for your introduction:

- Background. Introduce the background to the research problem. In applied research this will relate primarily to the organizational/business context; in pure research relevant context is likely to be the area of theory to which the research will contribute. This part of the introduction should be self-sufficient and non-controversial and establish 'common ground' with the reader (Booth et al. 2008: 235).
- The problem. Introduce the 'complication' (Minto 2009: 27) that disrupts the situation you have described in the background and that gives rise to the problem that motivates your research.
- The solution. This is where you indicate how your research will contribute to resolving the problem. You have two options here (Booth et al. 2008: 241): you can give either a taste of the solution in the form of a brief summary of your findings or a 'promise' of one to come by indicating the overall aims of the research or an outline of your research questions.
- Report structure. Finally, your introduction should provide the reader with the structure of the report, giving indications of the content and running order of chapters or sections.

The length of the introduction depends on the length of the overall report and any word count restrictions or guidance. We illustrate these elements in use in Research in Practice 15.2; for a longer introduction each element should be expanded as required to provide adequate coverage. Your introduction should also be appropriately referenced and make use of supporting data, such as industry statistics, particularly in the background section. In the case of the research into shopping by smartphone reported in Research in Practice 13.6, for example, the introduction included data on online shopping and smartphone usage to set the context for the research.

PART V

RESEARCH IN PRACTICE 15.2

Writing your introduction

Here we show you the way in which we can use the framework to write a short introduction. Note that your own introduction is likely to be much longer and contain more detail under each of the four areas shown in bold type.

Concerns about the environmental impact of commercial waste have emerged in the recent past few years. The United Kingdom currently recycles less than 3 per cent of used portable batteries that are discarded for waste disposal. **[Background]**.

The European Directive on Batteries and Accumulators, however, sets a collection target for commercial organizations of 25 per cent for waste batteries and accumulators for 2012, requiring major improvements in UK collection rates. **[Problem]**.

This research investigates factors inhibiting the UK's ability to meet its obligations under the EU Directive and identifies options for overcoming them. **[Solution]**.

The report is organized . . . **[Structure]**

Literature review

Chapter 3 gave advice on the role of the literature review in research and how to carry one out. We will not repeat all of that advice here but instead stress the need to ensure that your review is successfully integrated into your research report. Remember that if you have adopted a deductive, theory-testing approach your literature review forms the basis for the development of your conceptual model and any hypotheses you are planning to test. In an inductive approach, your literature review will frame the problem and may provide sensitizing concepts that will have informed your data collection and analysis.

Research questions hypotheses

This may be a relatively short section but is very important to the reader's understanding of the research. Here you should state your research questions, numbering them if you have more than one, so that they are clear to the reader. If you have adopted a deductive approach you may also choose this point, rather than the end of the literature review, to present the full version of your conceptual model, along with any hypotheses.

Research design

As we noted earlier, one of the characteristics of academic research reports is that they contain details of the research methods used. This section may go under different labels such as 'research methodology', 'research methods' or 'investigation design', but, whatever the terminology, it should provide a comprehensive account of the research design which will allow the reader to evaluate the approach taken and whether or not it was suitable. Key elements in this section include:

- overall approach to the research, including the philosophical orientation taken (Chapter 4 provides additional guidance on describing your overall approach)
- research design adopted
- sampling method used and details of the sample obtained
- data collection techniques used (such as questionnaire, in-depth interviews), including:
  - o data collection instrument, for example, how you developed your question-naire and the measures used
  - o pre-testing and piloting of your data collection techniques
  - o field procedures used in interviews or observation, or details of questionnaire administration

- data analysis techniques used to analyse your data (although results are not presented until later)
- quality control measures used in the research (see Chapter 4 for additional guidance)
- ethical issues faced and how they were dealt with (for example, gaining informed consent).

The detailed structure of this section and the language that you use should reflect the research design that you have adopted, but the above headings provide an outline structure. Throughout this section you should aim to describe what you did and how you did it, and to justify why that was appropriate. This includes the strategic-level decisions about why a particular research design was chosen and the more tactical-level choices of particular techniques, such as telephone rather than face-to-face interviews.

Results

In this section of your report you provide the reader with the results of your data analysis. You will therefore need to decide what to include. Go back to your research questions and consider how each can best be answered by the data analysis you have carried out. Be selective in what you use and do not overwhelm your reader with too much raw data or pages of graphs, tables or visual displays. Instead include the material that most clearly illuminates the points you wish to convey. Remember that in a research report the data that you present in your results section provide the evidence for your conclusions and subsequent recommendations.

When presenting your results, whether in the form of tables, charts, quotations or visual displays of qualitative data, make sure that you provide supporting commentary. Use the hamburger or sandwich technique as we have recommended in earlier chapters to top and tail each piece of data or analysis output:

- introduce the data
- present the data in a suitable format
- bring out the 'so whats?' by commenting on its relevance.

In addition, if you are using charts, tables or figures, ensure that each is clearly numbered, captioned and referred to in the text.

Think about how you will structure your results section. A common mistake in student projects is simply to organize and report the results one question at a time with each question forming, in effect, a separate section. Aside from taking up a lot of space, it is difficult to convey a coherent message to the reader. Instead, try to group your results into logical sub-sections. When reporting quantitative research, this may involve presenting related questions, such as classification variables, together. In qualitative research you can use your higher-level codes (Chapter 14) to help you structure your results in a thematic way. If you have conducted a mixed methods project you should also think about how to organize your results. For sequential designs, a simple technique is to report each as a separate stage of the project. For parallel mixed method designs, a thematic presentation of the results, in which findings from both the quantitative and qualitative components of the research are discussed together for each theme, may be more suitable.

Discussion

Having presented the output from the analysis of your data, the next section moves to a discussion of the significance of the findings that you have made. Here you are discussing what you have found (via your own research) in relation to existing knowledge and theoretical understanding (identified in your literature review), as well as how it informs your research problem. If your research adopted a deductive approach you should discuss the results of your hypothesis tests and other analysis in terms of the statistical and practical significance in relation to your original conceptual model. If your research adopted an inductive approach, you should discuss the extent to which your findings provided a fresh understanding of the research problem. Revisit your literature review and ask yourself 'are my findings consistent with the existing work on the topic?' If they are, then you can write about the consistency found in your work; if not, then discuss how your findings diverge or are different from existing theory. In your discussion section, try to be aware of the difference between description of your findings and your interpretation of them. Description merely retells what is in the data; interpretation brings out what is significant about them.

Conclusions and recommendations

The focus of the conclusions section is on the contribution of your research to answering the research questions. It can therefore be helpful to start your conclusions section with a brief reminder of the research problem and research questions that you set at the start of the project and to structure the presentation of your conclusions so that they clearly answer the research questions. A mistake sometimes made at this point is to confuse conclusions with findings. Your findings are the outputs from your data analysis. The conclusions are statements that are based on these findings. For example, the findings of a survey may be that '85 per cent of men compared to 30 per cent of women' prefer to shop online. Further analysis suggests that this difference is both statistically and practically significant for the target population. From these findings we conclude that there are gender differences in the usage of online retail websites amongst the target population.

Your conclusions should form the basis on which you make any recommendations regarding your research problem. In pure research, this may involve drawing out the implications for the existing theory in your topic area and how it may need to change to accommodate the results of your project. In applied research, on the other hand, the focus of the recommendations will be in the area of management practice. Ensure that your recommendations are grounded in your research findings and avoid speculation that is not justified by your own research.

The conclusions section should include a discussion of any limitations of your research (although this may also be done in the discussion section) by reflecting on your research in the light of the quality criteria for research discussed in Chapter 4. No research is perfect, and it is important to be reflective about limitations in your own research, for example, in relation to your sampling strategy or data collection procedures. Finally, you can end your report by discussing how further research may be undertaken in order to progress the investigation of the research problem or to further understand some of the new insights thrown up by your research findings.

Reference list

Referencing is a key part of academic writing. Ensure that you follow the guidelines in Chapter 3 and include a full reference list (or bibliography if required) in the format expected by your institution.

Appendices

Your appendices should contain information that the reader may need to access but that is not part of your main report. Typical material includes:

- copies of your data collection instrument (questionnaire, interview guide etc.)
- additional output from your analysis (such as more detailed SPSS tables) to support the analysis in the main body
- examples of briefing letters sent to participants and informed consent forms to document procedures that were followed.

The decision about what to include in your appendices is yours, and you need to be selective in what you include in order that the appendices do not grow too large. In most institutions the appendices and reference lists do not form part of the final word count but this should not be a reason to pack them too full. Make sure that you title and number all appendices, cross-reference them in the main text and include them in your table of contents.

PART V

15.2.2 Telling the story

Table 15.1 has provided a formal structure for your report, but you will also need to think about the storyline for your research report. This storyline should take the reader along a journey from the research problem, via the literature and your research design, to your results and conclusions. This means not developing each section of the report in isolation but seeing instead how they link together to provide a coherent account of your research. You also need to communicate that to the reader. A good introduction will help, but, especially in a long report, you should also provide regular signposts or pointers in the report that enable the reader to keep on track. You should also think about the 'shape' of your report. Bem (2003) uses the analogy of an hourglass to describe this idea. The report begins with the broader background to the problem and increasingly narrows its focus through the literature review to the research questions. The research design and results sections are the 'neck' of the hourglass, which starts to broaden out again as you discuss your findings, move on to conclusions and recommendations and, finally, recommendations for further research. By thinking of the hourglass shape of your research report you can avoid losing focus at the critical point where you present your own research design and your results whilst ensuring that the research is placed in context.

15.3 Writing for a practitioner audience

Communicating the results of your research to practitioners is an important part of many research projects. For some projects, particularly in commercial or policy-making environments, practitioners rather than academics will be the primary audience. Even if your project is for an academic qualification, you may still be expected to communicate your results to other stakeholders, such as members of the organization that requested the research or supported it in other ways. In other situations you may have offered to share your findings with research participants. An academic research report is unlikely to be suitable for a broader audience because of its size, style and focus. Instead you will need to produce a report (or more than one) tailored to the needs of a different audience.

15.3.1 Understand your audience

You should start, therefore, by understanding what your audience expects. If you have carried out the research for a client organization, you should have agreed the reporting format in the planning stage, so you should revisit that agreement and confirm that it is still applicable. If not, you should discuss the format with the intended recipient if possible or, if not, seek guidance from experienced colleagues, other researchers, your supervisor or others who have produced similar reports in the past. You should also consider whether a single format will suit everyone. You may, for example, need to tailor your report to meet the needs of particular groups; for example, a very short non-technical summary for a broad audience and a more detailed report containing recommendations for managers wanting to use your research to support their decision making or as a basis for setting future policy.

15.3.2 *Structure and content of a practitioner report*

Given the diversity of potential audiences, a practitioner report can take many different formats. It will still need to address the four key questions of what you did, why you did it, how you did it and what your conclusions were, but the emphasis will be different compared to an academic report. Table 15.2 shows what a typical practitioner research report might include.

Table 15.2 Structure and content of a typical practitioner report

Part	Component	Description
Front matter	Title page	Indicates the title and author
	Executive summary	A concise, non-technical summary of the report for the reader (replaces the academic abstract)
	Table of contents	Section headings and page numbers. Keep this simple
	Lists of tables and figures	If required, lists of tables, figures or other numbered items, with page numbers. Only include in longer reports
	List of abbreviations or technical glossary	If required (may be needed in some research projects, depending on the subject matter)
Body of report	Introduction	Background to the research problem, why it is significant, the overall purpose of your research and the structure of the report, emphasizing the practice-related dimensions of the research rather than the literature-related ones
	Method	A brief, non-technical overview of how the research was done
	Findings	Non-technical presentation of the research findings; more detailed analysis
	Conclusions and recommendations	Conclusions of the research in relation to the practical dimensions of the research problem; presentation of recommendations
End matter	Reference list	List of any works cited in the report; number-format referencing may be more suitable for a practitioner report
	Appendices	Additional information that may be relevant to readers of the report but does not form part of the main body (if required)

PART V

You will notice three key differences in structure and content, as compared to an academic report (Table 15.1). Firstly, an executive summary replaces the academic abstract. This is not just a change in name. An executive summary is intended to be read by a busy reader such as the CEO or head of policy who wishes to understand the project in an efficient and quick way. It should provide a non-technical summary of the report that can be understood by a competent lay reader without specialist expertise. The executive summary should typically cover the following:

1 What the research was about.
2 Why the research was done.
3 How it was done.
4 Main conclusions drawn from the research.
5 Recommendations made as a result.

Keep the executive summary short, and focus on those aspects of the project that are relevant to your audience. Note that for very large research reports, such as a major policy review, the executive summary may be somewhat longer and issued as a separate document.

The second area of difference is the absence of a literature review. This does not mean that the research project did not include one, but a formal literature review does not usually form part of a report intended for a practitioner audience (unless one is requested). In some research projects a literature review is included as an appendix or issued as a separate document for those who are interested. If, however, you are writing a practitioner-style report to be included as part of an assessment for an academic or professional qualification you may still be expected to include some discussion of literature in the main body. Ensure that you understand what is required if that is the case.

The third area of difference is the method section. This is usually much briefer and less technical than the academic equivalent. It should give the reader an outline of the key features of how the research was conducted, but not attempt to provide an in-depth, critical discussion of design issues. More details can be given in an appendix, if required.

In general, reports for a practitioner audience should focus on what is relevant to that audience. That will usually mean addressing the implications of your research for practice rather than engaging in 'academic argument' (Craswell 2005: 142). As a result, writing a practitioner report can be very demanding because it involves hard decisions about what is included and what has to be left out. Always start by understanding your audience's perspective when writing your report.

15.4 The process of writing

If you are new to research, you may find the idea of writing a lengthy report quite daunting. Even if you are used to writing big documents, preparing a research report may be new to you. In this section we will therefore offer some guidance on the process of writing and share some techniques that may be useful.

15.4.1 Understanding what is expected

Begin the planning process by reviewing any guidelines that you have been given regarding your report. For an academic qualification these will normally include recommended section headings and a maximum word count. Indicative content and word count within each section may also be provided. Alternatively, a percentage split for the marking may suggest the approximate length of each section. Knowledge of the allocation of words per section enables you to set a target for your writing. Exceeding (or falling short) of that target will alert you to the likelihood that your final report is going to be unbalanced in terms of the contribution of the main sections. If no written guidance is available, discuss expectations with your supervisor or other the intended recipient of the report. Tables 15.1 and 15.2 can also be used to help you decide on an overall structure. At this point you should also remind yourself of the criteria by which your report will be assessed, if it is for a qualification, or revisit any commitments you have made regarding deliverables in your research proposal.

15.4.2 Planning what you are going to write

The guidelines may provide an outline structure for your report but you still have to decide what to write, to create your storyline linking the different parts together and establishing a logical flow between them. You will also need to plan what you are going to say in each section. To help you do this, we recommend that you start by developing an outline plan for your report using one or more of the following techniques.

Develop a linear outline for your report

Developing a sequential, linear outline is the most obvious way of developing your overall report content. Start by listing all of the major section headings for your report; usually this will be based on guidelines you have been given. Next, identify what each section should contain and list these as sub-headings. Note what each sub-section will cover, adding sub-sub-headings if necessary. Note the planned word count for each section. Now review the structure to check that the flow is logical and that you have covered all of the key points that need to be made. Check also that the balance between the sections is appropriate, for instance, in terms of the word count. The main advantage of linear outlines is that they provide an immediate structure for you to write against. They are also easy to create in a word processing package. The disadvantage is that it can be difficult to visualize the connections between the parts of the report. In addition, creating a linear structure very early can lock you into a way of organizing your report that later may turn out to be unsuitable.

Use visual mapping techniques

Visual mapping techniques are an alternative planning device that can help you to make connections and visualize the relationships between the different components of your report. Mind mapping (Buzon 2006) is a very useful technique for doing this. Start with a blank sheet of paper. In the centre of the paper write the title of your report (or the relevant section heading if you are mapping only a part of it). Draw some lines coming out of the central title and label each one with your proposed section headings. Add branches to each line to represent sub-headings or the key content that will be included. Continue this until you have mapped out the report or the section in sufficient detail. You can use colour, arrows, pictures and so on to help you develop your thinking. A mind map can capture a whole report on a single piece of paper, making it easier to see how the different components fit together and to gain sense of the coverage. Mind maps can be drawn by hand or using one of the specialist software packages available. Figure 15.1 shows an example of a mind map developed for this chapter by one of the authors.

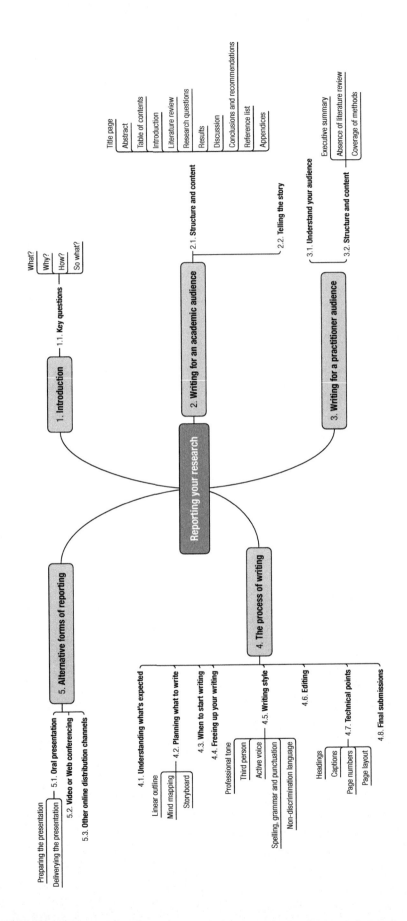

PART V

Figure 15.1 Example mind map

Developing a storyboard

In this technique you start working on the structure of your report by viewing it as a story which you are creating on a series of 'boards'. This is very similar to how film-makers or advertisers develop a storyline for a film or advert. It involves the following steps (Hunter 2009):

- On a large, blank piece of paper draw a series of boxes. Alternatively, you can use sticky notes or PowerPoint slides.
- Each box represents a section or sub-section of your report.
- In each box, write down the main point it will cover, e.g. 'impact of changes in information technology'.
- Next, rewrite the points as active phrases to indicate what you plan to cover in that section, e.g. 'describe how changes in information technology are impacting on the decision to outsource'.
- Add notes on key content, including data, key references and so on that you will include in the section.
- Check the structure and the flow. Reorder or regroup sections and sub-sections as necessary.

Using sticky notes or PowerPoint slides gives more flexibility to rearrange the structure and to add or remove sections as required. The completed storyboard then becomes the structure for your report. Storyboarding provides some of the flexibility of visual display techniques, whilst offering the sequential structure of a linear outline.

15.4.3 When to start writing your final report

Even a small research project report can take lot of time and effort to write, so do not leave it until the end of your project, and definitely not just before the submission deadline. Instead, start writing your research report as your project progresses or, as a colleague told one of the authors, don't write up, write down. In other words, write as you go. As well as using your research diary to record what you have been doing and your emerging thinking about your research questions, start drafting the major report sections as you carry out the work. Composing the final report then becomes more a matter of structuring, crafting and editing than just brute writing. Not only can this make it easier for you to hit your delivery deadline, it can also help you to create a better-quality report.

Writing can also help you to develop your ideas, and once they are on paper it is easier to share them with others and get feedback, so start early in the project. Once you have started, try to write regularly, every day if possible, to form what Creswell (2009: 80) calls the 'habit of writing'. Not only does this give you practice in writing, it can help you not to lose contact with your project and so find it hard to get started again.

15.4.4 Freeing up your writing

It can be hard sometimes to find time to write, so it is incredibly frustrating to find that the words will not come when you do sit down at the computer. Free writing is one technique that can be helpful in such situations (Wolcott 2001). As its name suggests, it involves writing freely without stopping to check for spelling or grammar. It means silencing what is sometimes called the 'internal editor', that voice inside us that keeps telling us to stop, go back and edit something. Write freely for a short period, such as 10 or 15 minutes. It is better to begin writing by getting your ideas onto the page and then editing them later. As Creswell suggests (2009), if you have an hour to write something, it is better to write four drafts, one every quarter of an hour, than just one which is usually written in the final 15 minutes. As the old saying goes: don't get it right, get it written. Once it is written, you can improve and refine it.

15.4.5 Writing style

Whether writing for practitioner or for academic purposes, you should always write as clearly and concisely as possible. Here we offer some tips on writing style for your report:

- Professional tone. Research reports should not normally contain slang, colloquialisms or jargon. Where technical, industry or other specialist terms, including acronyms, need to be used they should be defined clearly and a glossary should be added if necessary.
- Write in the third person. It is still standard to write reports in the third person in business situations. Although there is more latitude in this respect than previously, you should use the third person unless advised or invited to do otherwise.
- Use the active voice. Where possible, use the active rather than the passive voice when writing.
- Spelling, grammar and punctuation. Check your report thoroughly for errors. Your report should be free from spelling mistakes and basic grammatical errors. Watch for punctuation, in particular the correct use of apostrophes, commas, colons and semi-colons. If you are concerned about the accuracy of your written English you should ask someone to check your work at the draft stage.
- Non-discriminatory language. When writing your report you should ensure that you avoid language bias or language that is discriminatory towards groups or individuals. For example, your language should be gender neutral, using terms such as flight attendant rather than air hostess or staff rather than manpower.

15.4.6 Editing

Editing should take place at both macro and micro levels. At the macro level, changes involve looking at the overall structure and the sequence of the report. Here you should focus on the logic of the storyline, the flow between sections and the appropriateness of the weight given to each section. Check your report against any marking criteria or other guidelines. Micro-level editing involves looking at the structure of sections and paragraphs, the logic of the arguments presented and issues of style such as grammar, punctuation and language use.

We strongly recommend that you prepare a draft of your work, either in sections/chapters or as a whole, and have this read by someone else. This can be particularly helpful in identifying areas where your writing is not clear or where you fail to explain a key concept adequately. If you are a student researcher you may be entitled to have drafts of your work read by your supervisor. Do take advantage of this but make sure that you allow sufficient time for your supervisor to review and return work and for you to make any changes as a result. When preparing and circulating drafts, make sure that you keep track of the different versions and always work on the latest one.

15.4.7 Technical points

As well as the structure and content of your report you will have to ensure that it is correctly formatted. Review any specific guidance that you have been given. Important points to note include the following:

- Headings. Use text formatting such as bold and italics to emphasize your headings and any hierarchy. Consider numbering your headings. For most reports, up to three numbered levels (as in this book) will be adequate.
- Captions. Ensure that you number and caption all figures and tables and use the figure and table numbers when referring to them in the text.
- Page numbers. Include page numbers; if not specified by a required format, place the page number in the header or footer on the right (or outside if printing double-sided).
- Page layout. Confirm what is expected regarding page layout. Points to consider include:
  o *Margins.* If your report is to be bound, you may need to have a larger left (or inside) margin.
  o *Line spacing.* For drafts and reports for academic qualifications 1.5 or double line spacing may be expected.
  o *Font.* If font type and size are not specified, use a clear, easy-to-read font such as Ariel or Times New Roman in 11 or 12 point.

15.4.8 Final submission

Lastly, make sure that you are aware of and follow any special instructions for final submission of your report, including supporting documentation if required. Allow sufficient time for binding and delivery if a bound copy has to be provided.

15.5 Alternative forms of reporting

Whilst the conventional form of research reporting is to provide a written document, alternative forms of reporting can also be used to share your research with others. We consider three here: oral presentation, video or web conferencing and other online distribution channels.

15.5.1 Oral presentation

Most often an oral presentation is prepared in conjunction with a more detailed written report. Do not be tempted merely to repeat or read the written report. The value of a face-to-face presentation is to provide richness and clarity, along with the opportunity to respond to questions or discuss particular points in depth. Presentations may range

PART V

from informal discussions with a key stakeholder in the research, through to very formal presentations to a large group. The audience may be made up of practitioners, such as the members of a client organization, or it may be composed of academics, for example, at a research colloquium or academic conference. Here we provide you with some points to consider when preparing to give an oral presentation.

Preparing the presentation

Ensure that you are clear about the purpose of the presentation. Consider the audience for your research and what their expectations are. Who is in the audience? How big will the audience be? What aspect of the research will be most relevant to them? Will a formal or informal style be appropriate? If you are presenting a piece of research undertaken by you as a student researcher in an organization you may need to agree in advance with the organization what particular topics it is appropriate for you to cover.

- Establish how much time you have available for your presentation and any expectations regarding format, time allowance for questions and what aspects of your research are of particular interest.
- Plan the structure of your presentation carefully. Think about the storyline you will use to convey your message. Make sure that you prepare a clear introduction that leads the audience into the presentation and an effective conclusion that leaves the audience with a clear understanding of your key points.
- Use visual aids thoughtfully (e.g. diagrams or graphs), to elaborate and clarify what you are saying. Do not make slides overly complicated or too 'busy' with too much text or elaborate graphics.
- If using slides, do not have too many. A useful rule of thumb when planning is to allow at least two minutes per slide.
- Practise your presentation in advance, for example, by doing a rehearsal in front of colleagues.

Delivering the presentation

When presenting, do not merely read out the slides in the presentation. Instead, use the slides as prompts to ensure your key messages are received and understood. During your presentation ensure that you maintain good eye contact with your audience, looking at them rather than at any slides or other visual aids you are using. Speak confidently and at a pace that allows your audience to follow what is being said. Ensure that you allow sufficient time for questions and discussion after your presentation.

If you are not an experienced presenter, seek advice from colleagues, tutors or others who can help you to prepare and deliver an effective presentation. Whatever else, it is worth heeding consultant Peter Block's advice about presenting research:

> The mistake with most presentations is that they are too long and too intricate. When we have spent all that time analysing data, we fall in love with it. . . . Go ahead and fall in love with your data – but don't tell everyone about it. Keep it short and simple.
>
> Block (2000: 228)

PART V

15.5.2 Video or web conferencing

It may be that the audience for your research includes people who are widely distributed geographically, for example, management of the organization in overseas locations for whom you have conducted the research. With the capability of communication technology today it is possible to provide presentations efficiently to a wide audience. Webinar systems enable the presenter to load and deliver a slide presentation using audio and visual channels (via webcam). All participants are able to access and view the slides, although the order and pace of presentation is controlled by the presenter. The presenter provides an oral presentation to all participants and questions and answers can be enabled via either voice or text (depending on the system being used). There are a number of advantages and disadvantages to such web-based reporting of research, as summarized in Table 15.3.

Table 15.3 Advantages and disadvantages of web-conference research presentations

Advantages	Disadvantages
• Able to reach a geographically dispersed audience	• May be less engaging for participants than a face-to-face presentation
• Cost-efficiency in terms of time and money	• Lack of visual cues from the audience can make it difficult for the presenter to judge pace and audience reaction
• Useful for short, immediate feedback of research findings or update on an on-going research project	• Control of the flow of questions and discussion can be difficult for the presenter, so interactions in a large group may be limited
• Can allow for two-way discussion between participants and for the capture of feedback (either audio or text, depending on the technology being used)	

15.5.3 Other online distribution channels

The capability of the Internet today enables us all to upload and share content of all types. This opens up new ways of sharing our research findings, for example, by self-publishing our research report via a personal website, sharing it via social media sites or through the websites of commercial or other organizations. This can allow the dissemination of findings to a much wider audience, if required. Neither are we limited to written formats; videos, podcasts, slide shows and other formats can also be used to share our research with others. Before doing so, however, you must always consider the confidentiality of the report and any agreements that you have made regarding who has access to it. Equally important, you must respect the confidentiality and privacy of research participants. If you intend to place the results of your research on the Internet, this information should be included in the briefing documents, and in your report you must ensure that it is not possible to identify the research participants or their organization from the material you publish online. We discuss the growth of Internet-based dissemination of research in Critical Commentary 15.1.

PART V

CRITICAL COMMENTARY 15.1

Disseminating research

In Chapter 1 we introduced you to the distinction between pure and applied research. Today in the UK and other countries there is a discernible move towards trying to achieve impact from pure research beyond the academic domain, where impact can be understood as 'the demonstrable contribution that excellent research makes to society and the economy' (RCUK 2013).

One way in which impact may be increased is by using more immediate and accessible forms of communication to reach wider audiences. An example of where this is occurring is via 'open access' forms of publication. In this context, open access is a term used to refer to the process of making scholarly articles freely available to everyone via the Internet. This may be via open-access journals or via e-documents made available via authors' websites or other repositories (Antelman 2004). This act of freeing up the channel of publication is fraught with many concerns on the part of academics, institutions and publishers. Concerns include the effect that this approach may have on the 'gold standard' of peer-reviewed articles, issues of copyright, the costs associated with publication, fees to authors and revenue to publishers.

Despite this, scholars and researchers are turning to open access to disseminate their work more freely. However, we can ask if opening up the channel of access will in itself increase the flow of knowledge from the pure to the applied domain. Some issues still remain, such as: will a wider audience necessarily understand the language of pure research? Should such research be made available in different formats? Who will make the assessment of the quality and standard of the research? Whilst these are concerns to be addressed as the practice of open access develops, it is obvious that practitioners can benefit from wider access to knowledge derived from outside their own organization or sphere of interest. Watch this (web) space.

KEY LEARNING POINTS

- At the end of a research project we need to communicate the outcomes to as wide an audience as possible, which may be academic or practitioner.
- A report for an academic qualification (often referred to as a thesis or dissertation) will have a specific structure, often dictated by the academic institution to which it will be submitted. It will be relatively detailed and will provide the reader with a review of the theoretical support for the research undertaken and full technical information regarding the research method applied and data analysis. A discussion of the relevance of the findings to both existing theoretical knowledge and current practice, with conclusions drawn, will be included.
- A practitioner report is likely to be shorter and more succinct. It will focus more on the practitioner's problem or opportunity that is the focus of the research and how the findings provide useful input to solutions.
- A number of techniques are available to help the researcher to prepare a written report. These include linear outline, storyboarding and mind maps.

PART V

- Whilst most research continues to be disseminated via written report and/or oral presentation, technology now enables us to use alternative channels through which to reach our audience(s). These include video recordings (potentially distributed online), webinars and teleconferences or podcasts. In the field of pure research, open access publication is now enabling a wider dissemination of research outputs.

NEXT STEPS

15.1 **Understanding what is required.** Locate any guidance document that you have been given by your institution for your qualification or other requirements for your research report. Read it thoroughly and find out the following points.

- Is there a required/suggested structure for the document? If so, look at it and consider how the proposed chapters/sectors relate to your own research.
- If there is no template structure provided to you, look back at Table 15.1 and Table 15.2 and create an outline structure for your report.

15.2 **Planning your report.** Use one or more of the planning techniques discussed in this chapter to develop the overall structure for your report. Make notes of the content that will occupy each section.

15.3 **Get writing.** Choose one of the sections of your report and try free writing on the topic for 10–15 minutes. After your session, reflect on the process and recognize the degree to which your 'internal editor' is influencing your flow of writing.

15.4 **Developing a timetable for writing.** Set out a time schedule for your writing and aim to generate some form of written output on a regular schedule (daily, every two days or weekly).

15.5 **Presenting your research.** If you are not already required to do so, find an opportunity to present your research to interested parties, for example, at a research colloquium or seminar. Use the opportunity to get feedback on your research to date.

Further reading

For further reading, please see the companion website.

References

Antelman, K. (2004). 'Do open-access articles have a greater research impact?', *College and Research Libraries*, 65(5), 372–82.
Armistead, C. G. and Clark, G. (1994). 'The "coping" capacity management strategy in services and the influence on quality performance', *International Journal of Service Industry Management*, 5(2), 5–22.

PART V

Bem, D. (2003). Writing the empirical journal article. *In:* Darley, J., Yanna, M. and Roediger III, H. (eds) *The compleat academic: A practical guide for the beginning social scientist.* Washington, DC: Americal Psychological Association.

Block, P. (2000). *Flawless consulting.* 2nd edn. San Francisco, CA: Pfeiffer.

Booth, W. C., Colomb, G. G. and Williams, J. M. (2008). *The craft of research.* Chicago, IL: University of Chicago Press.

Buzon, T. (2006) *Mind Mapping.* Harlow: BBC Archive.

Craswell, G. (2005). *Writing for academic success.* London: Sage.

Creswell, J. W. (2009). *Research design.* 3rd edn. Los Angeles, CA: Sage.

Etheridge, H. L., Hsu, K. H. Y. and Wilson Jr, T. E. (2001). 'E-business education at AACSB-affiliated business schools: A survey of programs and curricula', *Journal of Education for Business,* 76(6), 328–31.

Hunter, I. (2009). *Write that essay.* North Ryde, NSW: McGraw-Hill.

Lambert, D. M., Sharma, A. and Levy, M. (1997). 'What information can relationship marketers obtain from customer evaluations of salespeople?', *Industrial Marketing Management,* 26(2), 177–87.

Minto, B. (2009). *The pyramid principle.* 3rd edn. Harlow: Pearson.

Neuendorf, K. A., Gore, T. D., Dalessandro, A., Janstova, P. and Snyder-Suhy, S. (2010). 'Shaken and stirred: A content analysis of women's portrayals in James Bond films', *Sex Roles,* 62(11–12), 747–61.

RCUK (2013). *What do research councils mean by 'impact'?* [online]. Research Councils (UK). Available from: www.rcuk.ac.uk/kei/impacts/Pages/meanbyimpact.aspx [Accessed 12 November 2013].

Rose, S., Clark, M., Samouel, P. and Hair, N. (2012). 'Online customer experience in e-retailing: An empirical model of antecedents and outcomes', *Journal of Retailing,* 88(2), 308–22.

Sotiropoulos, V. and d'Astous, A. (2013). 'Attitudinal, self-efficacy, and social norms determinants of young consumers' propensity to overspend on credit cards', *Journal of Consumer Policy,* 36(2), 179–96.

Tyler, M. and Abbott, P. (1998). 'Chocs away: Weight watching in the contemporary airline industry', *Sociology,* 32(3), 433–50.

Warhurst, C., Nickson, D., Witz, A. and Cullen, A. M. (2000). 'Aesthetic labour in interactive service work: Some case study evidence from the "new"' Glasgow', *The Service Industries Journal,* 20(3), 1–18.

Wilson, H., Daniel, E. and McDonald, M. (2002). 'Factors for success in customer relationship management (CRM) systems', *Journal of Marketing Management,* 18, 193–219.

Wolcott, H. F. (2001). *Writing up qualitative research.* Thousand Oaks, CA: Sage.

PART V

Glossary

a priori codes In qualitative data analysis, codes that have been developed prior to analysis (e.g. from the literature).

Abduction/Abductive approach An approach to research involving inference to the best explanation response to an observed anomaly and characterized by the interplay of theory and observation. The terms retroduction and retroductive approach are sometimes used as alternatives to abduction and abductive approach.

Action research A research design involving collaborative partnership between researcher and a group in a cyclical process of joint planning, action, observation and reflection that contributes to actionable knowledge for both the practitioner and academic communities.

Alternative (alternate) hypothesis Another term for the research hypothesis.

Analytic survey A survey study that tests theories by investigating the associations between variables of interest.

Axiology The study of values.

Bar chart A chart showing data in the form of a vertical or horizontal bar used for displaying frequency counts or other data.

Bias A systematic error in a particular direction.

Bibliography A list of all the works consulted during the preparation of the report, whether cited in the text or not.

Bimodal A frequency distribution with two modes (peaks).

Bivariate analysis The analysis of two variables simultaneously.

Box plot A chart showing summary measures of an ordinal or metric variable's distribution. Also known as box-and-whisker plots.

CAQDAS Computer-aided qualitative data analysis software.

Case In sampling, an element within a sample. Also referred to as an observation. In case study research, the case which is the object of the study.

Case study A research design involving the study of a relatively small number of naturally occurring cases, in depth and in context, often using multiple sources of evidence.

Causal description   Identifying that a causal relationship exists between X and Y.

Causal explanation   An explanation of how X causes Y, for example in terms of causal mechanisms.

Causal mechanism   Causal mechanisms explain how and why a hypothesized cause contributes to an effect.

Census   Research which collects data from all members of the target population.

Chi-square (χ^2) test of independence   Significance test of association between two categorical variables (non-parametric).

Closed questions   Questions with a set of predefined responses from which to answer.

Cluster analysis   A multivariate statistical analysis technique used to sort cases (e.g. respondents to a questionnaire) into groups whose members have similar properties.

Cluster sampling   A form of probability sampling in which the target population is grouped into clusters from which a sample is drawn, before further sampling from each cluster.

Clustered bar chart   A bar chart in which the observations for each category are clustered side-by-side.

Code   A numerical or textual label applied to segments of raw data to facilitate subsequent analysis.

Coding   1) In quantitative analysis, the process of assigning meaningful numerical values to non-quantitative data (such as responses to open-ended questions) to facilitate analysis. 2) In qualitative analysis, the process of applying thematic codes to data segments.

Coding schedule   A document that specifies which actions or behaviours are to be recorded during an observation and how they will be categorized.

Coefficient of determination (R^2)   In regression analysis, a measure of what per cent of the variability in the dependent variable is explained by the regression model.

Coefficient of variation   A measure of dispersion for metric data: usually calculated as the standard deviation divided by the mean; it can be used to compare the degree of dispersion between variables measured on different scales.

Computer simulation   The use of computer software to model the behaviour of a real-world process or system.

Concept   A mental category that groups observations or ideas together on the basis of shared attributes.

Conceptual model   Diagrammatic representation of a theory or real-world phenomenon, usually identifying concepts (variables) and their relationships.

Confidence interval   An interval estimate, giving a range of plausible values for a population parameter to a given confidence level (typically 95 per cent).

Confirmability   A dimension of trustworthiness. Showing that the findings of the study are shaped by the respondents and not by researcher bias, motivation or interest.

Confirmation bias   The tendency for the collection or analysis of data to be biased in a way that confirms the researcher's preconceived opinion.

Constant comparison   In grounded theory, the process of constantly comparing emerging theory with data.

Construct validity   The extent to which a measure actually measures the underlying concept that it is intended to measure.

Content analysis   A research design for the systematic analysis of text through the application of a structured coding scheme for purposes of description or prediction. Used here to refer to quantitative content analysis; a variant form is qualitative content analysis.

Content validity   The extent to which a measure captures all of the dimensions of the concept that it is intended to measure.

Contingency table   A cross-tabulation showing the relationship between two or more variables and displaying the frequency counts and/or per cents for each combination of categories. Described in terms of the number of rows × number of columns (r × c), so a 3 × 4 contingency table has three rows and four columns.

Control group   In an experiment, a group that does not receive treatment.

Convenience sampling   A non-probability sampling method in which participants are chosen on the basis of their accessibility or availability.

Convergent validity   The extent to which a measure for one concept is correlated with another measure that measures the same underlying concept. Contrast with discriminant validity.

Conversation analysis   The detailed study of talk in interaction.

Correlation   A relation between two entities (e.g. two variables) such that they vary together. A positive correlation means that as the value of one increases, so does the other; a negative correlation means that as the value of one decreases, the other increases.

Correlational study   A non-experimental quantitative research design in which the researcher measures two or more variables as they exist naturally for a set of individual cases (e.g. people) and then tests the association between them. (Note that the analysis procedures used in these studies are not limited to correlation but include regression analysis and related techniques.)

Cramer's V   Measure of the strength of association between two categorical variables (non-parametric).

Credibility   A dimension of trustworthiness. Giving confidence in the 'truth' of the findings, in terms of the alignment between the researcher's findings and the lives and experiences of respondents.

Criterion validity   The extent to which a measure of a chosen variable predicts the value of another variable known to be related, for example, how well a score on a course entry test predicts performance on that course.

Critical discourse analysis   A form of discourse analysis that investigates the relationships between text and talk and wider social relations, practices and structures.

Critical incident technique (CIT)   A technique that can be used to investigate significant happenings identified by the interviewee and how they were managed, why they happened, what the consequences were and so forth.

Cronbach's (coefficient) alpha   A measure of reliability of multi-item scales.

Cross-sectional study   A study in which data is gathered at a single, specific point in time. Also known as a one-shot study. Contrast with a longitudinal study.

Data collection instrument   A means by which we collect research data, such as a questionnaire.

Data matrix   Visual display in which the data are presented as a cross-tabulation.

Data reduction   Techniques to make large datasets more manageable by identifying the aspects of the raw data that are relevant for the project at hand.

Data transformation   In quantitative data analysis, the process of changing the format of the original data to a new format to facilitate analysis or reporting.

Deductive approach   A research approach that seeks to test theory against data.

Degrees of freedom (df)   The number of values that are free to vary when calculating some common test statistics (such as the t-test).

Dependability   A dimension of trustworthiness. Demonstrating that the findings are consistent and could be repeated.

Dependent variable   The variable that is identified as the effect; it is dependent on changes in other variables. Also referred to as the outcome variable. Conventionally labelled Y in diagrams, graphs and mathematical models.

Descriptive statistics   Statistical techniques used to analyse, summarize and report sample data.

Descriptive survey   A survey study that generates a description of phenomena in terms of the distribution of variables of interest.

Digital Object Identifier (DOI)   A unique digital identifier for an electronic document such as a book or journal article.

Directional hypothesis   A hypothesis in which the expected direction of the association is specified (e.g. A is greater than B, or X is positively associated with Y).

Directionality problem   The problem of deciding, if two variables co-vary, which one is the cause and which is the effect.

Discourse   A term with a wide variety of meanings. Used here to refer to the linguistic and other social practices that constitute the objects and subjects to which they refer.

Discourse analysis   The study of discourse. See also critical discourse analysis.

Discriminant validity   The extent to which a measure for one concept is not correlated with another measure that measures a different underlying concept. Contrast with convergent validity.

Dummy variable In regression analysis, an independent variable with two levels coded 0 and 1 used to incorporate the effect of different levels of a nominal variable (such as gender).

Ecological validity The extent to which findings from a research in an artificial environment, such as a laboratory, hold in natural settings, such as the home or workplace.

Effect size The magnitude of the effect being measured, such as the difference between pre- and post-treatment in an experiment.

Emic perspective Adopting the perspective of those in involved in the situation being investigated. Often associated with qualitative research.

Empiricism The view that valid knowledge must be based on observation and experience.

Epistemology Epistemology refers to questions of how we know what we claim to know.

Ethnography Used here to refer to a research approach involving in-depth investigation of a culture-sharing group in which participant observation and/or informal interviews play a significant role.

Ethnomethodology The study of how people produce and reproduce social structure through their everyday actions.

Etic perspective An approach in which concepts are specified by the researcher, based, for example, on the theory being tested. Often associated with quantitative research.

Experiment A research design involving manipulation of a variable to observe its effects.

Experimental control The management of extraneous variables that could threaten internal validity of a study by direct intervention by the experimenter, for example, by ensuring standardization of treatment.

Experimental design Research designs that involve the manipulation of an independent or treatment variable by the researcher to observe the effect.

Experimenter-expectancy effects Influence on the conduct of a study as a result of the researcher's expectations about the findings, for example, by behaving differently towards the treatment group, as compared to the control group, in an experiment.

External validity See *Generalizability*.

Extraneous variable A variable that produces a correlation between two variables that are not causally related.

Face validity A subjective judgement of the extent to which a measure appears 'on the face of things' to measure what it is supposed to measure.

Field experiment An experiment conducted under conditions that are not created by the researcher.

Field notes   The notes produced by the researcher during fieldwork, for example, as a participant-observer.

Fisher's exact test   Significance test of association between two categorical variables (non-parametric).

Focus group   A form of interview where research participants are interviewed in a group setting because the researcher wants to study not only the participants' views or experiences of the topic under discussion, but also the interactions between members of the group.

Frequency distribution   The number of observations or cases that fall within each category of a variable.

Frequency table   A table showing the number and per cent of observations or cases that fall within each category of a variable.

Gantt chart   A form of bar chart used to depict a time schedule.

Generalizability   The extent to which your research findings are applicable to people, time or settings other than those in which the research was conducted. Also known as external validity.

Grand theory   A theoretical system applicable to large-scale social phenomena.

Grounded theory   A research design in which the aim is to build theory systematically from data through an iterative process of constant comparison.

Hierarchical coding   An arrangement of codes in a way that reflects increasing levels of abstraction.

Histogram   A form of bar chart used to display the frequency distribution of a metric variable.

Hypothesis   A testable proposition about the expected association between two or more concepts or variables.

Hypothetico-deductive approach   A deductive research approach involving the formulation and testing of hypotheses derived from the theory under investigation.

Idealism   The ontological position that only minds and their ideas exist.

in vivo codes   In qualitative data analysis, naming codes based on a word or phrase used in the data being coded.

Independent two-sample *t*-test   Significance test of the difference between the means of two independent (not related) samples (parametric).

Independent variable   The variable that is identified as the cause of changes in the dependent variable. Also referred to as a predictor or treatment variable. Conventionally labelled X in diagrams, graphs and mathematical models.

In-depth interview   A format of interview where the researcher asks open-ended questions and where the choice of words and order of the questions is flexible.

Indicator   Something used as a measure of a more abstract concept, for example, answers to questions in a questionnaire to measure attitude.

Inductive approach   A research approach that seeks to build theory from data.

Inferential statistics   Statistical techniques used to make inferences about a population on the basis of sample data.

Internal consistency reliability   The extent to which items in a multi-item scale are related. Often measured using Cronbach's alpha.

Internal validity   The extent to which causal inferences about the relationship between two or more variables can be supported by the research design.

Interpretivism   A philosophical orientation that stresses the difference between the objects of natural science and the subjects of social science and emphasizes the importance of understanding and meaning in social research.

Interquartile range   A measure of dispersion: the difference between the top 25 per cent and the bottom 25 per cent of the distribution.

Inter-rater reliability   The degree of consistency between two or more coders when coding the same set of data. Also known as inter-coder reliability.

Interval data   Data measured at the interval level can be placed in rank order but it is also possible to measure the size of the difference between the values. Interval data do not have a naturally occurring zero point.

Interval estimate   An interval calculated from sample data to give a range of plausible values for a population parameter.

Interview guide   The topics or questions to be used in a qualitative interview. Also referred to as an interview schedule or interview protocol.

Interview study   A research design in which qualitative interviews are the means of data collection.

Investigative question   Questions asked in interviews or questionnaires that generate the data needed to answer your research questions.

Kendall's tau (τ)   Measure of the strength and direction of association between two ordinal variables (non-parametric).

Kolmogorov-Smirnov test   Significance test of whether or not the sample is drawn from a normally distributed population.

Kurtosis   A measure of the extent to which a distribution is flat (platykurtic) or peaked (leptokurtic), as compared to a normal distribution.

Laboratory experiment   An experiment conducted in a laboratory or other artificial condition created by the researcher.

Level of precision   The maximum difference that the researcher is prepared to tolerate between the estimated sample value obtained and the actual value that would be obtained in the population.

Likert scale   A widely used type of multi-item rating scale used to indicate level of agreement or disagreement to a series of statements.

Linear regression   A statistical technique for predicting the value of a metric dependent variable from knowledge of the value of one or more independent variables.

Literature   The body of written material on a particular topic, whether published or unpublished.

Longitudinal study   A study which gathers data on subjects or events over time. Contrast with a cross-sectional study.

Mann-Whitney test   Significance test for difference between two groups (non-parametric).

Maturation effects   A threat to internal validity that arises from changes in a participant over the course of a study and that can influence the results irrespective of any treatment, for example, the effects of growing older or gaining experience.

Mean   A measure of central tendency: usually refers, as here, to the arithmetic mean, which is the arithmetic average of the data.

Measures of central tendency   Statistics such as the mode, median and mean that measure the average or typical value for a variable.

Measures of dispersion   Statistics such as range, interquartile range and standard deviation that measure degree of spread or dispersion among the observations in a sample.

Median   A measure of central tendency: the value that is in the middle of the distribution.

Mediating variable   A variable that represents a mechanism through which an independent variable influences a dependent variable. Also known as an intervening variable.

Member checking   See *respondent validation.*

Memo   A term originating in grounded theory to refer to notes written by the researcher for their own use to track progress, record emerging ideas, serve as a basis for writing up and so on.

Memoing   The act of creating memos.

Meta-analysis   The use of statistical techniques to synthesize the findings from multiple studies to provide a single quantitative estimate (for example, as part of a systematic review).

Metric data   Used in this book to denote data measured on an interval or ratio scale.

Middle-range theory   A theory providing an explanation of a particular phenomenon.

Missing value   In quantitative data analysis, a value for a particular observation that is missing, due to non-response, data entry error or other reason.

Mixed methods study   A study combining quantitative and qualitative methods.

Mode   A measure of central tendency: the most frequently occurring value in the data.

Model   The term 'model' may be used to convey a number of meanings, including: 1) a synonym for theory, 2) a mathematical representation of a theory or real-world phenomenon, 3) a diagrammatic representation of a theory or real-world phenomenon.

Moderating variable   A variable that influences the nature of the relationship between an independent variable and a dependent variable.

Mono method study   A study using either quantitative or qualitative methods but not both.

Multi-item scale   A scale which consists of several questions (items) that are combined (summated) in some way to produce a single measure for the chosen variable. Also known as a summated scale.

Multimodal   A frequency distribution with more than two modes (peaks).

Multiple regression   Linear regression featuring more than one independent variable.

Multivariate analysis   The analysis of more than two variables simultaneously.

N / n   Upper case N is usually used to refer to the population size and lower case *n* to the sample size, e.g. *n* = 25 would indicate a sample size of 25.

Natural experiment   A research design in which the researcher looks for a naturally occurring comparison between a treatment and a control condition that is as close as possible to that which would have been created in a true experiment.

Netnography   A form of ethnography that studies behaviour in online environments. Also referred to as webethnography, online ethnography and virtual ethnography.

Network   Visual display in which the data are presented as a network of nodes and links.

Nominal data   The lowest level of measurement used when numbers are applied to distinguish different categories such as gender (male/female); the categories have no natural rank order.

Non-directional hypothesis   A hypothesis in which the direction of the association is not specified; non-directional hypotheses are the most commonly encountered type in business and management research.

Non-experimental design   Research design that does not involve manipulation of a treatment variable.

Non-parametric tests   Statistical tests that do not make assumptions regarding the type of probability distribution of the population from which the sample was drawn.

Non-probability sampling   Any non-randomized procedure for generating a sample from a target population.

Non-response bias   Bias introduced when non-respondents are systematically different from respondents.

Normal distribution   A probability distribution sometimes called the bell curve because of its shape. It is an important distribution in statistical analysis. Also known as the Gaussian distribution.

Null hypothesis The reverse of the research hypothesis indicating that what you expect to find is not present (for example, that there is no difference or no association).

Objectivism An epistemological position that assumes the possibility of gathering data through theory-neutral and value-free observation.

Observation A data collection technique involving the purposeful observation, recording and analysis of activities, events or behaviours. Also used in sampling and quantitative analysis to refer to individual elements, such as respondents.

One-sample *t*-test Significance test of whether the sample comes from a population with a specified mean (parametric).

One-tailed test A significance test of a directional hypothesis.

One-way, independent analysis of variance (ANOVA) Significance test of the difference between the means of three or more groups (parametric).

Online survey Survey method that uses questionnaire delivery via an Internet browser.

Ontology Ontology is concerned with the nature of what is out there to know in the natural and social world.

Open questions Questions that do not have a definitive set of option answers but, rather, the respondents answers freely in their own words.

Operationalization The process of turning concepts into measurable variables.

Ordinal data Data measured at the ordinal level can be placed in rank order from highest to lowest but do not allow measurement of the difference between categories.

Outcome variable See *Dependent variable*.

Outlier An observation or combination of observations with characteristics that are distinctly different from other observations in the dataset.

Paired (or dependent) 2-sample *t*-test Significance test of the difference between the means of two paired samples (parametric).

Panel study A longitudinal study that follows a specific group of subjects (the panel) by repeated observations over time.

Parametric tests Statistical tests that make assumptions regarding the type of probability distribution of the population from which the sample were drawn. If using a parametric test, you must ensure that any required assumptions are met by your data.

Participant-observation A form of data collection in which the researcher is an active participant as well as an observer.

Participatory research Research involving collaboration between researcher and respondents with respect to the goals, process and outcomes of the research.

Pearson's correlation coefficient (*r*) Measure of the strength and direction of linear association between two metric variables.

Peer review   The process of expert review of work prior to its being accepted for publication (also known as refereeing).

Phi   Measure of the strength of association between two categorical variables (non-parametric).

Pie chart   A chart that represents the relative proportion of each category of a variable by representing it as a slice of a pie.

Pilot study   A small-scale study carried out to test aspects of a research project such as a questionnaire, ideally with a group from the intended sample and using the same administration methods, prior to beginning full data collection.

Plagiarism   The representation of someone else's work as your own.

Point estimate   A single-number statistic estimate of a population parameter.

Population   The universe of people, entities or events in which the researcher is interested and from which a sample is drawn.

Population parameter   A statistic that characterizes a population.

Positivism   A philosophical orientation that seeks to apply the methods of the natural sciences to the social sciences.

Post-positivism   A philosophical orientation that shares some features of positivism but accepting the conjectural and fallible nature of knowledge. (Note: the term is also used by other writers to refer to a range of philosophical orientations that came 'after' positivism.)

Predictor variable   See *Independent variable*.

Pre-test   A test of a data collection instrument, such as a questionnaire, to check clarity, time to complete and so on prior to a pilot test.

Primary data   Data that are collected specifically for the purposes of the research project being undertaken.

Probability sampling   A procedure for generating a sample from a target population that involves randomization.

Process model   Conceptual model showing stages or event sequences over time.

Projective technique   A technique for eliciting responses in an interview whereby the researcher taps into the respondent's underlying feelings and attitudes that may remain dormant, by use of ambiguous objects or stimuli.

Proportionately stratified sampling   A form of stratified random sampling in which the sample size for each sub-group in the population is proportionate to its size within the total population.

Prospective study   A longitudinal study that follows events as they happen.

Pure research   Research associated with an academic agenda that focuses upon adding to the existing body of theoretical knowledge in relation to a particular topic.

Purposive sampling   A form of non-probability sampling which involves the selection by the researcher on the basis of theoretical relevance to the study.

***p*-value**   The probability of observing a test statistic at least as extreme (positive or negative) as the one observed, assuming the null hypothesis is true.

Qualitative content analysis   A qualitative variant of content analysis.

Qualitative interview   Refers to in-depth, semi-structured or unstructured interviews used to generate qualitative data.

Quasi-experiment   An experiment in which individuals are not assigned randomly to groups.

Questionnaire   A data collection instrument that uses a standardized, structured set of questions to measure variables that are of interest to the researcher.

Quota sampling   A form of non-probability sampling in which the researcher determines quotas for specific sub-groups within the population.

R²   See *Coefficient of determination.*

Randomized control trial   A term referring to a true experiment; often used in evaluation research, including pharmaceutical trials.

Range   A measure of dispersion: the difference between the maximum and the minimum values for a variable.

Ratio data   Data measured at the ratio level can be placed in rank order, have equal distance between measurement intervals and a meaningful zero point.

Realism   1) The ontological position that there exists a reality independent of the mind of the observer, 2) a philosophical orientation that combines ontological realism with epistemological subjectivism.

Reference list   A list of all the works cited in a text.

Reflexivity   The practice, as a researcher, of reflecting on one's own position and role in research.

Regression coefficient (b_i)   In regression analysis, a measure of the strength of the relationship between an independent variable and the dependent variable; it shows the change in the dependent variable associated with a one-unit change in the independent variable.

Reliability   The degree of stability and consistency of the measures used in a study.

Research   A purposeful, systematic process of investigation in order to find solutions to a problem.

Research diary or log   A record of relevant information and activities that take place which you document as you proceed through your project.

Research ethics committee (REC)   Refers to the appropriate conduct of research in relation to participants and to others affected by it.

Research hypothesis   A statement about what you expect to find in your data in terms of, for example, an association between two variables or differences between two or more groups. Typically written as $H_1 \ldots, H_2 \ldots, H_n \ldots$ etc. Also referred to as the alternative or alternate hypothesis.

Research problem   The specific problem, issue or opportunity that is the subject of your research.

Research proposal   A document that provides an overview of the intended research. It sets out the purpose of the research and a plan for how it will be carried out and is often the basis for research approval.

Research question   The specific question(s) that your research needs to answer in order to resolve your research problem.

Respondent validation   A process used in some research in which respondents are asked for feedback on emerging and/or final findings of the research. Feedback may be seen as part of a validation process or as a means of gathering additional insight into the research findings. Also referred to as member checking.

Response rate   The proportion, expressed as a percentage, of those contacted who actually participate in the research as respondents and whose data is included for analysis.

Retrospective study   A form of longitudinal study that takes place after the event of interest has happened.

Reverse coding   The process of reversing the direction of an ordinal or interval scale; usually carried out to ensure that all scales run in the same direction prior to analysis.

Sample   A smaller set of cases or observations drawn from a larger target population.

Sample statistic   Statistics that characterize a sample.

Sampling   The process of selecting a sample from the target population.

Sampling error   The naturally occurring difference between a sample statistic and the true population parameter.

Sampling frame   A listing of all the elements that make up the population from which the sample will be drawn.

Scatterplot   A chart plotting one variable against another; used with metric or ordinal data.

Secondary data   Data that were collected, usually but not necessarily by someone else, for purposes other than your own investigation.

Secondary data analysis   The re-analysis of secondary data to answer a research question that is distinct from that for which the data were originally collected. Also known as secondary analysis.

Selection bias   Bias arising as a result of systematic error in sampling leading to a non-representative sample.

Self-selection sampling   A form of non-probability sampling in which participants self-select to take part in a study.

Sensitizing concept   Concepts that are tentative and subject to change and which can guide data collection by suggesting initial lines of enquiry and can help to structure data analysis. Sensitizing concepts can be drawn from existing literature.

Shapiro-Wilk test   Significance test of whether or not the sample is drawn from a normally distributed population (non-parametic).

Significance level   In statistical significance testing, the level at which the null hypothesis will be rejected. Also referred to as α. For business and management, commonly set at 0.05. It represents the risk of committing a Type I error.

Simple random sampling   A form of probability sampling in which each individual is drawn at random from the target population.

Skewness   A measure of the extent to which a distribution departs from symmetry. Positive (right) skewness indicates that the observations are clustered around the lower values of the distribution with a tail of higher values. Negative (left) skewness indicates the opposite.

Snowballing   A form of non-probability sampling in which the researcher starts with a few known members of the population who meet the sample characteristics and these are approached to participate and also identify others whom they know who also meet the sample characteristics.

Social constructionism   A philosophical orientation that emphasizes the 'constructed' nature of phenomena which are seen as constructed through our social processes and, in particular, through interaction and language.

Social desirability bias   The tendency for respondents to choose answers that conform to what is seen to be socially desirable or responsible.

Spearman's rho (ρ)   Measure of the strength and direction of association between two ordinal variables or between one ordinal and one metric variable (non-parametric).

Stacked bar chart   A bar chart in which the observations for each category are stacked in a single bar rather than clustered side by side.

Standard deviation   A measure of dispersion: for metric data, measured in the same units as the mean, it indicates how far the distribution is spread out from the mean (the standard deviation is the square root of the variance).

Statistical control   The use of statistical techniques to identify and control for the influence of extraneous variables.

Statistical inference   The process of using inferential statistics to draw conclusions based on data; in research it commonly refers to drawing conclusions about a population on the basis of data drawn from a sample of that population.

Statistical representativeness   The extent to which a sample is representative of the population from which it was drawn.

Stratified random sampling   A probability sampling method in which the population is divided (stratified) into separate sub-groups and sample sizes are calculated for each sub-group.

Structured interview   A format of interview where the researcher asks closed-ended questions, in the same order, the same way, and only the predefined answer choices can be given, e.g. surveys.

Structured observation   A form of observation that involves the coding of observed behaviour or activities against a defined coding schedule for subsequent numerical analysis.

Subject-expectancy effects   Influences on research findings as a result of participants reacting to being part of the research, irrespective of any actual treatment administered.

Subjectivism   An epistemological position that assumes all observation is, at the very least, value laden.

Substantive theory   A theory providing an explanation of a specific phenomenon in a specific setting.

Survey study   A non-experimental research design that collects and analyses quantitative or quantifiable data on variables of interest for the population being studied.

Systematic random sampling   A probability sampling method involving the systematic selection of sample elements from a list at a predetermined sampling interval.

Systematic review   A type of literature review that seeks to provide a systematic, transparent and reproducible method for locating, appraising and synthesizing all of the relevant studies in the chosen topic area.

Systems model   Conceptual model showing system components and their inter-relationships.

Target population   The totality of all elements (individuals, organizations, documents and so on) of interest to our research problem.

Taxonomy   A classification scheme derived from data.

Test statistic   A value that is calculated as part of statistical testing and used to determine the degree to which the sample data are consistent with the null hypothesis.

Test-retest reliability   The extent to which a measure will give the same result if it is repeated.

Theoretical sampling   Another term for purposive sampling.

Theoretical saturation   A term originating in grounded theory to refer to the point at which the cycle of data collection and analysis generates no new categories or new dimensions of existing categories. Can be used as a guide in qualitative research that the sample size is adequate.

Thick description   A form of description associated with ethnography allowing an interpretation of the understanding of those involved in a particular situation or action.

Time series   A form of longitudinal data that consists of a sequence of observations, usually the observations are of a single entity at regular intervals over a fairly long period.

Transferability   A dimension of trustworthiness. Providing sufficient information to allow the reader to assess the relevance of the findings to other contexts; analogous to generalizability (external validity) in traditional quality criteria.

Treatment group   In an experiment, a group that receives a treatment.

Treatment variable   A term used in experimental designs. See *Independent variable*.

Trend   The long-term direction of a time series (e.g. up, down or stationary).

Triangulation   The process of using multiple sources of data or multiple methods to cross-check the validity of your findings.

True experiment   An experiment which uses random assignment of participants to groups.

Trustworthiness   A set of quality criteria proposed for qualitative research consisting of credibility, transferability, dependability and conformability.

Two-tailed test   A significance test of a non-directional hypothesis.

Type I error   Rejection of the null hypothesis when it is, in fact, true.

Type II error   Acceptance of the null hypothesis when it is, in fact, false.

Typology   A classification scheme derived in advance and then applied to the data.

Uniform Resource Locator (URL)   A unique address for a resource on the Internet.

Unimodal   A frequency distribution with a single mode (peak).

Unit of analysis   The unit of analysis refers to the level of aggregation of the data used during analysis and for reporting your results.

Univariate analysis   The analysis of single variables individually.

Validity   The extent to which research findings are really about what they claim to be about.

Variable   A concept, characteristic or attribute that can take on different values (e.g. satisfaction, income or gender).

Variance   A measure of dispersion: for metric data, it indicates how far the distribution is spread out from the mean.

Variance model   Conceptual model specifying cause-and-effect relationships between concepts, identifying dependent and independent variables.

Author index

When the text is within a table, the number span is in *italic*, e.g., abstracts *180, 371, 372–3, 379*

When the text is within a figure, the number span is in **bold**, e.g., binary choice questions 219, **219**

When the text is within a 'Research in Practice' box, the number span is <u>underlined</u>, e.g., observed behaviour 258, 263, <u>264</u>

Alvesson, M. 26
Andrews, R. 37, 40
Aneshensel, C. S. 35
Argyris, C. 12
Atkinson, P. 262

Barbour, R. 247
Bearden, W. O. et al. 215
Beile, P. 44–5
Bell, E. 150, 159
Bem, D. 378
Bennis, W. G. 11
Blaikie, N. 15, 78, 79–80
Block, P. 386
Blumer, H. 79, 340
Bono, J. E. et al. 123
Boote, D. N. 44–5
Bougie, R. 4, 32
Bowey, A. M. 271
Brannick, T. 132
Bresman, H. <u>112</u>
Britten, N. <u>106</u>
Brüggen, E. et al. 203
Bryman, A. 150, 159, 168
Burbules, N. C. 17
Burrow, R. <u>136</u>

Campbell, C. et al. 203
Canhoto, A. I. <u>245</u>, <u>261</u>
Casey, M. 247

Checkland, P. 65
Chell, E. 241
Christensen, C. M. 11, 12
Christopher, M. G. <u>124</u>
Churchill, G. A. 26–7
Clark, M. 154, 155, <u>197</u>, <u>245</u>
Clarke, J. 273
Coghlan, D. 132–3
Cooper, B. et al. 85, 90
Corbin, J. 12, 39, 346
Cramer's V *318, 320, 333*
Creswell, J. W. 39, 61, 86–7, 126, 261, 383–4

Datta, P. P. <u>124</u>
Davis, J. P. et al. 123
de Vaus, D. 34, 98, 110, *321*
Delbridge, R. 127
Denzin, N. K. 17, 237
Dhandayudham, A. <u>157</u>
Dibley, A. <u>80</u>, <u>197</u>

Emerson, R. M. et al. 262

Fairclough, N. 135, 137
Finch, H. 248
Flanagan, J. C. 241
Flick, U. 39, 41, 80, 195
Forzano, L.-A. B. 109
Foucault, M. 135

Gebauer, J. et al. 125, 270
Geertz, C. 102, 126
Gergen, K. 106
Gilbert, N. 123
Gill, J. 11
Glaser, B. G. 127
Glassner, B. 254
Gold, R. L. 259
Gomm, R. 86
Gorard, S. 109
Gravetter, F. J. 109
Gray, D. 4, 66
Greene, J. C. et al. 87
Grix, J. 46
Guba, E. G. 93–4, 361, *362*
Gubrium, J. F. 253

Hair, J. F. J. et al. 283, 284, <u>291</u>, 327
Hair, N. 154, 155
Hammersley, M. 159–60, 262
Harrison, J. R. et al. 113
Harwood, T. G. 154
Hodgkinson, G. P. 11
Holstein, J. A. 253
Holt, R. 102
Hong, W. 154
Horrocks, C. 242
Huberman, M. A. 108, 338, 348, 355–6,
    360, 362

Jain, V. et al. 125
James, A. 272
Johnson, P. 11

King, N. 240, 242, 338, 342
Kozinets, R. V. 265
Krön, V. <u>270</u>
Krueger, R. A. 247
Kvale, S. 243

Langley, A. 36, 110, 111
Legard, R. et al. 237, 242
Letza, S. et al. <u>62</u>
Lewin, K. 65, 130–2
Lewis, J. 248
Lincoln, Y. S. 17, 93–4, 237, 361, *362*
Llewellyn, N. <u>136</u>

MacAnaney, D. <u>79</u>, <u>225</u>
Markham, C. 31
Marshall, C. 238
Maxwell, J. A. 33, 36, 108, 178, 196, *197*

Mays, N. 138
McCloskey, D. N. 328
Meister, D. B. <u>133</u>
Meyer, J. P. et al. <u>222</u>
Miles, M. B. 108, 338, 348, 355–6, 360,
    362
Miller, J. 254
Mintzberg, H. 12, 61, 63, 99, <u>100</u>, 262
Morgan, D. L. 88
Morgan, S. J. 244
Moroko, L. <u>134</u>

Naccarato, J. L. 125
Neuendorf, K. A. 125, <u>125</u>

O'Toole, J. 11

Parasuraman, A. et al. <u>214</u>
Parker, A. 247
Patterson, A. 272
Peirce, C. S. 81
Petticrew, M. 48, 61, 69
Pettigrew, A. M. 111
Phillips, D. 17
Pope, C. 138
Popper, K. 78
Price, J. L. 215
Przeworski, A. 180

Rafaeli, A. <u>89</u>
Ragin, C. C. 86
Raynor, M. E. 11, 12
Roberts, H. 48, 61, 69
Robson, C. 4, 37, 40, 86, 91
Rose, S. <u>157</u>
Rosenberg, M. 106
Rossman, G. B. 238
Roth, A. V. et al. 215
Rousseau, D. M. 11
Roy, D. 127

Saldaña, J. 353, 355, 357
Salomon, F. 180
Sandberg, J. 26
Saunders, M. et al. 4, 19, 67, 181
Sayer, A. 13, 105
Schön, D. A. 12
Sekaran, U. 4, 32
Senge, P. M. 65
Shadish, W. R. et al. 103, 107, 117
Shapiro, M. <u>203–4</u>
Sigurdsson, V. et al. <u>120</u>

Silverman, D. 91, 254, 363–4
Starkey, K. 11
Strauss, A. 12, 39, 127, 346
Street, C. T. 133
Sutton, R. I. 89
Symon, G. 244

Tashakkori, A. 20, 40, 88
Teddlie, C. 20, 40, 88, 108
Thong, J. Y. L. 154
Thorpe, R. 102, 271
Toulmin, S. 46–7
Tranfield, D. 11
Tritter, J. 247
Troitzsch, K. G. 123
Tsoukas, H. 36

Uncles, M. D. 134

Valor, C. 129
Van de Ven, A. H. 11, 24, 26, 27, 30–1

Wallace, M. 48, 53
Ward, J 154
Watson, R. T. 60–1
Webb, E. et al. 274
Webster, J. 60–1
Wilson, A. M. 150
Wilson, H. et al. 131, 131, 356, 372
Wolcott, H. F. 384
Wooffitt, R. 339
Woolcott, I. 198
Wray, A. 48, 53

Yin, R. K. 34

Ziliak, S. T. 328

Subject index

When the text is within a table, the number span is in *italic*, e.g., abstracts *180, 371, 372–3, 379*

When the text is within a figure, the number span is in **bold**, e.g., binary choice questions 219, **219**

When the text is within a 'Research in Practice' box, the number span is <u>underlined</u>, e.g., observed behaviour 258, 263, <u>264</u>

5-stage research model 6–7, **6**

a priori codes 340, 353
abductive (retroductive) research approaches 16, 81, *85*, 95, 111
abstracts *180, 371, 372–3, 379*
academic journals 8, 29, 48–9, *50*, 215, *372*
academic qualifications 5
academic report writing 370–8, *371, 372*
action research: data collection *212*, 237, 258, 267; designing research 81; planning research *166*; research designs **126**, 130–3, **132**, <u>133</u>, 139
active listening 243
administration methods 133, 154, 231, 232–3, 234
affective commitment 221, <u>222</u>, 224, **281**
affiliations *145*, 150–1, *156*
aggregate properties *85, 86*, 101, *166*, 195, 345
analysis of variance (one-way independent ANOVA) *314*, 317, 324, **325**, 333
analytic generalization 92
analytic surveys **118**, 120–<u>1</u>, 122, 139, *166*, <u>225</u>
anonymity: ethics *145*, 151–2, 155, *156*, 161; interviews *238*, 245; qualitative data analysis 363, 365; questionnaires *212*, 228, 231, 232–3; sampling <u>207</u> *see also* privacy

ANOVA (one-way independent analysis of variance) *314*, 317, 324, **325**, 333
appendices *371, 377, 379,* **382**
applied research: analysis 362; applying research designs 121–2, 130; background 8, 9–10, <u>10</u>, 26–7; formulating the problem 32, 35, 36, 41; literature reviews 45, 48, 66; reports *373*, 377, 388
arguments: literature reviews 46–7, **47**, 49, 60, 67; planning research 181; reports 380, 384
artefacts 188, 273–4, 275
artificial settings 260, 262
asynchronous communication 243, 245, 250
attribute coding 353
audio recordings: data collection <u>229</u>, 248, 252, 265; ethics <u>149</u>; reports 336, 337–8; research designs **136**
author-centric structure 60, *60*
avoidance of harm 145–6, *145*, <u>157</u>, 160, 161
axiology 19, 20

bar charts 287–8, 296–8, **297**, 300–1, 305, **331**
bibliographic databases 49, *52*, 55, 59, 70–1, 268
bimodal distribution 292, **293**
binary choice questions 219, **219**
bivariate analysis 285, 294, 322–6, **325**, 329

bivariate (simple) linear regression 322–3, 324, 326
body language 243, 248, 250, 251 *see also* non-verbal data
Boolean operators 55
boundary setting 6, 31, 33, 39, 181
box plots *286, 290, 294–7,* **295,** *296*
brainstorming 29 *see also* mind mapping
briefing: interviews 255; observations 263; questionnaires 227, 228, 231, 232, 234; reports 377, 387; sampling 206

CAQDAS (computer aided qualitative data analysis software) 346–8, **347,** *347–8*
categorical scales 219, **219,** 231
categorical variables 298–9, 317, *318, 319,* 333
causal explanation 16, 103, 104–5, 107–8, 114, 129
causal mechanisms 18–19, 105, 114, 130, *166,* 355
causal paths 104, 110, 111, 114, 348
causality: data analysis 327, 355; formulating the problem 35; research designs 102–3, 105, 107, 108–10, 114, 129, 130, 138, 139
CDA (critical discourse analysis) 137, 140, *166,* 266
census data 83, 188, *269,* **304**
central tendency **285,** 290, 296, 329
checklists 218, **218,** 224, 248
chi-squared test of association 317–18, 318–19, 320, 327
CIT (critical incident technique) 241
citation indexes *52,* 55
classic experimental design **118**
classification questions 227, 230–1, 234
classification schemes 99–100, 100, 113
closed questions 222–3, 242 *see also* open questions
closing comments 227, 231, 234
cluster analysis 122, 327
cluster sampling **192,** 193, 198
clustered bar charts *296, 298, 300,* **331**
code management 341–2, **341,** *342*
codes of practice 151, 158–61, *158*
coding hierarchies 342–5, **343, 344, 345**
coding process 128, 263, 340–2, 340, **341,** *342*
coding schedules 263, 264, 275–6
coding schemes: data analysis 281–2, *282, 284,* 338–45, 342–5, **344;**

data collection 263; research designs **124,** 125, 139
coding table (Excel) **347**
coefficient of determination ($R2$) 323
collection speed 212
common mistakes 224, *224, 362, 376*
comparisons: data analysis 350; descriptive research 34; designing research 79; ethics 160; linking research questions to design 99, 113; observations 273; qualitative data analysis 353, 355, 356, *359, 360, 361;* quantitative data analysis 305, 313; research designs 118, 120, 128, 139; sampling **192,** *197*
complex constructs 215, 221
computer aided qualitative data analysis software (CAQDAS) 346–8, **347,** *347–8*
computer simulation 113, **118,** 123, 167
concept-centric structure 60, *60,* 67, 70
concept matrix *61*
conceptual models: concept maps 61, 352; data 225, **323,** 326; literature reviews 62–5, **64,** *66,* 69, 70; research designs 77, 79, 107, 121
conclusions and recommendations 376–7, 378, **382**
conditional routing questions 229–30, **230**
confidence intervals 307–9, **308,** 313, 324, 328, 329
confidentiality: data analysis 363; ethics *145,* 152, 154–5, *156,* 160–1; interviews 238, 242, 249; reports 387; sampling 206, 207
confirming findings 361–2, *362*
conflicts of interest 150–1 *see also* affiliations
constant comparison 81, 128, 139, 361 *see also* comparisons
content analysis: data analysis 336, 361; data collection 266, *267,* 270; linking research questions to design 101, 102; planning research *166;* research designs 118, 124–5, 125, **126,** 135, 139–40
content information *58,* 60
contingency tables 298, *299, 300,* 317–18, 320
convenience sampling 194, 202, 247
conventional sampling 201
conversation analysis (CA): data analysis *339,* 353, 364; linking research questions to design 113; observations *258,* 265; planning research *166;* research designs 126, 136, 137, 140

corporate governance <u>62</u>
corporate reputation (CR) <u>9</u>
correlational studies 120–1, 139
covariance 103
covert data collection 149–50
covert observation 149–50, 259–60, 263, 265, 274–5
critical discourse analysis (CDA) 137, 140, 166, 266
critical incident technique (CIT) 241
critical incidents charts 357, 359
critical reviews: literature reviews 44–7, 47, <u>62</u>, 67–9, 68; planning research 165, 169; reports 370, 371
CRM (customer relationship management) system <u>131</u>, <u>372</u>
Cronbach's alpha 93, 284, 310
cross-case comparison 355, <u>356</u>
cross-sectional studies 81–2
cross-tabulations 61, 342, 349–51, **351**, 357, 364
customer relationship management (CRM) system <u>131</u>, <u>372</u>

data collection instruments: background 58; linking research questions to design 101; planning research 169, 170, 172; questionnaires 211; reports 375, 377; sampling 205
data collection matrices <u>225</u>, 226, 227, 228, 234
data display limitations 353
data management 59, 176, 282, 346
data matrices: data collection <u>225</u>, 226, 227, 228, 234; qualitative data analysis 349–50, 350, <u>350</u>, 351, 354, <u>356</u>; quantitative data analysis 281, **281**, 283
data preparation 212, 282–4, 330, 337
data protection: data analysis 282; data collection 205, 253; designing research 84; ethics 145, 152–3, 154, 156
Data Protection Act (1998) 152
data reduction 338, 340, 342, 346, 353
data storage 156, <u>177</u>, 205, 253, 282
data transformation 284, 329
deception in research 145, 146–7, <u>147</u>, 150, 259
decision problems 27, 27
deductive approaches: background 14–15, 14, 21; data analysis 340; designing research 76–8, 77, 78–80, <u>79</u>, <u>80</u>, 85;

formulating the problem 39; literature reviews 65, 66, 70; reports 376; research designs 101, 117, 120
definitions of research 4–5, 4
degrees of freedom (df) 312, 312, <u>315</u>, <u>318</u>
depth realism 18
descriptions 99–100, 100–1, 101–2
descriptive research 34–5, 100–1, 102, 113
descriptive statistics 286, 305, 313, <u>315</u>, 329
descriptive surveys **118**, 122, <u>123</u>, 139, 166, 215
developing research questions 33–41
development processes 111
diaries (data collection) 271–2, <u>272–3</u> see also research diaries
Digital Object Identifier (DOI) 57, 59
dignity 145–6, 145, 156, 160
directional hypotheses 310, 313
discourse analysis **126**, 135–7, 140, 166, 266
discussion outlines 249
discussion section 376–7, **382**
dispersion 285, 286, 290, 296, 329
disseminating research 388
dissertations and theses: background 20; formulating the problem 25, 31; literature reviews 50, 66; planning research 176, 178; reports 370; research designs 132
distribution methods 200, 232–3
document formats 270–1, <u>270</u>
documents: as data sources 266–7; designing research 83; diaries 271–2, <u>272–3</u>; interviews 237; linking research questions to design 101; literature reviews 59; planning research 167, 174, 176–7, 179–80; research designs 128, 130; sampling 205–6; sources 267, 268–71, 269, <u>270</u>
DOI (Digital Object Identifier) 57, 59
'don't know' option 229–30
drug users <u>207</u>

Economic and Social Research Council (ESRC) 150, 151, 158, 160, <u>179</u>, 182
editing 169, **382**, 383–4, 384–5
elite interviewing 238, 238, 244, 247
emerging themes **343**, 360, 365
emic (insider) view 85, 86, 101
empiricism 17, 18
Endnote (software) 59

enterprise resource planning (ERP) systems 121
epistemology 15–16, *16*, 17, 19
ERP (enterprise resource planning) systems 121
error checking 283
ESRC (Economic and Social Research Council) 150, 151, *158*, 160, *179*, 182
ethical principles 144–5, *145*, 154–5, *157*, 160, 250
ethical questions *156*, 259
ethical regulation 159–60, 161
ethics 144–61; conduct 144–5; data 149–50; loss of dignity 145–6; online research 154–5; research projects 155–7, *155*, *156*, *157*; researchers 150–1, 153–4; right to privacy 151–2, *152–3*; sample forms *148*, *149*; standards 158–60, 161, 167; transparency and honesty 146–51
ethics committees 158–60, **354**
ethnography: data collection 198, 237, 258, 260, 265, 267; ethics 154; linking research questions to design 108, 113; planning research 126–7, *126*, *128*, *166*, 182
etic (outsider) perspective *85*, 86 *see also* emic (insider) view
evaluating sources 56–7, 58, 66, 69
events frequency 263, *264*
events listings 357, *358*, 359
events network **360**
experimental research designs 117–20
experimenter-expectancy effects 119
explanatory effects matrix **355**, *355*
Express Scribe (software) 338
external validity (generalizability) 91, 92–4, *92*, *93*, 95

facilitator (moderator) 246, 250
feasibility 32, 167–8, 181, 187, 200, 205
field experiments 119, *120*
filter questions 191, 228, *229*, 230, 283
final topic 242, 250, 365
Fisher's exact test 320, 333
flow charts 359
focus groups: interviews 246–7, 247–50, 250–1, *251*, 252, 254; planning research *175*; research designs 88, 134
formulating research questions 33, 37–9
framing 20, 25–6, 36, 40, 41, 222
free writing 383, 389
frequency counts *218*, 287, 298, 317, *348*

frequency distribution *166*, 285–90, *286*, *287*

Gantt charts **171**, 173, 184
gap spotting 26
gatekeepers 205–6, 261–2
generalizability (external validity) 91, 92–4, *92*, *93*, 95
generic sampling process 187–90, **188**, **189**
glossary of terms 391–406
Google Books *52*
Google Scholar *52*, 59
grand theories 13–14
graphical techniques 61, 70, 285, *286*
grey documents 49, 269
grounded theory: applying research designs 126, 127–9, *129*, 139; data collection 237, 258, 267; planning research 81, 108, 111, 113, *166*
group interviews 246–7, 247–8, 248–50, 254

Harvard Law Review 151
hierarchical coding 342–5, **343**, **344**, **345**
hierarchy of methods 109
histograms *286*, *287*, **288**, **294**, **331**
Homeworker Project Companies (HPC) 10
homeworking 10
'how' questions: data analysis 357–60, *358*, *359*; data collection 238; formulating the problem 34, 35–6; research designs 99–100, 110–13, 113–14, 129, 132
hypothesis testing 77–8, 308–13, **309**, 329, 376
hypothetico-deductive approaches 76, 90, 107, 127

idealism 15, 17, 18
identifying research topics 28–30, *28*, 41
in-depth interviews *see* interviews
in vivo codes 341, 353
incentivization 151, 191
independent 2-sample *t*-test 311–12, *315*, *315–16*, 333 *see also* one-sample t-test; paired (dependent) 2-sample *t*-test
index cards **341**, 342
indicators 39, 89, 135, 140, 215, *224*
inductive approaches: background 14, **14**, *16*, 17, 19, 21; data 241, 336, 360; designing research 78–80, *79*, 80, *112*; formulating the problem 39; literature reviews 45, 65, 66; reports 374, 376

industry databases *53*
inferential statistics 305–6, 309, 329
inferring causality 102–3, 109, 139, 327
informed consent: data collection 228, 231, 248–9, *249*, 255, 259; ethics *145*, 146–9, 149–50, <u>149</u>, *156*; online data collection 154, <u>155–7</u>; planning research <u>175</u>; reports 375, 377
insider (emic) view 86, 101
insider researchers 5, 165, 174–5, <u>175</u>
institutional talk 137
internet sampling 201–2, *202–4*
internet searching 49, *52–3*
internet telephony 244, 252
interpretivism *16*, 17–18, 21, 86, 90, 138
interquartile range *286*, 290, **290**, 294
interval data 216–17
intervening (mediating) variables 104, **104**
interview data 135, 188, 251–3, *253–4*
interview forms <u>148</u>, *149*
interview guides: data collection 239–40, 242, 243, 248, 252, 254–5; planning research *169*; reports 377
interview protocols *see* interview guides
interview schedules 239–40 *see also* interview guides
interviewing skills 238, 243
interviews 236–55; data collection 215, 223, *237*, 254; groups 246–7, *247–8*, 248–50, 250–1, 251–3; individuals 236–7, *237–8*, 239–40, 240–2, 243–4, 244–5; linking research questions to design 102, <u>106</u>, 108; planning research *166*, 167, 170; research designs **126**, 128–*9*, 133–*4*, 139
introductions 45, *180*, 373, <u>374</u>
investigative questions 33

Kendall's tau *318*, 320–1, 333
keywords 54, *58*, 70
kurtosis *286*, 292–4, **293**, **331**

laboratory experiments 119
language analysis 134–7
language differences 55
leading questions 241
Levene's test <u>315–16</u>
libraries 49, *50*, *52–3*, 56, 268–9, 274
library databases *52*, 56
Likert scales 216, 217, 228, 283, 284
linear outlines *381*, **382**, 383, 388
linear regression *318*, 322–4, 333
linear relationships 299, **302**

literacy levels 213, 224, 233
literature maps 61, **63**, 70
literature reviews 44–70; capture 56–9, *58*; critical review process 44–7, **47**; presentation 65–9; reports *371*, 374, 376, 378, 380, **382**; research planning 165, *172*; search 48–56, *50–1*, *52–3*, <u>54</u>; synthesis 60–5, *61*, <u>62</u>
literature sources: literature reviews 48–9, *50–1*, 55, 57, *58*; online sources *52–3*; research planning *172*, <u>177</u>
longitudinal studies: data collection 266, 269; designing research 82–3, 95; linking research questions to design 98, 110; research designs 120, 122, 125, 130; time series data 303, 329
low cost options *50*, 201, 212, 233

main research topic questions **227**, 228–30, 234
manipulative questions 242
Mann-Whitney test *314*, 317, 333
matrices: literature reviews *61*, <u>62</u>; qualitative data analysis 349–51, 354–5, 355–7, <u>356</u>, 359, 364–5 *see also* data matrices
maturation effects 119
mean 286, 291–2, **293** *see also* median
measurement levels: data analysis 285, *286*, 288, 296, *314*, *318*; data collection **214**, 216, 217–18, *218*, 234
measures of association 299, 318–27, <u>318–19</u>
median 286, 290, 292–4, **293**, 295
mediating (intervening) variables 104, **104**
memoing 345–6
Mendeley (software) 59
meta-analysis 69
meta-theories 13
methodological reflexivity 20
metric variables 287, 291, 294, *296*, 299–302, *318*, 320
micro-level analysis 253
middle-range theories 13–14
mind mapping 29, 61, 178, 381, **382**, 388
misrepresentations *145*, 152, *156*
missing values *282*, 283, 287, 329
mixed methods: data 267, 356, 361; designing research 76, 81, 87–90, **88**, <u>89</u>, 95–6; linking research questions to design 101, 108, 111, 114; planning research 165; reports 376

mobile telephony <u>79</u>, 252, 271
mode 286, 290, 292–3 *see also* median
moderating variables 104, **105**
moderator (facilitator) 246, 250
mono-method research 87
multi-item scales 93, 221–2, <u>222</u>, 224, 284,
    <u>307</u> *see also* summated rating scales
multidimensional classification schemes 99,
    <u>100</u>
multimodal distribution 292, **331**
multiple choice questions 219, **219**
multiple regression analysis <u>326–7</u>
multivariate analysis 285, 294–8, *296*, 327

naming systems 337, 365
natural experiments **118**, 120–1, 139, *166*,
    313
natural settings *85*, 86, 92, 119, 126, 260
netnography 127, 265, 275
network displays 351–2, 354, **354**, 356,
    <u>359</u>, 360
new topics *51*, 55, 168
newspapers 45, 49, *51*, 195, 267
NGOs (non-governmental organizations) *51*,
    53
nominal data 216, 218, 219, 284, 290
non-compliance <u>106</u>
non-directional hypotheses 310
non-experimental designs 107, 109, 114,
    121, 139
non-governmental organizations (NGOs) *51*,
    53
non-numerical data 95, 335
non-parametric tests 311, 317–*18*
non-probability sampling: data analysis 361;
    data collection **192**, 193–5, 196, 201,
    205, 208
non-response bias 191
non-verbal data: data analysis *339*;
    interviews 244, 250, 252; observations
    266, 275 *see also* body language
normal distribution 286, 291–4, **292**, **293**
normative questions 36
'not applicable' option <u>148</u>, <u>149</u>, 229
null hypothesis 309–12, <u>315</u>, 317, 320, <u>322</u>
numeric rating Likert-type scale 220, **220**

objectivism 15
observation skills 243
observations: forms 259–60; qualitative
    approaches 260–2, <u>261</u>; quantitative
    approaches 262–4, <u>264</u>; research designs
258–9, *258*; technology-mediated
    approaches 265
observed behaviour 258, 263, <u>264</u>
observer effects 259, 263, 274
official documents 269
one-sample t-test 313–14, *314 see also*
    independent 2-sample *t*-test; paired
    (dependent) 2-sample *t*-test
one-shot studies 81–2
one-way independent ANOVA (analysis of
    variance) *314*, 317, 324, **325**, 333
online communities: data collection 232,
    265; ethics 154; research designs 127;
    sampling 194, 202–3, <u>203–4</u>, 208
online data 57, 154–5
online data sources 83–4, 269
online distribution channels **382**, 385, 387
online ethnography 127, 265, 275
online focus groups 250–1, <u>251</u>
online groups 202, <u>203–4</u>
online literature sources *52–3*
online panels 202, 203, 205, 208
online questionnaires 154, 201, 233, 234
online research 154–5, <u>155</u>, <u>157</u>
online secondary data 269
online shopping: background 14; data
    analysis <u>326</u>; data collection 200–1, **221**,
    <u>225–6</u>, <u>251</u>; designing research <u>79</u>; ethics
    <u>155–7</u>
ontological realism 15, 19
ontology 15–16, *16*, 17
open questions 39, 219, 222–3, **223** *see also*
    closed questions
opening questions **227**, 228, 234
opening topics 249
operationalization 77, **77**
opportunistic projects 28, 29, 41
oral presentations 151, 176, **382**, 385–6,
    387, 389
ordinal data 216, 217, 287, 331
outcome (dependent) variable 103, 107, <u>225</u>,
    299, 322, <u>326</u>
outliers 287, 291–<u>2</u>, 294–5, 299, 302, 332
outsider (etic) perspective 86
overt observation 259–60, 265, 275 *see also*
    covert observation

p-value (probability value), *312–13*, <u>315</u>,
    <u>318</u>, <u>322</u>, <u>327</u>, 328
paired (dependent) 2-sample *t*-test 314, 334
    see also independent 2-sample *t*-test; one-
    sample *t*-test

panel studies 82 *see also* online panels

parametric tests 311

partial completion 213, 233

participant effort 206

participant observation 86, 126, <u>128</u>, 139, 203–4

participatory research 133, 154–5

past research projects 28, 29, 41

Pearson's correlation coefficient (r) *318*, 320–1, **321**, <u>*322*</u>, 333

peer review 48–9, *50*, 55, 56, 388

Phi *318*, 320, 333

philosophy 13, 15–22, *21*, 40, 86, 138

pie charts *286*, 288, **289**, 331

pilot studies: interviews 243, 247, 255; planning research *169*, 170, *172*; questionnaires 213, **214**, 229–30, 231–2, 234–5; reports 375; sampling 205 *see also* pre-tests

plagiarism 68

population parameters 306–8, 329

Porton Down <u>147</u>

positivism: background 16–19, *16*, 21; linking research questions to design 104, 114; research designs 78, 90, 138

potential research topics 28–30, *28*, 41

practical significance: applying research designs 138; data analysis 313, 324, <u>327</u>, 328, *360*; reports 376

practitioner literature 28, <u>38</u>, 45, 48, 55, 144

practitioner report writing *8*, *9*, *21*, 378–85, *379*

pre-tests: data collection **214**, 231–2, 234–5; ethics 146, *156*; planning research *169*, 170, *172*; reports 375 *see also* pilot studies

predictor (independent) variable 103, <u>**225**</u>, 298, 322, <u>326</u>

presenting research 386

primary data *83*, 84, <u>*131*</u>, 237, 258, 267

privacy: designing research 84; ethics *145*, 150, 151–3, 154–5, <u>*157*</u>, 160–1; interviews 246, 248, <u>251</u>; reports 387; sampling <u>207</u> *see also* anonymity

private domain: documents 268–9, 271, 274; ethics 154; interviews <u>251</u>; observations 258, *265* *see also* public domain

probabilistic understanding of causality 110

probability sampling 191–3, **192**, 196, 198, 208, 232

problem-centred approach 1, 24–5

problem-solving activity 24–33

problematization 26

process models 1, 64–5, **64**, 69, <u>112</u>, <u>133</u>

process theories 35, 111, *166*, 357

product development 14, **25**, 27, *131*, 271

project timetables 56, 389

projects of opportunity *28*, 29, 41

prospective studies 82

public domain 154, 268, 275 *see also* private domain

publishers' websites 53

pure research 8–9, *8*, 26

purposive (theoretical) sampling 127, 134, 194, *195*, 196–8, 237

QCA (quantitative content analysis) 124–5, <u>*125*</u>, 135, 140

qualitative data analysis 335–65; conclusions 360–2, *360*, *362*; data coding 338–45, *339*, <u>**340**</u>, **341**, *342*, **343–5**; data preparation 336–8; memoing 345–6; presentation of findings 363–4, *363*; process 335–6, **336**; research questions 353–4, 354–7, <u>**356**</u>, 357–60, <u>**358**</u>, *359*; using computers 346–8, *347*, *348*; visual data display 349–52, *350*, <u>*350*</u>, **351**, *352*; visualization 348–9

qualitative research 126–37; action research 130–2, 132–3, <u>133</u>; case studies 129–30, *131*; ethnography 126–7, <u>128</u>; grounded theory 127–9, <u>129</u>; interview studies 133–4, <u>134</u>; language analysis 134–7, <u>136</u>; methods 84–7, *85*, 101–2; observations 260–2, <u>261</u>; sampling 199–200, 202–4, 205–6

quality in research 90–4, 361

quantitative content analysis (QCA) 124–5, <u>*125*</u>, 135, 140

quantitative data analysis 279–334; data 280–2, *282*–4; exploration techniques 285–94, 294–302, 303–5; presentation of findings 328–33; process 279–80, **280**; research questions 305–6, 306–8, 308–13, 313–18, 317–27

quantitative research: designs 117–25, **118**; methods 84–7, 100–1; observations 262–4, <u>264</u>; sampling 198–9, 201–2, 205

quasi-experimental research designs 117–20, 212

questionnaires 211–34; administration/distribution 232–3; concept/variable identification 213–15, <u>*214*</u>; design process 211–12, 212–13, **214**; measurement levels 216–18, *218*; pilot studies 231–2; question evaluation 224–6, *224*, <u>225</u>; question format 215–16, 218–23, **218**, **219**, **220**, **221**, **223**; question management <u>226</u>, 227; structure and layout 227–31, **227**, <u>229</u>, **230**

quota sampling 194

quotations 363–4

R&D (research and development) teams <u>112</u>

randomized controlled trials 109

range 285–8, *287*, 290, 296–7, 306–<u>7</u>

rank preference scales 220, **220**

ratio data 217, 311, 314

realism 15–16, *16*, 18–19, 21, 105

reason explanation 105–6

reciprocity *145*, 153

recording apps 253

RECs (research ethics committees) 158–60, 354

reference data 57, *57–8*

reference lists: literature reviews 49, *50*, 55–6, 59, 68; planning research *180*; reports *371*, 377, *379*, **382**

reference management software. 57, 59

referencing 67–8

refining research problems 26, 30–1, 39

reflexivity 20–2, 86

regression analysis 322–7, **325**, <u>326–7</u>

RELATE model <u>9</u>

research and development (R&D) teams <u>112</u>

research designs 76, 164–8, **164**, *166*, *212*, 375

research diaries: data analysis 345, 352; formulating the problem 29; planning research 163, *172*, 176–8, <u>177</u>; reports 383 *see also* diaries (data collection)

research ethics committees (RECs) 158–60, 354

research hypothesis 309–10, 313

research objectives 39–40, 176, *180*, <u>291</u>, 305

research project management 173–4, 174–6, <u>175</u>

research project planning 168–9, 169–70, *169*, 170–3, *171*, *172*

research proposals *169*, *172*, 178–82, <u>179</u>, *180*, 182–4

research questions 33–41, *166*, 374

research reports: ethics 150, 155, *156*; final report 367, 374, 375, 378; literature reviews *51*, *53*, 66–7; planning research 170; sampling 190

research techniques 46, 75, 109

research terms 26–7, 28, 30, 36

research titles <u>372</u>

researcher bias 16, *93*, 138

researcher-instigated documents 271–2, <u>272–3</u>

researcher preferences 168

researcher role 259, 262

resource limitations 167

respondent literacy levels 213, 224, 233

respondent validation *94*, 362, 365

response rates: data analysis 345; questionnaires 213, 223, 227–8, 232–3; sampling 190, 200–1, *200*, 205, 208

results section 375–6

retroduction (abduction) 81

retrospective studies 82, *267*

reverse coding 284

risk assessment 170–3, *172*

risk management 173

sample interview forms <u>148</u>, <u>149</u>

sampling 187–209; access 204–5, 205–6, <u>207</u>; error 305–6, 308, 310–11; internet 201–2, 202–4; methods 191–5, **192**; problems 263; process 187–90, **188**, **189**; qualitative research *195*, 196–8, *197*, <u>197</u>; quantitative research 195–6, *195*; size 198–9, *199–200*, 200–1

sampling frame: access 201, 205; data collection 232, 234, 268; planning research *172*; sampling methods 192–6; sampling process 189–91, **189**, 207

scale reliability 283, 284–5, 329

scatterplots: exploring associations *296*, 298–302, **302**, 317; linear regression 323–4; Pearson's correlation coefficient (r) 320, **321**

scheduling interviews 238

scope: interviews 239, *240*, 249; projects 26, 31–2, 37; research design 87, 101; research management <u>177</u>, 181, 182; research questions 40; sampling 199; search terms 54; theories 13–14

scope creep 31, 170

search terms 54–5, 70

secondary data: access 167; documents 266–71, *267*; online data sources 83–4,

269; questionnaires *212*, 231; research designs 101, 112, 122; sampling 189
selection bias 190–1, 194, 196, 202, 205, 208
self-selection sampling *192*, 194, 195, 202, 232
semantic differential scale 221, **221**
semi-structured interviews 134, 239 *see also* structured interviews
sensitive research topics 207
sensitivity 206, 207, 232, 237, 240, 250
sensitizing concepts 79, **79**, 340, 360, 374
sequencing interviews 242, 248–50, *249*
SERVQUAL 214
'should' questions 36–7
significance levels **309**, 310–11, 312, 315, 327, 328–9
significance tests 313–17, *314*, 317–27
simple random sampling 192
simulation-based research: linking research questions to design 110, 113; planning research *166*, 167; research designs **118**, 122–4, 124, 139
single item response 222, **223**
skewness 286, 292–4, **293**, **331**
Skype 154, 244, 250, 251, 252
smartphones: data 225–6, 230, 252, 326–7; reports 373; research designs 79, 104, **105**
snowballing (sampling) 194, 202
social constructionism 18–19, 21, 253
social desirability bias 129, 242, 258–9, 266
social media: formulating the problem 34, 38; interviews *240*, 244, 245; questionnaires 232; sampling 194, 202, 206
social media comments 202, 270
social networks 245, 271, 354, **354**
social processes 15, 17–18, 35, 110, 112–13, *166*
software packages: literature reviews 59; qualitative data analysis 335, 346–7; quantitative data analysis 279, 294, 329; reports 381 *see also* spreadsheet software
sources of ideas 28–30, *28*, 41
Spearman's rho *318*, 320–1
speed of collection 212, 233, 244, 260, 265
sponsors/clients: data analysis 356; designing research 83; formulating the problem 28–9, *28*, 31, 41; planning research 173, 176, 177, 178; reports 378, 386; sampling 205

spreadsheet software 59, 61, 212, 279–80, 346, **347**
stacked bar charts 298, **301**, **331**
stakeholder expectations **164**, 165–7, 174, 183, 200
standard deviations *200*, 290–1, **292**, 305
standpoint reflexivity 20–1
stimulus items 241
storyboards **382**, 383, 388
storylines 378, 381, 383, 384
strategic management 61, **63**
stratified random sampling 193
structured interviews 236, 239 *see also* semi-structured interviews
structured observation 89, 122, 260, 262–3, 264
student research projects 5, *169*, *172*, 174
sub-categories 343, **343**
subject-expectancy effects 119
subjectivism 15, 18
substantive theories 13–14
summated rating scales 221, 234, 284, *284 see also* multi-item scales
survey studies: designing research 78, 88, 93, 101; ethics 151; questionnaires *212*, 225; research designs 122, 123, 133, 139; sampling 188, 201, 208
synchronous communication 244, 250 *see also* asynchronous communication
systematic random sampling 192–3
systematic review 68–9
systems 113, 139
systems models 64–5, **64**, 69

tables of contents 56, *371*, 373, 377, *379*, **382**
target population: data analysis 283; documents 268; planning research *172*; questionnaires 224, 230–1; reports 377; sampling 187–8, 191–3, 195–6, 200–2, 205, 207–8; sampling process **189–90**
taxonomies 99, 354
technical points **382**, 385
technology-mediated data collection 255, 275
technology-mediated focus groups 250–1
technology-mediated interviews 243–6
technology-mediated observation 265
terminology: interviews 242; literature reviews 45, 54–5; reports 370, 375; research designs 88, 103, 117
test output 311–*12*, 318, 327

test statistics *312*, <u>315</u>, 317, <u>318</u>, 324, 328
testing findings 361–2, *362*
tests of association 318–27, *319*, 333
tests of difference 313–17, *314*
text-based focus groups 250, <u>251</u>
text-based interviews 244–5, 254
theoretical generalization 92
theoretical literature 45, 48
theoretical (purposive) sampling 127, 194, 195, 196, <u>197</u>, 237
theoretical reflexivity 20
theoretical saturation: data analysis 336; interviews 237, 247; research designs 128, <u>129</u>, 139; sampling *195*, <u>197</u>, 198, 199, 208
theory 11–12, *12–13*, 13–14, *14–15*
thick description 102, 126, 139, *166*, 260, 275
time horizon 76, 81–3, 95
time sampling 263, <u>264</u>
time schedules 169–70, **171**, 173
time series analysis 111, 303–5, **303, 304**, 332
title page 370–2
transcription <u>136</u>, 245, 337–8, *339*, 364
transcription software 338
treatment (independent) variable 103, 107, <u>120</u>, 139
triangulation: applying research designs 128, 130; data analysis *362*, 365; data collection *212*, 266; designing research 87–8, *94*; linking research questions to design 111
Trickle Out Africa Project <u>179</u>
true experiments **118**, 119, 139
trustworthiness criteria *93*, *94*
Twitter 38, <u>245</u>, 246
two-tailed tests 313
Type I errors **310–11**
Type II errors **310–11**
types of interview question 240–2, *240*
typologies 99, <u>100</u>, <u>134</u>

UGC (user-generated content) <u>270</u>
Uniform Resource Locator (URL) *57*, *59*, *71*, 232
unimodal distribution 292, **293**, 314
unit of analysis 31, 38, 349
univariate analysis 285, *286*
unobtrusive measures 274
unstructured interviews 239
unstructured observation 260–1
URL (Uniform Resource Locator) *57*, *59*, *71*, 232
user-generated content (UGC) <u>270</u>

validity 91–4, *92*, 95, 119–20
variable response rates 213, 233
variance models 64–5, **64**, 69
video conferencing 382, 385, 387
video recordings: data analysis 337–8, 364–5; data collection 18, 248, 252, 254, 262, 265; reports 389
visual data displays 349–52, 353, 364
visual mapping techniques 381
visualization *347*, 348–9
voice recognition software (VRS) 338
VRS (voice recognition software) 338
vulnerable groups 149, 153, 154, 159, 167

web conferencing **382**, 385, 387, *387*
'what' questions: data analysis 353–4; formulating the problem 33–4, 36, 37; research designs 98, 99, 99–100, 100–1, 101–2, 113
'why' questions: data analysis 354–7, *355*; formulating the problem 34–5, 36, 41; research designs 102–3, 103–4, 104–7, 107–8, 109–10, 114
word-processing software 59, 61, 346, 381
wording research questions 38–9
writing down 32–3, 37
writing style 67, **382**, 384

Zotero (software) 59